PENGUIN BOOKS

FROM THE VELVETS TO THE VOIDOIDS

Clinton Heylin is the author of the highly acclaimed biography of Bob Dylan, *Dylan: Behind the Shades* (1991, Penguin 1992), and of *Stolen Moments: The Ultimate Dylan Reference Book*, as well as books on Public Image Limited, Joy Division, Richard Thompson and Sandy Denny. He is the editor of *The Penguin Book of Rock & Roll Writing*, published by Viking and forthcoming in Penguin.

Clinton
Heylin

From
the
Velvets
to
the
Voidoids

*A
Pre-Punk
History
for a
Post-Punk
World*

PENGUIN BOOKS

PENGUIN BOOKS

Published by the Penguin Group
Penguin Books Ltd, 27 Wrights Lane, London W8 5TZ, England
Penguin Books USA Inc., 375 Hudson Street, New York, New York 10014, USA
Penguin Books Australia Ltd, Ringwood, Victoria, Australia
Penguin Books Canada Ltd, 10 Alcorn Avenue, Toronto, Ontario, Canada M4V 3B2
Penguin Books (NZ) Ltd, 182–190 Wairau Road, Auckland 10, New Zealand

Penguin Books Ltd, Registered Offices: Harmondsworth, Middlesex, England

First published 1993
10 9 8 7 6 5 4 3 2

Typeset by Datix International Limited, Bungay, Suffolk
Set in 10/13 pt Monophoto Janson
Printed in England by Clays Ltd, St Ives plc

Contents

Acknowledgements

From the Velvets to the Voidoids has been a long time coming. I conducted my first interviews back in 1989, before I had even started on my Dylan biography, *Behind the Shades*, published in May 1991. Inevitably there has been a long retinue of people who have been invaluable to the project.

I'd especially like to thank Roberta Bayley, Alan Betrock, Leee Black Childers, Bob Gruen, Jerry Harrison, Richard Hell, John Holmstrom, Jim Jones, Lenny Kaye, Craig Leon, Tony Maimone, John Morton, Charlotte Pressler, Bob Quine, Tommy Ramone, Joey Ramone, Allen Ravenstine, Jonathan Richman, Andy Shernoff, Pete Stampfel, Chris Stein, Tish & Snooky, Marty Thau, David Thomas, Alan Vega, Tom Verlaine, Michael Weldon, Chris Whent, and Tim Wright, who all generously gave of their time to tell their part of the story.

Vital contacts and personal access were facilitated by the endeavours of Mitch Blank, Victor Bockris, Raymond Foye, Nicholas Hill and Barry Miles.

A book like this is only partially composed from first-hand interviews. A considerable amount of cross-checking, searching out secondary sources, and securing access to archive recordings was required. For their help in this more mundane, but equally vital, part of my researches I extend much thanks to Nina Antonia, Bob Bettendorf, Ken Dixon, Richard Lewis, Tony Legge, Alan Licht, Doug Morgan, Chris Stigliano, Scott C. and Pat Thomas. (No thanks are due, however, to Lewis Gerendasy, who so meticulously documented the CBGBs years on audio and video but now sits in his apartment, huddling up to these private mementoes of his lost youth, secure in his self-appointed task as solitary keeper of the flame.)

Thanks also to my American friends, who shared their homes, allowing me to impose myself for days at a time, all the while acting as answering services, during my regular forays to the States. So thanks, Mike and Susie, Scott and Suzie, Rob and Lynne, and Steve K, without whom . . .

Finally, thanks to those who took time to read and comment on the many drafts this book passed through: Bob Cooke, Steve Sheppard, Dan Levy, Mat Snow, Peter Vincent, Chris Charlesworth, who convinced me it was a worthwhile project, Michael Jacobs, for putting up with my neuroses about American publishers, and, above all, to my editor Tony Lacey, for his belief in the book's viability and his enthusiasm for my endeavours to drag rock history out of the godforsaken sixties . . .

Picture Acknowledgements

The photographs in this book are reproduced by kind permission of the following:

Section One (*between pp. 80 and 81*)
p. 1 Billy Name; *p. 2* LFI; *p. 3* author's collection; *pp. 4 and 6* Michael Weldon; *p. 5* Chris Stigliano; *pp. 7–8* Roberta Bayley.

Section Two (*between pp. 144 and 145*)
p. 1 Richard Hell; *p. 2* Charles Pritchard; *p. 3* Redferns; *p. 4* Jay Craven; *pp. 5–7* Roberta Bayley; *p. 8* Chris Stigliano.

Section Three (*between pp. 224 and 225*)
pp. 1–3 and 5–7 Roberta Bayley; *p. 4* Tim Wright; *p. 8* author's collection.

Section Four (*between pp. 288 and 289*)
pp. 1–8 Roberta Bayley.

Credit Where it's Due – The Appropriation of Punk History

Though the history of British punk continues to intrigue sociologists in music critic's clothing, its elder New York cousin, residing among the Bowery bums at a small rock club called Country Blue Grass and Blues,* has received scant attention. Yet the New York and London scenes shared similar antecedents, reflecting a common disenchantment with the rock & roll status quo. The New York scene contained figures of a significance equal to Johnny Rotten, Glen Matlock, Joe Strummer or Mick Jones. Patti Smith, Tom Verlaine, Richard Hell and the Ramones were all responsible for stylistic and musical traits evident in many latter-day New Wave bands. Their history remains untold, despite their profound influence.

The first problem to confront is one of terminology. Applying the words 'punk' and 'New Wave' (or indeed rock & roll) indiscriminately only compounds the general lack of awareness of the chronology for this third generation rock & roll revolution. So the first demarcation is most important – punk and New Wave are two separate, distinct movements. Punk predates the New Wave and American punk predates British punk. *From the Velvets to the Voidoids*, in dealing with American punk, seeks to provide a context for both the American and British new waves. Not just a who's who, but a what's what!

The origins of punk may be found initially in America's post-*Pepper* underground. The main American precursors of punk were the Velvet Underground, the MC5, the Stooges, the Modern Lovers and the New York Dolls. Britain's progenitors were the Sixties bands that combined a

---

* Though CBGB may be more correct, I have chosen throughout this book to refer to the club by its more common name, CBGBs.

keen pop sensibility with ballsy rhythm & blues – the early Stones and Who, the Small Faces, the Yardbirds – and those glam bands who gave noise back to teenagers in the early Seventies – T. Rex, Slade and Roxy Music. The first section of this book is about America's underground vanguard. For subterranean they truly were. Between them, the five significant American precursors could not muster one album in *Billboard*'s Hot Hundred (even if the Velvet Underground remain the most influential American band in contemporary rock music).

The central bands making up American 'punk' in the years 1974–6 can be divided into two distinct 'waves'. The first wave in New York, who made their debuts at CBGBs and Max's in 1973–4, were Television, Patti Smith, the Ramones and Blondie. Cleveland was the only other US city to have a contemporary wave of pre-punk exponents: Mirrors, the Electric Eels and Rocket from the Tombs were playing clubs like the Clockwork Orange and the Viking Saloon in the years 1973–5. All these bands were directly influenced by America's precursors (and in most cases by England's too).

A second wave, still predating the British punk explosion of 1976–7, then includes outfits like Suicide and the Dictators, who both existed before the CBGBs bands but were largely detached from the New York underground before 1976; splinter groups like the Heartbreakers, Richard Hell and the Voidoids and, from Cleveland, Pere Ubu; and, finally, bands who came to New York in response to the positive pulse that the first wave was generating, notably Talking Heads and the Dead Boys.

Though the important bands in the British 'punk' movement shared common influences and were a later phenomenon – and despite some ill-founded suggestions in the music press through the years as regards the Ramones' alleged influence on the Sex Pistols – they took little direct inspiration from the CBGBs and Cleveland bands, of whom they were only dimly aware. These British 'punk' bands, who began gigging between November 1975 and April 1977, included the Sex Pistols, the Clash, the Damned, the Buzzcocks, Subway Sect, Adam & the Ants, Generation X, the Adverts, X-Ray Spex, Wire, Siouxsie & the Banshees and the Slits. These bands played clubs like London's 100 Club and the Roxy and Manchester's Electric Circus.

New Wave is not an interchangeable term for punk. It was what punk became as influences became more disparate, musicianship improved, bands fragmented, new permutations emerged and record labels realized that punk was unmarketable. It was spawned from and influenced by its punk predecessors (and occasionally survivors). It also transcended the Atlantic divide. It took in everyone from the B-52s to the Bunnymen. In the New Wave ragbag can be included powerpop merchants like the Jam, the Police and the Pretenders, British guitar/synth bands like Joy Division, Echo & the Bunnymen, Magazine, latter-day Wire, PiL and the Cure, ska revivalists like Madness and the Specials, thrash exponents like X and Black Flag, the no wave of DNA and the Contortions and a million other splinters of inspiration.

From the Velvets to the Voidoids does not deal with the period after British punk when American music temporarily lost its own identity, before learning to assimilate influences and remake/remodel them anew. *From the Velvets to the Voidoids* deals with the origins, not the eventual course, of the New Wave.

There is a book to be written about the continually interchanging relationship between British and American rock & roll. This is not it. I only touch upon the British punk scene as it directly affected the US. Much − indeed too much, too soon − has been written about the similarities between American and British punk scenes. The differences were considerable. Only with the New Wave did bands synthesize the bam-a-lam rebelliousness of British punk with the self-conscious artistry of American punk.

An essential difference between British and American punk bands can be found in their respective views of rock & roll history. The British bands took a deliberately anti-intellectual stance, refuting any awareness of, or influence from, previous exponents of the form. The New York and Cleveland bands saw themselves as self-consciously drawing on and extending an existing tradition in American rock & roll.

Jerry Harrison: All of this is somewhat continuous. It started with the Velvet Underground and all of the things that were identified with Andy Warhol . . . Then that kind of faded, and . . . the Modern Lovers and the New York Dolls were the next carriers of the flame. Then, when we faded, it went into Patti Smith and through the whole CBGB scene.

Lenny Kaye: There was a direct line from the 'Nuggets' groups to the

Stooges, the Dolls and the glitter bands: there was an alternative recognized music scene ... [but] the Velvet Underground were certainly the most important band. They were the one group that proved you could scissor together the perverse side of art and the pop side of rock & roll. After them, the Stooges and the MC5.

A second difference between the British and American punk scenes was their relative gestation periods. The British weekly music press was reviewing Sex Pistols shows less than three months after their cacophonous debut. Within a year of the Pistols' first performance they had a record deal, with the 'major' label EMI. Within six months of their first gigs the Damned and the Clash also secured contracts, the latter with CBS. The CBGBs scene went largely ignored by the American music industry until 1976 – two years after the debuts of Television, the Ramones and Blondie. Even then only Television signed to an established label.

Debbie Harry: [The CBGBs scene] started in about '73 [but] it wasn't given any kind of credibility until about '75 ... I think the Ramones were the first ones to be signed and they were signed in what, '76. I think there was a pretty long time for everybody to get a nice development. And everybody to have an independent style ... The press wasn't there interpreting everything, and making everybody a little bit self-conscious.

Ironically the octane-charged British scene quickly began to have a notable – and detrimental – effect upon the American scene. With the emergence of the Pistols, Clash and Damned, American bands began copying their sound, often without consciously realizing that they were drawing aspects of this music second-hand from American bands like the Stooges, the Modern Lovers and the Dolls.

The failure of the original American punk bands – Television, Patti Smith, the Ramones, the Heartbreakers, and Pere Ubu in particular – to endure or to continue their commitment to their original aesthetic had a discernible effect on the wave of bands that succeeded this current of new American rock & roll. Their commercial failure – Patti Smith excepted – suggested the need for a new approach. Yet the conclusion that their successors seemed to reach was that rock & roll and commercial pop had become incompatible bedfellows and so, rather than seek a reconciliation, New York became a centre for 'no wave' and Los Angeles for thrash-metal in the decade following the CBGBs scene. These musical movements have been essentially peripheral to 'pop' music, hidden from the mainstream.

For a brief period it seemed possible that the American punk bands could have the same effervescent effect that British punk outfits had on their own country's pop scene. *From the Velvets to the Voidoids* is about that promise, in the brief period when everything seemed possible and the only limit was ambition.

Clinton Heylin, March 1992

Precursors

Modern music begins with the Velvets, and the implications and influence of what they did seem to go on forever ... The only thing I think would be a mistake ... would be romanticizing them too much.   – *Lester Bangs*

Like other forms of 'art', high and low, the history of popular music contains its fair share of fractures, moments when fissures appear in the edifice of accepted forms and something new and significant spouts forth from the cracks. Sure, what Elvis Presley recorded in Sun's studios in Memphis had clearly discernible antecedents, but what he produced was so much more than the sum of previous parts.

When Lester Bangs recalled the formation of the Velvet Underground as the beginning of something new, he was placing them in a position of pre-eminence not recognized by contemporaries. The Velvets were an entirely underground phenomenon during their actual existence. When they were finally rent asunder (by the usual 'musical differences'), five years after their formation and four years after recording rock & roll's most revolutionary debut album, they had never even risen to the intoxicating heights of the *Billboard* Hot Hundred.

The revolution instigated by *The Velvet Underground and Nico* was still germinating. Even as the Sixties were keeling over, the Velvets remained steadfastly left-field. They had nothing in common with either of the two 'rock' sounds to dominate the period when they were at their creative peak: Folk-Rock (1965–6), largely a phenomenon of New York and Los Angeles, and its wandering son, the San Francisco Sound (1966–7). Not for the Velvets the folk sensibility, the righteous calls to action, nor the symbolic obtuseness of Dylan and his fellow Village folkies; nor the West Coast's predeliction for lilting, Beatlesque harmonies. The members of the Velvets approached music from four unique perspectives, with just one strand in common – rhythm & blues. Out of synthesis came innovation.

The Velvets' singer-songwriter Lou Reed, born in Brooklyn, New York, in March 1942, showed an early commitment to rock & roll, recording a single with a high-school band called the Jades when he was just 16. But his fervour for the music seemed to wane as he moved on to college. When attending Syracuse University in the years 1961–4 he kept his love of rock & roll known only to a select few. After all, 'pop' music was puerile, 'kid's stuff', teen fodder in the eyes of his classmates. Reed seems to have shown an uncharacteristic willingness to conform to the college stereotype.

Sterling Morrison: He liked it to be known that he studied literature and wrote poetry, but he never mentioned anything about playing music.

In fact literature had not entirely subverted Reed's first love. During his time at Syracuse he assembled several brief-lived combos, all playing a watered-down form of black rhythm & blues. These outfits spent considerably more time jamming than playing live. They generally had one other regular member – Sterling Morrison.

Sterling Morrison: We had to change the name continuously so people would keep calling. We used to do covers of black music. When the Rolling Stones appeared we liked them. They did the same thing we did, only better.

Though Morrison himself briefly attended Syracuse, within two semesters he decided that he preferred the less orthodox discipline of New York's City College. He still made regular sorties out to Syracuse, to play with Reed and hang out with mutual friend Jim Tucker at Reed and Tucker's fraternity house.

The Syracuse Reed did not confine his musical interests to rock & roll. He had developed extremely catholic tastes. His love of black forms of popular music was the only common thread in his exploration of rhythm & blues, less traditional forms of jazz music ('I was a very big fan of Ornette Coleman, Cecil Taylor, Archie Shepp . . .') and doo-wop. If later statements are to be believed, he even dipped into the avant-garde, listening to Stockhausen while just a sophomore.

With such an eclectic background of musical interests, his next move seems all the more surprising. On graduating from college, he returned to his parents' home in Long Island. From there he commuted daily to Pickwick Records' HQ on Staten Island, where he was one of a rota of hack songwriters churning out formulaic, copy-cat compositions for Pickwick to release on budget-bin compilations. As Phil Milstein observed in the Velvet Underground Appreciation Society's critical discography, 'In many ways, this is the craziest part of the entire crazy Velvet Underground story. No work Lou has done is so trivial, so pre-fabricated, so tossed-off.'

Yet it would be Pickwick that would provide the vital link between Reed and John Cale, the other primary architect of the Velvet Underground.

It would be difficult to conceive of backgrounds more markedly different than those of Cale and Reed. Born in South Wales in December 1940, Cale's undergraduate education at London's Goldsmiths' College was in classical music, even if he did display an early leaning towards more avant-garde modern compositions. Under the direction of his tutor Cornelius Cardew, he began to learn about the works of Stockhausen and John Cage, seemingly unaware of the revolution in rock & roll taking place within spitting distance of his place of study. From 1960 to 1963, as other young London art students discovered American rhythm & blues, he completed a classical music degree.

In the summer of 1963, having finished his studies at Goldsmiths', Cale was awarded a Leonard Bernstein scholarship to study Modern Composition in Lenox, Massachusetts, but once in Lenox he failed to establish a rapport with Aaron Copland, under whose auspices he had secured the scholarship.

John Cale: Copland said I couldn't play my work at Tanglewood. It was too destructive, he said. He didn't want his piano wrecked.

Cale was soon on his way to New York, where his first activity was to work with John Cage in an eighteen-hour piano marathon that involved playing a short piece by Eric Satie 888 times, something that required a relay of hardened piano players.

If the actual performance was long, Cale's association with Cage was extremely brief, though he soon became embroiled in a long-term project with New York's other notable avant-garde classical composer, La Monte Young. In May 1963 Young, hand-drummer Angus MacLise, vocalist Marian Zazeela and violinist Tony Conrad had begun rehearsing together and that month, with four other musicians, performed a piece of music with no evident beginning or end, *Second Dream of the High Tension Line Stepdown Transformer*, at George Segal's farm in New Jersey.

The following month the quartet began to play a few concerts at the Third Rail Gallery in New York. In August, Young and Zazeela found a large loft downtown where they could rehearse all night. Cale, an enthusiast of Young's work, sought him out shortly after his arrival in New York in September. He was soon enlisted into the ensemble, Young convincing him to adopt the electric viola. The Theatre of Eternal Music, nicknamed the Dream Syndicate by its members, was born. As Alan Licht has written, in his definitive history of the group in *Forced Exposure*, its aims were not merely unorthodox but largely beyond the bounds of classical structure:

The group's work with excessive amplification, light projection, and Indian music-derived drones in the early Sixties predates nearly all other examples of their use in Western music ... Young developed an unusual approach to modal blues, which retained the usual I–IV–I–V–IV–I progression, but left open-ended the amount of time spent on each chord.

Though membership of the Theatre was always in a constant state of flux, the basic core was always permed from Young, Zazeela, Cale, Conrad and MacLise. The concept of eternal music also remained a perpetual undercurrent and the ensemble's approach was always entirely improvisational. As Licht has observed:

In rehearsal and performance, Young would define the harmonic structure (which notes could and couldn't be played) and the group improvised under those rules ... [Their major work] *The Tortoise [His Dreams & Journeys]* ... would continue unchanged forever. To help get across this idea at concerts, the group would start to play before the audience was allowed to enter, giving the impression that the piece was continuing, not starting ... The amplified viola drone, the numbing volume, the helter skelter piano of the Velvets all stem, to a certain extent, from the Theatre's work.

By the beginning of 1965 Cale had devised a unique approach to the electric viola. He had flattened the bridge of the instrument so that he could bow three or four strings simultaneously. He also used electric guitar strings on his viola which, combined with the overwhelming amplification the group was using, achieved 'a drone like a jet engine!' The trademark Cale viola would prove to be the most distinctive element in the Velvets' early sound.

Yet Cale suffered from a nagging feeling of dissatisfaction. Just as he had previously reacted against his orthodox classical training, he began to realize that New York's so-called avant-garde was just another esoteric clique, influencing nobody. In transcending the avant-garde, he sought to locate a more populist means to fulfil his musical ambitions.

John Cale: There was a certain futility in avant-garde music that was really mystifying, people were really interested in extreme statements . . . performance pieces like *Climb into the Vagina of a Live Female Whale.* But there is no futility in rock & roll, it's too urgent, that's what's great about it.

According to Tony Conrad, with whom Cale shared an apartment in the fall of 1964, a large part of Cale's dissatisfaction with the avant-garde stemmed from his discovery of rock & roll at the hands of Conrad, who, after a day of rehearsals, was wont to return home and sit around listening to records from his huge 45 collection.

Tony Conrad: [When] John started getting interested in rock & roll . . . there was a great ambiguity in his mind about how somebody could be interested in both rock and classical music.

John Cale's eventual meeting with Lou Reed confirmed in him the need for a new direction. It was the result of a chance encounter between Tony Conrad, John Cale and Reed's fellow Pickwick hack Terry Phillips, at a party. Phillips was looking for a band of musicians to promote a single recorded by the non-existent Primitives, a Reed spoof on dance crazes entitled 'The Ostrich'.

Why Phillips should hit on Conrad and his room-mate Cale as possible members of this imaginary ensemble remains a mystery. It was hardly the sort of music they were used to playing! Nevertheless Cale and Conrad, after enlisting Walter DeMaria, sometime drummer for the Theatre of Eternal Music, were escorted out to Pickwick's Staten Island headquarters to meet the author and singer of 'The Ostrich'. As soon as Reed began to teach the song to the newly constituted Primitives, there was an unexpected connection.

Tony Conrad: [Reed] said, 'Don't worry, it's easy to play because all the strings are tuned to the same note,' which blew our minds because that was what we were doing with La Monte.

Though Conrad, Cale and DeMaria joined Reed for a few out-of-town gigs, it quickly became apparent that 'The Ostrich' was going to remain with its head in the sand. Thus endeth The Primitives. However, Cale and Reed were fast forming their own mutual appreciation society, realizing that they had the common ground necessary to create something genuinely innovative and exciting.

John Cale: When I first met Lou, we were interested in the same things . . . We both needed a vehicle; Lou needed one to carry out his lyrical ideas and I needed one to carry out my musical ideas . . . This was about 1965, and he'd written 'Heroin' already and 'Waiting for the Man', but [Pickwick] wouldn't let him record it.

Cale and Reed had already started 'rehearsing' together at Tony Conrad's Ludlow Street apartment when they ran into Sterling Morrison on a subway train. He was still attending City College and had not seen Reed in over a year, so was presumably unaware of Lou's Pickwick sabbatical from rock & roll. He was more than willing to return with Reed and Cale to the Ludlow Street apartment and indulge in some spontaneous music-making.

Conrad had already made it clear that he was uninterested in playing with Reed and Cale. His interest in rock & roll did not extend to making a career of it. Reed quickly became a permanent resident at Ludlow Street and by the spring of '65 Conrad was moving out. Morrison was soon recruited into the fledgling outfit. His musical influences were considerably more mainstream than Cale's and his guitar-playing brought a requisite hardness to the duo's sound.

Sterling Morrison: A good guitar riff is better than a solo. There are songs like 'The Last Time' by the Stones that are just one big riff.

The use of the Ludlow Street apartment and Cale's previous avant-garde associations meant that the new combo's first percussionist was an obvious choice. Angus MacLise had shared membership of the Theatre of Eternal Music with Cale, and was a true experimentalist. His idiosyncratic approach to percussive sound made him an ideal foil for Cale's sawing viola. And, frankly, they had few other potential candidates.

Sterling Morrison: We played once a week, twice a week, three times a week, until we finally ended up living together on Grand Street ... At Ludlow Street, Cale never played keyboards, just viola, bass, and sometimes guitar. The minimalism in our sound was already apparent, and things just kept getting more and more weird.

Spring had barely turned to summer when the new outfit made its first recording. In July 1965 Cale, Reed, Morrison and MacLise recorded a demo tape, featuring prototype versions of the three central songs on the Velvets' inaugural album – 'Heroin', 'Venus in Furs' and 'Black Angel's Death Song' – plus 'Wrap Your Troubles in Dreams' (later recorded for Nico's first album) and a song (now lost) apparently entitled 'Never Get Emotionally Involved with Man, Woman, Beast or Child'.*

The fact that by the summer of 1965 Reed had already written 'Heroin' and 'Venus in Furs', perhaps – with 'Sister Ray' – the most important songs to result from the Cale/Reed association, is certainly significant. In 1965 *nobody* wrote songs called 'Heroin'† – though it would not be accurate to suggest that Heroin was the first 'drug-song' ever to be written, nor indeed rock & roll's first 'drug-song'. The Byrds were at number one on the *Billboard* singles chart with a song widely interpreted to be about a 'drug-induced experience', Bob Dylan's 'Mr Tambourine Man'.

The harrowing nature of 'Heroin' lies in its sheer matter-of-factness. Reed sings about addiction to hard drugs in a wholly believable, first-person manner which has the addict on the one hand rationalizing his habit – 'When I put a spike into my vein/I tell you things aren't quite

---

* This is the only known recording of the band with MacLise, but all copies appear to have been mislaid.
† According to Reed, in his *Selected Lyrics*, he wrote the song in college.

the same' – and at the same time showing the addict's awareness that only the ultimate escape awaits him – 'I'm closing in on death'. (It is tempting to consider the song to be not about a single fix but The Final Fix, that the addict's vision of a sailor on a clipper ship is not merely a drug-induced vision but a near-death experience.)

Likewise, in the song 'Venus in Furs', in many ways a straightforward recounting of Sacher-Masoch's tale of masochistic fervour, the use of the first-person viewpoint for Severin, cowing at the feet of his mistress Wanda, is totally convincing as a means of detailing the psyche of this willing underling.

Reed was aware that such subject-matter was potentially shocking. Indeed, the ability to shock was a key element in the Velvets' aesthetic.

John Cale: There was commitment there. That was the powerful advantage that all of Lou's lyrics had. All Bob Dylan was singing was questions – How many miles? and all that. I didn't want to hear any more questions. Give me some tough social situations and show that answers are possible. And sure enough, 'Heroin' was one of them. It wasn't sorry for itself.

Reed, like all of rock & roll's great wordsmiths, was reflecting his own concerns in these songs. When it came to the band choosing a name, it was no coincidence that they took their moniker from a book which claimed to be 'a documentary on the sexual corruption of our age', the cover of which consisted of a picture of a whip, a high-heeled shoe, a mask and a key. The book was entitled *The Velvet Underground*. Though Morrison later denied that they chose the name because 'of the S&M theme of the book', Reed clearly considered dealing with such taboo subjects to be an integral part of the band's radical stance. His well-known penchant later in his career for more androgynous aspects of sexual identity presupposes a budding interest as early as 1965.

Drugs were also not alien to Reed. He later wrote that he was forced to leave Syracuse University prematurely, after intending to do a postgraduate class in journalism, 'because of various clandestine [drug] operations I was alleged to have been involved in ... I had recently been introduced to drugs at this time by a mashed-in Negro ... named Jaw.'

A third song recorded by the Velvets in July shows the extent of Cale's influence at this juncture in their development. 'Black Angel's

Death Song' was *not* rock & roll. It was almost entirely free-form, as close to an amalgam of avant-garde and free jazz as the Velvets ever came. It was also the only Cale–Reed composition later included on that remarkable debut album, and the song that would cause the band's first confrontation with a club owner when played at the Cafe Bizarre that very Christmas. It was surely what Cale had in mind when he talked about Reed improvising lyrics over 'orchestral chaos'.

John Cale: When I played viola [with Reed] . . . I thought we had discovered a really original, nasty style. The idea was that Lou could improvise lyrics, and that was where the idea of space and scale from drone and hypnosis came to be. The idea would be that we could create this orchestral chaos on stage and Lou could improvise.

Throughout the summer the newly christened Velvet Underground worked on fusing their avant-garde and garageband aesthetics. Yet, with MacLise still in the band and Cale very much a dominant influence, the Velvets were still tending towards more avant-garde terrain. Though this may suggest that Cale was having an undue influence on the Velvets' direction, Reed was at this stage as affected by MacLise's notions as Cale's. An article co-written by Reed and MacLise at the time implied that the Velvets were striving to place Eastern notions of tone in a Western context:

Western music is based on death, violence and the pursuit of PROGRESS . . . The root of universal music is sex. Western music is as violent as Western sex . . . There is no such thing as the Indian influence. It's freaking around riffs aloft serpentine SCALES . . . The V.U. is the Western equivalent to the cosmic dance of Shiva. Playing as Babylon goes up in flames.

Their choice of 'Black Angel's Death Song' and 'Venus in Furs' to demo in July certainly supported their connection to the avant-garde, as did their involvement in a project which was really an extension of certain ideas first propagated in the Theatre of Eternal Music: The Launching of the Dream Weapon.

The project was partly Angus MacLise's idea, having been jointly organized by him and his old friend, film-maker Piero Heliczer. The Dream Weapon was a primitive mixed-media show. The basic idea was that Piero's films would be shown through a series of veils on to a screen while dancers danced around and 'behind the screen a strange music was being generated' (by Reed, Cale, MacLise and Morrison). The experience convinced the more mainstream Morrison of the validity of what the Velvets were trying to do.

Sterling Morrison: For me the path suddenly became clear – I could work on music that was different from the ordinary rock & roll, since Piero had given me a context to perform it in.

Yet the Velvets' contribution to The Launching of the Dream Weapon simply served to confirm Cale and MacLise's enduring association with their avant-garde friends, rather than asserting a relevance to contemporary rock & roll.

Thankfully, MacLise's single-minded commitment to the Art of it all precipitated his departure from the band. When the Velvets were offered a gig at a high school in New Jersey – for the modest payment of $75 – MacLise quit, apparently on the grounds that he didn't want anyone telling him when they could and couldn't start and finish their set.

Reed and Morrison recalled that their good friend Jim Tucker had a sister called Maureen, who played the drums. She even had her own drum kit, and the band she had been playing in – a three-piece outfit called the Intruders, whose set was primarily composed of Chuck Berry songs – had recently disbanded.

Though she was not offered a permanent position in the Velvets for some time, Maureen played on the first billed Velvet Underground gig on 11 December 1965, at Summit High School. Like her new musical cohorts, Tucker's musical tastes were eclectic, aligning that essential love of rock & roll – particularly the Who and the Rolling Stones – with a desire for experimentation.

Maureen Tucker: I started playing drums because I liked Olatunji ... what I'd always wanted to do was get an African drum sound, so I got a bass drum and turned it on its side, so I'd sit on the floor and play that ... And when I started enjoying rock & roll with more than just a listening enjoyment, I wanted to play something – something to smack on.

At Summit High School – the first performance of the Reed–Cale–Morrison–Tucker Velvets – the reception was typically polarized, recognition and revulsion in not-so-equal doses. The history of antagonism and confrontation that characterizes the Velvets' career had begun.

Sterling Morrison: The murmur of surprise that greeted our appearance as the curtain went up increased to a roar of disbelief once we started to play 'Venus', and swelled to a mighty howl of outrage and bewilderment by the end of 'Heroin'.

If you want to write the story of the Velvet Underground, you have to begin far beyond any of the physical things that actually happened. You first have to look at New York City, the mother which spawned them, which gave them its inner fire, creating an umbilical attachment of emotion to a monstrous hulk of urban sprawl. You have to walk its streets, ride its subways, see it bustling and alive in the day, cold and haunted at night. And you have to love it, embrace and recognize its strange power, for there, if anywhere, will you find the roots.   *– Lenny Kaye*

Some context is required. When the Velvet Underground began gigging on Manhattan's Lower West Side in December 1965, Greenwich Village was once again a vibrant scene. The Velvets, though, were the very antithesis of the folk-rock lightweights habitually haunting the better-known clubs. Yet, thanks to journalist and early Velvet advocate Al Aronowitz, within a week of their first gig the Velvets were playing nightly in the Village.

Whatever the owner of the not-so-appositely-named Cafe Bizarre thought he was getting, the Velvets were not it – even if their sets at this point were not extended excursions into white noise, feedback and distortion. Even these determined radicals realized that an unknown band playing in the Village was required to play largely recognizable tunes.

Sterling Morrison: We got six nights a week at the Cafe Bizarre, some ungodly number of sets, 40 minutes on and 20 minutes off. We played some covers – 'Little Queenie', 'Bright Lights Big City' . . . the black r&b songs Lou and I liked – and as many of our own songs as we had. We needed a lot more of our own material, so we sat around and worked. That's when we wrote 'Run Run Run', all those things.

After three weeks of 'some ungodly number of sets', the Velvets' capacity for tolerance – never one of their strong points – had been stretched to the limit. When the owner attempted to censor one of their own songs they responded with a commendable display of defiance.

Sterling Morrison: One night we played 'The Black Angel's Death Song' and the owner came up and said, 'If you play that song one more time you're fired!' So we started the next set with it.

A potentially exciting opportunity had opened up just two days before this Christmas catharsis. Andy Warhol had been one of the club's few customers to recognize the unique quality in the Velvets' sound. As one of New York's best-known and most successful visual artists – his famous Factory was already operating as an umbrella for diverse 'art'/film projects – Warhol was in a position to pull the Velvets up from this mundane bottom rung on rock & roll's slippery ladder.

Warhol had been looking to expand his operations to incorporate some undefined dimension of rock & roll. Right-hand man Paul Morrissey had convinced him that he could make money from putting his underground films 'in a rock & roll context'. The Velvet Underground were as close to art-rock as New York could provide in 1965. When Warhol offered them the opportunity to revert to a Factory regime they were happy to sign up.

Lou Reed: We looked at each other and said, 'This sounds like really great fun and a lot better than playing in this tourist trap in the Village.'

In popular perception, the Warhol association is the beginning of the Velvets' story. Indeed the degree of influence he exacted on the Velvets has often been misrepresented. It is important to recall that by the time they met Warhol the Velvets had already worked up the bulk of the songs they recorded on their first album.

Sterling Morrison: Andy gave us his opinion and we listened ... But if you asked him something directly, something like, 'What do we do now?', he would answer with one of his typical sarcastic answers, like, 'Well, what would you like to do?' Thus was his advice: 'Think what you would like to do and do it' ... That helped us, because we didn't waste any time thinking about how to get our songs on the radio.

Lou Reed's former professor at Syracuse, poet Delmore Schwartz – to whom the Velvets would dedicate the final cut on their first album – had already drummed into Reed the importance of maintaining faith in one's inherent worth in the face of ignorance and/or commercial constraints. Schwartz's bitter, cynical air, brought on by years of lack of recognition, made Reed profoundly aware of the potential cost of such integrity. He was certainly conversant with Schwartz's essay, 'The Vocation of the Poet in the Modern World', in which Schwartz had written, 'In the unpredictable and fearful future that awaits civilization, the poet must be prepared to be alienated and indestructible.'

Despite Warhol's general policy of non-interference, he did make one suggestion – and immediately caused dissension in the ranks. He wanted the Velvets to be augmented by a Hungarian chanteuse called Nico, who had come to New York in the summer of 1964, after Dylan had stayed at her Paris apartment, donating her one of his finest songs, 'I'll Keep It with Mine'.

Gerard Malanga: Andy decided to throw Nico into the act because the Velvets themselves were not very charismatic onstage, and Andy wanted a spotlight on someone. So Andy threw her in on the act against the wishes of the Velvets.

There was very little suitable material for Nico in the Velvets' current repertoire, and Reed was required to write new songs specifically for her. 'I'll Be Your Mirror' and 'Sunday Morning' showed that he was as capable of writing wistful ballads as the *Götterdämmerung* of 'Black Angel's Death Song'. Nico, though, was never fully accepted as an integrated member of the Velvets.

Sterling Morrison: There were problems from the very beginning because there were only so many songs that were appropriate for Nico and she wanted to sing them all – 'Waiting for the Man', 'Heroin', all of them. And she would try and do little sexual politics things in the band. Whoever seemed to be having undue influence on the course of events, you'd find Nico close by. So she went from Lou to Cale, but neither of those affairs lasted very long.

Yet Nico's importance in the early Velvets' set-up should not be underestimated. Her winter-day voice and icy beauty did add an extra dimension. Cale was certainly impressed by her singing, going on to produce her first four solo albums. The first Nico solo album, *Chelsea Girl*, recorded between the first two Velvets albums, could easily have been an alternative *Velvet Underground and Nico*. With Cale producing, Reed, Cale and Morrison providing musical accompaniment, and five songs written by Cale and/or Reed, *Chelsea Girl* is *Nico and The Velvet Underground*. It represents threads of the Velvets' sound largely discarded when they left the Warhol cocoon. 'Wrap Your Troubles in Dreams' and 'Little Sister' had both been recorded for the first Velvets album, while 'It Was a Pleasure Then' developed out of 'Melody Laughter', an early Velvets instrumental. The album would have been even more obviously in Velvets territory if producer Tom Wilson had not over-dubbed string arrangements on most of the songs.

Lou Reed: [I wish] they'd just have allowed Cale to arrange it and let me do some more stuff on it. Everything on it – those strings, that flute – should have defeated it. But with the lyrics, Nico's voice, it somehow managed to survive. We still got 'It Was a Pleasure Then' on, they couldn't stop us. We'd been doing a song like that in our beloved show; it didn't really have a title. Just all of us following the drone. And there it sits in the middle of that album.

'Our beloved show' was a multi-media presentation, *Andy Warhol – Uptight*, which opened at the Cinemateque in February 1966. The Velvets accompanied a 70-minute silent black and white film entitled *The Velvet Underground and Nico: A Symphony of Sound*. The idea quickly evolved into something more ambitious, utilizing dancers, lights, strobes and slides, as well as film, presenting a truly multi-media performance. It became known as the Exploding Plastic Inevitable. By the time the Velvets & Co. had returned from a brief out-of-town excursion, Warhol had arranged a residency on Manhattan's Lower East Side.

Sterling Morrison: When we opened the Dom, a nice setting in a spacious hall in St Marks Place, people didn't talk yet about the East Village ... When we started moving around, things changed. Never again did we have a place like that. We needed a base of operations, and the Dom was an ideal place.

The Velvets had always delighted in improvisation, but the Exploding Plastic Inevitable gave them an unprecedented opportunity to extemporize while kaleidoscopic images projected around them, dancers acted out conceptions, and people were encouraged to participate actively in the whole sensory experience. The downside: the EPI was restricting opportunities for the Velvets to work on new songs.

Sterling Morrison: We just played and everything raged around us without any control on our part.

The only extant recording of the Velvets with the EPI comes from a show in Columbus, Ohio, in November 1966, by which time the EPI had been up and running for nine months. On this evidence, the Velvets' EPI performances very much continued ideas originally explored by the Theatre of Eternal Music. What the Velvets' early experiments lacked was a sense of structure like that achieved with the Theatre. The Velvets needed to leave the confines of Warhol's grand experiment and rely entirely on their own presence, instead of subsuming their music to a series of sensory distractions. In describing one of their numbers, 'Melody Laughter' (which would form the basis for Nico's 'It Was a Pleasure Then'), Tucker hints at a tendency for indulgence which the EPI only encouraged.

Maureen Tucker: 'Melody Laughter' was another one. We used to play it when Nico was with us. I think there weren't any actual lyrics, just warble ... That would go anywhere from two minutes to forty-two ... It used to drive me crazy, because it started off with a certain beat, and Lou would just do what he wanted, and the next thing you know, John would be doing what he wanted, and I had to stay at the same beat, and you're hearing this definite other beat ... Cale would play the viola, put it down and pick up the bass, put it down, and if we had an organ or something he'd play that. It just went on and on.

Their time in the EPI illustrated an important aspect of Velvet pyschology. They had so many strings to their electric bow that they could manifest themselves in myriad, almost mutually exclusive ways. They could be a straight r&b band; an avant-garde ensemble on the outer edges of music; a light, melodic pop combo; a haunting wave of noise designed to complement Nico's occasionally over-strident vocals;

or indeed any combination of the above. The EPI allowed them to push one aspect of their complex makeup to an extreme, but it was never a direction that could be fully satisfying. After all, they had all these songs they wanted to record.

The Velvet Underground and Nico is an album even the band members never thought they would be allowed to cut. It seems to have been Warhol who made the decision to record the album and *then* try to sell it to a record label, rather than the more conventional route of securing a contract first. The advantage was obvious – no interference. As was the disadvantage – no funds. The results reflect both the sense of freedom and the economic limitations. Prior to the sessions the Velvets rehearsed constantly, working on new arrangements, determined to transfer as much of their unique sound to vinyl as possible.

The lack of funds meant that the number of studios available to them was seriously curtailed.

John Cale: This shoe salesman, Norman Dolph, put up the money, and he got a deal at Cameo-Parkway Studios, on Broadway. We went in there, and the floorboards were torn up, the walls were out, there were four mikes working. We set up the drums where there was enough floor, turned it all up and went from there.

If conditions were anything but ideal, the quality of the results says a lot for the Velvets' determination to compensate for primitive facilities, and for the engineer's ability to get the best from very basic equipment. There has been a lot of speculation in the intervening years as to Warhol's role in the making of this historic album (as there has been about his role in the Velvets' entire development). The album credits him as producer. In a conventional sense there was no producer. What Warhol did qualified more as executive input. Nevertheless, his role was central to the completion of the album, and its eventual sale to Verve.

Lou Reed: Andy was the producer and Andy was in fact sitting behind the board gazing with rapt fascination . . . at all the blinking lights. He just made it possible for us to be ourselves and go right ahead with it because he was Andy Warhol. In a sense he really did produce it, because he was this umbrella that absorbed all the attacks when we weren't large enough to be attacked . . . As a consequence of him being the producer, we'd just walk in and set up and do what we always did and no one would stop it because Andy was the producer. Of course he didn't know anything about record production . . . He just sat there and said, 'Oooh, that's fantastic,' and the engineer would say, 'Oh yeah! Right! It is fantastic, isn't it?'

The Velvets' determination to avoid compromises is reflected best by the two cuts which conclude the album. After the sensuous guile of 'I'll Be Your Mirror' comes the determinedly opaque 'Black Angel's Death Song' and the cacophonous 'European Son', which Reed dedicated to Delmore Schwartz because of his hatred for pop forms, 'European Son' being a long way from any rock music being made in 1966. They did not confine the song's sounds to musical instruments.

Maureen Tucker: [There's] a chair being scraped across the room by Cale, at which point he stops in front of Lou, who drops a glass . . . The engineer, he's saying, 'My God, What are you doing?' . . . It was tremendous, because it is in time, and the music starts right up. I don't know how we timed it like that . . . [but 'European Son'] was just different every time. There was no structure, we just did it.

With the album largely complete when the Velvets went looking for a record deal, there could be no misunderstanding as to what any potential label might be getting. Not surprisingly, this was a major problem. Atlantic were interested in signing the band – minus 'Heroin' and 'Venus in Furs'! In their search for a label not afraid to handle a band who were a little out of the ordinary, the Velvets had one useful ally. CBS producer Tom Wilson had seen the band playing in the Village, wanted to work with them, and already had a label in mind.

Sterling Morrison: Tom Wilson . . . was still at Columbia. He told us to wait and come and sign with him when he moved to Verve because he swore that at Verve we could do anything we wanted. And he was right. We gave something up of course, because there was no effective marketing on Verve . . . The album was ready by April 1966, but I don't think it even made a '66 release.

Eventually released in March 1967, *The Velvet Underground and Nico* is an extraordinarily assured debut album. Within its grooves lay not only the seeds of subsequent Velvet albums – *White Light/White Heat* ('Black Angel's Death Song', 'European Son'), *The Velvet Underground* ('I'll Be Your Mirror', 'There She Goes Again') and *Loaded* ('I'm Waiting for the Man', 'Run Run Run') – but a thousand innovations drawn upon by later bands. The Velvets never again allowed the hypnotic drone of Cale's viola its full impact. 'Venus in Furs' and 'Heroin', in particular, defined the Velvets sound for some time to come. Yet the album went largely ignored by contemporaries.

If the Velvets were operating outside conventional parameters, they did not see themselves as working entirely in a vacuum. Within the East Village itself were a couple of other bands striving to widen the limits of popular music.

Sterling Morrison: The Fugs, the Holy Modal Rounders and the Velvet Underground were . . . [all] authentic Lower East Side bands. We were real bands playing for real people in a real scene.

In fact the Holy Modal Rounders, whose fusion of bluegrass, country and folk into something truly original was equally at odds with the times, had been the original back-up group for the Fugs, at a time when Sanders and Kupferberg lacked even the basic musical knowledge required to realize the wilful parodies of rock forms that they had in mind.

Pete Stampfel: When they started they sat down and decided to form a dirty rock & roll band. Knowing nothing about rock & roll whatsoever they proceeded to write sixty songs, like 'Bolt On Clip' and 'Coca Cola Douche', exactly like punk ten years later. Just taken with an abrasive vision which, despite the fact they had no technical knowledge or chops or expertise or skill to do it in the standard way, did it anyway on pure balls . . . Sanders had this toy organ, and Ken Weaver had various hand drums which kept on getting stolen from him, and Kupferberg didn't play anything, so I volunteered the Rounders to be their backing band.

If the Holy Modal Rounders could be considered a folk version of the Velvets, there was one more band that the Velvets took seriously among the jumble of folk-rock exponents and West Coast rockers, the only outfit to have had a commensurate influence on modern rock & roll – the Byrds. Though the Byrds achieved considerable chart success, like the Velvets their innovations were largely ignored in their day.

Sterling Morrison: I always liked . . . the Byrds . . . Roger McGuinn was always at an incredible level. If I had to admit that something called folk-rock existed . . . then the Byrds were it.

Bob Quine: When I met Lou Reed in 1969, the only guitarist he would say anything positive about was McGuinn. When 'Eight Miles High' had just come out he saw them in a club in the Village. He was thinking along the same lines too. He was listening to Ornette Coleman.

If the Velvets were painting themselves in black and white, and the Fugs and the Byrds in sepia tones, the remainder of the American music scene they perceived in garish technicolour. Rather than indulging in the contemporary fascination with hallucinogenics, the Velvets were an amphetamine band – in every sense – loud, cynical, brutal and frenetic. They were not interested in mellowing out an audience.

Sterling Morrison: Drugs didn't inspire us for songs or anything like that. We took them for old-fashioned reasons – it made you feel good, braced you for hostile audiences and criticism.

Of course the Velvets' association with amphetamines and – it was assumed – heroin, only confirmed their Satanic mission in the eyes of their most vehement critics.

Pete Stampfel: Amphetamine was considered the Bad drug, it was what evil people took to make 'em more evil, or nice people took it and became evil!

If the Velvets seemed confrontational, this was absolutely deliberate. The band was formed to shake people up. Confrontation (in all its forms) was a major part of both Cale's and Reed's psyches at the time.

John Cale: I had no intention of letting the music be anything other than troublesome to people. It was a revolutionary, radical situation. We really wanted to go out there and annoy people.

If their music sounded extreme within the jaundiced confines of Manhattan, then a trip to the West Coast in the summer of 1966 offered the Velvets a rare opportunity to take their sound to the heart of the hip(py) underground and confront the gurus of Soporifia. The Velvets' main concern on arriving in Los Angeles was to complete some 'retouching' on their debut album with Tom Wilson.

Maureen Tucker: When MGM bought [the album], and agreed to put it out, they gave us three hours in California in the studio to fix ten songs.

The Velvets ended up re-recording four songs – 'Waiting for the Man', 'All Tomorrow's Parties', 'Heroin' and 'Venus in Furs' – though at least one band member was unhappy with the released version of 'Heroin'.

Maureen Tucker: 'Heroin' drives me nuts . . . It's a pile of garbage on the record . . . The guys plugged straight into the board. They didn't have their amps up loud in the studio, so of course I couldn't hear anything . . . And when we got to the part where you speed up . . . it just became this mountain of drum noise in front of me. I couldn't hear shit . . . So I stopped, and being a little wacky, they just kept going, and that's the one we took.

The Velvets and the EPI slotted in some shows in Los Angeles. They quickly found that they had already been tried, judged and sentenced by the West Coast media.

Sterling Morrison: The West Coast music scene was then a very strong force trying to predominate within the music industry. I remember that we rented a car at the airport, and the first thing we heard was 'Monday, Monday'. We knew that it was going to be hard to please these people on their own turf.

John Cale: Our attitude to the West Coast was one of hate and derision.

In San Francisco, where they played two shows at the legendary Fillmore West, the Velvets were equally at odds with the prevailing wave. The world media would soon designate San Francisco as the veritable pulse of what was happening in contemporary music, thanks to local outfits like the Grateful Dead, Jefferson Airplane, Great Society and Big Brother & the Holding Company.

Sterling Morrison: When we finally made it to San Francisco we were attacked directly. They convinced themselves that we were there to destroy the innocence and purity of their music. Ralph Gleason said that we were the urban evil of New York, and we were there to corrupt the simple beauty of the California music.

Though the Velvets would return to San Francisco on an annual basis until the fall of 1969 (when they played a long residency at the Matrix, from which much of the *1969* album comes), very little would change in the intervening three years. The wind would continue to be filled with a pungent smoke.

By the spring of 1967 – their debut album finally in the shops – the Velvets were outgrowing their association with Warhol. The EPI had become a means to avoid working on new songs and, despite the Warhol connection, the debut album was selling poorly. The art connection also meant that the Velvets were failing to reach a rock & roll audience.

Maureen Tucker: We played one place in Philadelphia . . . at some art show, and I'm telling you . . . I'd be beating the shit out of those drums, and I'd look up and see – Urgh! – it was 50-year-olds, people who came to see a soup-can, and this is what they got. And Gerard swooping around in his bikini with the American flag.

The band had tired of working with Nico on stage and Reed felt that Warhol had now made his grand rock & roll gesture.

Lou Reed: Andy came up to me and said we should have a talk. He said, 'You have to decide what you want to do, Lou. Do you want to start expanding into the outside world, or do you want to keep doing museums and art shows?' And I decided – 'Well, we're leaving you.' He was furious.

Between May and December 1967 the Velvets, unimpeded by the EPI, worked on a live sound that meshed the abstract noise of 'European Son' with modern pop-rock structures. They often opened shows with a powerful instrumental christened 'Booker T' (which was so far removed from 'Green Onions' that 'Purple Hearts' might have been a more apposite title). They also worked up a monumental tale called 'Sister Ray' around a riff they had first devised in Chicago, in June 1966, during an EPI residency, when the Velvets were playing without Reed, who was sick. Cale had assumed vocal duties, Tucker had become bassist, while Angus MacLise had temporarily returned to play tabla drums sitting on the floor.

'Sister Ray' could run anywhere from fifteen to forty minutes, depending on which version of the saga Reed wanted to relate that night.

John Cale: In the Velvet Underground the idea was to go out there and improvise songs on stage. I talked to Andy Warhol about it and he said we should actually go out there and rehearse. Like, stop and go back and teach each other and the audience the songs.

There are no circulating recordings of any Velvets show from 1967 (though a 58-minute tape of an April show at the Gymnasium in New York remains in the hands of John Cale). Two songs from the Gymnasium – one broadcast by Cale on a New York radio station some years later, 'Guess I'm Falling in Love', the other, 'Booker T', included on Cale's 1992 soundtrack album *Paris S'Eveille* – indicate the Velvets' renewed delight in distortion and feedback as the two principal pillars of their temple of sound. The problem that they now faced was how to get this 'off-the-dial' sound on to vinyl.

John Cale: When it came to *White Light/White Heat*, it was like a road band, improvising songs on stage . . . We decided to make that album as live as possible, we told Tom Wilson we were gonna do it as we do it on stage.

The resultant album may well be the most extreme committed to vinyl in the name of rock & roll. The title itself, *White Light/White Heat,* sums up the sound they were trying for. But Tom Wilson, sitting in as producer, lacked the technological expertise to capture the Velvets' live sound and was 'more interested in the blondes running through the studio', while the engineer merely grew increasingly exasperated at the Velvets for attempting to record such unconventional sounds.

Sterling Morrison: There was fantastic leakage because everyone was playing so loud and we had so much electronic junk with us in the studio – all these fuzzers and compressors. Gary Kellgran the engineer, who is ultra-competent, told us repeatedly: 'You can't do it – all the needles are on red.' And we reacted as we always reacted: 'Look, we don't know what goes on in there and we don't want to hear about it. Just do the best you can.' And so the album is all fuzzy, there's all that white noise . . . We wanted to do something electronic and energetic. We had the energy and the electronics, but we didn't know that it couldn't be recorded . . . What we were trying to do was to really fry the tracks.

There was at least one song whose impaired state on the album was not a result of Wilson's inability or the studio's capabilities, but rather Reed's attempt to remake the Velvets entirely in his own image. The seeds of division were being sown.

Maureen Tucker: 'I Heard Her Call My Name' was ruined in the mix – the energy. You can't hear anything but Lou. He was the mixer in there, so he, having a little ego-trip at the time, turned himself so far up that there's no rhythm, there's no nothing.

All the members of the Velvets now admit that perhaps they overdid it on *White Light/White Heat*. On one song though – 'Sister Ray' – the Velvets captured the sound that proved elusive on the remainder of the record, a morass of noise from which each instrument is required to assert its own identity by cranking up and blasting out. The story of 'Sister Ray' is largely lost in the ongoing battle but even the least attentive listener could not ignore the repeated refrain about 'sucking on my ding-dong'. The Velvets had succeeded in pushing rock & roll off the dial.

Listening again to *White Light/White Heat*, it is astonishing that Verve ever countenanced its official release, particularly when the Velvets provided as front-cover artwork a photo of a black skull printed on a pitch black sleeve. Still, it was released, and fared even worse than the debut album.

In fairness to Verve, there was no way to market *White Light/White Heat* in 1968. It made Jefferson Airplane's *After Bathing at Baxters* sound like the Everly Brothers on Mogadon. Indeed the album was so far off the path of contemporary rock & roll that the Velvets themselves were constrained to retrace some of their own steps in order to produce something that their contemporaries could deal with. The remaining history of the Velvets is essentially one of attempting to commercialize innovations that date from the first two years of their existence.

If the Velvets' was the sound of New York City, then clearly they were giving the rotten apple a bad name. After a second album where references to drugs and deviant sex remained as overt as album number one (witness 'Lady Godiva's Operation' and 'Sister Ray'), the Velvets found it almost impossible to get radioplay in New York. They also found it increasingly difficult to locate suitable venues prepared to book them. The Velvets decided that, if New York didn't want their brand of musical mayhem, they would not foist their form of indigenous music upon it. As Sterling Morrison concisely put it, 'Our reaction was: fuck 'em. And we stopped playing in New York, despite the fact it was the prime market in the country, and our home.'

The Velvets did not play New York between the Gymnasium shows in the spring of 1967, and a residency at Max's in the summer of 1970. With the Velvets went the underground. The simultaneous abandonment of New York by its folk-rockers, heading for the mountains or the (other) coast, meant that the city became merely a stopover for bands seeking industry backing and publicity. It would be another five years before New York once again heard the beat of its own sound.

Having acquired a new manager, the unprepossessing Steve Sesnick, the Velvets' most regular hunting ground became the Boston Tea Party, a 1,200 capacity ballroom in which Sesnick had a controlling interest. From May 1967, when they played their first post-EPI shows there, the Velvets were rarely absent from the Tea Party for more than a couple of months.

Sterling Morrison: Boston was our second home. We had a large audience there. On one occasion we played in Boston 'against' the Doors. They had to come to our party, and they didn't like it.

The second most important venue for the Velvets was also within striking distance of New York. Cleveland's La Cave played host to the Velvets throughout 1968 and into 1969. At La Cave, like the Tea Party, the Velvets felt comfortable enough with their audiences to play whatever they considered appropriate. On one occasion their entire set consisted of a version of 'Sister Ray' prefaced by a 40-minute instrumental (christened 'Sweet Sister Ray').

Although the Velvets toured sporadically throughout 1968, ostensibly promoting their second album, they rarely performed much from *White Light/White Heat* save for 'Sister Ray' – which rarely bore much resemblance to the released version – and the title-track. They seemed genuinely unsure of what direction to pursue, given the resounding failure of the second album.

Reed had always retained a keen pop sensibility, dating back to his days at Pickwick, and in February 1968 the Velvets went into a New

York studio to record their first non-album single, two unashamedly pop-oriented songs, 'Stephanie Says' (later reworked as 'Caroline Says' on Reed's 1973 album *Berlin*) and 'Temptation Inside Your Heart'. The songs ended up unused. In May they recorded a further new song. 'Hey Mr Rain' seemed more like a return to forsaken territory, at least in its use of Cale's viola as the fulcrum of the band's sound.

No further studio recordings are known from the first nine months of 1968, as the two ostensible leaders of the Velvets vied for the future direction of the band. Inevitably, the songwriter won out and Cale was ousted from his own band.

John Cale: There were a lot of soft songs and I didn't want that many soft songs. I was into trying to develop these really grand orchestral bass parts, I was trying to get something big and grand and Lou was fighting against that, he wanted pretty songs.

Sterling Morrison: [Cale] was going in a more experimental direction, while Lou wanted something within a more 'pop' context . . . John and I were very happy with Sister Ray-type music . . . Lou placed heavy emphasis on lyrics. Cale and I were more interested in blasting the house down.

It may well be that Cale's 'more experimental direction' was simply an attempt to return the Velvets to their original aesthetic, which he felt they had strayed from.

John Cale: In the beginning, Lou and I had an almost religious fervour about what we were doing – like trying to figure ways to integrate some of La Monte Young's or Andy Warhol's concepts into rock & roll. But after the first record we lost our patience and diligence. We couldn't even remember what our precepts were.

The Velvets had always been the product of unresolved tensions, Cale and Reed always representing two contrary figures. But Cale's virtuoso grasp of instrumentation was largely irreplaceable. The Velvets would never recapture the unique, modal sound that Cale had brought to the band.

Sterling Morrison: John was playing great at the time. He was always exciting to work with. If you listen to his bass part on 'Waiting for the Man' it's illogical – inverted almost. He had really good ideas on bass. Or take a song like 'What Goes On': if you'd heard us play that in the summer of '68 with Cale on organ you would have known what it was all about . . . He was not easy to replace. Doug Yule was a good bass player, but we moved more towards unanimity of opinion, and I don't think that's a good thing.

It was as a recording band that their identity most dramatically changed. The third Velvets album seemed to continue the direction Reed had sought to steer the band in with the aborted February 1968 single, save for the surrealism of 'Murder Mystery'. According to Morrison, *The Velvet Underground* was not originally devised to sound the way that it came out.

Sterling Morrison: All our effects boxes were locked in a munitions box that was stolen at the airport when we were leaving for the West Coast to record. We saw that all our tricks had vanished, and instead of trying to replace them, we just thought that we could do without them.

It is difficult to give credence to Morrison's explanation, that the 'closet sound' of the third album was simply down to circumstance. Even the previously manic 'What Goes On' is a muted performance on record. Studio recordings that the Velvets made within six months of finishing their self-titled third album only affirmed the new direction. (These tracks make up the bulk of the two official collections of Velvet Underground out-takes, *VU* and *Another VU*.)

The Velvets were finally dumped by MGM in the fall of 1969 – without even releasing the tapes provided for a fourth Velvet Underground album – and had to record their final album for Atlantic. *Loaded* – 'with hits!' – ensured that the movement towards a more 'pop' orientation was evident to all. Reed seemed happy as a writer of orthodox rock songs rather than an exponent of the more free-form experiments that the Velvets had originally pioneered. Of course *Loaded* was in part an attempt to salvage for the Velvets a marginal commercial credibility. If so, their image was still far too daunting for *Loaded* to reverse their fortunes.

In concert the Velvets were not so conciliatory, continuing to indulge in exuberant self-expression. Though Cale's sawing viola was now absent from the mix, Reed and Morrison's twin-guitar attack was if anything turned up in intensity. Songs like 'Run Run Run', 'Waiting for the Man' and 'I Can't Stand It' became extended guitar duels, only tenuously connected to their studio prototypes. 'What Goes On' once again became an astonishing *tour de force*, as organ and guitar vied for attention. Their twelve-minute performance of the song at a hillside festival in New Hampshire in August 1969 (featured on the Italian *Wild Side of the Street* CD) remains one of the Velvets' most dramatic live recordings, illustrating perfectly the Velvets' notion of pushing rock music to the cliff-edge of a droning monotony before turning intensity up to white light/white heat proportions.

The live versions of 'What Goes On', 'Ocean', 'I Can't Stand It' and 'Waiting for the Man' on *1969* also hint at the Velvets' ability to transport their songs to another plane when extending them in performance. Despite the esteem that this belated collection of live Velvets cuts has enjoyed since its 1974 release, the bulk of *1969* is drawn from a sedate October 1969 performance at Dallas's End of Cole Avenue club.

Sterling Morrison: The [*1969*] tapes were recorded by the owners at the Matrix and End of Cole Ave. I don't like it, because it was taped in small locations . . . Generally our sound was bigger. On this record everything is subdued, there are no really loud songs . . . At the Boston Tea Party, a bigger location, the ideal size for us, about 1,200 people, we could really play.

If *1969* was recorded as the Velvets were descending from peak performing powers, the Dallas version of 'Sister Ray', omitted from *1969* but available on the Italian *End of Cole Avenue* CD, is an impressive example of how the Velvets could still build a song up in performance. It begins as if the Velvets were simply tuning up for an EPI-style symphony of sound, but then the bizarre tale begins to audibly unfold as the music teeters on the brink of a storm. First it spits, then it pours down like silver.

By the time of the November Matrix shows – from which the remainder of *1969* would later be drawn – the Velvets were fast disintegrating. They had lost the one label that had given them *carte blanche* in the studio, and though audience recordings from the beginning of 1970 show them extending 'Train Round the Bend/Oh Sweet Nuthin' into a seventeen-minute opus, and attempting ambitious new material like 'Sad Song', 'Men of Good Fortune' and a prototypical 'Oh Jim', the outfit that began recording *Loaded* – all the while performing their first New York residency in over three years at Max's Kansas City – had largely abandoned major extemporizations.

'Sister Ray' was now rarely performed. On *Live at Max's* no song clocks in at longer than five minutes, as if Morrison and Reed were too weary to blast away. The Velvets were certainly burnt out. By the end of the Max's residency, Reed was heartily sick of what his band had become. After a five-year tightrope walk between avant-garde ideals and commercial constraints, Reed realized that he had become nothing more than a circus performer.

Lou Reed: I hated playing Max's. Because I couldn't do the songs I wanted to do and I was under a lot of pressure to do things I didn't want to do . . . I was giving out interviews at the time saying yes, I wanted the group to be a dance band, I wanted to do that, but there was a large part of me that wanted to do something else. I was talking as if I were programmed . . . I didn't belong there. I didn't want to be a mass pop national hit group with followers.

If the Max's concerts were viewed by New York fans as something of a homecoming, the spirit of America's rock & roll underground was passing beyond the five boroughs. The torch was being carried not by fellow New Yorkers, but by bands who had been exposed to the Velvets during their regular sorties to second homes like Boston and Cleveland; and, most importantly, by two bands at the heart of an effervescent Detroit scene, the Stooges and the MC5, who fused their garageband aesthetic not to an avant-garde classical but to a free-jazz sensibility, searching for free-form with substance.

While the Velvets were vacating New York and the mainstream American media were centering their attention on the West Coast's gentrified version of rock & roll, the centre of white trash garage-rock was the home city of the soul brothers of Motown, then dominating the pop sensibilities of black America – Detroit, the Motor City.

If the Velvets can be considered to have fathered art-rock, then Detroit's two chief rock exponents, the MC5 and the Stooges, represented a more primitive tradition – rock & roll as the people's music, requiring nothing more than commitment from its participants, an approach best expounded by that godfather of punk-journalism, Lester Bangs:

Rock & roll, as I see it, is the ultimate populist art form, democracy in action, because it's true: anybody can do it. Learn three chords on a guitar and you've got it. Don't worry whether you can 'sing' or not. Can Neil Young 'sing'? Lou Reed? Bob Dylan? . . . For performing rock & roll, or punk rock, or call it any damn thing you please, there's only one thing you need: NERVE. Rock & roll is an attitude, and if you've got the attitude you can do it, no matter what anybody says. Believing that is one of the things punk rock is about. Rock is for everybody, it should be so implicitly anti-elitist that the question of whether somebody's qualified to perform it should never arise. But it did. In the Sixties, of course. And maybe this was one reason why the Sixties may not have been so all-fired great as we gave them credit for. Because in the Sixties rock & roll began to think of itself as an 'artform'. Rock & roll is not an 'artform'; rock & roll is a raw wail from the bottom of the guts. And like I said, whatever anybody ever called it, punk rock has been around from the beginning – it's just rock honed down to its rawest elements, simple playing with a lot of power and vocalists who may not have much range but have so much conviction and passion it makes up for it ten times over. Because PASSION IS WHAT IT'S ALL ABOUT – what all music is about.

If rock & roll is indeed 'a raw wail from the bottom of the guts' and punk 'rock honed down to its rawest elements', then their home in the late Sixties was undoubtedly Detroit. The Velvets flirted with the effects of distortion and feedback, but the MC5 based their entire sound on them. They had consciously assimilated the precepts of free-jazz pioneers like Albert Ayler and John Coltrane and now sought to place their innovations in a 'rock' setting. Their historic first album contains an adaptation of a Sun Ra song, 'Starship', and covers in their set at the time were drawn from Coltrane, Pharoah Sanders and Archie Shepp. The appeal of the free-jazz approach was obvious. To quote Valerie Wilmer in her history of the new jazz:

For the player, the new music has been concerned with ways of increasing his freedom to improvise, but to the listener, its most obvious characteristic was that the musicians constantly explored, and exploited, new systems. No sound, in fact, is considered unmusical in the New Music.

It was the MC5 who were largely responsible for turning Detroit into the centre of American underground rock & roll in the late Sixties. The Motor City Five, to give them their full name, had already been in existence some considerable time when they signed to Elektra Records in September 1968, predating even the Velvet Underground in formation. For the first two years of their existence (1964–6), they were essentially a covers band in the tradition of fellow Detroit combo the Amboy Dukes (the A-side of their privately pressed first single, released in 1966, was Van Morrison's 'I Can Only Give You Everything', a good indication of their early roots).

A change in rhythm section in the fall of 1965 – Michael Davis and Dennis Thompson enrolled on bass and drums respectively – to augment vocalist Rob Tyner and guitarists Wayne Kramer and Fred 'Sonic' Smith, allowed a shift towards a more improvisatory, jazzier approach. By the summer of 1965 they had introduced their most famous free-form song, an extended improvisation called 'Black to Comm'.

In the early months of 1967 they began to be managed by radical journalist John Sinclair, who quickly augmented their raucous rock & roll sound with a chic revolutionary stance. Sinclair shared the MC5's love of free jazz – he was the author of a regular jazz column in *Downbeat* – and openly encouraged them to travel further in this direction, at the same time cementing a link between the MC5 and his radical Trans-Love Energies organization. Under Sinclair's direction the band soon worked up several confrontational blasts of radioactive rock & roll, including 'Kick Out the Jams' and 'The Motor City is Burning'.

The considerable press that the MC5 were generating was bound to pique record company curiosity, but their radical stance was a dissuading factor for most major labels. The field was clear for a newcomer like Elektra, seeking to transform their 'folkdom' image into one that accorded with the rock & roll audience they had begun to attract with the popular success of the Doors. On 22 September 1968 Danny Fields, publicity director for Elektra Records, attended an MC5 benefit for the Children's Community School at the Union Ballroom on the University of Michigan's Ann Arbor campus.

By this point, the MC5 had ascended to the crest of their own personal wave, though Detroit's alternative scene had barely begun to coalesce. In concert they were fusing gut-wrenching originals like second single 'Borderline', the infamous 'Kick Out the Jams', and 'Come Together' with raucous covers of rock & roll classics like the Who's 'Can't Explain', Bob Dylan's 'Ballad of a Thin Man', Little Richard's 'Tutti Frutti' and Screaming Jay Hawkins' 'I Put a Spell on You', and versions of free-jazz epics like Pharoah Sanders' 'Upper Egypt', Coltrane's 'Tunji' and Archie Shepp's 'Hambone' (reworked as 'Ice Pick Slim'), all topped off nightly with their own 'energy orgy', 'Black to Comm'.

But there was serious dissension in the ranks.

John Sinclair: The Elektra contract came at the end of September 1968 – and the peak of their discontent. Just before Danny Fields came out to hear the Five and sign them up, we had a decisive argument. We were returning from a manufacturer's party, which we had attended to look at some new equipment. The band had all drunk a lot of alcohol at the party, and I was as pissed off as usual. They started attacking me on the way home, telling me that they were tired of living with my Trans-Love Energies crowd, and demanding that they be allowed to get a house of their own. I really got pissed off at that, and told them it was fine by me – that they could move out just as soon as they could afford it. I also told them that if they didn't start taking their work more seriously, I didn't want any more to do with them anyway . . . because I wasn't interested in playing nursemaid to a bunch of drunks.

Fields was not to know that the Sinclair/MC5 coalition was breaking apart. Perhaps it was the sense of an outfit straining at the seams that impressed Fields. He returned two weeks later with Elektra president Jac Holzman, who agreed to sign not only the MC5 but also a second act witnessed by Fields in September. At the MC5's insistence Fields had gone to see an even rawer Detroit outfit, the Psychedelic Stooges.

The MC5 were keen to document their own extraordinary live show as soon as possible. They arranged to record two shows at the end of October at the Grande Ballroom, a 2,000-seater venue in Detroit proper, where they had regularly appeared since October 1966 and were always assured of a rapturous reception.

The resultant album, *Kick Out the Jams*, is an appropriate document of the Motor City's premier underground band firing on all cylinders. The thunderous pounding dispensed by the rhythm section, aligned to a guitar-sound with the sort of distortion they usually measure on the Richter scale, was the perfect antidote to a bath at Baxter's. However, the album did not reflect the cross-section of material that the MC5 were playing, omitting the legendary 'Black to Comm', as well as 'I Believe In My Soul', 'Upper Egypt' and 'Tunji', all staples of their live set at the time. It was as if the MC5 were unsure about the likely reception for songs overtly reflecting their rock/free-jazz fusion.

By the time *Kick Out the Jams* was released in the spring of 1969 the MC5 were champing at the bit, angry at Sinclair's parochial politics and what they saw as his mismanagement. Sinclair later claimed that the band was showing its true colours, betraying a long-latent desire to move in a more mainstream direction. When the MC5 became embroiled in a controversy about the use of the word 'motherfuckers' on the title track to *Kick Out the Jams* and finally agreed to Elektra censoring the record on subsequent pressings – though not before taking out ads in the local Detroit press castigating one particular record chain for refusing to stock the album – Sinclair realized that pressure was being brought to bear, transforming his ultra-radical vision of the MC5 into a rock & roll band. No more, no less.

John Sinclair: I kept hoping they would wake up one day and realize what was going down. They never did. In fact, they kept going further in the other direction. As the band got more national publicity and exposure, the industry people started getting to them more and more, it seemed, trying to convince them that they would have to give up their 'political', revolutionary stance altogether if they planned to make it big in the biz. This fit right in with their own fears – that they had worked this long and this hard only to be denied their rightful position as a s*t*a*r band because their manager had mis-led them and had got them to do all the wrong things . . . and they began to plot their break from me.

When rock journalist-cum-aspiring record producer Jon Landau moved into the MC5's Detroit home in May 1969 to help put together a second MC5 album, this one for Atlantic Records (Elektra had sacked them as a result of the 'motherfucker' incident), the original exponents of free-form distortion in rock & roll were dead in the water, even if the body stayed afloat for another two years.

The MC5 were the first important American underground rock band to forsake their previous sureness of direction, and ultimately disintegrate, when unable to reconcile the need for commercial success with an original integrity. They would not be the last. Their natural heirs as Detroit's premier ambassadors of subterranean rock & roll, the Stooges, never had any such illusions of reconciling their outrageous approach, both musically and visually, with a mass market. Their shows were a form of terrorist assault resonating deep into witnesses' psyches.

The Stooges had made their live debut just six months before signing to Elektra in October 1968. Part of the difference between the vinyl legacies of the Stooges and the MC5 may be due to the former being signed to Elektra at a point when they were still experimenting with their music. They were thus able to sustain their brand of garage-rock long enough to record two of rock & roll's most powerful collections of 'raw wails from the bottom of the guts', before they too imploded under the intolerable burden of a public demand for excess in its many malignant forms.

The Stooges, when seen and heard by the shell-shocked Danny Fields in September 1968, may have been gigging barely six months but they already had their own 'sabre-toothed fury'. Their standard set never lasted more than 25 minutes, the bulk of which was taken up with such abstract constructs as 'The Dance of Romance' and 'Goodbye Bozos'.

Iggy Pop: We weren't interested in anything like writing a song or making a chord change. I didn't bother with anything like that until I had a recording [contract]; once I had the contract I thought I'd better really learn how to write some songs – so I did. Our [early] music was flowing and very conceptual. We'd have just one given song, called 'Wind Up', or I'd change the title to 'Asthma Attack' or 'Goodbye Bozos', or, I don't know, 'Jesus Loves the Stooges'. So, la de da, that's how we started out.

Iggy Pop's natural showmanship mitigated for a band who had barely made it out of the garage. Unremittingly inept, the Asheton brothers, who were largely responsible for the Stooges' pneumatic noise, were only just beginning to master their instruments when they signed to Elektra. What they did have was an ability to extemporize while Iggy did his stage acrobatics and indulged in his unique audience interplay.

Ron Asheton: Usually we got up there and jammed one riff and built into an energy freak-out, until finally we'd broken a guitar or one of my hands would be twice as big as the other and my guitar would be covered in blood.

Even in the early days their shows required an unusual degree of audience participation. The MC5's bass player, an early devotee, remembers the form Iggy's onstage stunts usually took:

Michael Davis: Iggy gyrated around the stage and usually made a crazy fool out of himself to everyone's pleasure. Everybody liked it. Everyone who was at those gigs was shocked in a pleasant way – not in a negative way. They weren't turning people off. They were just weird and different and didn't play songs like everybody else.

Having barely advanced beyond the stage where they 'didn't play songs', the Stooges were patently unprepared to record an album when signed to Elektra in October 1968, and were not much more prepared when they actually began recording their debut album in June 1969. They arrived in New York with just five songs – barely half an album – so Jac Holzman sent them away, telling them to return when they had enough material. They composed 'Not Right' and 'Real Cool Time' in the space of two days, but still required the largely improvised ten-minute opus, 'We Will Fall', to pad out their debut album. On 'We Will Fall', John Cale, the Stooges' chosen producer, added the trademark drone of his electric viola to the hypnotic quicksand of sound the Stooges spontaneously created, establishing a direct link between the Stooges' and the Velvets' improvisations.

The Stooges reflects a midway point in their passage from early, purely abstract structures to the coherence of their third and most conventional album, *Raw Power*. It had no more initial impact than *Kick Out the Jams*, despite being the first American rock & roll album to strip the early Rolling Stones' sound down to a swamp of jagged guitars and vocal histrionics.

Thankfully, the debut Stooges album, though met with general bemusement by critics divorced from its sister city sounds and indifference by the record-buying public, was only the first step in the Stooges' grand strategy. As the MC5's power began to fade, the Stooges, whenever they played at Detroit's Grande Ballroom, were cranking up the volts. The sheer unpredictability of Iggy in performance warranted regular examination:

John Sinclair: Iggy had gone beyond performance – to the point where it really was some kind of psychodrama. It exceeded conventional theatre. He might do *anything*. That was his act. He didn't know what he was going to do when he got up there on the stage. It was exciting. I'd just watch him and I'd think, 'Wow, this guy will stop at nothing. This isn't just a show – he's out of his mind!' . . . I remember when he started taunting the crowd with broken bottles . . . I think he got to where he didn't really have any respect for the audience. So he'd do things to see what would get a response.

On 29 August 1969 both of Detroit's arch-exponents of garage-rock shared a New York bill, at the State Pavilion in Queens. Though the Stooges would later make some of their most infamous appearances in New York, on this occasion they were watched by just a small enclave of New York rock fans who had come to see what all the fuss was about with these Detroit punks. Iggy's final act before leaving the stage was to pick up two drumsticks and 'cut long welts into his chest with the tips of the drumsticks'.

At subsequent New York shows Iggy would be far more extreme. He seemed to respond to the typical Manhattan 'let's wait and watch' attitude like a bull to an audience of Redcoats, and would do anything simply to engender a reaction. Photographer Bob Gruen recollects the effect of Iggy's attempt to reproduce his famous 'walking on the crowd' stunt from the 1970 Cincinatti Pop Festival, when playing New York's Electric Circus in the spring of 1971:

Bob Gruen: I'd heard of [the Stooges] and I got there and there's this guy covered in oil and glitter and peanut butter. There was this famous picture of him walking out on the people and he tried that in New York and he stepped off the stage – and these are New Yorkers, they don't touch the performers – and they all jumped back, 'Don't step on me asshole,' and he hit the floor eight feet down. And he's lying on the floor. We're all looking at him, 'What you doing on the floor, fella?'

Ron Asheton was now inflicting a guitar sound of wilting intensity on those fortunate audiences who saw the Stooges in the fall of 1969 and the winter and spring of 1970. That spring, in the wake of the release of the MC5's 'collaboration' with Jon Landau, *Back in the USA*, the Stooges recorded one of the two albums which define Detroit garage-rock at its best, *Funhouse* (the other, Alice Cooper's *Love It to Death*, Bob Ezrin would produce later that year). *Funhouse*, not *Back in the USA*, was the logical successor to *Kick Out the Jams*.

The Stooges had decided to embellish their raw(cous)ness with a saxophonist, Steve MacKay. If the MC5 had turned their backs on their early jazz/rock fusion, the Stooges were keen to add jazziness to jaggedness and Sinclair was once again an important influence in the process.

Ron Asheton: John Sinclair introduced us to Coltrane and we loved it ... We got Steve MacKay from the Charging Rhinoceros of Soul and Carnal Kitchen to play saxophone, because we liked the Coltrane stuff and wanted to have better freak-outs at the end of songs.

Recorded in May 1970 in Los Angeles, *Funhouse* redefined the Stooges' sound. It featured their most extreme statement, 'LA Blues', a five-minute sonic wave of feedback and noise that, as with 'We Will Fall', came into being simply because they lacked enough quality material to complete the album. However, in the case of *Funhouse* it was the only possible conclusion to an album that reached deep into the darkened pit of degradation and emerged with the unrefined essence of rock & roll.

In the summer of 1970 the Stooges headed in the direction that 'LA Blues' had given them, i.e. towards 'Energy Freak-Out Freeform' (the original title of 'LA Blues'). New songs with titles like 'Way Down in Egypt', 'Searching for Head' and 'Private Parts' were 'more jazz-influenced and less structured', and the Stooges, further augmented by second guitarist Billy Cheatham, allowed Ron Asheton to play more and more lead solos. Unfortunately Billy Cheatham was replaced in the fall of 1970 by a superior technician, James Williamson – shortly after the departure of saxophonist MacKay, who wished to form his own band – and the original Stooges ceased these explorations as Williamson began to steer the band in a more orthodox direction.

Despite the introduction of Williamson's brand of accessible high-energy rock & roll, in June 1971 Elektra decided not to take up an option on a third Stooges album and Pop decided that their expulsion from Elektra was a perfect reason to break up the band. The Stooges' lack of commercial viability had long been apparent even to Elektra, but the label had probably made a final decision to unload the Stooges the previous August. Iggy had insisted on a $400 advance to purchase enough cocaine to get him through four nights at New York's Ungano's, personally requesting the funds from Elektra president, Jac Holzman.

The Stooges' disintegration in June 1971 was part of a general fragmentation of Detroit's garage-rock scene, which was in an advanced state of collapse by the end of the year. Late in the day the MC5 seemed to realize the error of their ways, rectifying some of the damage caused by *Back in the USA* with the flawed but worthwhile *High Time*. Issued in October 1971, it features perhaps the MC5's quintessential rock & roll statement – 'Sister Ann'. The MC5 played their final show, appropriately, at Detroit's Grande Ballroom, on New Year's Day 1972.

Meanwhile Bob Seger had gone back to college in 1969 and Alice Cooper, who moved from Los Angeles to Detroit at the beginning of 1970, believing that it was a more conducive locale for their brand of theatrical garage-rock, returned to the West Coast after the commercial success of their 'Eighteen' single. Though their next album, *Killer*, was still very much in the garage-rock vein of *Love It to Death*, it was the last of the Alice Cooper albums to run on Motor City fuel.

Even the re-formed Stooges were now based five thousand miles away. If the Stooges had supposedly given their final show in June 1971, a lengthy post-Stooges respite did little to cure Pop or lead-guitarist James Williamson of junk habits. They unwisely reassembled in London in the summer of 1972, after David Bowie offered to produce an Iggy Pop album. They continued to produce music of stark primitivism but recorded only one more studio album, the disappointingly restrained (indeed ill-named) *Raw Power*, which suggested that Bowie's main forte was sanitizing genuine innovators for public consumption, particularly when taken in association with the results he achieved on Lou Reed's *Transformer*.

The reincarnated Stooges were billed as Iggy and the Stooges, and compositions which had previously been constructed by the band as a whole were now seen as the exclusive domain of Iggy Pop and his new confidant, James Williamson. The history of Iggy and the Stooges is one of a return into a maelstrom of physical excess but without Pop and Williamson's indulgences feeding back into the music. Partially this was due to a muting of Ron Asheton's role in the band. Though Williamson had originally been recruited as a second guitarist, Asheton was relegated to bass duties in the newly reconstituted Stooges.

Iggy finally cut loose from Mainman's financial talons in May 1973 and attempted to resurrect the Stooges in all their profane glory, but his own drug dependency and compulsive need to live up to his reputation for excess – created on the back of stories of him rolling in broken glass, gouging himself with a bottle and fighting the more adept bruisers from his audiences – was already tearing the band asunder.

Ron Asheton: [Iggy] started out doing self-destructive things because that was the way he felt. Then it got to be expected. He'd just try to top himself for the crowd. We would often say, 'Give it up Iggy' . . . He tried to top himself every time. I was waiting for him to kill himself.

Iggy and the Stooges would make one more major contribution to the punk aesthetic. Shows in Detroit in October 1973 and February 1974 (their final show) were compiled into a live document, *Metallic K.O.*, perhaps the most confrontational live album in rock music, Iggy determined to prove his willingness to push the boundaries of the artist—audience love—hate relationship beyond previous norms.

The Stooges' influence on the New Wave would far exceed that of the MC5, both in terms of lead singer Iggy Pop's onstage antics (and attendant lifestyle), and the metal-crusher sound they developed. Yet their influence would rarely be an accurate reflection of what the Stooges themselves had been about. As Lester Bangs later wrote:

I'd just like to ask some of these spikedomed little assholes if they think when Iggy formed the Stooges he sat down and said, 'Okay, boys, let's be punks: we'll get fucked up all the time and act like assholes and make a point of not knowing howta play our instruments! It'll make us famous!' ... Iggy was just a fucked-up kid who took too many drugs and wanted to have the most fucked-up band in history so as to externalize his own inner turmoil.

During Detroit's temporary primacy in underground rock & roll, Bangs worked for the Motor City's own rock & roll magazine. Just as Detroit's music was intended to be the very antithesis of all the West Coast artists that *Rolling Stone* doted upon, so *Creem* was a necessary alternative to *Rolling Stone*'s 'rock as Art' approach. Throughout the Detroit years (1969–71) it maintained its underground status, thanks largely to its enduring coverage of the Detroit bands and the 'degenerate drool' of Lester Bangs and Dave Marsh. Lester Bangs had started out writing the occasional piece for *Rolling Stone*, but soon realized that his aesthetic had little in common with theirs. So he moved to Detroit, working throughout the early Seventies for *Creem*:

Lester Bangs: Rolling Stone had flown me up to [San Francisco to] check me out, since I had been writing for them for about six months. I guess they wanted to see if I was executive timber. I guess I wasn't, because not only did I get moved from Greil Marcus's to Langdon Winner's house after about two days, but I thought it was as curious that they sat around, not even smoking pot, but listening to Mother Earth and Creedence with absolute seriousness, as they were bewildered by my penchant for guzzling whiskey all day while blasting 'Sister Ray' at top volume ... to make a dismal story mercifully short, I discovered a magazine in Detroit called

Creem, whose staff was so crazy they even put the Stooges on the cover. Of every issue! So I left my job and school and girlfriend and beer-drinking buddies and moved to Detroit, where my brand of degenerate drool would be not only tolerated but outright condoned, and over the five years I worked at *Creem* we used our basic love for it to exploit the punk aesthetic and stance in just about every way humanly possible.

Though *Creem* would make its own gradual transition into a mainstream magazine during the Seventies, it was one of the Motor City's more enduring legacies from its buoyant late-Sixties scene. It still espoused the Detroit creed in its pages as late as 1974–5, when, aside from Bangs, their very own godfather of punk journalism, they published the work of two figures central to America's mid-Seventies rediscovery of a rock underground: Patti Smith from New York and Peter Laughner from Cleveland.

The first significant band to fully embrace the Velvets' – and to a lesser extent the Stooges' – approach to rock music emerged in the early months of 1971 from Boston, where the Tea Party had played host to remarkable shows by both bands in recent years. In his sleeve-notes to *The Original Modern Lovers*, the Modern Lovers' leader and founder, Jonathan Richman, admits, 'If it weren't for [Iggy] and Lou Reed this record wouldn't have existed.'

Richman had been a regular attender at the Velvets' Tea Party gigs and often socialized with the band. Though he was profoundly affected by the power of the Velvets' sound, his own message was largely at odds with the amphetamine darkness of the Velvets.

Richman's early songs celebrated the ordinary – 'I Grew Up in the Suburbs', 'Modern World' and 'Don't Let Our Youth Go to Waste' – displayed a refreshingly uncloying form of romanticism – 'Song of Remembrance for Old Girlfriends', 'A Plea for Tenderness', 'Someone I Care About' and 'Womanhood' – and generally advocated the joys of the open road/sky – 'Roadrunner', 'Riding the Highway' and 'Fly into the Mystery'. They also insisted on physical well-being at a time when the rock underground generally subscribed to the 'road of excess leading to the palace of wisdom' principle. 'I'm Straight' and 'She Cracked' disputed the theory.

Peter Laughner later recalled that as soon as he could play guitar, Richman would 'stalk through the parks of Cambridge, declaiming his songs to anyone within earshot, yelling things like "I'm not a hippie! I'm not stoned!"'

Jerry Harrison: Jonathan had a message that went against the grain of the times in that he was against drugs. To me he captured a certain kind of teen frustration practically better than anything that's ever been written . . . [but] sonically, we were into the idea of noise and into using distortion and hard sounds. Jonathan was using a really clipped, transistor distortion [on his guitar] and I would run my Fender-Rhodes piano through a fuzztone. It was a very aggressive, hard music.

The Modern Lovers, consciously adopting the twin-engined organ/ guitar sound that the Cale/Reed Velvets had pioneered, relied on Richman's idiosyncratic vocal delivery and heartfelt lyricism to add an authentic stamp of originality. The irony of Richman's career is that his way of 'outgrowing' the influences of Lou Reed and Iggy Pop was to not only gradually strip his music down – a process also evident in Reed's late-Sixties and early-Seventies work – but also to regress lyrically to a point where direct honesty often gave way to platitudes.

A prototype Modern Lovers had been formed in 1970, featuring Richman, John Felice, David Robinson and Rolfe Anderson. They lasted barely six months, only drummer Robinson and Richman himself surviving the spring 1971 transition into a band of real potential, the true Modern Lovers.

Jerry Harrison: Ernie [Brooks] and I were having a party in the apartment we shared in Cambridge. Jonathan wandered in with all these people who had acted in Andy Warhol movies. He had the new Velvet Underground album, *Loaded*, which I had not heard, and he was very excited by it. He put it on and sort of danced in our kitchen singing about it. He had just formed a band and wasn't sure if it was going to be called the Modern Lovers. Jonathan's whole rap about the beauty of commercial enterprises, the signs on the highway and Howard Johnson's, fitted in with the idea I had for a movie I was making at the time . . . So Jonathan came over and started talking about whether we would play with him . . . First Ernie joined, and then about a week or two later I joined.

The Modern Lovers' early Boston shows soon generated an impressive reputation, which extended as far as New York, where Lillian Roxon of the *Daily News* was an important media supporter, encouraging her fellow journalists to go see the band and predicting great things of them. Though they would play surprisingly few shows in New York, the

Modern Lovers always had a considerable reputation in the city. Sadly the Lovers' – or perhaps more accurately Richman's – elitist distaste for the New York scene did them no favours.

Jerry Harrison: We seemed to be more well-known in New York than we were in Boston, which was our home base. We only played New York a couple of times, but we were very popular among the music critics centered around Danny Fields and Lillian Roxon and Steven Gaines and, later, Lisa Robinson.

Despite the relative isolation of Boston and the reluctance of the Modern Lovers to expand their horizons, their enthusiastic, unpaid publicists ensured that A&R men were soon descending on New England to see them perform, prepared to wine and dine these slightly emaciated young men. In April 1972 they were finally convinced by Warner Brothers and A&M to fly to Los Angeles to record some demos, the band's passage being financed jointly by the two labels. John Cale, whose post-Velvets work had been primarily in the guise of a producer (most notably for Nico and the Stooges) was Richman's preferred choice to produce the Warners demos.

Though the nine demos recorded with Cale eventually convinced Warner Brothers to sign the Modern Lovers, there was a considerable delay while options were considered. They had recorded some further demos, this time at A&M's expense (the Warners and A&M demos constitute the bulk of *The Modern Lovers*, released in 1976), but A&M were less impressed.

The Modern Lovers is the only real document of the Lovers at the time when they were seeking to combine the roar of the Velvets with Richman's eccentric suburbanism, and it 'remains a souvenir of what was and a hint of what might have been', to quote *Rolling Stone*. The album's sweep, particularly for a collection of demos, is impressive. From the contagious 'Pablo Picasso' to the rip-roaring 'Roadrunner', *The Modern Lovers* is the work of a supremely homogenous outfit.

Despite being very interested in signing the Modern Lovers, Warner Brothers were unable to stop them hotfooting it back to Boston and then seemed equally incapable of getting them to furnish evidence of the new songs they were allegedly working on. When the Lovers did go into a studio, Intermedia in Boston, they came out with the maudlin

'Hospital', a song about the narrator's fascination with a comatosed patient, and inferior takes of 'Someone I Care About' and 'Roadrunner'. In despair, the label asked the New York Dolls' manager, Marty Thau, if he would like to represent the band.

Marty Thau: WEA [sic] approached me. I was managing the [New York] Dolls – we're up to '72 – and they sent an emissary to New York to ask me if I would manage the Modern Lovers too, because of the problems they had in relating to the band. So I went to Boston and lived in their house that the company had rented for them to get their material together and I didn't quite communicate with them. I felt there was some kinda inner difference that existed in Jonathan's brain as it related to the other members of the band. It was just neither here nor there ... Jonathan's fantasy about how a rock star should behave, and appear and record. He just didn't want to fit into the system.

By the end of the summer of 1972, when Thau went to Boston, the Modern Lovers were already losing their previous sureness of direction, without even recording an album and with little of substance to show for all the hyperbole and attention. Richman's ideas about the sound the Lovers should advance were now veering towards his later minimalism. Out of accord with the rest of the band, Richman was failing to take account of the Modern Lovers' strengths.

When Kim Fowley entered the picture, matters only grew more confused. Hollywood entrepreneur Fowley had come across the Lovers in Boston, shortly after their return from Los Angeles, and was instantly impressed. He persuaded them to go into Dinky Dawson's basement studio and record some more demos with him, hoping to get results that Richman would be happy with, but the demos recorded that summer were patently inferior to the Warners and A&M demos – even if Fowley seems to have endeared himself to the Modern Lovers.

Jerry Harrison: We didn't have a manager at the time and we wanted to go with Steve Paul. He had a record label [in mind] at the time. And Clive Davis at CBS was a big fan of the band. We decided that we would [go with Davis] and then he changed his mind and then later Steve backed out after we had tried to sign for the Epic label ... That took about six months. We eventually went with Warner Brothers because we felt John

Cale would be a good producer [but] ... by the time we got there Jonathan had begun to really lose interest in his early songs and had stopped caring about the Velvet Underground [sound].

When they flew to the West Coast early in the fall of 1973 – after a year of prevarication – at last prepared to record a debut album for Warners, Richman was clearly at odds with the remainder of the band.

It had been nearly eighteen months since the Modern Lovers had recorded the demos which had so impressed Warner Brothers. The label was therefore understandably concerned when producer John Cale, again drafted in at Richman's request, reported back that Richman was refusing to recut some of the stand-out songs that they had demoed earlier. Instead Richman wanted to record a series of entirely new songs.

He certainly had a plentiful supply of songs. The problem was that songs like the largely spoken eight-minute 'Plea for Tenderness', the wistful 'Song of Remembrance for Old Girlfriends' and the hymnal 'Fly into the Mystery' hardly maintained the high energy quotient that Warners had expected on the basis of Cale's earlier demos, while 'Hey Mr Insect' was just absurd. The rest of the Modern Lovers were as unhappy as Warners with Richman's new direction. As Matthew King Kaufman wrote in his notes to the 1989 CD reissue of *The Modern Lovers*:

By now Jonathan was developing a more sedate, child-like optimism which characterizes his work today. He wanted to turn down the volume, cut back the distortion, and record an entirely new batch of songs. The rest of the band, while not necessarily opposed to such a transition later, felt strongly that they would be better off recording as they sounded now. Cale didn't understand the problems Richman was having as he and the band started to grow apart.

A decision was made to resume recording the album with a new producer – enter Kim Fowley once again, with whom the Lovers proceeded to record 'I'm Straight', 'Government Center', 'She Cracked', 'I Wanna Sleep in Your Arms', 'Girlfriend' and 'Roadrunner'. Despite the up-tempo nature of these songs, only 'I'm Straight' and 'Government Center' were really usable (both were eventually released on Warners' various-artist sampler *Troublemakers*) and the Fowley sessions were soon aborted by Warner Brothers, who decided to write off their investment, blaming the Lovers' removal from the label on vinyl shortages and adverse economic conditions. The reality was that Richman was beyond anyone's command, and the band were as tired of his antics as Warners.

Robinson quit within a couple of weeks of the Modern Lovers' return from LA, and by January 1974 Harrison had also reached the point of no return. At a show in Cambridge, Richman pushed his luck too far.

Jerry Harrison: After the first set Jonathan started ... arguing that I was playing too loud and he couldn't hear his voice ... He was always saying, 'I saw someone out there with his hands over his ears. Please turn down!' He just went on and on. Finally Bob Turner, the new drummer – I was already a lost cause – said, 'What the fuck are you tryna do?' And that was it ... we went out and played and got three encores. Then we did this impromptu song with Jonathan making up words about how he needed silence and no one understood.

The Modern Lovers' failure to live up to the promise of their 1972 demos has meant that they have commanded only a footnote in rock & roll history. Yet the truth is that on their day they were one of the few genuinely exciting bands around at a time of retrenchment in rock music. Theirs was a promise perhaps the equal of the Velvets, but largely still-born.

Jerry Harrison: The Modern Lovers were an attempt every evening at seeing what would happen and adjusting to the acoustics of the hall, seeing where that would lead to and having a very strict structure and sort of a droning that would provide you with the basic idea from where you would go ... Certain songs were arranged but, with the best, accidents would happen and you'd pick up on 'em ... It was a very exciting band and [at] that time ... it was very counter to what was going on. We felt very much alone and very much ahead. Even though we were primitive there was an energy there that no one [else] seemed to have.

5 The Underground Jukeboxes

If Boston's Modern Lovers quickly came to the attention of the record industry, as had the Stooges in Detroit and the New York Dolls in New York, there was one budding alternative scene that went largely ignored during the early Seventies – Cleveland. In a post-Velvets world, Cleveland's premier band was powerpop combo the Raspberries. Raspberries aside, the city's bars were full of bands playing a steady diet of Top 40 sounds and – at least as far as the industry was concerned – very little else.

Michael Weldon: Cleveland has a strong tradition of bands playing cover versions in bars and sometimes getting very popular locally.

In this vacuum of indifference, original ideas had time to develop. Potentially innovative bands could work on a sound (and the musicianship required to achieve it), and in the early Seventies that sound was largely Velvets- and Stooges-inspired.

David Thomas: [We] were working in isolation – we had no hope of ever being taken seriously by the mainstream establishment. All the other bands in town played Top 40 sort of stuff – the mainstream bands. They thought we got stoned and got on the stage and made stuff up as we played. So we had no hope of ever being successful, which is a heartening and creatively positive thing . . . So a lot of stuff was developing at that point that later, when the marketplace opened [up], had access to the market.

Despite being a very small, insular scene, Cleveland's Seventies underground was divided from the start into two camps – what might be considered the Lakewood and Disc Records brigades. The prime movers in the Electric Eels – John Morton, Dave E, Brian McMahon and Paul

Marotta – and Mirrors – Jamie Klimek and Jim Crook – all attended Lakewood High School. The two frontmen in Rocket from the Tombs, Peter Laughner and David Thomas, did not.

Charlotte Pressler: It is important to Cleveland punk history that Cleveland punks are West Side, almost exclusively. People from Cleveland Heights liked jazz and progressive music and folk music. It wasn't a working-class social background, it was precariously middle class ... John [Morton] ... had been to one of the local private schools and gotten kicked out for being obstreperous. So Morton finished up at Lakewood High School ... Jamie Klimek's family had moved to Lakewood [and] Jamie was a high-school dropout. Peter [Laughner] grew up in Bay Village, which is a sterile little bedroom suburb, a WASP suburb ... David Thomas was from Cleveland Heights. His father taught for many years at one of the community colleges here ... [All of us] emphatically did not want to join the class that our parents struggled into.

If there was one central figure in Cleveland's alternative rock scene, it would have to be Peter Laughner, even if his earliest musical influences were rather traditional, primarily the blues of Robert Johnson, Leadbelly, Willie Dixon, etc. His first band, Mr Charlie, formed in 1968 while still in high school, played in the style of early Yardbirds/Stones until Laughner heard the first Captain Beefheart album, *Safe as Milk*, after which they began playing their blues 'Beefheart-style'.

At the same time as his discovery of Beefheart, Laughner became seriously immersed in the recordings of the Velvet Underground. The impact of the Velvets was such that Laughner would later write:

When I was younger, the Velvet Underground meant to me what the Stones, Dylan, etc. meant to thousands of other midwestern teen mutants ... All my papers were manic droolings about the parallels between Lou Reed's lyrics and whatever academia we were supposed to be analysing in preparation for our passage into the halls of higher learning ... I had a rock band and we played all these songs, fuelled pharmaceutically by our bassist who worked as a delivery boy for a drugstore and ripped off an entire gallon jar full of Xmas trees and brown & clears. In this way I cleverly avoided all intellectual and creative responsibilities at the cleavage of the decades.

Whenever the Velvets would play at La Cave, Laughner, along with

Lakewood High student Jamie Klimek, would hang out in the back room between sets, 'listening intently while Lou Reed strummed his big Gibson stereo and talked about chord progressions and life on the road'. Soon enough, Laughner was steering Mr Charlie away from its rhythm & blues origins.

Charlotte Pressler: The band worked up a thirty-minute, feedback-filled version of 'Sister Ray', at the close of which Peter generally leaned his guitar against the amp and walked away, letting it scream. They did originals too; there was a quasi-blues Peter had written called 'I'm So Fucked Up'. It wasn't your average high-school band.

Laughner's tastes were not confined to rock and its blues-based ante-cedents. He was also a fan of free jazz, in particular of one of Cleveland's more innovative sons, Albert Ayler. Charlotte Pressler, who would later marry Laughner, recollects their first meeting.

Charlotte Pressler: I went over to Peter's parents' house, 'cause he was still in high school, and I walked in the living room and there were his albums on the floor arranged in alphabetical order and the first one in the stack was Albert Ayler's *Bells*, and I said to myself, 'Boy, I think I want to get to know this person.' 'Cause that was hip. He got me a job at Disc Records with the intention of seducing me.

Disc Records was a centre for those Cleveland rockers interested in less orthodox pop exponents. Jim Jones, later of Mirrors, recalls working alongside not just Laughner, but also fellow teenage dropouts Tim Wright and Scott Krauss. All four had among the hippest record collections west of the Cuyahoga, and all would play their part in Cleveland's mid-Seventies rock renaissance.

If Jamie Klimek knew Laughner from Velvets shows at La Cave, another Lakewood reprobate only came into contact with Laughner at Disc Records. John Morton's tastes were even more unorthodox than Laughner's. When Laughner encountered him, Morton had 'peroxided blonde hair down to his shoulders, [and was] wearing secretary-blue eyeshadow and giant earrings shaped like Pepsi-bottle tops', which in Cleveland in 1970 definitely qualified as off-beat. Morton had come into the Disc Records Westgate store to order most of the ESP jazz catalogue. Not surprisingly, Laughner struck up a conversation.

John Morton: I remember listening to free jazz, Ornette Coleman ... we listened to John Cage, and Sun Ra and Ayler. That's what [the Eels] was supposed to be [but] we didn't really understand it.

At this juncture Laughner was between bands while Morton's interests still lay largely outside rock. Mr Charlie had disbanded the minute they graduated from high school. The rest of the band had their eyes on college and, frankly, had little in common with a self-appointed leader who listened to the likes of Captain Beefheart and Albert Ayler.

Charlotte Pressler: The other guys in Peter's band had never liked him very much. They all smoked a lot of dope and did a lot of acid; they liked to stay back from situations, calculating their next move. Peter drank instead, and was too full of restless energy, too full of scraps of knowledge picked up from William Burroughs and *The Magus* and the backs of album jackets to stay back from things long.

Laughner decided that Cleveland was not the place to make his reputation and, with Pressler in tow, headed for California. Given that this was the summer of 1970, Kent State riots *,et al,* San Francisco did not seem the obvious locale for a Velvetized folksinger to make a name for himself.

Charlotte Pressler: We took off for California to make things better in a completely new environment ... He was 18, I was 20. He was, believe it or not, going to make a living as a folksinger. He was into old timey/bluegrass ... [but] it was a mess out there and you don't just walk in and take San Francisco. And he was also getting very strong pressure from his family to come back.

By the time Laughner returned to Cleveland, he found that fellow Velvets groupie Jamie Kimek had begun to assemble a formative version of his very own Velvet-derived rock band, Mirrors. After attending a gig by Mr Charlie at a canteen at Bay High, Klimek had come away sufficiently inspired to get his friend, Jim Crook, to show him the E and A chords on a guitar so that he could begin writing songs. Soon enough Klimek and Crook were making some home recordings and at the end of 1971 Klimek finally put Mirrors Mk 1 together.

Michael Weldon: Mirrors began with Jamie Klimek and Jim Crook being friends, playing together and being Velvet Underground followers. They had already recorded together, just home studios that friends had. I don't know how far back they go playing music together but they had always wanted to have a band.

Having recruited Weldon on drums, Klimek blackmailed bassist Craig Bell into joining Mirrors in order to gain access to Klimek's sister, Karen. Mirrors could now begin rehearsals, ever alert to possible venues to play. Though gigs in Cleveland were extremely hard to come by for a band who concentrated on original material, Mirrors made their first couple of appearances at a private party and a show at the local YMCA.

Michael Weldon: We did play out and we actually were paid a few times, which was quite an accomplishment for somebody that wasn't doing covers, because at that time ... if you didn't play cover songs people would heckle from the audience and demand cover songs ... When we were doing cover versions it was for the most part Velvet Underground songs, and then after a while we expanded the covers list to include songs by the Troggs, and Pink Floyd ... The first places we started playing were a YMCA [and] a bowling banquet in somebody's basement ... [We were] playing for a very middle class suburban bowler [crowd] who drank beer and liked to dance. They didn't care that we weren't playing songs that they were familiar with, they just cared that it sounded good and had a beat you could dance to.

Though Mirrors played a cross-section of originals and covers, they recognized few antecedents save for the Velvets and Syd Barrett. Incorporated into their live set were such Velvets favourites as 'Foggy Notion', 'There She Goes Again', 'Some Kinda Love', 'That's the Story of My Life', 'Here She Comes Now' and 'Sweet Sister Ray' (Klimek had had the foresight to record this song at La Cave back in April, 1968). Their originals boasted titles like 'Amputees', 'Cheap and Vulgar' and 'She Smiled Wild' and combined the Velvet-style delight in feedback and guitar noise with a keen melodic sensibility.

Up and gigging, Mirrors faced their first major setback when, in the early months of 1973, Bell found himself blackmailed once again – this time by the American government – and was drafted into the army. It seemed that Mirrors might have to disband when, at Craig Bell's final gig, closet-guitarist Jim Jones, who had also been a regular attendee at the Velvets' La Cave shows, volunteered his services.

Jim Jones: This kid used to come into the store, named Brian Kinshey at the time, [but better known as] Brian Sands. This guy was only into Captain Beefheart and David Bowie . . . He said his band, Milk, was going to be playing [a gig] . . . On the bill was another group called Mirrors, and here I'm watching this band doing Syd Barrett songs and Velvet Underground songs and Troggs songs, which were three of my favourite bands, and I was completely flabbergasted. So after the gig I went up to them and told them how great I thought they were, and how outrageous that they should be doing this material. Most people didn't care for what they were doing at all, this is '72/3 . . . They said, 'Yeah, it's too bad our bass player got drafted, if you know a bass player, let us know.' So I said, 'I play bass!' which was a total lie – I played guitar! I said, 'There's only one problem. I don't have a bass right now,' and Jamie was able to find one, an old Rickenbacker six-string, and they had put bass strings on it.

It was not until the end of 1973 that Mirrors at last established their own weekly residency, at a club called Clockwork Orange, run by the notorious Clockwork Eddie. They had previously been sharing the ocassional bill at the Viking Saloon with Laughner's post-Mr Charlie outfit, Cinderella Backstreet, but it was at the Clockwork Orange that they were at last able to develop their own material.

Michael Weldon: In later years we were booked into two different clubs that were in downtown Cleveland, one was just down the street from the bus terminal, and we played there one night a week . . . We played on a free-beer night a couple of times, again with the encouragement of Peter Laughner who was trying to get things going on a lot of different levels. There was a story in the *Plain Dealer*, by Jane Scott, who was important to what was happening in Cleveland at the time because she would write about anything. She did this feature story, 'The New Underground?'

At the same time as Mirrors began gigging with a cross-section of Velvet and Velvet-influenced material, Laughner was putting together his own Velvet-derived combo, Cinderella Backstreet. Cleveland was taking its first tentative steps toward its very own, fully grown, two-hundred-pound underground.

The prodigal son had returned from California at the end of 1970 to few exciting vistas. If Laughner's flair for the guitar and eclectic tastes meant that he could always play the odd acoustic gig at a 'folk' venue, his first post-California stint in a band was an unsatisfactory four or five months in the local equivalent to John Mayall's Bluesbreakers, Mr Stress's Blues Band. The tenure proved short-lived because, although Bill Miller, aka Mr Stress, was fully aware of Laughner's ability, he was not entirely happy with Laughner's jagged guitar solos, continually resisted his attempts to introduce more rock & roll material, and disliked the idea of trying to get his band to record some songs, something Laughner was constantly pushing for.

Laughner needed his own band – like Klimek, but with musicians.

Charlotte Pressler: There seemed to be nobody who would play his music. He envied Jamie at times; what Jamie was doing with Mirrors was in some ways what he would have liked to do. But Peter, unlike Jamie, could never have put up with the slow process of teaching non-musicians to play; he wanted people who were already competent. Though Peter never valued technical skill for its own sake, it was for him a necessary precondition for making music.

Laughner eventually placed an ad in Cleveland's *Plain Dealer* newspaper, hoping to find some fellow punks he could play with. Among the few replies were two genuine musical misfits, guitarist Gene O'Connor and drummer Johnny Madansky. Though they jammed with Peter on a couple of occasions, nothing came of their association. As yet.

Meanwhile Pressler – whom Laughner had married shortly after their return from California – had come across an experimental trio by the name of Hy Maya, composed of two synthesizer players, Bob Bensick and Allen Ravenstine, and string bass player Albert Dennis. Hy Maya were approaching their music strictly from an art perspective. There was no knowledge of, or desire to emulate, rock & roll practices.

Allen Ravenstine: In 1971, I came back from Mexico to Cleveland and I got an apartment in Lakewood ... and a guy moved in underneath me who was an art student at Cleveland State [University] ... and he was doing these things where you take fuzztones and rewire them into oscillators ... I [became] involved in this community of people who were working in the Art Dept at Cleveland State, but they were not musicians *per se*, they were painters and sculptors, but there were a couple of them who played instruments on the side . . . We would sit in [Bob Bensick's] apartment and plug these things into his stereo and make noise . . . We even did a couple of gigs, we went out to a couple of art galleries and we did things with lighting and me making noises with these boxes, playing a processed flute . . . There was no music *per se*, it was more in the category of a happening, no drums, no guitars, just oscillators, and a flute.

Hy Maya may have suggested an untapped well of original musicians in the Cleveland area, but it was the informal jams that Bensick arranged at a house on 23rd Street that most interested Laughner.

Allen Ravenstine: Periodically, we had these jams where guys would come down from Cleveland State, one guy would play congas, there was a bass player, and Bensick, on flute . . . Scott Krauss was a friend of both of those guys, he played drums and he started to hear about what was going on out there.

When Laughner got around to calling Bensick he was invited down to jam with this loose association. After one jam session, Laughner asked bassist Albert Dennis, guitarist Rick Kallister and drummer Scott Krauss if they would like to form a band. Space Age Thrills, as the new combo was briefly dubbed, played their first gig at a 1972 midwinter party at the Cooper School of Art.

The band soon changed to a more cryptic *nom de plume*, Cinderella Backstreet, an obscure in-joke referring to the band's sometime mellotron player/backing vocalist Cindy Black. Black had been drafted into Cinderella shortly after the Cooper gig as one half of the Leatherettes, whose job, to quote Pressler, was 'to sing backup and look good – they were better at the latter than the former; in their feather boas, rhinestone-studded cutoffs and low-cut lace and velvet tops, they were beautiful, but chronically off-key.'

Cinderella Backstreet, like Cleveland's surfeit of 'Top 40' bands, stuck to cover material, but their sets consisted almost entirely of ten-minute versions of Velvet Underground classics plus the occasional Richard Thompson or Bob Dylan song, all cranked out and metallicized à la *Rock & Roll Animal*. As such, Cinderella Backstreet did not really reflect the depth of Laughner's musical interests.

Charlotte Pressler: Peter was listening to a fair amount of AACM-style jazz, Albert Ayler, Pharoah Sanders ... fair amount of blues ... lots of Jimmy Reed albums, a fair amount of the weird folk stuff, Holy Modal Rounders. A little bit of Cage, Yardbirds – they were very important – the Velvets, Stooges albums as they were coming out, the post-Velvets stuff. He [even] listened to a bit of Terry Riley, Michael Hurley ... [but] Peter liked to hide behind covers. He did not have much confidence in his own writing.

The policy of 'hiding behind covers' did little to help Cinderella Backstreet develop more than a local reputation. Yet, if Laughner was happy to perform other people's songs, his choice of covers was not really in accord with Cleveland's late-night revellers. When he booked Cinderella to play a regular gig at a gay club, the residency proved predictably short-lived.

Charlotte Pressler: It simply didn't work. He was up there every week emoting in a black vinyl jumpsuit and red lipstick and doing his best to look like a transexual-Transformer type. It wasn't what the gay people in the club were at all interested in – they wanted disco. Anyway, Peter would go just so far and then he wouldn't put out.

Despite his frustration at the lack of originality on the local scene, Laughner was reluctant to allow Cinderella Backstreet to perform a cross-section of originals and covers like Mirrors, even though he had several noteworthy originals to hand, including a rather fine Dylanesque song, which bore the same name as the band.

Charlotte Pressler: It is important to know this about Peter's personality; it is part of his tragedy: acceptance meant everything to him ... Peter had a deep need for approval; he could feel real only if he saw himself reflected in other people. As long as he was alive, he had great difficulty bringing out his original songs. He was convinced that no band would play them, and that, even if a band could be found, no one would want to hear them. The bands he was associated with, and especially the bands he led, always played a great deal of cover material; they were underground jukeboxes.

The preponderance of covers in their set did give Cinderella Backstreet a far greater chance of establishing a regular gig than Mirrors. Sure enough, they secured the Wednesday slot at the Viking Saloon, a hard-rock bar close to Cleveland State (Laughner then managed to coax the owner into booking Mirrors). But Laughner was taking Cinderella far more seriously than his fellow Backstreeters.

Charlotte Pressler: Peter . . . wanted a tight, committed band that would stand shoulder-to-shoulder against the world, a duplication of the camara-derie he imagined had existed in his high-school band . . . [the others] thought he meant a band along the lines of [their loose jamming ensemble] Froggy and the Shrimps; five or six people all used to each others' styles who would work up four sets in a week and play out for fun.

In August 1973, Cinderella Backstreet played their final gig. But Laughner wanted another shot, and quickly formed a sequel band, Cinderella's Revenge. The slimmed-down four-piece remained a covers band, and lasted less than a year. Laughner required an outfit with more conceptual integrity.

Though Cinderella Backstreet – and its 1973–4 incarnation Cin-derella's Revenge – were hardly pushing back the boundaries of rock & roll, they provided a useful training ground for several Cleveland musicians: Scott Krauss and Laughner himself both became founding members of Pere Ubu; Sue Schmidt and Deborrah Smith – both members of the Revenge incarnation of the band – would later play in Laughner's post-Ubu outfit, Friction, before founding Akron's Chi-Pig; even Chrissie Hynde (yes – that Chrissie Hynde), whose brother Terry played in Akron's Numbers Band (aka 15–60–75), is alleged to have played in one of Cinderella's incarnations.

Yet it was not as a musician but as a rock & roll journalist that Laughner first achieved a small degree of notoriety. Like Lester Bangs, who was Laughner's primary inspiration as a rock & roll writer and soon a close friend, it was the Velvet/Stooges/Dolls garage-rock tradition that he sought to propagate in his articles, most of which were for *Creem* magazine. As early as 1974 he was writing (this time for Cleveland's *Plain Dealer*):

I want to do for Cleveland what Brian Wilson did for California and Lou Reed did for New York. I'm the guy between the Fender and the Gibson and I'm singing about you.

If Laughner's own music was not yet at a stage where he was likely to inspire a generation of recalcitrant rockers, he could steer them towards bands who might – notably his most enduring love, the Velvet Underground. He was also keen to advocate the one local band he considered both talented and original, Jamie Klimek's Mirrors:

Mirrors are as far from r&b as you can get. They're so white they disappear in the daytime. Their sound is a composite of all that was promising in the Sixties ... Pink Floyd, the Velvet Underground, the raunchiness of the Troggs and the Stooges.

If Cinderella Backstreet and Mirrors maintained only a poor gig/rehearsal ratio, they were considerably more successful in their attempts to perform in public than Cleveland's other first generation underground rockers – the Electric Eels.

Charlotte Pressler: The Electric Eels were high concept, low gig.

The Electric Eels came into existence via an appropriately negative form of inspiration.

John Morton: Me, Brian and Dave E went to see Captain Beefheart, and Left End were [supporting]. And they were real bad. And I said that we could do better than that. We started practising on the back porch. I played guitar and Brian played piano 'cause he didn't want to play guitar. We figured Dave E could sing 'cause he didn't do anything else. We had our ideas about playing anti-music back then.

If their intent all along was to play 'anti-music', they required some musical input to play against. Morton had gone to Lakewood High with Paul Marotta, one of those rare figures whose avant-garde musical ideas matched his technical competence.

Paul Marotta: We used to have this thing in high school when we were hippies and most of the jocks used to try to beat us up. I would start fights and John would finish them. That was like our friendship.

Marotta was invited to join the Eels sometime in the fall of 1972. The Electric Eels have had their performances described as a form of Art Terrorism – a very accurate term of reference. But early gigs were not few and far between – they were non-existent.

Charlotte Pressler: [Early on it was] hard to say whether [the Eels] were even a band ... The Electric Eels seemed more to be the name of a concept, or perhaps a private club.

In the winter of 1973 they finally secured a job opening at a local bar for legend-in-his-own-lunchtime Jamie Lyons. After their debut show, John Morton, an intimidating hulk of peroxide-bedecked muscle at the best of times, and Dave 'E' McManus were arrested for being drunk and disorderly. Morton was apparently wearing a coat hung together with safety pins and McManus's stage 'attire' was covered with rat traps. The cops generously broke Morton's hand during the arresting procedure.

When the Eels resumed their brief residency, Morton had a slide-rule taped to his cast and wrenches taped on his arm. When they introduced a new instrument to their repertoire – a large sheet of metal which Morton hit with a sledgehammer – the owner pulled the plug and they were minus a gig. Forced to organize their own gigs, they spent the remainder of 1973 and 1974 relocating to Columbus and rehearsing. Gigs in Columbus were no easier to come by than in Cleveland. After all, Art Terrorism was not the easiest concept to sell to a club- or bar-owner.

Michael Weldon: Mirrors was unusual enough to not get bookings, but were civil enough to get bookings if they tried. The Electric Eels looked stranger, played stranger and either didn't care or purposely wanted to antagonize people, or a combination of the two.

Though Morton has attempted to downplay its bearing on Eels performances, violence was a central part of their aesthetic. It was not restricted to their shows, either, often carrying over to rehearsals.

Paul Marotta: An Eels practice was like literally breaking chairs over people's heads.

Morton, at some point, physically attacked all three residual members of the Eels, and the others frequently left the band, only to return when they had licked their wounds, literal or metaphorical. Morton's penchant for violence – or in his terms, confrontation in a direct, physical sense – was such that he and Brian would sometimes go to working-class bars and dance together until the inevitable fight broke out.

John Morton: We didn't go out to be terrifying. We just were. We didn't have any thought for what we were doing, we were acting on our instincts. Dave E felt himself a sinner who was going to hell and he didn't have any choice. He knew he was wrong but he had to do what he was doing . . . I never planned any violence. We would plan certain things, like to wear power tools, but that was entertainment, but the philosophy sort of evolved . . . We were more like the Detroit [bands], we were unaware . . . we thought what we were doing was right, it was just that the other people didn't know it. We didn't have the facility to sell ourselves to the public . . . we were a dichotomy, to have that fragile and explosive a thing made it exciting but it also made it doomed.

Anti-music or not, Morton was most definitely influenced by America's underground forerunners. That element of immediacy and confrontation that Iggy Pop brought to the live 'rock' performace had an obvious appeal to Morton who – like many of his contemporaries in New York and Cleveland – entered the rock arena from a most obtuse angle. His enduring vision was as a visual artist.

John Morton: It was our music. We heard the Velvets and the Stooges and Beefheart and we felt that's what we should be doing. I liked the excitement of being a 'rock star' but I also liked doing artwork and I wanted to combine the two, because doing artwork didn't have the excitement of performing.

The Eels' self-conscious punkdom predates and previews many punk outfits on both sides of the pond, even if they gigged barely half a dozen times in the three years they existed.

If their form of Art Terrorism could involve the use of anvils, gas-powered lawnmowers and, more often than not, fists, it was their songs – with titles like 'Agitated' ('5 a.m. and I'm crawling the walls/waiting for imaginary telephone calls'), 'Anxiety', 'Cyclotron' and 'Jaguar Ride' ('there are no words to describe our jaguar ride') – that presaged the amphetamine-fuelled early English punk bands.

Charlotte Pressler: John and Dave E [once] refused to ride in Marotta's Volkswagen Microbus because hippies had microbuses and they were not hippies . . . you could describe them, pretty accurately, as spoiled rotten but looking at it another way they were very uncompromising.

Above all else, the Eels were totally original. Their roots, like Suicide in New York, led them to deconstruct rock & roll, retaining only the noise element, the polemical nature of the rock lyric and the confrontational aspect of the live performance.

Paul Marotta: There was no drummer in the band. That was part of the reason it didn't catch on – it was ridiculously loud and noisy and . . . it was pretty confrontational.

Though their lack of musicianship – Marotta excepted – meant that the Eels' attempts at anti-music were largely unconscious and lacking in direction, they were taking the Stooges' original aesthetic to its logical conclusion. This set them apart from both Mirrors and Cinderella Backstreet, who were derivative of the Velvets in both style and content. When Cinderella Backstreet played Columbus, Laughner called on the relocated Eels during one of their rehearsals. His wife, recognizing in the Eels an essential quality of originality that Cinderella lacked, tried her best to convince Laughner to offer them his services.

John Morton: I remember Charlotte saying she would divorce Peter if he didn't join the Eels. That's when he had the band Cinderella Backstreet. They came down to play Columbus and where we were practising she heard us and said that. They actually had a big fight about it . . . he couldn't understand any of us. He read Bukowski and we read Burroughs, he liked the Grateful Dead.

It is quite possible that the impact of that visit on Laughner was more profound than Morton realized. Cinderella Backstreet was in reality Cinderella's Revenge, which was on its last legs by the spring of 1974. Laughner needed to channel his gifts down a more productive boulevard. Soon after his return from Columbus, Laughner saw the first performance of David Thomas's new band, Rocket from the Tombs, at the Viking Saloon on 16 June 1974. They were billed as The World's Only Dumb-Metal Mind-Death Rock & Roll Band.

In the early Seventies, the rather imposing Thomas had briefly fronted a spoof rock band called the Great Bow Wah Death Band and was writing for a local paper about rock music, with Mark Kmetzo under the joint pseudonym of Croc O'Bush, and under the alias Crocus Behemoth in his own right. But when he formed Rocket from the

Tombs, Thomas was largely detached from Cleveland's small scene of original musicians. Like Laughner at this stage, Thomas's primary role was as a professional cynic of rock & roll, even if his own tastes as journalist and fan leaned more towards the Stooges than Laughner's beloved Velvets.

David Thomas: I was reviewing stuff. We'd go to shows and he was reviewing things for other people so that's how I ran into him. Peter was always really into the Velvets. I thought the Velvets did interesting music but I thought the rest of it was baloney. I tended to be more into Zappa, Beefheart, MC5 sort of thing ... the Stooges, but Peter was into the Stooges, too.

Laughner realized that the Rockets had potential at a time when Thomas saw it purely as a vehicle for parody, and conceived of an outfit that could fuse the pretensions of the Velvets with the performance art of the Stooges. The sporadic gigging and marginal public profile of Cleveland's first generation underground bands, and the isolation of Cleveland itself from the major meccas of American music, precluded any awareness of a new movement in the early to mid Seventies. But Cleveland's subterranean strata were mobilizing by the summer of 1974, having survived into the punk era.

On 22 December 1974 the Electric Eels, Mirrors and Rocket from the Tombs played the Viking Saloon, billed as a Special Extermination Night. The Viking was the one local venue to endorse original music – the Rockets had debuted there, Cinderella had played a regular Wednesday night gig, and even Mirrors had enjoyed Viking hospitality. Aside from affording the Eels their first gig in many months, it was the first gig for a new incarnation of the Rockets, featuring Peter Laughner, David Thomas, Craig Bell from Mirrors, and two of Laughner's old partners-in-jamming, Gene O'Connor and Johnny Madansky. They were soon to become Cleveland's leading garageband and one of America's most important precursors to punk.

The first New York outfit to draw directly upon aspects of a Velvets/Stooges aesthetic were formed not within a rock context but – like Hy Maya and the Eels in Cleveland – from an art perspective. Their intent was not to celebrate but to deconstruct rock & roll. Suicide was comprised of two native New Yorkers, Brooklyn-born Alan Vega and Bronx-boy Martin Rev. Vega had actually been a sculptor of no fixed renown when he first considered applying his concepts to rock & roll.

Alan Vega: I had a couple of shows already at O.K. Harris, this big gallery in New York, but I felt the art thing was coming to an end . . . music was just a freer thing, the performance thing . . . [My roots] were more rock & roll, the Velvets, the Stooges, blues, Marty [Rev] was more into free jazz . . . Marty has a very classical education. Eventually we just put our heads together, me coming from this place and Marty coming from that place and that's how Suicide started in a 'free-rock' place!

Vega's first attempt at developing his radical notions within American rock & roll had been a brief-lived combo whose pretensions far outweighed their technical competence. He needed a more audacious regime in order to enter the Velvets' domain. When he met Martin Rev, Rev was working in a musical form entirely divorced from rock. He was fronting a band playing a hybrid form of avant-garde free jazz. Vega's notions needed something considerably less grandiose than Rev's existing ensemble.

Alan Vega: Marty was coming out of a jazz thing, with his own band. The most way out stuff in the world! He was the only one playing the electric keyboard at the time . . . Martin Rev was the first guy to bring an electric keyboard into a jazz thing. And he had three drummers and four trumpet players and five guys with clarinets. Sometimes some of the trumpet players would walk off, it was a continuous gig, all night long, it wouldn't stop for eight or nine hours. It was called Reverend B, and they did a few things around town and had a great thing happening, but Marty was looking for a new thing.

Suicide offered a stark contrast to contemporary trends in both rock and jazz, which were tending towards ever more complex arrangements and convoluted structures. As early as 1970, Vega and Rev conceived of the need for a new minimalism in music. Like the early Stooges and Velvets, the embryonic Suicide preferred to forsake songs *per se*, presenting one not-so-seamless performance piece. Reflecting their 'art' background and New York's surprising lack of alternative rock venues in the early Seventies, Suicide's first live performance – as a three-piece – was a typically ill-attended loft gig. The Velvets had just disbanded and the Stooges just completed a famous residency at Ungano's.

Alan Vega: It was at the end of 1970, at a thing called the Punk Best, this was before the word punk was ever used ... in a loft in a place in Broadway, and we had a riot. At that gig Marty Rev didn't even play keyboards, he actually played drums. I had a trumpet and a guitar and we had a guitar player and we just played noise, we didn't have songs ... we didn't even know where we'd start. The next gig was about a year later, in '71 ... nobody ever wanted to give us a gig, we already had a rep. from that one gig, and that's the way things started. At that time in New York there was nothing, there was no music.

The immediate reaction to Suicide was undisguised revulsion, a response which was only marginally diluted in the coming years. Vega's stage manner did little to assuage any initial fears that the band's cacophonic approach might have instilled in the audience.

Alan Vega: It was actually like an environmental piece, the music was creating a sound environment, and then with that sound environment – which was driving people nuts – I'd be going out and jumping around ... The way we dressed was completely bizarre. Now, everybody has black leather jackets, but [not] in those days ... and I studded it up, it said 'SUICIDE', it had chains and we put the rips in.

Clearly the element of confrontation, which had always been central to the Velvets/Stooges *raison d'être*, was equally fundamental in a Suicide performance. At these early shows Vega would sometimes spend nine tenths of a performance in the audience. He was not merely jumping into the crowd, but sometimes knocked chunks out of the wall with a bicycle chain he carried. Vega's stage guise came across as extremely threatening, not to say sinister. Not surprisingly this had repercussions when it came to socializing with other disenfranchised New Yorkers.

Alan Vega: In the early Seventies people were actually afraid to talk to Marty and I. I'd hang out at Mercer. People were still afraid to come up to us – I'd stand at a bar and there'd be space at either side of me!

Much of Vega's adopted persona – Alan Suicide – was a Brooklyn take on Iggy Pop's more famous antics. Vega had been profoundly influenced by seeing the Stooges at their shows in New York in 1969 and 1970.

Alan Vega: When you see Iggy, that was for real. That guy just did what he did and everything was not thinking up there, that was live, that was like a jazz thing, a sense of performance. Totally open . . . Iggy, I went to see him every chance I could, there was never any performance that was like any other and you never knew what was going to happen, and the same musically with them, you never knew where they were going to go musically and that was the excitement of the thing, 'What's he going to do tonight?' . . . When I saw Iggy I realized that this man had just changed my whole perception of the world at that point, and me as an artist, if I was going to be truthful to being an artist, I would have to change, because this man just opened up a whole new vista for me. He changed my life. Like the first time you heard the Velvet Underground . . . you could no longer say you were the same person any more.

After their live debut Vega and Rev decided that their sound was still too close to the rock & roll forms they were seeking to deconstruct. They jettisoned the second guitar player, and Rev's classical musical background was put to better use on an electronic keyboard. Rev's toy 'synthesizer', not a guitar/drums mix, would be at the centre of Suicide's sound. Though Vega would contribute some guitar-work at the next couple of performances, the dissonantly repetitive refrains that Rev extracted from his cheap Japanese keyboard would be the sound original enough to disorient Suicide's early witnesses.

Alan Vega: We found a 10-dollar Japanese keyboard, it was probably the first prototype computerized keyboard, but we couldn't get a sound out of it, it was a piece of shit, so what we did was get a load of effects boxes, Electro Harmonix, we must've had ten in a row! All lined up! Just to get the sound out of this keyboard we needed all this juice . . . The sound itself . . . psychologically created an ambience, so people were looking at me now through a sound thing as well, because the sound was so overwhelming . . . People were coming in off the streets, coming into a performance arena where they were hoping they'd be escaping and all we were doing was shoving the street back in their face again.

If Vega's performances drew most obviously on Iggy, the Suicide sound was a self-conscious attempt to develop the notions of repetition, monotony and dissonance first introduced into the rock arena by the Velvets. None of this was unconsciously arrived at. One of Suicide's early performance-pieces was simply a *reductio ad absurdum* version of 'Sister Ray', titled 'Sister Ray Says', which made dominant those aspects of the original song (like Reed's repeated refrains – 'sucking on my ding-dong' and 'just like Sister Ray says') most in tune with the Suicide creed.

Alan Vega: The Sixties thing after a while was so ridiculous and monotonous . . . so Marty and I said the first thing that has to go is the drums, and the next thing was the lead guitar. Enough of these guitar solos and drum solos!! The Velvets came along and they were intimating something new with that continuum sound, that monotonous thing, it was also happening in classical music with La Monte Young, and Philip Glass . . . the Stooges too, in a way, were intimating that kind of monotonous, one-note thing . . . The keyboard thing had never been tried before . . . [Rev] knew that even for a jazz guy it had come as far as Albert Ayler and that [was] as far as it had got.

If Rev was creating a sound that verged on the atonal, Vega's vocal histrionics compounded the alienation that audiences were quick to feel. Suicide's early 'constructs' were basic affairs at best, lyrical complexity being secondary to immediate sensory impact.

Alan Vega: I started [out] going 'Rocket Rocket USA' and that was a lyric. Or 'Ghost Rider' and repeat it a hundred times.

Not every member of the audience at early Suicide gigs was repulsed by this wave of noise. Some recognized something vital and original that questioned the direction of rock music, when confronted by these two harbingers of doom. The sheer intensity that Vega and Rev brought to each performance made each infrequent gig an event.

Marty Thau: Most people were scared shit of Alan, who would have a black leather jacket and a chain wrapped around his arm and wouldn't hesitate to smash the wall with the chain. Some of the early Suicide shows were just Alan basically screaming at the top of his lungs and Marty banging away on a Vox organ with a 1957 rhythm machine – which was the basic equipment we used to record the 1977 Suicide album that people said, 'This is the new synthesizer sound.'

Craig Leon: They were actually the first New York band I saw when I first moved to New York – much earlier than the whole CBGBs [scene]. This has gotta be 1973, at Max's Kansas City, as the opening act for a really naff band. There were about six people in the audience. Here was this guy doing James Brown and I think he had a whip, he was beating himself with chains and everybody was walking out. And I said, 'Well, this is definitely where it's at.'

Thau and Leon would jointly produce the first Suicide album in 1977, but at this stage it would have been impossible to conceive of Suicide on vinyl. As Lester Bangs would write in his sleeve-notes to *Half-Alive*, 'the onstage carnage which frightened early audiences ... wouldn't have transferred to tape.' A review of a Suicide performance at the Mercer Arts Centre in October 1972 noted the reputation acquired by Vega and Rev in a handful of actual gigs:

Allen Suicide [sic], face grotesque with sequined mask-like effect, is out front singing with growling tight voice and repetitive lyrics. During one piece called 'A Punk Music Mass', he struts, dances, is on and off stage, intimidates those in front, especially femmes, blocks the door to hinder those trying to escape, and beats his face with the hand mike. Actually, it's tamed down since Suicide's past shows included use of daggers and chains in the audience.

Unfortunately Suicide's reputation made it extremely difficult for them to find gigs. It is not too surprising that club owners were extremely reluctant to book such 'challenging' artists, given that they were likely to drive paying punters screaming into the streets. Even if they could convince a club boss to give them a break, they were rarely invited back. Even during the 'Mercer years' – between April 1972, when the New York Dolls debuted at the Mercer Arts Centre, and its collapse in the summer of 1973 – when it seemed like New York's underground was coming up for air, Rev and Vega were given few opportunities to spread the Suicide gospel. The owner of Mercers, then booking the likes of the New York Dolls, Teenage Lust and Wayne County, drew the line at Suicide and took some painful convincing.

Alan Vega: [The owner] literally slammed the door on my foot … I wouldn't let it go, the guy was killing me. I said, 'I wanna play here.' 'You can't draw shit.' And I said, 'Come on, man,' and finally he let it open and gave us a gig. That's how I got our first gig at the Mercer Arts Centre.

Though they would make a few appearances at Mercers in the final eighteen months of its existence – thanks to the Dolls' significant endorsement – other options were few and far between. Max's generally only booked record-label acts – though, as Craig Leon has observed, Suicide did sneak on to a couple of Max's bills as support acts (it would be as a Max's act in 1976–7, when the club had changed management, that Suicide would at last establish a regular gig). One of the only other potential openings was a rather pungent establishment recently opened, Hilly's on the Bowery. Though not a regular rock venue, owner Hilly Kristal had put on a couple of Mercers acts when, at the tail-end of 1972, Suicide made its Hilly's debut.

Alan Vega: We had done a gig at CBs, when Hilly's had first started in the early Seventies … this is really early Seventies, he didn't even have a stage, he had a tiny little stage at the other side of the place and he had a pool room in the back where the stage is now. You could buy a whole pitcher of beer for a quarter. So it had nothing but the Hell's Angels and the bums from the Bowery.

It would take Vega and Rev another four years to convince Kristal to rebook them. By then the club, renamed CBGBs, was one of the most famous rock venues in the world. But in 1972–3 it was Mercers that was the new centre of New York's underground music scene and it was the New York Dolls who were turning the New York scene around. Thankfully their manager, Marty Thau, and lead singer, David Johansen, were big fans of Suicide.

Alan Vega: We used to rehearse three or four days a week ... David Johansen walked in one night, just playing keyboard with us ... at some point he got so engrossed in his thing he didn't notice that Marty and I had walked away and were just hanging out, smoking cigarettes ... These guys were all in rock bands and everything was structured ... and in some ways [we gave them] a free head.

Yet Suicide needed to make an important shift if they were to bridge the gap between art project and rock outfit, and so become a galvanizing force in the new New York underground. At the end of the Mercers era they went into a period of hibernation to work on a reformulation of their sound – without sacrificing the Suicide aesthetic.

Alan Vega: Marty and I knew we could never be part of anything – just the way we smelled or looked or whatever. To begin with, musically we weren't about to change our sound. Marty Rev avoided that anyway ... [but] maybe we did say, 'Come on, we've got to be more commercial.' Maybe we did say that. I think we did. If it was anybody, it was me who suggested to Marty, 'We got to start putting in different kinds of beats, we gotta write a ballad. I gotta start singing more words.'

When they were ready to re-emerge, it would be as the enemy within.

If America's rock & roll underground had taken up residence outside New York in the years immediately following the Velvets' residency at the Dom, it returned with a vengeance in the spring of 1972. The New York Dolls, as their name implies, were proud of the mother that spawned such second-generation musical degenerates. With the exception of their lead singer, the Dolls comprised ex-Brooklyn junior hoods.

Jerry Nolan: There were lots of gangs in Brooklyn; the Ellery Bops, the Hell Burners, the Jesters . . . but the best gang was the Phantom Lords. I was in the Young Lords, which was like a junior branch . . . We were really into dressing very cool – we were a very well-dressed gang . . . black shark-skin style suits, tab-collar shirts, and thin ties. The sort of clothes that Dion & the Belmonts and Gary US Bonds used to wear.

The Dolls were the gang who took to guitars rather than guns – not that they could have caused more uproar if they had set up Child Kidnappers, Inc. From their very formation, the Dolls adopted a trash-rock aesthetic that was a hall-of-mirrors refraction of the nascent English glam scene. But in America in 1972 the ambiguous sexuality of the Dolls' image was largely unpalatable outside that Gomorrah of decadence, New York.

The Dolls' original incarnation was a trio named Actress, formed early in 1971 by guitarist Arthur Kane, drummer Billy Murcia and rhythm guitarist Rick Rivets. The threesome soon realized that they lacked a bassist. At a Manhattan bar that catered to everybody and was known as Nobody's, a favourite hang-out for the late-night-or-is-it-early-morning set, they met Johnny Volume (né John Anthony Gezale Jr) who expressed a ready willingness to join Actress, even adopting a more appropriate alias for his bass duties, Johnny Thunders.

Despite being recruited as bassist, Thunders soon realized that he was a superior guitar technician to either Kane or Rivets, and Kane was relegated to bass, while Thunders promoted himself to lead guitarist *and* singer. Such a barefaced coup not surprisingly brought Thunders into conflict with Rivets, but Murcia and Kane were convinced that Thunders was their main asset and Rivets was soon despatched, replaced by a friend of Thunders and Kane, Sylvain Sylvain (né Ronald Mizrahi). In the fall of 1971 Actress were able to get down to some serious rehearsing.

Actress's rehearsals were generally held at night, in the back of a cycle shop owned by one Rusty Beanie, and lasted until the morning. Rehearsals at Rusty's continued throughout the winter of 1971–2, even as the four-piece was metamorphosing into the Dolls.

David Johansen: Up on Columbus Avenue, around 82nd Street, there's a bicycle shop, and in the winter, when it wasn't busy, we'd go up there, because the guy who owned the shop had these huge Fender amps and some other equipment, and we'd give him five or six dollars, and get up there about midnight, and play until light, with the space heaters going. He'd lock us into the crummy old shop so we couldn't steal anything, and he'd come back at dawn to let us out. So we were banging it out nightly for about six or seven hours, for several months, until we decided we had a band.

The only known recording of Actress dates from a rehearsal at Rusty's on 10 October 1971. With Thunders on lead vocals, they run through seven songs,* of which only 'That's Poison' would survive the transition to the Dolls, and even then new lead singer Johansen would provide his own set of words, 'Subway Train'. The rehearsal tape confirms that they were capable of playing a suitably raunchy, derivative form of rock & roll, but badly needed a singer with more projection than Thunders could muster.

Actress had already spotted a potential recruit at their favourite hang-out, Nobody's. Tall, skinny Jagger-clone David Johansen was a regular Nobody. He already had considerable musical experience.

---

* 'That's Poison', 'When I Get Back Home', 'Talk to Me', 'I Need You', 'Human Race', 'I Need Your Love' and 'Why Am I Alone?'.

David Johansen: When I first started [singing] I'd do Archie Bell and the Drells' songs, whichever was the hit at the time. I was in my first group, called the Vagabond Missionaries. I was about 15. All from Staten Island. After that I was in a group from Staten Island again, called Fast Eddie & the Electric Japs ... We were doing all covers then – 'Uptight' by Stevie Wonder, Motown stuff, while at the time every other rock band was doing psychedelic music ... We used to hang around this place called Nobody's, on Bleeker Street, and we'd hang around at Max's. Those were our places. You'd go to Nobody's for girls. You couldn't pick up girls at Max's except there would be one or two beauties, but they were usually very elusive.

Despite sharing a hang-out, Actress were reluctant to approach Johansen, possibly intimidated by his greater musical pedigree. Instead they let it be known that they were looking for a singer, and relied on a mutual acquaintance to relay the message.

David Johansen: There was a guy called Rodriguo, who lived downstairs from me on the Lower East Side; he played congas, and I played harmonica and guitar – so we used to get together at night, smoke reefer, drink beer and jam. He knew Billy Murcia because they'd both come to the States from Bogota, Colombia, around the same time ... and when Billy and Arthur were looking for a singer, he told them about me. We went over to see Johnny, who I was always seeing on the street, jammed a little and became a band.

The New York Dolls was no art-rock combo. The Dolls had far more in common with the Stooges than with their fellow New Yorkers the Velvets. Other primary influences included the Brit-Invasion bands – notably the Stones, the Who, the Kinks and the Yardbirds – black r&b artists like Bo Diddley, Sonny Boy Williamson, James Brown, Chuck Berry and Otis Redding, and doo-wop bands like Archie Bell & the Drells and Dion & the Belmonts. Theirs was a simple drive – to play good ol' rock & roll in an era of prog-rock and FM mush. The Dolls were reactionaries, in sound if not in image.

The newly formulated Dolls rehearsed throughout November and December 1971 before making an unexpected debut on Christmas Day, in front of perhaps the strangest audience they would ever play to.

David Johansen: Our first gig was at Christmas time, and it was a complete accident. Across the street from the bicycle shop there was this old welfare hotel, and they were having a Christmas party, and these two old guys from the hotel showed up and said that the band hadn't showed up for their party, so we hauled the junk across the street and played for these people. They were mostly black and Spanish, so we played 'Don't Mess with Cupid' by Otis Redding, 'Showdown' by Archie Bell and the Drells, old songs like that.

The Dolls in street-attire debuted as an orthodox rock band that Christmas Day but their next show, after a further three months of solid rehearsing, represented their pukka unveiling. In March 1972 at the Diplomat, a downmarket hotel near Times Square, they at last appeared in all their resplendent glory, more trash than camp, but not exactly diplomatic! Nevertheless, they did succeed in reminding a couple of A&R men in attendance what rock & roll had once been about.

David Johansen: That was the first time we ever got dressed to play ... We got a great response. There were a couple of people from the music business there, Danny Fields for one told me he thought the band was great, and all this heavy stuff, so I figured we would stick to it.

At the time of the Dolls' emergence there was a distinct lack of places where new bands could play in New York. If you didn't have a contract, and didn't play an unending diet of covers, then New York was no more a creative hubbub than Cleveland. Even the legendary Max's was not a venue that booked unsigned bands. It was simply a place to be seen. Eventually local scenester Eric Emerson, who fronted one of New York's best unsigned bands, the Magic Tramps, found a new locale and they began playing regularly at the Mercer Arts Centre on Mercer Street.

David Johansen: Kenny's Castaways, when it was uptown, had this ethnic scene going up there, blues and jazz, and Max's would have the Wailers or Waylon Jennings, or just generally established acts ... [but] Eric [Emerson] had this room [at Mercers]; it was called the Kitchen, like a video room, and he said he wanted us to come down and open for him ... Then the owner of the place approached me and offered to give me the Oscar Wilde room, every Tuesday night.

The Mercer Arts Centre had only recently opened its doors to rock & roll, needing the necessary funds that off-Broadway plays were not providing. It was a place fondly remembered by all its *habitués*.

Marty Thau: The Mercer was like a complex of small theatres that was designed by an air-conditioning mogul whose heart was in theatre. This was his dream come true. They had one or two little things that made a little bit of a buzz in off-Broadway circles and it was nicely put together. It was interesting and modern and the design of it was very comfortable [but] they could not attract enough shows to keep all the theatres running, so in an attempt to bring some more money into the cash register from time to time they allowed artistic rock, and the Dolls seized upon this and started appearing there in what was ... a back, long rectangular room.

The Mercer's change in image was bound to attract local press. Ed McCormack, in Warhol's *Interviews* magazine, wrote about 'this strange new Le Drugstore type nightclub complex ... which seems to be trying to touch all bases by presenting several types of attractions simultaneously in different rooms: video-tape shows, a cabaret featuring jazz greats like Charlie Mingus, a discotheque called aptly enough the Oscar Wilde Room.'

The Dolls soon found a substantial, previously subterranean, following for their brand of trash-rock. At Mercers they were able to work on both a repertoire and a reputation, and before long attracted the entrepreneurial skills of a manager.

Marty Thau: In '71 I took a job, became the head of A&R at Paramount Records and I stayed there for six months and was very unhappy with that ... In maybe April/May of '72 I had given in my resignation and I was out with my wife celebrating. We went down to the Village and had dinner. We're walking around the Village and came past this place – the Mercer Arts Centre – and saw the signs: the New York Dolls. And I had remembered that Danny Goldberg had mentioned [them] to me when I had asked him the question a couple of months before, 'What is happening really in New York?' And he said, 'The only thing I can think of downtown is the New York Dolls but it's like so underdeveloped.' When I saw their name on the marquee I said, 'Let's go in and see this.' It was like two dollars ... They had played there like one or two days before that. They did one show at the Diplomat Hotel, some big debauched spectacular. I was walking out and commenting to my wife, 'We've either seen the best group or the worst group.' We got to the door. I said, 'Come on. Let's go back.' We went backstage and approached them and over the next couple of weeks [I] met them further, was very impressed with them and their clarity as to who they were and what they wanted to be.

The Dolls/Mercers combination gave New York its first underground rock & roll scene since the EPI had established the Dom back in 1966. The Dolls' fans, though, were very different from the Velvets' devotees. This was no coterie in search of a new coat, they were rock's third generation, gaudy glam-kids.

David Johansen: You'll see younger kids at the Dolls' gigs in New York than at any other. Of course they're sophisticated, hip, little New York kids, not the kids who come in from Long Island to see the Osmonds [but] the kind who try and sneak out at night to hang out in Max's backroom, wear what their parents feel is obscene clothing, and have nasty thoughts.

Though the Dolls were viewed as the premier band on the Mercers rostrum, they were just one of the unsigned bands that had at last found a place to play in Manhattan. All the bands playing Mercers adopted a camp/glam image and trash-rock aesthetic, giving the fans a sense of common identity. But the Dolls, with representation from Thau, who had retained Leber and Krebs as their booking agents, were the standard-bearers. If they could secure a recording deal, then the other acts could ride on their tailgate. Many rock journalists, who had despaired of the descent into soft-rock then prevalent in the industry, welcomed the Dolls with besequinned open arms.

Lenny Kaye: The New York Dolls ... were a very influential band. They were the first native Lower Manhattan rock & roll band to really make it ... So by their very existence, the Dolls gave a certain focus to the glitter/New York rock scene that gave us groups like Forty-Second Street Harlots, the Miamis and Teenage Lust.

The Dolls were not Mercers' most outrageous exponents of this brand of trash-rock. If there was an element of parody about the whole semi-drag aspect of the scene, it was the outrageous pastiches performed by Wayne County, a transvestite going on transexual, who provided the best (worst) copy for worried parents. County had long ago developed a wicked sense of humour as his primary weapon against those who sought to ridicule his androgyny. A feature in *Crawdaddy* about one of County's performances at Mercers ably communicated the cause for parental concern:

County's act is carried on in total drag; he wears a plastic cunt with straw hair, sucks off a large dildo, shoots 'come' at the audience with a squirt gun, and for an encore, eats dog food out of a toilet bowl. County's act is the logical culmination of a scene which consumes more glitter, more mascara, wears out more platform shoes and more boutique costumes than a travelling theatrical company ... While these groups and their fans on this burgeoning scene profess to be parodying or 'camping on' various sexual styles (bisexuality, transvestism, sadomasochism), it is difficult to say where affectation ends and reality begins.

Inevitably the Dolls became tarred with the same make-up brush as County, whose act was simply designed to outrage and amuse – even if his band was perfectly capable of playing high-energy garage-rock (County would be performing largely the same act five years later as the New York scene moved beyond the trash-rock of Mercers).

The one ensemble to transcend the camp-rock tag was Suicide, who were one step beyond even County's attempts at outrage. Though the owner of Mercers was understandably reluctant to let such disturbing performers into his domain, Marty Thau added them to both the New Year's Eve 1972 and Valentine's Day 1973 extravaganzas he organized. Though Suicide ended up not playing the New Year's Eve show, their Valentine performance, on a bill that included both the Modern Lovers and the Dolls, was typically memorable.

Alan Vega: These things were going on simultaneously, Suicide'd be playing in one room and I remember David [Johansen] walked up on stage, I think he had just come off [from] his gig with the Dolls or they were taking a break, and he started playing mouth harp with Suicide ... People used to stand about 20 feet away, people would never come up they were too afraid 'cause they knew I was coming ... [That] was the night that Rev played one note. I found this hunk of wood that looked like a big cross and I walked out on stage with this cross ... I'm walking out on stage in leather and chains and studs and the whole bit, and everybody else was still into glitter, the fancy clothes, everybody was walking round in platform boots.

The initial reaction of noted rock photographer Bob Gruen reflects most contemporaries' perception of the Dolls and the Mercers scene:

Bob Gruen: I stopped in at the Mercer Arts Centre [sometime in 1972] ... It was the weirdest group of people I'd ever seen in my life: 13- to 14-year-old girls in mini-skirts and make-up and plastic clothes and guys that were just so effeminate and prancy. And then some guy I knew walked by with eyeshadow on and that was too much. I split ... [The Dolls] were totally outrageous. They were setting the pace. The thing that was funny [was] they said uptown, 'Oh, they're gay. They dress like girls.' Well, no girls dressed like that. No girls walk around in cellophane tutus with army boots. They mixed the genders ... The Dolls blew up more equipment than anybody because they were just over the top. They did everything to the fullest, to the maximum.

Throughout the spring and summer of 1972, the Dolls remained New York's best-kept secret. Ed McCormack, in his *Interviews* feature, recognized a central dilemma:

The Dolls are a totally New York phenomenon. If they succeed and make it big, they will come practically as a revelation to the rest of the country. In order to comprehend what I mean by such a statement, it is necessary to understand what fantastic creatures in the New York underground, who hang out in the back room of Max's Kansas City, have made of themselves – as though to give birth in some weird onanistic fashion to some wholly different creature from the ones their parents birthed.

Marty Thau remained convinced that a Dolls audience existed all around America, even if it was only in New York that the more developed English glam scene was having any real impact (save for Bowie's growing national following). A real difference existed between English and American glam exponents. The English scene was perceived, internally at least, as somewhat juvenile. The glam-rock audience were 'just kids' and 'would grow out of it'! Marc Bolan was considered a teen-idol, not a radical, undermining sexual stereotypes, whose performances had an intensity absent from ELP, Yes and the 'older brothers' music' that the English music press had embraced so readily. The Dolls were perceived as a threat.

Not surprisingly, the Dolls received media attention from a glamorized England before they had any wide national exposure. In September 1972, Roy Hollingworth, correspondent for England's long-standing music weekly *Melody Maker*, devoted a major spread to the Dolls, in which he wrote that they were 'the best new young band I've ever seen'. Marty Thau realized that perhaps his carefully orchestrated campaign of hype could be best served by going to England, where glam-rock was firmly established as the dominant form of teen-music, and where he could hopefully secure European record deals. Leber and Krebs had managed to secure the Dolls a mid-bill slot for a major show at Wembley Arena, headlined by the Faces.

The Dolls had always skirted the border between simple gestures of outrage and sheer recklessness. If the androgynous aspect of their image was perhaps saleable in the UK, particularly after a successful support slot at Wembley and good press, the death of their drummer, Billy Murcia, in an apartment in London in early November seemed to confirm that the Dolls were consciously flirting with one of rock's most dangerous aesthetics – 'too fast to live, too young to die'.

Marty Thau: The night that Billy died I was sitting with Kit Lambert and Chris Stamp, myself, Tony Secunda, his girlfriend Zelda, my wife and Steve Leber, and we had received a wire that day from Ahmet Ertegun saying, 'I'll give you $50,000 sight unseen.' He knew of all this noise and tumult that was taking place very quietly away from New York. All the rest of the record industry was sound asleep at the time. And I was talking to Kit and Chris about $350,000 for a European signing, which was unheard of in those days, when I received a phone call, 'Marty come quickly. Billy Murcia just died.' I just dropped the phone, ran out and grabbed a cab and I was over there in about five minutes and I identified his body for Scotland Yard. It seems he went to a party in the midst of a whole bunch of people that he didn't know and took various things that driven and excitable young men do. Anything he ever did he was always able to handle but unfortunately it worked against him, the mixture of whatever he took, which was some downers and champagne and [stuff] like that. And

The Velvet Underground, Nico, Gerard Malanga and Andy Warhol at the Factory,
New York 1966.

The original Stooges circa 1969.

Warners' solitary promotional shot of the original Modern Lovers circa 1973.

Mirrors Mk 1 (*left to right*): Jamie Klimek, Craig Bell, Paul Marotta, Jim Crook, Michael Weldon. Painting by John Morton.

Charlotte Pressler, Peter Laughner and affectionate friend.

The remainder of the
Electric Eels hide from
John Morton

Alan Vega and Martin Rev of Suicide stalk the New York streets.

The New York Dolls' not-so-legendary Gem Spa reunion.

somebody put him in a bathtub when he passed out, thinking that he was in a coma, and tried to pour coffee down his throat to revive him and he died by choking on his own regurgitation like Jimi Hendrix. The reality probably could have been had they let him dry out he would have been alright. There were like fifty people at this party of which like forty-eight of 'em ran out not giving a damn that somebody was having a hard time in the back and this one guy tried to help him and finally called an ambulance.

The Dolls returned to New York, unsure whether they had the will to continue. In less than a year they had become an important new band, 'the next big thing', with a respected manager providing guidance, a fanatical following in New York and seemingly on the brink of major success. But they also had one dead drummer and at least two other members mixing booze and blues on a daily basis.

Marty Thau: What [Murcia's death] succeeded in doing – as is so often the case in rock & roll – it made them even more notorious ... When I came back from London I got sick. I was in bed for a month. I was getting phone calls from all around the world. The Dolls didn't do anything, they just grieved. And then finally we got together and we went down and had dinner, all of us, down in Little Italy. And they said, 'We've decided we're gonna continue and we have this drummer in mind – Jerry Nolan.' The first show they played as the newly reconstituted Dolls with Jerry Nolan on drums was on December 19, 1972, at the Mercer Arts Centre, not at the Oscar Wilde room but in the Eugene O'Neill Theater which was the biggest room. There was like 600 people who showed up at a theatre that had a legal capacity of 299 – and [they] packed 'em in. It was like a record convention, every record exec and honcho was there – still missing the point, not relating to it, with the exception of Paul Nelson! At this point they were larger than life: they had a death in the group, they had played in London, and they were in the blurb columns with all kinds of suggestions.

Though a huge personal blow, Murcia's death was no great loss musically. Jerry Nolan's playing was considerably more three-dimensional than Murcia's. He was far more inventive with his fills and maintained a more robust rhythm. Yet, despite an added depth to the Dolls' sound, and the huge industry presence at their Christmas show, nobody seemed willing to take a risk on signing them. The Dolls had become a hot potato everyone was waiting to see cool down. A&R man Paul Nelson, though, was determined to ensure that Mercury held on to this exciting new property.

Marty Thau: [But for] Paul Nelson's interest and belief in them [they] wouldn't have got a contract when they did get it. It's really a statement on the record business – about the leaders and the followers. I would have thought that was the exact setting to sign somebody. Others exercise morality into it. It becomes a moral judgement. They feel like they're in trust of the public conscience or something.

It would take another three months for the Dolls to sign to Mercury, and not before Nelson convinced them to go into a local studio and demo every song in their repertoire, hoping to prove to the upper echelons that the Dolls really could play – contrary to industry tittle-tattle. The twenty-two-song tape, which mixed a dozen originals in with r&b covers like Gary US Bonds' 'Seven Day Weekend', Chuck Berry's 'Back in the USA' and Sonny Boy Williamson's 'Don't Start Me Talking', provided ample evidence of an outfit for whom gutsy authenticity was more important than technical flair, but who still retained that unmistakable dynamic found in all great rock music.*

Though the Dolls had already cut nine demos with Marty Thau in the summer of 1972, four further songs at a studio in Kent during their stay in England, and the twenty-two songs with Nelson, their official recording career would be concise to the point of terse. Within four months of signing with Mercury, their self-titled first album was in the shops. Their second, the ironically titled *Too Much, Too Soon*, followed exactly a year later, and would be the last Dolls vinyl studio outing. Though the Dolls themselves considered both studio albums slightly disappointing, they have stood the exam of epochs well. Next to what their primary influence, the Rolling Stones, could summon up in these two years (*Goat's Head Soup* and *It's Only Rock & Roll*), the Dolls' output represents a far more authentic take on the spirit found on the Stones' debut album.

* This tape has been bootlegged on vinyl under the title *Seven Day Weekend*.

If Todd Rundgren's production let the first album down, the real sticking point commercially may have been the album's cover, which emphasized the camp aspect of the Dolls' image. Though the band's outrageous image was generating press, it might have been more prudent to tone it down on the album, at least superficially. The actual contents were unabashed rock & roll, even if song titles like 'Personality Crisis', 'Vietnamese Baby', 'Frankenstein' and 'Trash' hardly corresponded to rock orthodoxy. *The New York Dolls* failed to crack the Hot Hundred.

Contrary to the implication in its title, the Dolls' second album was a better balanced, more raunchy artefact. Driven by the exuberant 'Who Are the Mystery Girls?', Thunders' acerbic 'Chatterbox' and the swaggering bravado of their rendition of Sonny Boy Williamson's 'Don't Start Me Talking', it should have consolidated the Dolls' reputation, even if it pales alongside an album's worth of songs they recorded in a single session with Paul Nelson, live at Media Sound studios, shortly before they began the sessions for *Too Much Too Soon*. Though the bulk of the fourteen songs recorded at Media Sound were covers – 'Great Big Kiss', 'Stranded in the Jungle', 'Milk Man', 'Don't Start Me Talking', 'Don't You Mess with Cupid', '(There's Gonna be a) Showdown', 'Seven Day Weekend', and 'Back in the USA' – Nelson's efforts were the closest anyone came to capturing the Dolls' live feel in a studio.

But the preponderance of covers at both the Nelson and second album sessions suggested that the Dolls were having difficulties coming up with new material. Of the ten tracks on *Too Much Too Soon*, only six were original Dolls compositions, of which four – 'Human Being', 'Babylon', 'Mystery Girls' and 'It's Too Late' – had been recorded for their Mercury demos in March 1973. Possibly the Dolls' failure to crack the American market had a bearing, making them unwilling to work on new songs. Certainly they did their best to promote both albums by touring the North American continent on the hindlegs of each release.

David Johansen: I really don't know why people didn't like us. Maybe it was too cacophonous for them. At the time we came out, the music scene was at its most middle-of-the-road.

The pop scene had certainly become decidedly bland. What should have been the quintessential rock & roll image of the Dolls was unacceptable in such austere times. Though the Dolls elicited all manner of opinions, without the benefit of a trend-driven weekly music press, and with charts at least partially reliant upon radioplay, they were at the mercy of 'self-appointed arbiters of taste'.

Marty Thau: One year *Creem* magazine did a poll and they had The Best New Group of the Year – the New York Dolls and The Worst New Group of the Year – the New York Dolls . . . I took an ad out in *Billboard* when their first album came out, that was entitled 'The Band They Love to Hate.' That was very controversial, too. Mercury expected them to sell 500,000 or more but we only sold 110,000 the first time around. But I thought that was great for a band who had to break down so many barriers.

If hindsight's colouring process makes *Too Much Too Soon* sound like a final effort, the truth is that – barely eighteen months after Murcia's premature death – the Dolls were no longer 'the next big thing' and were being debilitated by drink and drugs. Maybe they felt that, with the Stooges' dissolution, the responsibility for redefining rock & roll's catalogue of excess had now devolved to them.

Jerry Nolan: '74, '75 – we're on tour and in Brussels. Then me and Johnny somehow got a bundle of pure Chinese rocks. Chinese rocks are tan and rocky; it looks exactly like cat litter. We crushed it up, snorted it, and got fucked up. Me and Johnny took a real liking to it.

Gene Simmons: The Dolls failed because they lived their rock & roll fantasy. They were supposed to be drunk, and they were.

The irony is that Dolls-copyists like Simmons' own band, Kiss, who, trading on the Dolls' image, toned up the glam aspect and toned down its drag orientation, eventually tapped into their intended market and through perspiration rather than inspiration achieved platinum-plated success.

In August 1973 the Dolls found themselves without their alma mater, and New York's briefly ascendant underground scene was left bereft of accommodation, when the Mercer Arts Centre literally collapsed. Eric Emerson and the Magic Tramps were rehearsing inside at the time.

Debbie Harry: The centre was integrally linked to the Broadway Central hotel, which had a glorious history but had now become a crumbling structure occupied by welfare recipients. It was so old and decrepit from years of people pissing on the floor and throwing up in the corner that it just caved in.

Alan Vega: Eric's band were in the place at the time, rehearsing and had to run out . . . The guys were running out, trying to salvage the equipment, the building is coming down on them . . . They were lucky to be alive. That part of the floor they were on didn't collapse . . . but because they were from California when things started to shake they just said, 'Aww, it's a little earthquake,' and then things started coming down. I was walking down the street at the time. It was the end of an era . . . In those post Mercer Arts Centre days, all that was available was lofts.

With the collapse of Mercers, and their failure to make serious inroads into the backwaters of America, the Dolls were becoming increasingly confined to New York's few clubs, notably Max's, where they were assured of an ecstatic reception and were guaranteed to meet their costs.

In the spring of 1974, the Dolls actually played a mini-tour of New York, which only served to illustrate the prestige their name held in the five boroughs – and their lack of commerciality elsewhere. The tour culminated at the Club 82, a late-night pick-up joint run by transvestites. As a gesture to the management, the Dolls played entirely in drag, though Johansen's leather jacket over his one-piece dress ensured that they did not entirely forsake their own brand of machismo.* With such stunts the Dolls seemed determined to confront and go beyond each exaggeration the media sought to attach to them.

In the early months of 1974 Club 82 was one of the few clubs to welcome the ex-Mercers acts, providing a temporary substitute for some of the better-known bands, though Suicide's tenure at the club was predictably fleeting.

Alan Vega: Club 82 opened up and that's where all the musicians went after hours. They started having a music thing happening down there, we played down there. We did one gig and the lady [owner] went nuts, 'Get

* This infamous show was filmed by Bob Gruen on open-reel video.

down off there, I can't take any more!' We were playing there with Billy Joe and Teenage Lust.

The failure of the second Dolls album, which peaked at a miserable number 167 in the *Billboard* charts (despite an impressive half-hour slot on Don Kirschner's national *Rock Concert* TV show), suggested that the Dolls needed a serious rethink of strategy. Of most pressing concern were Thunders and Nolan, who now had serious habits, and Arthur Kane, who seemed bent on becoming a dissolute alcoholic.

Thau realized that unless the Dolls shaped up they were finished as a creative entity, and threatened to drop them until they decided that they were serious about what they were doing. The Dolls' reputation, though, at least locally, was such that their booking agents, Leber and Krebs, increasingly estranged from Thau, could continue to book them gigs until they dropped from exhaustion or OD'd from drugs and drink – new product or not.

Marty Thau: I in essence dropped the Dolls. In a dispute with Leber and Krebs I told them that they didn't understand what they had and they didn't know how to work this properly or develop it properly and that they were also stealing ideas from it for Aerosmith who they were also managing. I told the Dolls that the trouble with them was they were beginning to believe their own press clippings, they take too many drugs and drink too much too often and are not professional enough and are selling their souls out for a shitty little $200 a week paycheck and if they were serious enough about their careers they would be more disciplined than they are and give people who are investing in them their moneysworth and time-worth. And when they put Leber and Krebs straight and get their own acts together, then I would come back. There was one alcoholic and two drug addicts in the group. Out of five people how could three perform under those conditions?

Of course, it was Leber and Krebs' money that was on the line if the Dolls went under. As such, it is not too surprising that they were prepared to deal with anyone who could keep the Dolls afloat long enough to recoup at least part of their considerable investment. But without Thau's guidance, Mercury were not prepared to provide further backing for the band.

   Enter Malcolm McLaren. McLaren's rock & roll revivalist store on the King's Road in London had been frequented by the Dolls during their stay in London at the end of 1973. He was a genuine fan and was even willing to provide the neccesary funds to relaunch the band with a new image, asking for little in the way of guarantees in return. It was the Dolls' last opportunity for salvation.

Bob Gruen: When Malcolm McLaren became involved, Marty Thau managed the band. Malcolm McLaren was not so much their manager as their haberdasher. He came over with their outfits – they all ordered these red clothes from him, a lot of 'em red leather . . . Malcolm showed up with the band's clothes and expected this exciting phenomenon he had seen last summer and walked into a dying scene. The band was on its last legs. They were totally drunk, they were addicted to drugs. There was very little life left in 'em. I credit Malcolm with saving their lives 'cause he put three of 'em into hospitals and drug-treatment programmes when everybody else had abandoned them because they'd been so abusive on the road. They had a $20 per diem and they would make $200 worth of room service and $400 worth of phone calls and just be drunk and say, 'Well somebody's gotta pay for it.' And finally the record label had [enough] and Leber– Krebs were in debt a hundred thousand dollars and Marty's trying to tell them, 'This is a brilliant band.' And they're going, 'They may be brilliant but we're going broke.' So they didn't want to hear it from Marty any more . . . There was a real vacuum.

McLaren felt that the Dolls required a new image, that perhaps the camp look was hampering the band. Perhaps he could even link a new image to his own dabbling in radical politics. Johansen was keen to adopt McLaren's ideas, perhaps viewing them as the only way out of the band's downward spiral. But McLaren's kitsch-politico concept of Red Patent Leather only confused existing fans.

Bob Gruen: Since they had red clothes, they [thought they] would have a red party and if it was going to be a red party why not a communist party. Instead of sending an invitation they sent a manifesto, where they accused Leber–Krebs of being a paper-tiger management. It was bad enough to be called gay but being communist was something people really couldn't deal with. You get beat up for being a fag, but you get killed for being a commie, and that frightened off a lot of people and confused a lot of people. It was meant as more freak-out and to take a little attention away from the gay aspect and take it one step more outrageous. It was another slap in the face at any kind of propriety. But by that point they were on their last legs and nobody would book them.

The new image was unveiled at an intimate little theatre in Manhattan, the Little Hippodrome, on 28 February 1975, with five further shows booked over two weekends. The Dolls had worked up a repertoire that included some new numbers like 'Red Patent Leather', 'On Fire', 'Pirate Love' and 'Teenage News', and for once they played like they had actually rehearsed for the shows.

Jerry Nolan: That's when me and Johnny got down and said, 'We either learn a new repertoire and put on a new show and get up to date . . . or forget it!' . . . And we did do it. We put on a show at the Hippodrome and it was the greatest. People that never liked the Dolls admitted that the Dolls had become a professional band.

Chris Stein: The Red Leather stuff that Malcolm presided over was the best they ever were. They were just great. They were [usually] very erratic with their playing but that bunch of shows they were very tight.

Sadly, the Hippodrome shows proved to be just a final spasm of the Dolls' corpse. The will to carry on was no longer apparent. Arthur Kane's drink problem was not under control, and when shows were scheduled for Florida in April, roadie Peter Jordan was required to play bass on the dates. Nolan and Thunders decided that they wanted out.

Johnny Thunders: I thought the band had gone as far as it could. Towards the end we had Malcolm McLaren managing us . . . he wanted us dressing in red leather and stuff . . . me and Jerry thought it was more important to get a new set together. We had five or six new songs and we wanted to get back to New York – we were in Florida – and work on them, but David thought we should stay with Malcolm.

According to Thau, Nolan and Thunders had a considerably more pressing reason for getting back to New York than working on new songs, and it was Johansen and Sylvain who despaired of Nolan and Thunders, not the other way around.

Marty Thau: Johnny and Jerry wanted to score some drug that they couldn't do down there [in Miami] so they decided to come up to New York to get it. And David and Syl looked at each other and said, 'If this is what we have to contend with in this newly revitalized Dolls we're better off not doing it. Don't we learn from past mistakes?' So then they said, 'Screw it.'

Even McLaren realized that the Dolls were finished as a creative unit, and that his concepts would be better utilized elsewhere. He returned to England to try to convince a bunch of lads who worked in his store and had a band of sorts to get their act together and start playing seriously. Wally Nightingale, Steve Jones, Paul Cook and Glen Matlock were just a bunch of Swankers, but you never know.

Perhaps he realized as early as the second weekend at the Little Hippodrome that the Dolls were just not going to 'get their shit together, maan'. He certainly seemed to spend most of his time backstage in earnest conversation with the bass player of the support act, Richard Hell of Television. Like Thunders and Nolan, Hell was looking for an out – despite having spent the last year building, with his co-founder Tom Verlaine, a New York club scene ninety degrees removed from the trash-rock of Mercers. The club they were playing every weekend was called CBGBs. It was here that New York would at last become the focal point of a new rock & roll.

The First Wave

Two of the three central figures in the revival of New York's pre-eminence in underground rock in the mid Seventies – Tom Miller and Richard Meyers – had been friends since the mid Sixties, when they had attended the same school in Delaware. Under their respective aliases, Tom Verlaine and Richard Hell, they would found Television, the first band to provide New York's post-Mercers scene with focus.

Richard Hell: I was brought up in Kentucky. I lived there till I was 16. When [my parents] moved away to Virginia I was sent to school in Delaware. The school was like a glorified reform school really, like a country-club reform school. It was where middle-class people sent their kids they couldn't deal with. And [Tom] was there too. That's where we met.

If Meyers and Miller were soon confidants, it was a joint attempt to escape the confines of their 'country-club reform school' that firmly cemented their friendship. It also provided the catalyst necessary to drive Meyers to New York.

Richard Hell: I had been kicked out and suspended from innumerable schools and my mother was just at the point of a breakdown and ... so she found a school after very deep, profound research that would accept [me]. Tom was another of the students there ... it wasn't so much we hated that school, we just hated school, and we felt like we were ready to go out and make our own way and so one night on impulse, we just walked out of the school grounds, pooled the pocket money we had to take a train and get as far away as possible so that we couldn't be picked up immediately. We got a couple of hundred miles away spending our money on a train ticket and then we started hitch-hiking. We were trying to hitch-hike to Florida ... We knew there was a seven-state alarm out for us and we'd been away for like three weeks. So we were only about two hundred miles from the Florida border and it was late at night and it was really cold and the redneck locals kept taunting us trying to hitch-hike on the highway. They'd pull up as if they were gonna stop and then stamp on the accelerator as we got near the car. So we realized we weren't gonna get a ride that night. We decided we'd go down in the field by the road and camp till morning and we made a little fire and we just started provoking each other. We used to do this kinda thing all the time. Just work ourselves into a giddy state where anything could happen. Where it led this time was picking up pieces of burning wood [and throwing them] into the field cursing all of Alabama and before we knew it – Woah! Fire engines and police with dogs. And we were taken to jail and reclaimed. Tom went back to school, finished high school and went to college and I made this deal with my mother ... I said, 'You don't wanna send me [back] to reform school, do you?' We worked out this deal where if I could earn a hundred dollars while staying in school she would let me go without calling the authorities. So I'd have a stake. And she thought she'd outsmarted me 'cause I was very irresponsible and she just couldn't imagine that I could ever put together a hundred dollars but I immediately got this job right after school in a porn bookstore in Norfolk and I had a hundred dollars in two weeks and I got a bus to New York. Tom followed ... a year and a half or two later ... We were in touch all the time.

Though Meyers shared with Miller an interest in rock music, when he came to New York it was to become a poet, not a musician. As Hell would later relate (during a symposium on the origins of punk rock), he was adopting an aesthetic that was modelled more closely on Arthur Rimbaud than James Dean.

Richard Hell: I came to New York to become a writer in 1967 – the tail end of the flower children – but I never felt comfortable with that mentality, that kind of consciousness, though I took my share of acid as all the punks did. Acid and speed chased with beer. But I felt very much an outsider, and as a teenager is likely to, I also felt like I was neglected – that I wasn't getting enough attention. I felt like I could see how the world operated and everybody else was pretending that things were running smoothly when they really weren't. I also had a history of interest in poetry. I was always a sort of literary type ... I kind of kept it a secret because I didn't want to have anybody walk over me because of that. I still wanted to hold my own on the street. I was really influenced by the twisted French aestheticism of the late nineteenth century like Rimbaud, Verlaine, Huysmans, Baudelaire, etc. Moving up into the twentieth century I also admired the surrealists Breton and Vallejo ... And a lot of my view of the world came from that.

Though Meyers was primarily interested in the power of the word, the friend who had stayed behind was more keenly concerned to learn how to be a musician. Miller's first chosen instrument was not the electric guitar but the saxophone.

Tom Verlaine: I started composing stuff on the piano when I was in the fifth grade, but I can't remember any of it. Then I heard John Coltrane ... So I got a saxophone; for about $30. I used to have these jam sessions with a friend. We couldn't play at all; we just used to like to make noise; fantastic noise, this raw expression ... I was especially into saxophone players then ... guys like John Coltrane and Albert Ayler. I played sax for maybe two years, but I never really played it well, because I was eager for expression before I'd got the technique right.

So Miller's first love was not contemporary rock & roll, but free jazz – a form of music that could be truly improvisational as rock & roll in the mid Sixties had yet to be, perhaps with the notable exceptions of the Velvets and MC5.

At around the time of his little jape with Meyers, the guitar began to replace the saxophone in Miller's affection. He even formed his first band, which was not dissimilar to latter-day Television, a combination of free-form jazz-rock and r&b. Though jazzier and less frenetic than Television, this high-school band shared another component with its illustrious successor. The drummer, a Delaware local, was none other than Billy Ficca.

Tom Verlaine: When I learnt guitar I had a group with Billy Ficca, but we only played a graduation party or something. They threw stuff at us. We wheeled the other guitar player out in a wheelchair, but we were serious about what we were doing. We were actually doing more complicated stuff than [in Television]. We were doing these real long pieces . . . not like Yes or anything, but they had a lot of changes in them.

Billy Ficca: It was pretty far out. Not at all commercial. We couldn't get any work. There weren't too many people in Delaware interested in that kind of crazy music. We just rehearsed, worked out some material and played for ourselves really.

The young Miller made it to college in Pennsylvania, but became rapidly disenchanted with formal education and soon dropped out. All the while he maintained a correspondence with Meyers, the only contact he had in New York. As the home of the Velvet Underground and John Coltrane, the five boroughs had an unmistakable resonance for Miller.

Tom Verlaine: I left [college] in November '67, messed around for nine months, just taking drugs and growing up . . . I was still a huge fan of Albert Ayler – he was my favourite – and the Velvet Underground . . . Then I came to New York.

Miller would later state that he came to New York with the purpose of starting a band. If so, he was unsuccessful, though he performed briefly as part of a folk duo during the summer of 1969, before subverting his musical ambitions to Meyers' avowed vocation – becoming a poet. Like Meyers, Miller was working at the cavernous second-hand bookstore the Strand, where the third central figure in New York's mini-renaissance, a budding poetess by the name of Patti Smith, would later seek employment (though when Meyers met Smith it was through fellow-poet Andrew Wylie, not at the Strand).

Miller also shared Meyers' early interest in hallucinogenics. This was, after all, the year of Woodstock!

Richard Hell: We were dropping acid – and he would really open up then; he more or less revealed that he had this fundamental belief in his absolute inherent superiority to everyone else on this earth.

Tom Verlaine: From 21 to 23 I was using all kinds of hallucinogenics. Just out of interest. To see what scrambling your senses could do to you . . . People who mess with drugs, I can't stand to be around them for too long. There are still a lot of people doing it to themselves. They also have so many illusions about things that they're totally boring to listen to.

Meyers had invested in a small printing press, and was editing his own small-circulation poetry magazine, titled *Genesis: Grasp*. Published under his own name, the magazine lasted barely four issues, the final one, published early in 1971, featuring cover pictures of Arthur Rimbaud, Antonin Artaud and the mysterious Theresa Stern, the first *alter ego* of Meyers and Miller.

In this last issue, *Genesis: Grasp* also carried several individual efforts by Miller and Meyers. Miller was full of helpful advice with his 'Three Good Answers for Troubled Minds':

> Feel like you're on a torture rack in your mind???
> Or maybe like you're on a bed of hot fingernails???
> Perhaps a thousand dead rats are your thoughts today hmmm???
> Your ol' lady got run over?? Ya know what I would do?
> I'd forget it as soon as possible.

Meyers' own poems reflected an early angst waiting to mutate into manic-depression. One of his final efforts for *Genesis: Grasp* was entitled 'You Don't Love Me':

> It must be about time to die, you worthless cement block, they said.
> I am the Test, the strange man others are locked in with for five days.

The use of Theresa Stern's portrait on the front cover was a little in-joke, unveiling Miller and Meyers' first truly collaborative project, a book of poems to be published under the *nom de plume* Theresa Stern.

Tom Verlaine: It turned out as time went by we had a series of collaborations and Hell decided, 'Let's publish this.' And I said, 'Let's publish it under a woman's name,' and then he got this mad idea of doing a composite photo of us in make-up and wigs. His girlfriend came over with this ridiculous wig. And then he started using the name.

The book they published, *Wanna Go Out?*, passed unobserved. The writing may have been on the wall, but who reads walls these days? *Wanna Go Out?* was the culmination of Meyer's early pretensions as a poet – the final proof that Theresa Stern, and therefore poetry, would not make Miller and Meyers legends in their own lunchtimes. Adopting a new persona also made Meyers muse upon whether the process of redefinition could achieve that all-important balance between instinct and self-conceit.

Richard Hell: The problem I used to have with poetry [was that] I was always censoring my 'expression' because of a wrong-headed conception of poetry, poets, and me that was finally overcome only by the extreme method of conceiving Theresa, which bypassed my inhibitions by writing in a new persona and collaboratively.

Just as *Wanna Go Out?* was about to be published, the Dolls began playing at Mercers, and Meyers and Miller were reminded of the possibilities this medium offered for asserting their world-view. Just as John Cale earlier realized a lack of urgency among avant-garde musicians, so Meyers and Miller reached the same conclusion about New York's enclave of would-be poets.

Tom Verlaine: There were lots of different cliques. People seem to form schools [in New York] very fast. Like all the poets would get together in various groups, and develop similar styles and share the same ideas and the same girlfriends. I don't know if incest is the right word, but it got to the point where everyone was just patting each other on the back and congratulating each other all the time.

Richard Hell: I was twenty at the time and it felt very futile. I wanted to shake up the world. I wanted to make noise, but nobody reads. I could identify with that, I wanted to be true to my heroes, but I could see reading could be very boring if you weren't conditioned to enjoy it . . . and I got to feel that was a dead end. About 1972–73 we decided we were going to make a band. I was real inspired by the attitude of the New York Dolls and the Stooges.

If Meyers had provided a large part of Miller's education in poetics, Miller was the more *au fait* with garageband rock & roll, even if he had come upon it via the unorthodox route of free jazz.

Tom Verlaine: The first rock song that really knocked me out was '19th Nervous Breakdown'; 'cause that seemed to me like Coltrane a lot, real barrage of sound.

Their common influences blended American and English, providing a potentially combustible synthesis of American garage-rock and Brit-beat merchants.

Richard Hell: [We] were [both] influenced mainly by the Velvet Underground and the sort of American punk of the late Sixties that was made by the groups on Lenny Kaye's *Nuggets* album, like the Standells, the Shadows of Knight, the Seeds, etc., and the Stooges. The other main line, at least for me (I got most of my music education from Verlaine), was the mid-Sixties English Invasion of the Beatles, Them, the Who, the Kinks, the Rolling Stones and the Yardbirds.

There was one incident which, in tandem with the Dolls' potent reminder, gave an important jolt to the Miller system. Having immersed himself in parochial media for too long, he was offered an opportunity to reacquaint himself with Sixties rock & roll.

Tom Verlaine: I remember a Hare Krishna kid came up to me in the street and I guess he was selling all his possessions and he had this little box of 45s. And he said, 'You wanna buy these? Here give me $5.' And this box was 'All Day and All of the Night', 'For Your Love', five Beatles [singles] and a bunch of other singles and I took them home and I thought, 'God these records still sound great.' The energy of these records was great. They were rhythm-guitar orientated songs. There's good solos on all those early singles. The rhythm guitar was way out front, that kinda riff thing . . . I heard that and I thought that's where the excitement comes from.

In recent years Verlaine's love of the riff-driven forms of rock & roll may have become less evident, but in 1972 he was entirely in accord with Meyers' commitment to the garageband sound, and shared his desire to form a band based around that sound.

Richard Hell: I was more into Iggy and the Velvet Underground but Tom introduced me to most of the stuff and he definitely has a side of him that's interested in it, but somehow it faded or something. The way that the Neon Boys sound on [the released] cuts . . . is the way Television sounded at its best as far as I'm concerned. That's when we were on the same wavelength.

The Neon Boys represent a step on from Theresa Stern in the

reinvention of Richard Meyers and Tom Miller. Like many contemporaries, they had become disaffected by the state of their beloved rock & roll. But the Dolls were reasserting rebellion as the rock & roll creed in their own inimitable way, and Meyers and Miller decided they wanted to join in the process of returning rock & roll to that half-remembered time when it 'meant something'.

Richard Hell: When I was a teenager in the Sixties, there was a period for a couple of years where the music was really the network of news for teenagers, where you defied the lives and conventions of the grown-ups and talked to each other over the airwaves about what life was really like and what it felt like to be alive. We wanted to bring that back, so part of the principle was that we were going to reinvent ourselves to be our own ideal picture of what we were like on the inside ... We were really angry and we were really laughing too.

The Neon Boys were a three-piece composed of Miller, Meyers and Miller's old friend from Delaware, Billy Ficca, who had been playing in a blues band when Miller invited him to come to New York to join his new band.

The brief chronology of the Neon Boys has never been clear, and has not been helped by the impression both Hell and Verlaine have given that there was a considerable gap between the demise of the Neon Boys and the birth of Television. In fact, the Neon Boys lasted from some time in the fall of 1972 until April 1973, at which point they made their one and only studio recording, a tape consisting of six songs, three sung by Meyers, three by Miller.*

The first problem that the Neon Boys needed to overcome was Meyers' status as a complete musical novice. By default he was required to be the bass player. Never having played bass, he had to be taught the parts for each song in turn.

Miller had originally attempted to audition a young New York musician he knew. Chris Stein had just begun playing with Debbie Harry in the Stillettoes but was unhappy with the nature of the Neon Boys' material, which was perhaps a little too brutal for his tastes.

---

* The three Hell songs, 'That's All I Know', the original 'Love Comes in Spurts' and 'High-Heeled Wheels', are now available on a Neon Boys CD single; the Verlaine songs, 'Tramp', 'Hot Dog' and 'Poor Circulation', remain unreleased.

Tom Verlaine: When I decided to try and put a band together . . . one of the guitar players turned out to be Chris Stein and he came and heard a few songs and played guitar and said, 'This stuff's too fast. I don't like this stuff. It's not commercial enough.' He could play it, though. Then Hell decided he was gonna learn bass and that was the Neon Boys.

Stein seems to think that it never got as far as an audition, though he certainly recalls Verlaine's approach.

Chris Stein: [Verlaine] called me up and asked me for a bass player. Actually my friend and I used to make fun of him because when he first came to New York he had shoulder-length hair and he had all these hippy love songs which he used to play acoustically, and we used to take the piss out of him basically. He called me up looking for a bass player but by that time I was already doing something with Debbie.

Even at this point, Meyers and Miller had a twin-guitar sound in mind, but aside from a makeshift bassist, the Neon Boys lacked a second guitarist. When they recorded their six songs in April 1973, Miller was required to play lead and rhythm. Though they never found a satisfactory rhythm guitarist they did audition at least one potential recruit, subsequently an important figure on the New York scene in his own right. At the audition he was introduced as Douglas Colvin, though it would be as Dee Dee Ramone that he would achieve prominence. He was simply incapable of meeting Miller's minimal technical requirements.

Richard Hell: Tom would say, 'We'll play a C,' and [Dee Dee] went from fret to fret, he would look up with these questioning eyes. He'd look up and we'd shake our heads.

Without a second guitarist, the Neon Boys had no real future and in the spring of 1973 called time on their endeavours. Meyers' and Miller's first venture into rock & roll might have passed without result had they not decided to record some songs as a memento of their efforts.

On the 1980 *Richard Hell – Past and Present* EP the prototype for Television can be heard in all its rusty glory. Though only the three

Hell tracks have been released,* they suffice to illustrate that Miller, Meyers and Ficca had been paying attention to their Stooges and Stones records. The sound is considerably less mellifluous than latter-day Television. Indeed the brutal guitars are barely recognizable as antecedents to Verlaine's later sound. But Miller and Meyers needed another guitar player if they were to bring the Neon Boys' sound to the world.

Richard Hell: There was like a year gap between the Neon Boys and Television. 'Cause we couldn't find another guitar player . . . In fact that's why we made these tapes, because we didn't have the other guitar player to play live.

---

* 'High-Heeled Wheels' was added to the 1990 CD re-release of the 1980 EP.

■t must have been something they were putting in New York's ink! Like Hell and Verlaine, the other major figure in the early New York punk scene started out as an aspiring poet.

Patti Lee Smith had been born into this world of sin in Chicago on 30 December 1946, and had spent her pre-teen years in Philadelphia, before moving to Woodbury Gardens, New Jersey in the year that rock & roll first assailed American consciousness – 1955.

> Mama filled me with fantasy . . . my bears danced at midnight
> even my toybox had a soul
> Mama called me her goat girl . . . little black sheep
> I loved my brother and sister; Todd and Linda
> we drank each other's blood . . . we were double blood brothers

Smith's conception of herself as a visionary in the Rimbaudian tradition had its origins early in childhood. At the age of four she came down with scarlet fever and malaria and subsequently suffered periods of hallucinations, which stayed with her well into her adolescence. In a 1974 article she would romantically describe her childhood as a state of limbo:

I lay there and listened for that future music, the track and phase of a fender whine, to lull me outta this separate limbo called childhood.

As adolescence stalked in, her fantasies inevitably became sexual. Even if her austere family background meant that she was innocent of the ways of the world, her fertile imagination soon manifested itself in a series of detailed (not-to-say convoluted) masturbatory fantasies, some of which suggested a masochistic fervour common among those inculcated from a tender age with religious doctrines of guilt and shame.

Patti Smith: I used to make up these long, dramatic poems about getting arrested by a beautiful blonde Nazi guy and having pleasurable torture, but that didn't mean I wanted Hitler back or I was a racist. It's just . . . you're in the adolescent terrain, which is very violent.

The religious schizophrenia which would colour Smith's entire work was in evidence from a very early age, as she came to realize the gulf in beliefs that existed between her father, Grant, and her Jehovah's Witness mother, Beverly.

Patti Smith: My father taught us not to be a pawn in God's game. He used to blaspheme and swear against God, putting Him down. I got that side of me from him. The religious part I guess is from my mother, who was a complete religious fanatic.

Though Smith displayed strong devotional traits as a child, and was an avid reader of the Bible, on entering her teens she began to perceive religion as a divisive force.

Patti Smith: When I was a kid I was real religious and I would love the idea of communicating with God . . . I spent all my time praying and I was really trying to get to God through a religion, and every single religion I ever got into had so many dogmas and rules that always shut people out. My father was an atheist and I was really nuts about my father. Every time I'd get into a religion, they'd say, 'Well, if your father doesn't do this and this and this then he can't really be a part of this with you' . . . I was a kid and I couldn't handle that . . . By the time I was about 12 or 13 I just figured well, if that was the trip, and the only way you could get to God was through a religion, then I didn't want Him any more.

It did not take the young Patti Lee long to find a substitute for her religious devotion – Art with a capital A. In her senior year at Deptford High School, her yearbook gave her interests as 'painting, folk music, progressive jazz', and her nickname as Natasha – largely because of her regular use of a heavy Transylvanian accent. Her ambition: to become an art teacher.

Patti Smith: I was real self-conscious about being skinny, and I had one teacher who said I shouldn't be. She took me to the school library . . . and she showed me the Modiglianis and she said I looked like an El Greco, or the Blue Period of Modigliani, and it was the first time I could relate to something physical.

Smith would later suggest 'Art totally freed me.' It certainly provided her with a direction. On leaving Deptford High, she was offered a partial scholarship to the Philadelphia Art Museum, but the shortfall in the scholarship was more than her parents could make up. So she attended the nearby Glassboro State Teachers College, which offered art classes, though geared towards the teaching of art, not art for its own sake. Though Smith was not a typical student she managed to find the first of many mentors among the teaching staff – Dr Paul Flick.

Patti Smith: He really got it through to me that often criminals were failed artists, like Hitler wanting to be a painter. I learned all the stuff you have to do – like TB, eat hashish, sleep in gutters – so I was all prepared when I came to New York.

Smith's desire to move to New York had to be temporarily put on hold due to an unexpected result of her sexual awakening – pregnancy. Leaving Glassboro in the fall of 1966, when she was three months pregnant, Smith decided to see the birth through and have the child adopted. Her one condition for the adoption – that the child not be raised a Catholic. Dr Flick devised a story about a special project in New York to cover her early departure from teaching college. In fact he wasn't far wrong with his white lie, for Smith had already tired of the sheer parochialism of New Jersey.

Patti Smith: I was so harassed in Jersey. My mother was a waitress, and I would go into the fountain and all they would say was 'Who's the weird one?' My mother would be ashamed that it was her daughter and I just couldn't stand it.

She would later detail her sense of disgust at New Jersey's neophobes on her first single, 'Piss Factory', which related her experiences in a factory during the summer following the birth of her baby. She had got as far as Pitman, New Jersey, in her leisurely progress to New York.

> Sixteen and time to pay off, I get this job in a piss factory . . .
> These bitches are too lame to understand,
> Too grateful to get this job,
> To know they're getting screwed up the ass.

Smith eventually made it to New York in the fall of 1967, staying with a friend while she found gainful employment. Appropriately, her first job was at a bookstore, Scribner's on Fifth Avenue. Her artistic impulses had not been supressed by years of Jersey conformity, and she began to hang out at the Pratt Institute of Art, a noteworthy centre for the visual arts, where she was soon employed part-time as a life model.

Patti Smith: I was reading all these romantic books about the life of the artists so I went to Pratt, in Brooklyn, where all the art students were. I figured I would find an artist and be his mistress and take care of him. I found this guy, Robert Mapplethorpe. He was about 19. He was real cute . . . He was an artist so I got a job in a bookstore and . . . he started teaching me discipline and structure to put my creative stuff in.

Despite his sexual proclivities being channelled elsewhere, Mapplethorpe was fascinated by Smith and adopted her as his very own sorcerer's apprentice. In Smith, Mapplethorpe found a mass of neuroses and took it upon himself to try to help her translate them into something productive, even artistic. They were soon living together.

Patti Smith: [Mapplethorpe] was kinda fascinated by my case because I suffered so many hallucinations. I lived a very hermetic life with Robert, and he was the one who spent five years getting me to the point where I could exorcise all the demons in me into good work. That was my peak period, 1969–70, when I made the transition from psychotic to serious art student.

Initially Mapplethorpe encouraged Smith in an ill-conceived desire to become a sculptress. She presumed that her love of Swiss sculptor Brancusi was reason enough to attempt the discipline, but quickly realized her profound limitations in this medium before turning to painting and drawing as a means to 'exorcise all the demons in me'. She seemed equally unhappy with these media. Perhaps she required a city with more artistic ambience. So in May 1969 she travelled to Paris with her younger sister, Linda, where they remained for two months.

Patti Smith: I was living in Paris, painting and messing around. And I started to notice that my paintings were becoming more and more like cartoons, and that the words in these cartoon-like things were becoming more important to me than the paintings. I had gone to Paris to immerse myself in painting and I came back wholly involved in words and rhythms. I returned to New York and concentrated on poetry.

When Smith returned to New York late that summer, she resumed living with Mapplethorpe. They soon relocated to the infamous Chelsea Hotel, home of itinerant wannabes and onceweres. If Mapplethorpe was determined to become a visual artist, Smith was still unsure of her own direction, despite her new-found leaning towards poetry.

Patti Smith: [When] I came back Robert had become a semi-hustler . . . Robert hung out at Max's every single night until like three in the morning trying to get a big break. I don't even know what we were trying to get a break for . . . We hung out there every night for about six months and nobody even said hello to us.

If Max's was a dead loss, living at the Chelsea inevitably brought Patti into New York's 'artistic' circles. Andy Warhol and William Burroughs were regular habitués of the hotel. But it was professional friend-of-the-famous Bobby Neuwirth who was Smith's next mentor. They met in the lobby of the Chelsea – inevitably. Neuwirth asked her where she had learnt to walk the way she did. She admitted it had been from watching Don Pennebaker's *cinéma-vérité* study of Dylan's 1965 UK tour, *Don't Look Back*. Neuwirth, Dylan's regular sidekick in those days, cracked up.

Patti Smith: He said, 'Come here, what do you have in that notebook?' I said, 'Nothing,' and I was really acting tough but I was instantly and totally in love . . . Bobby looked in my book and asked me who wrote that stuff and I told him I did . . . I think he immediately recognized something in me that I didn't even recognize in myself, and he took me under his wing.

I was writing a lot of poetry then, a real rhythmic kind of poetry . . . He really loved the poetry. To me he was a real hot shit. *Don't Look Back* and all that . . . I thought he was the classiest, sexiest guy. It was 1970 and the guy had dark glasses . . . Bobby started me out . . . tried to inspire me with the poetry. He built up my confidence. Treated me like a prodigy. He'd say, 'Don't treat Patti Lee like a groupie, she's a poet.' I never got laid because people don't think poets fuck. He taught me how to drink tequila, too. I got in my rock & roll period then 'cause I was hanging around his friends . . . I lived at the Chelsea and every night was a fuckin' party. Someone was always fighting or Nico was slashing some person.

At the same time as Smith immersed herself in the Chelsea scene, she became involved in her first notable New York affair, with aspiring playwright and part-time drummer Sam Shepard.

Pete Stampfel: [Patti] came to review the Holy Modal Rounders, and fell in love with Sam Shepard. He was really pissed off and he wrote this song called 'Blind Rage' which he sang while playing drums, it was great. Patti heard him perform this song – which he only did once – and he cocked her entire mind. So she decided she wanted to write about Sam Shepard.

They initially shared an apartment near the Chelsea Hotel, in an apartment building over the Blarney Stone tavern, but soon moved back into the hotel itself, where they attempted to write a play together. Shepard had left his wife, O-Lan, temporarily captivated by Smith. The relationship proved a tempestuous one, and few could see any lasting future for the pair.

Patti Smith: He was an important force in my life. We wrote one play, *Cowboy Mouth*, together on the same typewriter – like a battle. And we were having this affair. He was a married man, and it was a passionate kind of thing. We wrote the play and took it right to the stage . . . It was sad at the end. We were talking about two people – two big dreamers – that came together but were destined for a sad end. It was the true story of Sam and me. We knew we couldn't stay together. He was going back to his wife, and I was going on my way . . . But even though it was an unhappy love affair, it was a very happy union. He inspired me to be stronger and move on – to make my move.

Cowboy Mouth gave an early intimation of Smith's belief in the rock & roll dream. Possibly the lifestyle at the Chelsea, particularly her association with Neuwirth and the Winter Brothers, Edgar and Johnny, had put stars in her eyes. In *Cowboy Mouth* the Smith character, written entirely by Patti, was named Cavale. In the notes, she described Cavale as 'a chick who looks like a crow, dressed in raggedy black'. The most significant part of the play, at least in relation to Smith's future plans, came when she revealed her belief in rock & roll as the new religion – replacing the High Church in pomp, ceremony and even revelation:

I mean I can't be the saint people dream of now. People want a street angel. They want a saint but with a cowboy mouth. Somebody to get off on when they can't get off on themselves. I think that's what Mick Jagger is trying to do . . . what Bob Dylan seemed to be for a while. A sort of god in our image . . . ya know? Mick Jagger came close but he got too conscious. For a while he gave me hope . . . I want it to be perfect, 'cause it's the only religion I got . . . in the old days people had Jesus and those guys to embrace . . . they created a god with all their belief energies . . . and when they didn't dig themselves they could lose themselves in the Lord. But it's too hard now. We're earthy people, and the old saints just don't make it, and the old God is just too far away. He don't represent our pain no more. His words don't shake through us no more. Any great motherfucker rock'n'roll song can raise me higher than all of Revelations. We created rock'n'roll from our own image, it's our child . . .

By the time that *Cowboy Mouth* received its one and only American performance on 29 April 1971 (Patti Smith playing Cavale and Sam Shepard as Slim: 'a cat who looks like a coyote'), Smith had already given her first live concert, fusing her two great loves – poetry and rock & roll.

The event, ostensibly a celebration of Bertolt Brecht's birthday, was held at St Mark's Place. The calendar read 10 February 1971. Smith read some of her own poetry accompanied on electric guitar by Lenny Kaye, a well-known New York rock & roll journalist. After opening with a version of Brecht's 'Mack the Knife', she performed several original poems, the first of which was 'Oath'. Its opening lines ran, 'Christ died for somebody's sins/ but not mine/ melting in a pot of thieves/ wild card up my sleeve/ thick heart of stone/ my sins my own.'

Lenny Kaye: She was actually working on *Cowboy Mouth* when I first really started getting friendly with her. I knew she hung out with Steve Paul, the Johnny Winters crowd a lot. But we never really actually talked until she read an article I wrote in *Jazz & Pop* magazine called 'The Best of Acapella', which was about doo-wop music in Jersey in the early Sixties.

Because she was from south Jersey and the Philly scene we had both heard a lot of these street-corner groups so she called me up one day out of the blue and told me how much the article moved her. Which I thought was really sweet, especially since I wrote the article 'cause I felt that nobody else knew about this music. So then she started coming into [the record store where I worked] Village Oldies, and we'd put on a couple of south Jersey favourites. I was from New Brunswick which is kinda equidistant 'tween Philly and New York so I got both worlds. We'd put on a few of our favourites and we'd dance around in the store and hang out. She knew that I played guitar and at the time I wasn't really playing in any bands. She said, 'You wanna play guitar behind some of these songs. They're just poems.' I went over to her loft on 23rd Street and it was kinda easy to figure out what to play guitarwise behind her, especially rhythmically, 'cause even then she kinda sung/talked her poetry. There was a real rhythm and almost a melody. And she did this reading and it went over great. In a weird way it had all the seeds of what we would later [do] . . . It was Bertolt Brecht's birthday — so we did a version of 'Mack the Knife' which was like our salute to the past, and then she did a bunch of poems including 'Oath', which we later adapted, and then we did a song called 'Fire of Unknown Origin', kind of a minor-key blues which we later did as a B-side. Then we did a song she wrote called 'Jesse James' and then this song called 'Ballad of a Bad Boy' which was about a car crash and [at] the end of it I simulate a car crash on the guitar. So that would be like our 'Radio Ethiopia'. So all the seeds. A little pop song, a little art ballad and a little anarchic lunacy.

The performance, which was taped by Brigid Polk, was well-attended — evidence of the many contacts Smith had developed since her return from Paris. Mapplethorpe had brought his Jet Set friends, Kaye had brought his fellow critics and Neuwirth his rock & roll comrades.

Smith, though, was reluctant to devote herself entirely to her performance art at this stage and chose not to repeat the experiment with Kaye — at least for the time being. The traumas she was experiencing in her relationship with Shepard cannot have helped her peace of mind. Indeed, after the premier of *Cowboy Mouth* at the American Place Theatre in April, Shepard disappeared and on the second night Smith had to go out and inform the paying punters that they could not proceed with the performance as nobody could locate the male lead. But the termination of *Cowboy Mouth* was not the end of Smith's interest in theatre, an integral aspect of the development of Patti Smith the Performer.

Leee Black Childers: Patti, Cherry [Vanilla], Wayne [County] were all in a show called *Island* which played three or four years before [CBGB] to absolute rave reviews and packed houses down on 2nd Ave and Bowery, not half a block from CBGB. It was theatre of the ridiculous, Patti played a very Brian Jones-esque sort of speed freak in it ... [It was] written and directed by Tony Ingrassia ... it was very anarchist, it was set on Fire Island, all that anyone did was gossip and eat and in the end they all get blown up, everyone dies ... All that theatre of the ridiculous stuff presaged all this [scene] and had a great influence on it. Patti knew what would appeal to [her audience], she knew she shouldn't come out dressed like Jackie Curtis, in sequins and glitter and stuff, because they wouldn't understand it.

Smith also continued to work on her poems, and in September 1971 *Creem* published a portfolio of her poetry, which included tributes to Sam Shepard and Bobby Neuwirth and, of course, 'Oath'. This was an unprecedented gesture by the editors of *Creem*. *Creem* was a rock & roll rag, not a poetry magazine. According to Smith's blurb accompanying the poems, 'If I found kids at high schools couldn't dig [my poetry], I'd give it up.'

As soon as Smith began writing prose for *Creem*, she reflected her love of rock & roll in a series of reviews and features. At the same time she rejected an approach from the Winter brothers' manager, Steve Paul, to use her voice in a rock & roll band. Though she had an abiding interest in rock music, the themes of her poems regularly touching on her personal icons, she saw herself as a poet, pure and simple. Her relationship with Allen Lanier, keyboardist for Blue Oyster Cult, whom she met in the fall of 1971, allowed her to witness all the trappings of rock & roll first hand. Lanier attempted, like Shepard and Neuwirth before him, to harness Smith's energies, still prone to being needlessly dissipated.

Patti Smith: Allen gave me a hard time for a while, saying that he would not stand behind my work unless I learned some skills to back up my

mouth, which was pretty big. I was like Muhammad Ali with no punch . . .
He forced me to discipline myself and go beyond image.

With her articles for *Creem*, the publication of two books of her poetry
– *Seventh Heaven* and *Witt* – and growing popularity for her unaccompan-
ied poetry readings, the two years following the completion of *Cowboy
Mouth* represent a period of successful retrenchment for Smith the
writer. In the summer of 1972 she returned to Paris, again with her sister,
at which time she visited the grave of Doors' leader Jim Morrison, who
had died there the previous July. She would later write about a vision
that she experienced at Morrison's grave in her 1975 composition, 'Break
it Up', and also in a 'final' essay for *Creem* magazine, 'Jukebox Crucifix':*

I went to paris to exorcise some demons. some kind of dread I harbored of
moving forward. I went with this poetic conceit that we would meet in some
melody hovering over his grave. but there was nothing. it was pouring rain and
I sat there trying to conjure up some kind of grief or madness. I remembered
this dream I had. I came in a clearing and saw a man on a marble slab. it was
Morrison and he was human. but his wings were merging with the marble. he
was struggling to get free but like Prometheus freedom was beyond him.

I sat there for a couple of hours. I was covering with mud and afraid to move.
then it was all over. it just didn't matter anymore. racing thru my skull were
new plans new dreams voyages symphonies colors. I just wanted to get the hell
outa there and go home and do my own work. to focus my floodlight on the
rhythm within. I straightened my skirt and said good-bye to him.

On her return from Paris, Smith came into contact with Jane Friedman.
Friedman was booking groups at the Mercer Arts Centre when, early in
1973, she came up with the unorthodox suggestion that Smith open for
the Dolls, reading some of her poetry. Though she struggled to be
heard above the background swell of sound and the inevitable bozo
shouting for rock & roll, Smith found a surprising degree of acceptance.
Finally, in the fall of 1973, Smith decided that a return to her earlier
fusion of rock & roll and poetry was her ordained direction.

Lenny Kaye: Around '73 she started doing more poetry readings. Jane

---

* Smith scribbled a note at the bottom of this essay to indicate that this was her final
article.

Friedman became her manager . . . *Witt* was definitely out and some time around then she came in Village Oldies where I was still working and [started] telling me she was gonna do a reading at Les Jardins, which was on top of the Hotel Diplomat on 43rd Street, and would I come along and do my guitar thing with her. We essentially did pretty much the same thing [as at St Marks but] I think we did a version of 'Annie Had a Baby'.

This time, though, the Smith/Kaye set was no one-off performance. Smith and Kaye began to appear regularly as a duo, and her solo poetry readings became another skin shed.

Lenny Kaye: It slowly grew . . . Every month or so she'd get a gig and I'd get up for three songs. By the end of '73 when we opened up Phil Ochs at Max's I was onstage all the time, though I wasn't playing for all of it. But the songs were interspersed and she had a piano player . . . [though] Richard didn't join until March of '74. Every gig we had a different piano player. We had a guy named James, and Patti's friend Matthew Reich played for one series of gigs [when] we opened up for Happy and Artie Traum . . . I remember Artie or Happy seemed really mad at us one day, talking about, 'What do you know about your three chords?' But we just did our thing and I'm not sure people really understood what we were doing but we were having a good time doing it and Patti even then was incredibly charismatic, and a totally heartfelt performer and her poetry really communicated . . . Her poems weren't based on intellectual judgements but were pure emotional torrents and we used to improvise a lot. [It was] one of the things we got into partially because one of my roots was free jazz and free rock improvisation. We'd just get on these rhythmic moves – we called them fields – where we just kinda rode around in them. And [with] a lot of our early songs that's all they were. 'Free Money' was just those chords repeated over and over again . . . 'Land of a Thousand Dances', 'Gloria' certainly, they weren't really songs but over the course of performing them we would get into things that we would come up with and they were incorporated into the song.

In the winter of 1973–4, Smith and Kaye still conceived of themselves as an art project whose connection with rock & roll was at best tangential. Chris Stein, then playing with the Stillettoes, recalls one of the duo's early shows:

Chris Stein: The first time I saw Patti she was speaking at some Notre Dame show where she did a poetry reading and then brought Lenny out to play with her and she just sorta made fun of him. It was more the image of this rock performer than an actual attempt at being a real rock performer. He was playing real lousy. He was just bashing these chords out and drowning her out and she abused him and it was almost a comedy routine that they did. She was just poking fun at the whole rock & roll syndrome.

If the 'fields' that Kaye and Smith were harvesting recalled the spirit of the Velvets, the two of them believed that they were working in a contemporary vacuum – that their form of art-rock had no parallels with any other band in New York. This was despite the fact that Smith was friendly with one of two Neon Boys seeking to change all that, Richard Meyers.

Smith's and Kaye's 'ignorance' lasted until 14 April 1974 when they decided to stop off on their way home from the New York premiere of the Rolling Stones' documentary film *Ladies and Gentlemen* to see Meyer's band play at a recently opened club on the Bowery called CBGBOMFUG (Country, Blue Grass, Blues, and other music for uplifting gourmandizers).

Smith and Kaye witnessed the fourth gig of Meyers and Miller's new band, Television. After the dissolution of the Neon Boys, Meyers' next scam had involved him managing Miller as a solo act, attempting to secure him gigs in the Village. Miller did not meet with instant recognition. After a few unpaid spots at Gerdes Folk City, he reached the dizzy heights of a fifteen-minute slot at Reno Sweeny.

Tom Verlaine: I decided to play the sets like I had a whole electric band behind me; so I just went in with an electric guitar and turned it up. They really hated it, [but] Richard [Lloyd] was there and he liked it.

Among the songs Lloyd heard was one that struck an immediate chord with him, '(I Fell) (Into the Arms of) Venus De Milo'. The presence of fellow guitarist Richard Lloyd at Miller's Reno Sweeny debut was no coincidence. Lloyd had been living at the loft of a good friend of Meyers and Miller, Terry Ork. Ork knew of Miller's long-standing quest for a second guitarist and had cajoled Lloyd into giving up practising the guitar for just one night.

Richard Lloyd: I was living in Chinatown in a loft, a huge loft, that this guy named Terry Ork had . . . Then one day he told me about this guy he knew, who he saw around the bookstores, whose name was Tom, and who did the same thing as I did, being all alone and playing electric guitar and singing, who was going to be doing a gig at this small supper club on audition night . . . Richard Hell was there acting as his manager at the time, and they both came in tattered, ripped t-shirts . . . We walked in and sat down at a table with a few other people there waiting. We got pretty loud and the manager was coming over and saying, 'You gotta be quiet.

You're bothering the other patrons.' And I'm going, 'Gee, this would make a nice rock club if you kicked out all the palm trees and tuxedoes.' Tom came in and plopped his amp on stage and turned it on and it went POP and the manager immediately runs up to him and goes, 'You gotta turn that down, that's too loud' . . . He played three songs . . . I thought 'My God, put us together Terry, then there'll be a band because I know I can flesh out what he's doing. I can augment it perfectly.'

Lloyd's own musical influences − more conventional than Miller's − were firmly rooted in the blues. As far as he was concerned, 'guys like Elmore James, Buddy Guy, Magic Sam, John Lee Hooker, have a rudiment that all guitarists have to have.' Lloyd had only recently arrived in New York from Los Angeles.

Richard Lloyd: I was 17 when my parents moved to New Jersey. I spent one year there before fleeing with all the strength I could muster − I went to Boston, I went to Los Angeles, I did all the usual sort of vagabond 20-year-old trip around America.

A week after the Reno Sweeny gig, Lloyd came around to Miller's apartment and they jammed together. Miller had found his Sterling Morrison, a guitarist who naturally complemented his more free-range way of playing. He set about reforming the Neon Boys as a four-piece. Billy Ficca was again recalled from some less audacious out-of-town outfit. Meyers' bass playing had made only marginal advances since the Neon Boys, and he was reluctant to be a part of the new band. However, there were no real alternatives, and Meyers' other inputs, as lyricist and ideas man, counter-balanced his musical deficiencies − at least at first.

Richard Lloyd: Richard and Tom had played together before, and Richard had played bass and given it up, but Tom and I convinced him to pick it up again − were going to be a rock & roll band . . . Richard at the time said he couldn't play bass, and we were going to be sorry, because he'd been through it all with Tom already, but we kept after him, and finally the three of us were playing together on these old beat up amps . . . we plugged the bass and both guitars in one amp for a while. Tom said he knew this great drummer who was up in Boston playing in a blues band, and he called up Bill.

The four-piece Neon Boys could now start rehearsing – thanks to the generosity of Terry Ork, who donated the sort of rehearsal space they could ill afford to rent.

Tom Verlaine: Terry Ork, who was the big support for the band, had a loft where we could rehearse . . . Hell said, 'Why don't we do this band? This guy Lloyd wants to play with you. He likes your songs.' So I said, 'Well, let's try it.' So . . . we started banging it out. I had a lot of reservations about it actually, [but] Lloyd was a good player. He began to practise right away . . . He would sit and learn parts.

The first requirement was a new name. The Neon Boys was part of the past. After rejecting the likes of Goo Goo and the Liberteens, Meyers suggested Television. Meyers, Miller, Lloyd and Ficca were ready to tune in.

Richard Lloyd: We wanted something that was really tinkly and mechanical and had a car radio . . . something that blared out. It's always there. It's so there that you lose your consciousness about it. 'Television' just seemed to fit that bill 'cause it's something that's in every home in America. It's so obtrusive, it's unobtrusive.

The two erstwhile leaders decided that onstage *alter egos* were in order. Miller chose to display an affiliation with the French symbolists by becoming Tom Verlaine, though he would later insist that his choice was made simply because it sounded suitable.

Tom Verlaine: It was just some kind of way of disassociating yourself from your own past, a way to be something that you want to be . . . You didn't have any choice in your name when you were born, so you realize that, and then figure that maybe you do have a choice.

For Meyers it was a more convoluted process. His choice of name was intended to convey more than an affiliation to a dead poet – it was how he felt! Richard Hell came with an entire wardrobe and attitude attached. Richard Hell was the image behind the man. The creation of Richard Hell was a statement in and of itself. It also contained the seeds of the eventual split between Hell and Verlaine.

Richard Hell: One thing I wanted to bring back to rock & roll was the knowledge that you invent yourself. That's why I changed my name, why I did all the clothing style things, haircut, everything. So naturally, if you invent yourself, you love yourself. The idea of inventing yourself is creating the most ideal image you could imagine. So that's totally positive . . . That is the ultimate message of the New Wave: if you just amass the courage that is necessary, you can completely invent yourself. You can be your own hero, and once everybody is their own hero, then everybody is gonna be able to communicate with each other on a real basis rather than a hand-me-down set of societal standards.

Television's first concert was at the 88-seater Townhouse Theater on 2 March 1974. They had solicited snappy quotes from artist-friends like Nicholas '*Rebel Without A Cause*' Ray and placed an ad in the *Village Voice* carrying these endorsements. According to Hell, Television actually played this show against a backdrop of television sets. Though the performance went well enough, they realized that another phase of serious rehearsing was in order.

Richard Lloyd: At that time we didn't have any specific idea of what we'd sound like . . . We all realized that we had to improve. If you realize that you are not technically proficient on an instrument, that shouldn't stop you from playing. But you have to be aware of the limitations of not being proficient . . . You have to work at it constantly.

Tom Verlaine: After we did that first gig . . . I remember thinking, 'We've got to rehearse a lot more. This sounds horrible' . . . We started rehearsing a lot more and writing more songs.

In fact, Television had very little prospect of any future gigs. In August 1973 the centre for new New York sounds, Mercers, had crumbled to the ground. There were no alternatives for an embryonic outfit like Television. Terry Ork suggested that they take a leaf from the Dolls' book and find a small club where they could establish a regular gig.

Tom Verlaine: There weren't even any other bands around then, apart from the leftovers from the New York Dolls [scene] . . . bands like Teenage Lust. I was just complaining to a friend that there was no place for an unrecorded band to play in New York, because even Max's at that time was taking acts through the record companies. So he suggested we find a bar with a cabaret licence where we could play once a week, which is what we did.

Barely three weeks after their debut, Lloyd and Verlaine came upon a small club on the Bowery, which had been a Hell's Angel hang-out during its few months of existence. The owner, Hilly Kristal, was looking to expand his customer base.

Richard Lloyd: Tom and I were walking down from his house to the loft in Chinatown, and we passed this place which the owner was outside fixing up. We asked if maybe we could play there – and he told us he was going to call the place Country Blue Grass and Blues. So we said, 'Yes, we play stuff like that; we do all kinds of stuff including our own original material.' He gave us a gig, so we got a whole bunch of friends down and convinced him to give us every Sunday for a month.

CBGBs, as the club became known throughout the world, had opened in December 1973, on the same site as Hilly's on the Bowery, a bar Kristal ran between 1969 and 1972, at which point pressures on his more profitable West Village locale, known simply as Hilly's, required his entire attention. By the time Hilly's on the Bowery reopened as CBGBs, Kristal had lost his battle with West Village residents to keep Hilly's open. Hilly's on the Bowery had already played host to a couple of Mercers acts. Wayne County and Suicide had both been prepared to brave the unique Bowery ambience for the opportunity to play live, but Kristal had decided that country music was going to be the next happening scene. He was attempting to put on country acts and poetry readings when Verlaine and Lloyd convinced him otherwise.

Television's debut at CBGBs was on 31 March 1974. It was the beginning of a six month period in which the post-glam New York rock & roll underground coalesced into a small but highly active scene. Throughout this period, Television continued to play every Sunday at CBGBs, regularly attracting between twenty and thirty people. The Stillettoes, the prototype for Blondie, began playing CBGBs in May, sharing the bill with Television. Meanwhile the Ramones were making their debut at a loft uptown, euphemistically christened the Performance Studio. In August Television graduated to Max's, where they played a weekend of shows with Patti Smith, while the Ramones and Blondie made their debuts at CBGBs.

All this happened without a great deal of media attention, though Television were reviewed in the *SoHo Weekly News* within a month of their debut, Josh Feigenbaum providing such memorable backhanded compliments as: 'The great thing about this band is they have absolutely no musical or socially redeeming characteristics and they know it.'

Television remained a ramshackle outfit for some considerable time, though they had the edge on the early Ramones or Blondie. Despite, or perhaps because of, their rickety nature, Television had some quality that marked them as different, just like the equally 'unprofessional' Beatles, twelve years earlier, in the Cavern. And they did have early supporters, notably David Bowie, who witnessed one of Television's May shows and gave a surprising endorsement – 'The most original band I've seen in New York. They have it.' This was assiduously given prominence on subsequent flyers for Television gigs.

Bob Quine: Ork said come see this band Television. They were playing this place, the 82 Club. Sort of a drag-queen hangout. And I was fairly well stunned by it. When I saw them I said, 'There's definitely a place for me [in rock music].' They were completely unprofessional. They were out of tune at all times. They were breaking strings tuning up, [taking] about four minutes between each song. An amp would blow up! I didn't know what to make of them. The thing that surprised me most was how unprofessional they were and how well accepted by everybody in the club. Verlaine's guitar-playing especially impressed me. He'd obviously listened to Albert Ayler, freaky Coltrane stuff.

Television's sound provided a stark contrast to the Stillettoes, with whom they shared CBGBs bills in these early days. The Stillettoes had a choreographed look, and since they played largely covers, they came across as a marginally professional outfit, even if a sense of pastiche remained the dominant impression from a Stillettoes show.

Debbie Harry: [Television] all wore ripped-up old shirts, except Richard Hell who would wear a ripped-up James Brown frilled satin shirt, and they all had short hair. As far as expertise went they were the same as the other bands, although they had a slightly different sound that was very droney. They weren't trying to be slick.

Yet Television soon came to the attention of at least one A&R man. In the fall of 1974 they were seen by Richard Williams, then working for Island Records. Despite reservations, he was greatly impressed by Verlaine's stage presence.

Richard Williams: I was shepherded to a grubby downtown theatre opposite Club 82 by Richard and Lisa Robinson, those eternal foster-parents of Manhattan's rock avant-garde, to see [Television] in concert. It was an odd event, the four musicians diffident but defiant in the face of a tiny audience and troublesome electronics. That defiance impressed me immediately, particularly when the equipment failed utterly in the middle of an already shaky ballad called 'Bluebird', and Verlaine fought through the song as though his life depended on it. Otherwise the playing was awfully rickety, almost amateurish, but there was something interesting happening, and most of it was vested in the gawky, angular, pained figure of Verlaine.

Though Verlaine's presence appealed to Williams, a large part of the visual impact of early Television resided on the other side of the stage, where Richard Hell was living up to his reputation, leaping around like a dervish tramp who had accidentally ingested some angel dust in his meths.

Chris Stein: I liked Television with Richard. With Hell I thought they were fantastic. It's a shame they never recorded, and so few people saw them and there never were any films or anything. They were really exciting. Even Richard's own performance was different from what he was known for in later years. He really used to do this Townshend thing, a whole series of leaps and bounds around the stage. It was more dynamic. Verlaine was on the end and Lloyd was in the middle. Then all of a sudden Verlaine was in the middle and it changed things. The band was more evenly dispersed with Lloyd in the middle. Lloyd was the lesser of the three of them so he evened it out, made Tom and Hell equal on the ends. It was a subtle thing.

Hell was most concerned with projecting an image for the band. The look of Television, with their ripped shirts and cropped hair, was deliberately anti-glam, a reaction as much to the Mercers scene as the excesses of the current rock scene. The basis for the look was actually considerably older than most people realized.

Richard Hell: There were some artists that I admired who looked like that. Rimbaud looked like that. Artaud looked like that. And it also looked like the kid in *400 Blows*, the Truffaut movie. I remember I had a picture of those three guys. I really thought all this stuff out in '73 and '74.

The anti-glam look, shared by the entire band, came as a shock to at least one old friend of Richard Lloyd's, photographer Leee Black Childers.

Leee Black Childers: I met Richard Lloyd in Los Angeles when I was working for Mott the Hoople, and he was a rock & roll fan, he had shocking pink lipstick, his hair was brown and he was just hanging out with bands. It wasn't long thereafter I was in New York and he comes up to me and he's platinum blond, completely punked out.

Hell conceived of a clear division of labour in Television. If Verlaine was assuredly the musical director, it devolved to Hell to project their visual stance. However, Verlaine seemed to grow increasingly resentful of anything that distracted the audience from concentrating on the music.

Richard Hell: To me it was part of the separation of duties in Television [that] I took charge of all the stuff which . . . wasn't musical. I wanted us to stand for something that showed in everything we did. And that included clothes and the look of our graphics and all that imagery kind of thing. The intention was to make it as true to life as possible in every way that we presented ourselves . . . It was this kinda anti-glamour, angry but poetic sensibility that Tom and I shared but that I was much more interested in translating into media than Tom was . . . And that was part of the disagreement. Tom resented my preoccupation with this imagery stuff.

As Chris Stein has suggested, an essential problem in conceiving of how the early Television sounded is a lack of any worthwhile recordings from this period. Both Hell and Verlaine were quite prolific in the early days, even if most of the songs they performed were never recorded and have been lost or forgotten.

Richard Lloyd: Originally, when we first formed the band, Richard Hell sang 40 per cent of the songs. Tom sang 50 per cent, and they wanted me to sing, but I really didn't want to sing . . . Tom was brimming with songs – 40, 50 songs came out of the period when we were together.

Lloyd sang at least one song in the early Television repertoire, 'Hot Dog', a Verlaine song that the Neon Boys had recorded. Though he preferred to remain 'a guitarist in a great band . . . I didn't want to sing;

I had no confidence in my voice', Lloyd also shared vocal duties on 'I Don't Care' (later rewritten as 'Careful'), each band member – save for Ficca – singing their own verse and sharing the chorus:

> I don't care . . . it doesn't matter to me,
> I don't care . . . it never enters my mind,
> I don't care.

Richard Hell: 'I Don't Care' . . . was one of the first songs we wrote, and that was really the root of the idea of the blank generation.

Richard Hell's '(I Belong to the) Blank Generation' was perhaps the most important, certainly the most anthemic, of the early Television songs. It was also the last Hell song to be excised from the Television repertoire.* 'Blank Generation' was intended as the Seventies' antidote to 'My Generation', i.e. a modern teenage angst song which claimed a right to define the future on its own terms. It also defined the Hell persona for some time to come.

Richard Hell: People misread what I meant by 'Blank Generation'. To me, 'blank' is a line where you can fill in anything. It's positive. It's the idea that you have the option of making yourself anything you want, filling in the blank. And that's something that provides a uniquely powerful sense to this generation. It's saying, 'I entirely reject your standards for judging my behaviour.'

Aside from 'Blank Generation' and 'I Don't Care' (both recorded in 1975), there were at least half a dozen songs demoed at some point in 1974, when Television was a genuine partnership, though the tape has been lost for many years. Verlaine recollects that the Hell songs they recorded included 'Change Your Channels' ('Just put a finger at that place on your panel and – click click – change your channel') and 'Eat the Light'. Lloyd sang a song which later became 'Postcard from Waterloo' (a 1982 single by Verlaine), and Verlaine himself sang a very fast version of '(You're So) Hard On Love' (which became 1981's 'Without a Word'), 'another song about purple velvet' and one called 'You Lied to Me'.

---

* It is the one Hell vocal to be featured on the bootleg album of early demos and live recordings, *Double Exposure*.

Also part of the early repertoire were songs like 'One on Top of Another', 'Love Comes in Spurts', 'High-Heeled Wheels' and 'Fuck Rock & Roll'. At this juncture most of the quotable lyrics (and titles) seemed to be coming from Hell's pen. Verlaine's songs tended to be drier, though equally loaded with wry wordplays (after all, 'Hard On Love' was a Verlaine original). Verlaine's early efforts included 'Horizontal Ascension', a song 'about a kid who got a lighter for his birthday and decided to burn things. He'd go to drug stores and movie theatres, and when nobody was looking – whoosh! – he'd burn everything up'; 'Enfant Terrible', which contained the immortal line 'So many personae, you're so death-loose'; and 'Bluebird', one of the lengthier early Television songs and again overtly sexual in orientation ('My horse run away, my hennypennies don't lay and my cock just don't git up no more.')

Television circa 1974 bore little resemblance to the outfit that would record *Marquee Moon* in November 1976, and the difference was not simply Hell. Verlaine's early Television material was considerably more whimsical than his later songs. The only song performed at the early shows to make it on to their debut album was 'Venus De Milo', and this shared the tongue-in-cheek flavour of Hell's songs:

> Richard said, 'Hey man, Let's dress up like cops,
> Think of what we could do.'
> Something, something, said we'd better not.

The songs also tended to remain resolutely in the three-minute domain established by 45 rpm singles – concise statements, full of verbal puns. The poets were at play. But it did not remain a game for long.

If, as has been pointed out by my market sample of attendees at early Television shows, they were no great shakes technically, that was partially the point – the notion that technical competence should not be a prerequisite for forming a rock & roll band. Television were very deliberately not 'in the tradition of the late Sixties worship of guitar playing, exquisite jams and precious music', to quote Hell. He considered their so-called amateurishness a positive aspect.

Richard Hell: One of the ideas that [I wanted] to convey [was] that anyone can go out and pick up a bass. The immediate publicity around Television always mentioned, and we encouraged it, that I'd just picked up a bass six months before, and it was scandalous except for the Dolls who had introduced some number of people to that idea already.

But Verlaine was becoming increasingly unhappy with Hell's approach. Television was not meant to be a joke, and playing with a bassist of at best average ability, who sang songs like 'Fuck Rock & Roll', seemed a little too much like burlesque for his taste.

Hell, though, received encouragement from both Lenny Kaye and Patti Smith, who shared his belief that rock & roll needed some serious shaking up, and technical competency was no substitute for commitment. And they were expounding their evangelistic views in the forums they wrote for – notably *Rock Scene*, *Hit Parader* and *Creem*.

Lenny Kaye: The first time we went to CBGBs was Easter '74 ... We started hanging out there on Sunday nights as a result of that. Television was the only band there – every Sunday night ... They were pretty rough and ragged. One of the nice things about that scene is that everybody had a long time to grow up in it. For a long time every Sunday night there would be like twenty people in the audience, just some local musicians ... We met Richard [Hell] before we met Tom because I know that Richard was at the auditions when we auditioned Richard Sohl ... We were definitely aware of them and ... we were [soon] becoming like a brother and sister band.

Smith and Kaye had considerably more in common with Television than the other first-wave bands at CBGBs like Blondie and the Ramones. Smith shared Hell and Verlaine's poetry background and – along with Kaye – a common view of rock & roll that asserted the pre-eminence of the British Invasion and the Velvets/Stooges brand of American garage-rock. Hell had been on the verge of publishing a volume of Patti's poetry, under his Dot Books imprint, when his disillusionment with the medium diverted his attention. They had both worked at Cinemabilia, a bookstore specializing in film, and Smith became very friendly with Verlaine after seeing the band in April. Two months later she was asking him to play on her first single; they later co-composed a small pamphlet of poetry called *The Night* and also co-wrote a couple of songs.

Two events bonded the bands together. In the summer of 1974 they shared a residency at Max's Kansas City, lasting from 28 August to 2 September. Though Smith was headliner, due to her reputation in poetry circles and her relatively high profile as a writer, the poster for the shows gave equal billing to Television. The Max's residency represented a step up from regular shows at CBGBs and a significant breach in Max's booking policy towards local unsigned bands. Patti Smith also gave Television their first major write-up in the October 1974 issue of *Rock Scene*, with a two-page feature entitled 'Learning to Stand Naked'. It placed them at the forefront of a long-needed renaissance in rock & roll.

The young gladiator clung to his sword and shield just as the child of rock & roll holds fast to the flash over flesh. This is cool it's the rule of rock & roll but somewhere somebody must stand naked. In the sixties we had the Stones Yardbirds Love and Velvet Underground. Performers moved by cold image. They didn't hide behind an image. THEY WERE THE IMAGE.

We are victims of media penetration. Television is image warm enemy number 1. It's like some alien form of life – flesherpoid parasites – sucking up the grand consciousness and translating it 2-D dot field. It's made our stars and our art (rock & roll) into limp pasteurized versions of a once high-raw process. Boycott rock & roll on TV. Who wants an image of the image. Rock & roll is not hollywood jive. It's becoming flash theatre with less emphasis on the moment – the movement – the rhythm and alchemy of hand to hand combat. When Midnight Special comes on TUNE OUT. Accessible middle class. Killing natural action.

Already a new group has begun an attack. Starting from the bottom with completely naked necks. A group called TELEVISION who refuse to be a latent image but the machine itself! The picture they transmit is shockingly honest. Like when the media was LIVE and Jack Parr would cry and Ernie Kovacs would fart and Cid Caesar would curse and nobody would stop them cause the moment it happened it was real. No taped edited crap. I love this group cause they focus on the face. Close-ups don't disarm them cause they reveal everything. And the lead singer Tom Verlaine (initials TV) has the most beautiful neck in rock & roll. Real swan like – fragile yet strong. He's a creature of opposites. The way he comes on like a dirt farmer and a prince. A languid boy with the confused grace of a child in paradise. A guy worth losing your virginity to. He plays lead guitar with angular inverted passion like a thousand bluebirds screaming. You know like high treble. And like Todd Rundgren he is blessed with long veined hands reminiscent of the great poet strangler jack the ripper.

Richard Hell on bass is another cool picture. Real highway 61. Perfect shades, tufted hair and a suit Philip Marlowe mighta left behind in a piece of blonde luggage circa 1946. His bass is pure trash – metallic gold fleck. His movements are maniac chuck berry. It's amazingly disorienting to watch a guy straight outta desolation row doing splits. Richard Lloyd plays emotional and highly sexually aware guitar. He's the pouty boyish one. The one most likely to get beat up in a parking lot. I love to watch him and Tom and Hell pumping on guitar. The three of them playing with such urgency as if each time is the last time or the first woman. Relentless adolescents. Backed by Billy Ficca (a tough Italian biker) on drums they present a picture made for the plague. A movement of inspired mutants that will take the slop out of rock. Television will help wipe out media. They are not theatre. Neither were the early Stones or the Yardbirds. They are strong images produced from pain and speed and the fanatic desire to make it. They are also inspired enough below the belt to prove that SEX is not dead in rock & roll.

Their lyrics are as suggestive as a horny boy at the drive in. Songs like 'Hard On Love', 'One On Top of Another' and 'Love Comes in Spurts'. Sexual energy is suppressed on tv is the main ingredient of Television. They got the certain style. The careless way of dressing like high school 1963. The way they pulse equal doses of poetry and pinball. Their strange way of walking. Hell is from Kentucky. A runaway orphan with nothing to look up to. The others grew up in Delaware: a land of grids – one long oppressive gymnasium. Tom and Hell done time in reform school. Lloyd done time in mental wards. Billy been round the world on his BSA. They came together with nothing but a few second hand guitars and the need to bleed. Dead end kids. But they got this pact called friendship. They fight for each other so you get this sexy feel of heterosexual alchemy when they play. They play real live. Dives clubs anywhere at all. They play undulating rhythm like ocean. They play pissed off psychotic reaction. They play like they got knife fight in the alley after the set. They play like they make it with chicks. They play like they're in space but still can dig the immediate charge and contact of lighting a match.

By the time Patti Smith resumed her alliance with Lenny Kaye in November 1973, both of them had become increasingly disillusioned with what contemporaries were doing to their beloved beat. Yet only gradually did they come to realize that the sea of possibilities might include them in the swim of things.

Both Smith and Kaye were writing regularly as rock journalists. This allowed them the perfect opportunity to expound upon their concern that American rock & roll was in need of some radical new impetus. Patti's own description of rock & roll, in an article on Edgar Winter in the March 1973 issue of *Creem*, reflected her belief that the form had irredeemably lost its innocence:

Rock n roll is a dream soup. whats your brand? mine has turned over. mine is almost at the bottom of the bowl. early arthur lee. smokey robinson. blonde on blonde. its gone. the formula is changed. there are new recipes. new ear drums. rock n roll is being reinvented. just like truth. its not for me but its there. its fresh fruit. its dream soup ... Personally I'd like to see it dirtier. Less homogenized. But then I'm of the old school. I still drool for Billy Lee Riley. Original James Brown. Hot buttered soul. But things are different now. More than 4 track. More than a microphone.

In this monologue on the state of modern rock & roll, Smith comes across as a detached observer, as if the beat had gone beyond her powers of receptivity. As this sense of disinterest began to fade, Smith's writings became more polemical. Her final article for *Creem* prior to her own assumption of the rock & roll dream, 'Jukebox Crucifix' (already quoted in Chapter 9), has her accepting a mantle of responsibility.

rhythms like rules shift. something new is coming down and we got to be alert to feel it happening. something new and totally ecstatic. the politics of ecstasy move all around me. I refuse to believe Hendrix had the last possessed hand that Joplin had the last drunken throat that Morrison had the last enlightened mind. they didn't slip their skins and split forever for us to hibernate in posthumous jukeboxes.

Smith and Kaye's vision of a revitalized rock & roll was, like the Dolls and Television, essentially reactionary. Unlike the English punks, who were only dimly aware of rock & roll's history and whose own 'raw wails from the bottom of the gut' took the form of a knee-jerk response rather than a carefully considered programme, Smith and Kaye were very much children of the Sixties. It was to the experimentation and inventiveness they associated with that era that they wanted to return rock & roll.

Lenny Kaye: Much of the [Sixties] era relied on older ways of thinking – the emphasis on hit singles to make or break a group, for instance, or the submergence of instrumental displays to the needs of the song at hand – but much clearly pointed forward: a fascination with feedback electronics, caged references to the drug experience along with more 'worldly' concerns, and a sense that, somehow, things were going to be a lot different from this point on.

But Smith and Kaye were also doing something new: a unique fusion of poet-rock & roll. If past critics had asserted that songwriters like Dylan were 'poets' (which Dylan himself ridiculed by suggesting that some people are POets and some are poETS), his so-called major lyrics were always intended to be performed in the context of song. Smith and Kaye were actually taking poetry and giving it a disarming relevance by placing it in this unfamiliar context, and their audience seemed willing to accept such a radical approach.

If the early Smith/Kaye experiments were crude in the extreme, when they united with pianist Richard Sohl in March 1974 the possibilities at last merged into some recognizable amalgam of performance poetry and improvisatory free-form rock & roll. Though they had already tried a couple of piano players at earlier gigs, it was the eclectic Sohl who steered them in the necessary direction.

Patti Smith: At first it was just me and Lenny Kaye on electric guitar farting around at poetry readings. Then it started to gather force. We advertised for a piano player. We were really just bluffing, y'know? And all these guys would come in and say, 'Hey, wanna boogie?' Me and Lenny were stoned, trying to talk all this cosmic bullshit to them, like, 'Well, what we want to do is go over the edge.' And finally Richard Sohl came in wearing a sailor suit, and he was totally stoned and totally pompous. We said, 'This guy's fucked up.' Lenny gave him the big cosmic spiel and Sohl said, 'Look buddy, just play.' We felt like we were the ones getting auditioned.

With her three-piece line-up Patti Smith, managed by the capable Jane Friedman, began to attract a healthy cross-section of hipper New Yorkers. It was also this line-up that recorded the first Patti Smith single – Piss Factory/Hey Joe – in June 1974, with the help of Tom Verlaine, lead guitarist on the B-side, 'Hey Joe'. The A-side was an astonishingly frank account of the time Smith spent working in a factory in Pitman, New Jersey.

Patti Smith: To me that little 'Piss Factory' thing is the most truthful thing I ever writ. It's autobiography. In fact, the truth was stronger than the poem. The stuff those women did to me at that factory was more horrible than I let on in the song. They did shit like gang up on me and stick my head in a toilet of piss.

'Hey Joe' was prefaced by a poem about Patty Hearst, christened 'Sixty Days'. In this context, 'Hey Joe' came to be about the revenge of a father, not the fury of a cuckold. This technique – of prefacing covers with snippets of her own poetry – was a logical extension of the early Smith/Kaye sets.

The most intricate fusion was 'Land', which combined Smith's own 'Horses' rap-poem with rock & roll standards 'Land of a Thousand Dances' and 'Bony Maronie', though there were several other contemporary examples, notably a doo-wop cover of the Quintones' 'Down the Aisle', during which Smith would do her 'do you take this woman' rap.

Patti Smith: All our things started out initially as improvisations . . . Lenny and I work out tunes as they go along. I have words and know how I think they should go, so we just pull it out and pull it out further until we get somewhere.

Such segues often transformed the material. 'Time is on My Side' was invariably prefaced with Smith's famous 'tick tock/fuck the clock' rap, while Van Morrison's 'Gloria' was introduced by the opening lines of 'Oath'. Smith had even written a couple of verses for the Velvet Underground's riff-looking-for-a-song, 'We're Gonna Have a Real Good Time Together', with which she now opened most shows. The verses were so much in a Velvets vein that fans could be forgiven for thinking Smith had access to some complete Velvet Underground version of the song:

> Went down to Harlem looking for something black,
> This black man looked at me and said,
> 'Darling don't you know the blackest thing in Harlem is white.'

The Max's residency with Television at the end of August 1974 coincided with the independent release of the Piss Factory/Hey Joe single, which had been largely financed by Robert Mapplethorpe and Kaye. Smith's initiative – releasing an independent single as a means of attracting media attention – would soon be copied by Television and Pere Ubu, and would have a major impact on the way that English punk bands 'spread the word'.

Smith's sense of theatre was now developing apace. A highlight of these Max's shows was a version of 'Paint it Black' where she did a mock strip with her black tie and white shirt, à la *Horses*, leaving her clothed entirely in black.

More importantly, Smith, Kaye and Sohl were performing several potent new works. Replacing some of the rhythmic rants that had been highlights at earlier shows were 'Kubla Khan', 'We Three' and an embryonic version of 'Land'. Smith was also doing far more singing than chanting.

A trip to California in November convinced Smith and Kaye that a further expansion in their art-trio was required. The need for someone to alternate between bass and guitar and help to fill out the sound was becoming a pressing concern.

Lenny Kaye: The end of '74 we actually went out to California and played the Whisky A Go-Go and stuff. Nobody knew who we were . . . We played the Whisky and then went up to San Francisco . . . we played an audition night at the Winterland with Jonathan Richman on drums. He was pretty good. We'd never played with a drummer before so it was interesting ... By this time the music had gotten such, we needed something 'cause I was really struggling. There was a lot of ground to cover ... When we had guitar auditions we put an ad in the *Voice* like everybody else does in New York. We had fifty guitar players come down. And it was the first time where we actually had to think: What are we doing and who do we need to do it with? Do we want this great blues guitar player? We were working in such weird formats that we needed someone who fitted us rather than would take us some more traditional place. The idea of having a rock & roll band we resisted for a long time ... We enjoyed staying outside of the tradition. We always felt it was important to keep a sense of surprise in the music.

Patti Smith: We had days and days of guitar players, all sorts of maniac baby geniuses from Long Island, kids with $900 guitars who couldn't play anything. Mother had sent them – in a cab! ... Finally Ivan Kral came in. This little Czechoslovakian would-be rock star. He said, 'I am here to be in your band' ... We did 'Land of a Thousand Dances' and it went on so long I thought I was gonna puke.

Smith's romanticized version of Kral's audition overlooks the fact that he was actually playing in Blondie, and therefore Smith and Kaye were surely already conversant with his guitar-work from weekends at CBGBs. Indeed both Chris Stein and Debbie Harry believe that Kral was deliberately purloined by Smith.

Despite Friedman's methodical management and the local popularity of Patti Smith gigs, the new four-piece Patti Smith Group was still only playing the occasional show in the winter of 1974–5, while Television had been cutting their teeth every weekend at CBGBs. Smith and Co. needed a regular gig in order to get their material to a stage where it could be recorded. Record labels had already expressed interest in her music, but what Smith had that winter was raw and unrefined.

Late in March 1975, Patti Smith and her band began a two-month residency at CBGBs, sharing each weekend bill with a reconstituted Television, who were working in a new bassist after the sudden and acrimonious departure of Richard Hell. Surprisingly, this was the first time that Patti Smith played at CBGBs, aside from a Valentine's Day weekend in February, despite regularly attending Television's Sunday night gigs there. Her presence was a major fillip to CBGBs' credibility – as well as the first time that the club had been packed out every weekend night. The Television/Patti Smith bills established CBGBs as New York's premier rock & roll club, at a time when the Ramones and Blondie could barely muster fifty people in toto at their shows. It also cemented a relationship between the art-rock crowd, who regularly attended Patti Smith gigs, and CBGBs' rock & roll crowd. This alliance had a major effect on the development of New York's new rock & roll scene.

Lenny Kaye: With Patti Smith we had a following drawn from the art fringes and we would play a lot of cabaret/folk clubs, mostly one-offs every month or so. We got very friendly with Television, 'cause we were working on the same outer limits.

The regular CBGBs shows formalized the Patti Smith Group sets, at least in terms of song-selection. They were now concentrating on the songs later included on the *Horses* album, plus new originals like 'Space Monkey', 'Distant Fingers' and 'Snowball', and recently introduced covers like Smokey Robinson's 'The Hunter Gets Captured by the Game'. All the songs were undergoing internal changes.

Lenny Kaye: It gave us a chance to continuously work on an act. We worked pretty much on improvisation. We became a real band after that gig. It was also around that time we signed to Arista ... A lot of songs started off as jams and soon we found that things would organically come together. 'Gloria' started as a jam. We'd do chordal riffs over which Patti would chant, poeticize and tell stories.

The CBGBs residency also introduced a new Television. Though barely six months separate Television's first joint residency with Patti Smith, at Max's in late August 1974, from their second dual residency, at CBGBs in March 1975, in that period Television, on the verge of a record deal, had fragmented and reconstituted, emerging a more single-minded outfit at the end of their tribulations. All the while their reputation remained in the ascendant. Aside from Smith's major endorsement in *Rock Scene*, they were now attracting comment in *Creem*, the *Village Voice* and its short-lived rival, *Soho Weekly News*.

Part of the original appeal of Television may have been the tension between the opposite poles of Hell and Verlaine, but their respective demeanours on stage meant that they had been at odds from the very first. Television's house was built on sand.

Richard Hell: I have a completely different attitude towards performance than [Verlaine]. To me, it's just a total catharsis, physically and mentally. To them, it's just mental. It reached a point in Television where we had entirely different ends in mind . . . I used to go really wild onstage, and the first thing that indicated I was on the way out was when he told me to stop moving onstage. He said he didn't want people to be distracted when he was singing. When that happened I knew it was over.

A second major source of acrimony came about because by the fall of 1974 Verlaine was gradually phasing Hell's songs out of Television's live repertoire, a process even the other members of Television were aware of.

Richard Lloyd: During that first year Hell and Tom pretty much sang evenly. Then Tom started to take over . . . I was sad to see it happen because I was just watching these two guys chewing themselves up, getting to the point where they wanted to kill each other.

The process was piecemeal, but by the beginning of 1975 Hell had been reduced to singing just two songs in Television's live set, 'Love Comes in Spurts' and 'Blank Generation'.

Roberta Bayley: We used to go see [Television] at Max's a lot and that's when Richard [Hell] sang about a third of the material. Richard Lloyd had his own song that Richard and Tom had written for him about putting his head on the railroad track. And Richard Lloyd always had the t-shirt which Richard Hell had made for him which said Please Kill Me. And he had blond hair but he always got his dye mixed up and so his hair was green. All the girls used to yell for Richard [Hell]'s songs, [like] 'Fuck Rock & Roll (I'd Rather Read a Book)' which really pissed Tom off. The song titles were good ones to shout out. They were the more novelty-esque, amusing songs. Little by little Tom cut all Richard's songs from the set except for 'Blank Generation' and then one day at rehearsals he's like, 'You know I was thinking of cutting "Blank Generation" out of the set.' And Richard said, 'Perhaps it's time to leave this band.'

Verlaine was not merely suggesting cutting 'Blank Generation' from one of Television's shows. After months of building a reputation, Television had been offered an opportunity to record some songs for a possible album on Island Records. The sessions would be co-produced by Richard Williams and Brian Eno (whose work with Roxy Music was known to both Hell and Verlaine). Verlaine refused to allow any Hell songs to be recorded for Island – even the ever-popular 'Blank Generation'. It was an impossible situation and Hell realized that there was no point in continuing his membership of the band. If all he was to be was the bassist, then they might as well recruit a superior player. It seemed to Hell that Verlaine was determined to turn Television into the Tom Verlaine Band.

Richard Hell: By that time I was just there in form. I already knew that I was leaving the group when Tom said that he didn't want to record any of my songs [for Island]. That was the last week or two I was in the group ... David Bowie and Bryan Ferry and a bunch of heavyweights came to our gigs and were spreading the word about us ... It was clear something very soon was gonna break. I was basically squeezed out. He was gradually depriving me of any role in the group and when it reached the point that it was just intolerable I left. And I felt totally betrayed. We'd been best friends, only companions.

Tom Verlaine: I do remember not being enthusiastic about hearing [Hell] sing, especially after we made a tape and I heard tapes of the band live. At that point I was really trying to concentrate on keeping the band focused. And I was already getting bored with playing [three-minute songs]. I didn't feel friction. I liked Richard but at that point he was using a lot of dope ... Hell in those days would say, 'Do you think we'll be a cult band or do you think we'll be as big as the Rolling Stones in a couple of years?' And I would never even have those thoughts. My whole thing was how do I get this song to sound better? ... How to develop the whole sound of the group so it communicated something? So my whole orientation was towards music and performance rather than getting the photographs right.

Given that Verlaine's 'whole orientation' was 'towards music' it came as no surprise when he informed the others that Hell's musicianship was no longer acceptable to him.

Tom Verlaine: Richard didn't play very well. He was more or less learning how to play bass. It didn't matter for a while . . . Then we'd hear a few tapes of the band and it would sound funny. Then it just got to the point where the whole group was missing a bottom. There was nothing which sank down in the sound, which is what you need in rock & roll.

Despite Verlaine's attempts to present a unified sound on Television's demos for Island, he was unhappy with the results. They recorded five songs – 'Prove It', 'Venus De Milo', 'Marquee Moon', 'Double Exposure' and 'Friction' – all outstanding examples of early Verlaine, and at least one of which indicated the direction he saw Television heading in – the eight-minute 'Marquee Moon'.

If Verlaine had been concerned that Hell's musicianship might hold the band back, the bass-playing on the actual demos sounds not only proficient, but appropriately rib-thudding. It was something less tangible that was missing.

Tom Verlaine: The band wasn't that bad, it was just the way it was recorded. There was no life or vitality, which are our strongest points . . . the guitars sounded like the Ventures; except not as good – the Ventures at least sounded warm and wet and [we sounded] cold and dry – very brittle with no resonance. They said, 'We'll sign you up and Eno will produce your record,' so I said 'OK, but let's get another producer.' There was a lot of runarounds and nothing ever happened.

Richard Williams: I [had] booked some time in a Broadway studio called Good Vibrations . . . With me was Brian Eno, who had also seen them and was anxious to participate and investigate them further. We spent three or four nights in the studio, cutting rough versions of five songs; in the beginning Verlaine was quiet, nervy and a little overawed by Brian's enthusiasm. On the second night he began to assert himself; I realized that he knew exactly what he wanted . . . On the last night Verlaine pulled me aside. He was unhappy about the way it had gone. He wanted the band to sound professional.

According to Verlaine, the intention all along had been to record an album for Island, rather than simply a set of demos ('We didn't finish the album they wanted those demos to be'). On hearing the results he became convinced that Television was not ready to make its first vinyl excursion. Verlaine would shy away from any further record deals for another eighteen months, until he felt entirely prepared. And with Hell on the verge of quitting, Television were really in no shape to complete an album.

A major part of the dissension with Hell had been about the scope of the songs that Verlaine was now introducing into the Television set. Though Verlaine's early material had shared the Hell aesthetic, and was firmly rooted in a garageband sound, he was quickly outgrowing the form and looking to expand the internal possibilities within each Television song. Hell was clearly unhappy with this direction, which did not sit easily with his preferred short, sharp shocks to the system.

Richard Lloyd: When the band was first formed, Richard said, 'I don't know how to play bass.' But the enthusiasm was great at the time just in terms of sheer vibrations. Tom and I said, 'Come on man, you'll learn as we go along.' We would teach him each song as we went along, but he would never play the bass, he would only practise the songs. Eventually, the band was progressing to the point that Richard didn't neccesarily want to make the effort to get to. It got to be tedious because you'd be jamming and really going out someplace and you'd find you were being held back and Tom had more and more songs that he wanted to sing.

It was probably the introduction of 'Marquee Moon' that first signalled the genesis of this new approach. Though, according to Verlaine, 'Marquee Moon' had been written as an acoustic ballad before Television was even formed, it became part of the Television set relatively late in the Hell/Verlaine era.* Though Hell manages to stay with the song on the Eno demos, and the March 1975 version is not greatly different in construction from the fall 1976 take used as the title track on Television's debut album, it is clear that Hell did not feel confident extemporizing in the manner that the other guitar players craved. Verlaine was seeking to produce a sound that was much more of a synthesis of his free-jazz roots and the best of Sixties rock & roll.

Tom Verlaine: I got bored with [those 3-minute songs] really quick and got more into the improvisational stuff. It wasn't wanting to play longer

---

* It was certainly in the set by the beginning of January 1975.

songs, it was just being onstage and wanting to create something. So I would play until something happened. That much more comes from jazz or even the Doors or the *Five Live Yardbirds* album – that kinda rave-up – dynamics.

Verlaine already knew whom he wanted to replace Hell – which adds credence to Hell's theory that he was squeezed out of the band. The prospective candidate was Fred Smith, then bassist in Blondie. Television must have seemed a much better prospect to Smith: Blondie at this point were dubbed by their peers 'The Least Likely to Succeed', while Television were the only regular CBGBs band to have generated any real press and industry interest.

Tom Verlaine: I had already played with another bass player. I don't know whether [Hell] got the drift of it or not, but I wanted to see what it was like. It was Fred Smith as a matter of fact . . . I invited him down one night just to fool around, because another friend of mine had been talking to him and he said how much he liked our material, because he'd been playing on the same bill as us a couple of times. Fred's a real fluid kind of bass player.

Verlaine had never lost his love of Coltrane and Ayler, and Ficca's drumming had always betrayed a very strong jazz influence. The addition of a bassist like Fred Smith to hold the sound down allowed the possibilities for improvisation to increase exponentially. From the point of Hell's departure in March 1975 – his final shows being the second weekend of the New York Dolls' ill-fated 'comeback' at the Little Hippodrome – the succinct little vignettes which Verlaine had contributed to the early Television sets began to be superseded by more musically audacious efforts.

Tom Verlaine: When [Hell] left the band Billy was indifferent but me and Lloyd were actually a little glad because we wanted something in there that would ground the whole thing. Even the best three-minute rock songs always touch some ground. Whether it was the Kinks or the Yardbirds it had a root which Television didn't have. Whether it had to do with simply a good bass player or a concept or a flow I don't know. All I know is when we got Fred it clicked immediately. At the first rehearsal me and Lloyd [were] looking at each other and thinking, 'God, this is a real relief.' It was like having a lightning rod you could spark around. Something was there that wasn't there before. Fred could follow stuff. I remember starting up in the longer songs and being able to do stuff that wouldn't throw everybody.

Smith's recruitment certainly unleashed Verlaine's muse. A veritable avalanche of new songs poured down, most of which were designed for twin-guitar embellishment. The CBGBs residency that spring, with Patti Smith and her band, gave the new Television two months of regular gigging to work on new songs. By the end of the residency 'Marquee Moon' was nudging beyond ten minutes and that Neon Boys stalwart 'Poor Circulation' was now a seven-minute creature of moods, while new material like the equally-extended 'Breakin' in My Heart' (which would eventually appear on Verlaine's first solo album, with a new set of words), 'Foxhole' (sometimes prefaced with a snippet of 'Star Spangled Banner' à la Hendrix and then a strangled cry of 'Soldier Boy!'), the sensual 'Judy', and 'Little Johnny Jewel', perhaps the most jazz-oriented number in their new set, were all expansive in structure.

Tom Verlaine: Johnny Jewel is how people were maybe two hundred years ago ... Nowadays, we have to decide what we want to buy in grocery stores, what job to take, what work to do. But not Johnny. For him, it's all right there – it's a freer state, and that's what my music is looking for. To understand Johnny, you should think of William Blake.

By July 1975, when they played their first out-of-town gig, in Cleveland, Television had also added the ten-minute 'Kingdom Come',* which would remain in their set right up to their final gig, without ever being recorded in the studio. It was perhaps the most 'open' of their work-outs, giving full rein not just to Verlaine and Lloyd, but also to Ficca.

Like the Detroit bands in the late Sixties, the mid-Seventies New York bands seemed reluctant to forsake home territory. Television's Cleveland gig had been arranged by musician/rock journalist Peter Laughner after he had seen them in New York, first with Hell, then during the Television/Patti Smith CBGBs residency. He convinced the Piccadilly Penthouse that here was a band with the same sort of

---

* This is not the song Verlaine recorded for his first solo album.

appeal as the New York Dolls, who had been firm favourites in Cleveland, and promptly placed his own band, Rocket from the Tombs, in the support slot for the two shows. Verlaine must have been impressed by Laughner's guitar-playing at these gigs as he was soon offering him a place in Television.

After it became apparent that Island Records was not going to follow through with a concrete record deal, Television decided that they would follow Patti's lead and record their own independent single, in the hope of generating a little media interest. They borrowed a simple four-track recorder from the Patti Smith Group's drummer, Jay Dee Daugherty, set it up in Patti Smith's rehearsal loft and recorded several tracks for a possible 45. Of the songs they recorded – which presumably included 'Hard On Love', 'Fire Engine', 'Friction' and 'I Don't Care', all of which were demoed at this time – the seven-minute 'Little Johnny Jewel', which needed to be divided over both sides of a 45rpm single, seemed a most incongruous choice as a debut single.

Tom Verlaine: Lou Reed asked me, 'Why'd you put out this song? This is not a hit.' I said, 'What band playing a bar in New York, issuing their own single, is gonna have a hit?' It seemed much more [the point] to put out something like what the band did live.

The choice of 'Little Johnny Jewel' as the single incensed at least one member of Television. Richard Lloyd threatened to quit if Verlaine went ahead but, unconvinced by Lloyd's objections, he proceeded with the release.

Richard Lloyd: After we recorded 'Little Johnny Jewel' and a few other songs . . . [we] decided that we were going to put out our own single . . . Of the songs that we had, I thought that 'Little Johnny Jewel' . . . had the least chance and didn't really represent the band . . . At the time I said, 'If that comes out, I'm going, forget it.' So I left, and laid around. In the meantime, we had a gig coming up [at Mothers], so Tom changed the ad to read Tom Verlaine instead of Television.

Coming hard on the heels of Hell's departure, Lloyd's resignation might have finished Television, but Verlaine was quick to recruit a replacement. He knew that Peter Laughner was a devoted admirer of Television, at least the equal of Lloyd as a guitarist, and was blessed with diverse musical tastes; and – whether Verlaine knew it or not – Rocket from the Tombs had now disbanded. They had played just one more show after their support slot at the Piccadilly Penthouse before internal divisions finally rent them asunder. Laughner was ready, willing and able. He flew to New York, where he spent three days rehearsing with Television. Then Lloyd decided that he didn't want to quit after all.

Richard Lloyd: We ran into each other at this restaurant – Tom and Fred were eating, and I walked in and I asked how they were doing. They looked at the floor and said, 'Well, you know how it is – it's rough.' And they asked how I was doing, and I said 'Well, the same. You know how it is – it stinks.'

Lloyd's version of Television's reunification naturally suggests that they were missing his unique feel – yet Laughner was already conversant with much of Television's set (he had taped their Piccadilly set to learn some of the songs) and regularly played 'Venus De Milo', 'Prove It', Verlaine's rewrite of 'Fire Engine' and 'Breakin' in My Heart' at solo gigs in Cleveland. He was also used to alternating rhythm and lead with Gene O'Connor (aka 'Cheetah' Chrome) in Rocket from the Tombs.

Laughner was crushed to have to return to Cleveland as an ex-member of Television. Yet within a month he had formed another band based around a twin-guitar sound. Pere Ubu would prove as important to the history of the New Wave as the band he had so wanted to join, though Ubu would also spurn him before making their most significant vinyl statement.

At the time that CBGBs was starting up in New York, Cleveland's premier rock & roll venue was the Viking Saloon, and its leading rock & roll outfit was Rocket from the Tombs. Formed in June 1974, the Rockets lasted barely a year, during which time they went through at least half a dozen line-up changes, before disbanding in July 1975, having failed to release a single vinyl memoir.*

Yet the Rockets were the originators of three of American punk's most potent anthems – 'Sonic Reducer', 'Final Solution' and 'Thirty Seconds Over Tokyo'. Of the two splinter groups that emerged from the Tombs, one would, for a brief period in the late Seventies, be perhaps the most innovative, challenging rock band in America, while the other remained among the most derivative and regressive.

The original Rockets' line-up had been of minimal significance. They were six months into their existence before they mutated into a true rock & roll outfit. Before this incarnation – which debuted at the Viking Saloon in December 1974 – Rocket from the Tombs had been decidedly left-field. Conceived by Crocus Behemoth (né David Thomas) – then working part-time as a bouncer at the Viking – with Charlie Weiner and Glen 'Thunderhand' Hach fulfilling guitar duties, and Tom Foolery (né Clements) on drums, the original Rocket from the Tombs was a spoof-rock band, playing primarily Fifties and Sixties songs, rewritten as skits on contemporary rock & roll. Thus 'Hey Joe' became 'Hey Punk', it's opening line, 'Hey punk, where you goin' with that glitter in your hair,' showing the early influence on David Thomas of Frank Zappa, someone Peter Laughner was rather disdainful of.

---

* Though Laughner, writing to a friend in May 1975, stated that Rocket from the Tombs were about to record a single – Wild in the Streets/Final Solution – neither cut has emerged.

Charlotte Pressler: Peter was very fond of Beefheart [but] hated Zappa! Just absolutely hated him. Not enough heart. Zappa seemed to him to be always playing with everything as a movie. David Thomas is a real chameleon. He's changed his influences, his pattern of thinking over the years, depending on which strong personality he was relying on. That was why he could write a song like 'Final Solution' and then deny it later ... [Laughner was] very dark. Anybody that he liked was liked because they had that streak of darkness in them. That's clearly there in Richard Thompson ... David Thomas is more into the life-as-a-movie thing. Peter wanted heart, real badly, and in that very detached, pseudo-surrealist atmosphere that you pick up from a lot of Zappa albums, he couldn't find anything that he could connect with emotionally.

Rocket from the Tombs's transformation was a direct result of Thomas's friendship with Peter Laughner. That summer Laughner was playing a weekly gig at a folk club called the Grapes of Wrath, a few blocks down from the Viking Saloon, and he would come and watch the Rockets between breaks. Soon enough Laughner was augmenting the Rockets on stage, assuming full-member status in September and in the process turning the Rockets into a far more potent vehicle for disinterring rock's real roots.

Charlotte Pressler: Crocus had started out doing Rocket from the Tombs as a joke band and I think it shows [that] he is better able to hold the world at a distance and think of it as a cartoon ... it was Peter who convinced him that something serious could be done out of the Rocket from the Tombs joke atmosphere and started pulling that together. When David started writing the songs that the Dead Boys later took over he was writing them consciously punky. It was probably how 'Final Solution' got to be named. [Peter] pushed Crocus into taking himself seriously as a singer and songwriter.

Laughner's previous 'full-time' band, Cinderella's Revenge, had dis-banded towards the end of 1973. He had briefly flirted with a Roxy/Eno-inspired version of Cinderella called the Finns (after Eno's first single, 'Seven Deadly Finns'), but they proved to be nothing more than an interesting diversion, recording a scintillating live version of Eno's 'Baby's on Fire'.

With Laughner's recruitment, the element of parody in the Rockets was considerably toned down. A third guitarist, Chris Cuda, was a short-lived addition, before Weiner, Hach, Cuda and Clements were all dispensed with. The first new recruit was Gene 'Cheetah' O'Connor, a guitarist Laughner had tried forming a band with back in 1972. O'Connor suggested as their new drummer Johnny 'Madman' Madansky, who had also jammed with Laughner back in 1972, and was now playing in a lacklustre Kiss/Dolls covers band, Slash. Finally Laughner convinced Craig Bell, who was still playing bass in Mirrors, to also gig with the Rockets.

The recharged Rockets' debut, at the Viking on 22 December, was part of a 'Special Extermination Night', sharing a bill with the other two Cleveland bands willing to forge an original approach – the Electric Eels and Mirrors. Though Thomas recalls that 'all three of us together could barely fill the place', it was a landmark gig, defining a small underground scene of local musicians reflecting the same spirit then inspiring New York.

The Rockets had changed into a high-energy hard-rock unit, playing a combination of Detroit covers and originals with titles like 'Seventeen' ('Your daddy beat you and took you to church/If he'd had a gun he would've done me in first'), 'Down in Flames' (from which the Dead Boys would take their name), 'Transfusion' and 'Redline'.

Also introduced that December night at the Viking was the Rockets' very own psychodrama, 'Thirty Seconds Over Tokyo', a cathartic tale of 'thirty seconds on a one-way ride', based on the book of the same title, with a guitar-crunching destructo-conclusion as the plane crashes 'over Tokyo', reduced to a ball of flame. Its performance could last anywhere between six and nine minutes. Lacking the sound effects that synth-player Allen Ravenstine would utilize on the later Pere Ubu version (released as their first single), the burden of the song's nagging riff devolved to the two guitarists, Laughner playing the clear, ringing refrain, O'Connor revelling in the sonic destruction, out of which – at the end of this 'one way ride' – emerges that same clear, ringing refrain. 'Thirty Seconds Over Tokyo' provided early notice of the direction Thomas wanted to steer the Rockets in.

An early local feature on the Rockets suggested that Laughner too was looking to make some kind of art statement with their music,

true life presents
TELEVISION

Suzan Carson/Sir Reel Productions

```
                    ...PROVE IT
             LOVE (COMES) IN SPURTS
    (I LOOK AT YOU AND GET A) DOUBLE EXPOSURE
                    MARQUEE MOON
            (THE ARMS OF) VENUS DE MILO
                   HARD ON LOVE
        (I BELONG TO THE) BLANK GENERATION
                    FRICTION...
```

at C.B.G.B.'s
315 Bowery at Bleecker 982-4052
for four weekends

In January: Sunday 12th; Fri., Sat., Sun., the 17th, 18th & 19th;
Fri., Sat., Sun., the 24th, 25th & 26th. Plus Sunday
Febr. 2nd. At 10:00 & 12:00 with guest bands.

A true-life poster of Television with Richard Hell, January 1975.

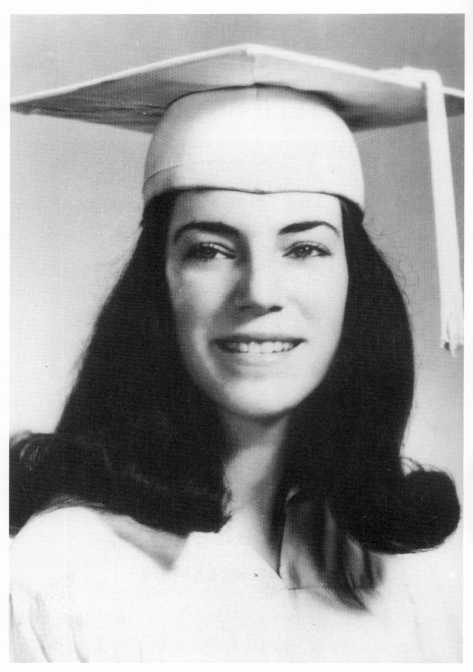

Patti Lee Smith's graduation photo, circa 1964.

Patti Smith rides the sea of possibilities, circa 1975.

The original Television,
circa 1974.

Television at CBGBs, with
Fred Smith and Talking
Heads' drum-kit.

Blondie at CBGBs with
Fred Smith.

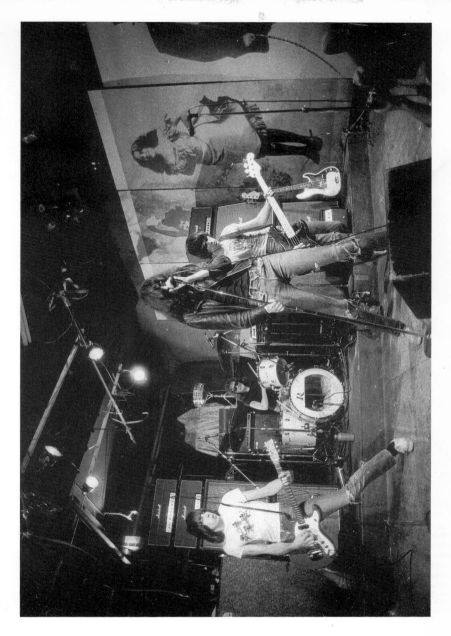

The Ramones, fully
punked-out, at CBGBs.

Rocket from the Tombs with Johnny Madansky, February 1975.
Rocket from the Tombs with Wayne Strick, July 1975.

though his comments were inevitably suffused with his own brand of rock & roll evangelism.

Peter Laughner: What we really want to do with our music is to change the audience's way of looking at things. If people leave a Rocket from the Tombs concert somehow changed in any small way, then we've succeeded . . . Rock & roll used to be able to get you to do things. It used to get you to think about what you were doing, but now all it does is sort of lull you into a state of complacency, the major concern being strictly to have a good time. Entertainment is fine, but there has to be something beyond that. It may sound pretentious to talk about making art statements, but it is possible to make an art statement with music.

Though a second 'Special Extermination Night' at the Viking was arranged for January, the Rockets were absent from the bill, possibly at the Eels' and Mirrors' behest. Morton had never been impressed by Laughner, who in his eyes was always trying 'whatever was hip, [while] we were doing something he couldn't do', and Klimek, who always looked down on Laughner, was now doubly incensed that Bell should wish to play in Laughner's new band.

Charlotte Pressler: Craig Bell's joining Rockets did not sit well with the people in Mirrors, who basically didn't really like Peter much at all . . . I'm sure that professional jealousy can be a motive in these things, but they never really thought that Peter was very cool. In some ways they were right . . . He was quite self-indulgent and I suppose you could say a chronic wannabe.

It was probably just as well that the Rockets stayed away given the fall-out that resulted from this one gig. Having survived through the years when gigs were nearly impossible to come by, Cleveland being largely devoid of an alternative scene, the Eels and Mirrors decided to implode when a fledgling scene was beginning to emerge. In the Eels case, it was simply a case of still being a little too unique for their hometown. Accounts vary as to the actual cause of the Eels' ban from the home of early 'alternative' rock in Cleveland. According to Stiv Bators it was the result of Morton's use of a gas-powered lawnmower.

Stiv Bators: They were hardly getting any gigs in the first place and they were playing the Viking Saloon, which was really the only place for the underground bands to play, and he revved up the lawnmower and the clubowner's cat got scared.

Michael Weldon, who was playing drums for Mirrors that night, suggests the cause was no more than a little dose of Art Terrorism.

Michael Weldon: Dave [usually] played clarinet [but] started a power mower during a song and, when John was preoccupied fighting with an audience heckler, entertained by singing TV commercials and theme songs from programmes like 'The Patty Duke Show' ... people in the audience were amazed by the show, but the owner locked up the Eels' equipment to pay for damages and banned them from his club.

If the Eels had come up against the brick wall their Art Terrorist approach had unswervingly steered them towards, there was also a major personality crisis epidemic that night at the Viking. Paul Marotta had been providing his electronic expertise for both Mirrors and the Eels. Taking a temporary loan on another band's most able musician was perfectly acceptable in Klimek's mind. However, Bell playing with both the Rockets and Mirrors was not. After the January gig Klimek made him choose. Mirrors were now minus one bass player.

At the same time, Marotta quit the Eels. Frustrated at the impasse they had reached, he was determined to assert a new musicality which seemed the very antithesis of his work in the Eels and refused to attempt such a change within either the Eels or Mirrors set-up. Klimek was becoming increasingly attracted to Marotta's ideas regarding a more musically ambitious band. Though Mirrors would stumble on for a further six months, their demise became inevitable.

Michael Weldon: Mirrors broke up because Jamie wanted to play a different style of music, and was playing more with Paul on the side, which led to the Styrenes. Paul had been playing in Mirrors and for a brief time both bands existed at the same time ... The Styrenes did some good music that I liked but it was different than what Mirrors did. Mirrors was pretty simple, raw and unpolished, whereas they were very polished and precise. Paul had been a child prodigy, playing many different instruments, and he brought a professionalism to the group that in some ways was helpful and in other ways destroyed it.

The Rockets were destined to be only marginally more enduring than their troubled contemporaries. They were always an inchoate amalgam of disparate tensions. Laughner's tastes were more eclectic than the remaining Rockets. Having been originally versed in the blues and blessed with a remarkable ear, he was into everything from the feedback/distortion kings of Detroit to the melancholy of Michael Hurley or Nick Drake. Unfortunately the remaining members of the Rockets, Thomas excepted, were considerably more rigid in their tastes, and inevitably the band settled on what little common ground its constituent members had:

Charlotte Pressler: Crocus's main influences were Hawkwind, Stooges, MC5-acid/Detroit destructo stuff. Gene pretty much went for that too. He and Johnny liked the Dolls as well, and just about anything that would have qualified as proto-heavy metal (Blue Oyster Cult etc.). Peter's musical influences as always were eclectic; but the glam-rock side of him was definitely de-emphasized in this band ... Craig was coming from a different place altogether: most of what he liked fell into the British art-rock category – the poppier the better, e.g. Sparks, Roxy Music, this kind of stuff. Loved the Kinks.

Thomas, like Laughner, had broad tastes and, though his main influences at this time were 'Hawkwind, Stooges, MC5-acid/Detroit destructo stuff', they also included Zappa and Beefheart (he would later recall that the first three albums he ever bought were *Hot Rats, Uncle Meat* and *Trout Mask Replica*) and the best of contemporary European rock music.

David Thomas: Everything that was interesting that happened in the Seventies had its roots in the period 73–74–75. At this point there was a generation that had come up – I guess it was my generation – who were the first generation that was brought up with rock & roll as the established cultural medium. It wasn't the music of rebellion in your teens and 'Summertime Blues' ... So this was a generation ... that was seeing it as a serious musical form. As a true art. This is the time that Soft Machine with Kevin Ayers had its greatest day, Can, all that German stuff, the early Eno, Warm Jets, Tiger Mountain, all that, the Roxy Music stuff. In America, Marc Bolan was seen as an underground thing and not as a teenybopper. Musically Marc Bolan was considered to be, quite rightly, a real radical 'cause he was producing a psychodramatic musical form and this is what we were picking up on, not all the teeny trash. What he was doing, he was doing incredibly intensely . . . The thing that marked Cleveland was, at that point, there were some very good record stores and some very good radio stations and everything that was happening from Can to Richard Thompson to Kevin Ayers to Roxy Music, Pretty Things was made commonly available . . . I still remember some of the most influential albums in Cleveland were the early Richard Thompson [records].

Although Laughner shared Thomas's love of Beefheart, their diametrically opposed views on Zappa perhaps suggested a vital psychological difference which made their eventual falling out inevitable and made it difficult for them to provide a united front against the other forces in Rocket from the Tombs.

For a brief period, though, the Rockets managed to coalesce into one relatively unified whole. In the new year they played their own shows at the Viking, even playing the occasional support slot at the Agora. They also made their first radio broadcast, on Cleveland's hip radio station, WMMS.

On 18–19 February they recorded eleven songs in the loft they used for rehearsals: covers of the Rolling Stones' 'Satisfaction' and the Stooges' 'Search and Destroy' and nine originals. Four of these would be subsequently released on Dead Boys albums ('Down in Flames', 'What Love Is', 'Ain't it Fun' and 'Never Gonna Kill Myself Again' – rewritten as 'Caught with the Meat in My Mouth') and two by Pere Ubu ('Thirty Seconds Over Tokyo' and 'Life Stinks'). The other originals included Laughner's chilling 'Transfusion' (co-written with his wife Charlotte Pressler and Gene O'Connor), with its insistent refrain, 'You didn't bleed', and Thomas and Laughner's 'So Cold', which Thomas described in the solitary Rockets newsletter as 'A hymn to numbness . . . a cross between *Night of the Living Dead* and the Utopia Lounge.'

A second radio broadcast, also on WMMS, was drawn from a live gig at the Agora three months later, and included three songs not demoed in February, most notably Thomas and Craig Bell's 'Final Solution.'* The bone-crunching riff for this song, which had been

---

* A cross-section of songs from these two sources was recently put out as the *Life Stinks* album, which contains detailed sleeve-notes on the Rockets' history.

'adapted' from Blue Cheer's 'Summertime Blues', best represents the synthesis of art-rock and garage-rock that was the Rockets at their peak, while the lyrics are a perfect pastiche of dumb teen-angst rock songs:

> Ma threw me out 'till I get some pants that fit,
> Just won't approve of my strange kind of wit.

In fact Thomas's parents really did throw him out, though not because his pants did not fit. When they finally saw the Rockets live, his parents were a little shocked by the onstage apparition greeting them in the guise of their son.

Charlotte Pressler: [Thomas's] parents were rather actively rejecting him. What got him thrown out was the Rocket from the Tombs gig at the Berea Community Centre. David's parents came along and he was in his Crocus clothes and he did the dance where you wallow along on your belly over the floor, and he had a box of dog biscuits and he was doing 'I Wanna be Your Dog' and he started throwing the dog biscuits but he was rather excited, it wasn't happening fast enough, so he threw the whole box and it hit his father on the head.

The title of 'Final Solution' hinted at one aspect of Cleveland's alternative scene that in later years its members have been keen to downplay – a flirtation with the imagery of fascism, something closely paralleled in the early British punk scene. Though Thomas would go to great lengths to deny the connection – for the actual lyrics exist in the same ain't-it-hell-to-be-young territory as 'Life Stinks', 'Ain't it Fun' and 'Never Gonna Kill Myself Again' – the swastika symbol was evident on the posters for the Special Extermination Night as well as on Johnny Madansky's drum kit.

Charlotte Pressler: They were all flirting with it. In part it was shock-value and it's a serious way to rebel against your middle-class parents – Oh God! It gets 'em upset.

Madansky and O'Connor would continue their flirtation in the early days of the Dead Boys. But it was the Electric Eels who most deliberately draw upon such symbols as part of their general policy of confrontation. Their overt use of these potent images was just one more dissuading factor when it came to securing gigs.

John Morton: That came from Burroughs and Lenny Bruce and semantics, those are symbols and it depends on what you bring into that . . . We knew that it was provocative. That is something we wanted, to have that provocation, we wanted to confront those issues.

One song in particular – 'Spin Age Blasters' – had some very disturbing images as part of its lyrical content.

Paul Marotta: 'Spin Age Blasters' . . . started because we went to the American Nazi Party Headquarters down on Lorain and 110th. And they had all this racist bullshit literature that was out on the front and one of the things – a headline, like 72-point type – was: Pull the Triggers on the Niggers. And Dave E was like, 'What a line for a song' . . . It was shock tactics. It was confrontational art. It was meant to be satire . . . And it did shock people. Peter Laughner . . . had a big party at his house and we all came wearing [American Nazi Party] t-shirts and nobody would come near us . . . Peter didn't want anything to do with us with these shirts on. He just couldn't handle it and of course that just made us want to shove it in your face [more].

By the time the Rockets made their second radio broadcast in May 1975, they had abandoned their tenuous internal equilibrium. Drummer Madansky, unable to decide whether he wanted to be in the Rockets or not, quit the band a couple of days before the Agora show, apparently due to 'parental/girlfriend pressure'. Don Evans was drafted in for this one gig. After two months with the mysterious Wayne Strick on drums, Madansky returned to the fold, only to find the Rockets even more divided than on his departure – the main source of contention being the relative (de)merits of Thomas's singing.

If Thomas had never been entirely sure of his own vocal abilities, Laughner had encouraged him from the start and continued to do so. O'Connor and Bell were less convinced. The tapes of the Rockets tend to bear out their suspicions. Though Thomas was an imposing presence as frontman at a gig, his vocals at this point were hardly the most harmonious noises to come out of the band. In fact, with the exception of 'Thirty Seconds Over Tokyo', which undoubtedly benefited from his speaking-thru-a-megaphone vocals, Thomas's singing largely took the form of atonal howling.

O'Connor and Bell temporarily prevailed and Thomas was reduced to stage left. Laughner, writing about the change to a friend in New York at the end of May, observed, 'Crocus is blowing alto sax, sounding freakishly like Steve MacKay on *Funhouse* or Albert Ayler without the vibrato. He being the conceptualist and lyricist *along with me* we couldn't very well set him adrift, despite his limited stage trip.' A young kid from Youngstown, Ohio, who regularly attended Rockets shows and had been singer in a Detroit/glam-copy combo, Mother Goose, was drafted in as singer. He went by the names of Steve Machine or Stiv Bators, depending on the weather.

Charlotte Pressler: Nobody in the band ever thought [Crocus] could sing except Peter, and even he was open to persuasion. That's how Stiv Bators got into Rocket for a while. But he was worse than Crocus – he could hit the notes all right, but everything he did came across like an Iggy parody.

Bators was soon expelled, though not before causing further strife in the Thomas household:

Stiv Bators: David's parents were Jehovah's Witnesses and they own this farm in Pennsylvania. So for 4th of July all the Rockets went down to his parents' place. We rehearsed in this big barn and had a holiday out in the woods. We used to do a lot of speed, me and Peter, and that was the first time I stayed up for a week on speed. I also took some mescaline and everybody was sleeping and I went to the barn and I had never played keyboards before. We had this Farfisa connected to a Morley pedal and an Echoplex and I ran it through the PA and played this song off the top of my head. A twenty-minute psychedelic number. And this music is pouring out over this Quaker area ... It ended with the police coming because people were going to church.

Thomas, though, did not return to centre stage. The Rockets set was starting to fragment into mutually exclusive sections. Each member was singing his own songs, backed by the remaining Rockets – like something out of the Beatles' *Let it Be* movie! Bell would perform 'Muckraker', Thomas would do 'Thirty Seconds Over Tokyo' and the recently written 'Sonic Reducer', while O'Connor would tackle 'Search and Destroy', O'Connor and Bell would duet on the MC5's 'Sister Ann', and Laughner would sing his rock & roll covers, 'Route 66' and 'Fire Engine', and originals like 'Amphetamine', a Velvetized saga about taking the guitar player for a ride.

Charlotte Pressler: [By July, Crocus] was only getting to do one song, 'Tokyo' – otherwise playing a little Acetone organ. Bators had come and gone. Gene was trying to take over the rawer vocals and not succeeding – his voice wasn't strong enough and too forced ... The band was starting to dissolve into eclecticism, had lost a sense of what it did well. Peter's old rock & roll standards were competing with Craig's Roxy/Velvets stuff which was competing with the Detroit stuff, which at least had fit in with the original sound of the band. Nobody was sure why they were doing this any more, or what they were doing ... There were some fistfights in the dressing room the second night at the Piccadilly.

The two shows with Television at the Piccadilly Penthouse in July, arranged by Laughner, marked the end of the line. O'Connor was in a bad way throughout both shows. Thomas recalls him falling over on his back in the middle of the second gig, though 'he [still] didn't miss a beat'; after the show, Verlaine ran into O'Connor sitting on the stairs crying because he had taken some particularly bad drug. Thomas had had enough. There was one more show at the end of the month, back at the Viking, the Rockets sharing the bill with an equally terminal Mirrors.

David Thomas: The band broke up because it was untenable ... just everything was a bit too schizoid. There was the Gene O'Connor, Johnny Madansky, Dead Boys thing – [Let's rock out] at all costs! Stiv Bators, Johnny Madansky, Gene O'Connor on one side, me, Peter and Craig on the other. It just wasn't going to hold together very long. It was a brave attempt, a brave experiment to fuse two incompatible forms ... I just remember sitting there [at the Piccadilly] thinking, 'Why am I doing this?'

Mirrors also felt the need for reformulation after their Viking gig. They had fallen victim to Paul Marotta's grandiose concepts just as they were finally transcending their Velvet roots and making the leap into real originality. Though they recorded a final set of demos at Owl Studios in June (with Bell lending a hand on bass), Mirrors had become a part-time concern for Klimek, who was subsuming his minimalist notions to become the minor partner in Marotta's Styrenes outfit.

Mirrors and the Rockets may have both called it quits after their July Viking show, but the Electric Eels had beaten them to the punch – literally, disbanding after one final display of fisticuffs from Morton at a show at the Case-Western Reserve University in May, the Eels' only gig with the drummer Nick Knox, later of Cramps fame.

Charlotte Pressler: Brian McMahon couldn't stand leading his double-life any longer. His was a very strict Irish Catholic family and then he goes and does all this stuff, right. But he would only do it for a few months at a time and then he'd collapse.

The premature disbandment of the Eels, Mirrors and the Rockets ensured that they would not benefit from A&R men's belated interest in the Cleveland-Akron scene in the late Seventies. But as the first Cleveland bands to perform original underground rock, breaking the Top 40 mould of local covers bands, they would have considerable influence.

While the Rockets splintered into Pere Ubu and Frankenstein (the prototype Dead Boys), the Eels/Mirrors camp made two attempts at a satisfactory resolution of the best of each band. The Eels' bastard son, the Men from UNCLE, featured all four original Eels – including Marotta – plus Jim Jones and Jamie Klimek, both of Mirrors, and Anton Fier, of no fixed outfit. It lasted exactly two rehearsals in August 1975. The Men from UNCLE was the first attempt to resurrect the Eels' concepts and align them to a more conscious anti-rock musicality. A second attempt in 1976, with Tim Wright, was equally short-lived. The Cleveland malaise of strong personalities ripping chunks off each other as a means of producing music was never more evident than in the Eels family.

The Styrenes made their first studio recordings a month to the day after the Men from UNCLE's final rehearsal. Composed of just Klimek, Marotta and Anton Fier plus, on occassions, Jim Jones or John Morton, the Styrenes' 'deliberately crafted melange', to quote Art Black's sleeve-notes to the 1991 Styrenes CD, 'incorporated distinct flavours of jazz, progressive, and even a languid sort of smack-addled swing.' But the Styrenes, despite their grand conceits and convoluted arrangements, were a considerably less radical 'melange' than either the anti-rock of the Eels or the keen melodies and brutal guitars of Mirrors.

Charlotte Pressler: Mirrors was already breaking up and being replaced by Styrenes. There you had a situation where you had two groups with the same key personnel but different concepts and they wanted to go in the direction of the Styrenes and not in the direction of the Mirrors. Mirrors was much more minimal, Velvet Underground-ish. Styrenes was much more complicated. Paul has a real taste for very complicated arrangements. Frankly, I always thought it was their weak point.

If Styrenes and the Men from UNCLE failed to develop on their predecessors' sound, the 'art' splinter from Rocket from the Tombs represented a very obvious advance. Pere Ubu would be the logical outcome of Laughner's and Thomas's determination to make an art statement with their music.

■nevitably, a history of Blondie resolves into the story of Chris Stein and Debbie Harry, guitarist and vocalist, Blondie' smost regular song-writers and sole permanent members. For much of the period between the fall of 1973 – when Stein joined Harry's outfit, the Stillettoes – and November 1975 – when Blondie finally settled on the line-up that would record its debut album – Harry and Stein's careers did not seem to be heading in an unduly auspicious direction. Their relationship with the CBGBs scene conveys, through its twists and turns, the process by which the highly successful pop band Blondie came about.

In 1972 Debbie Harry was living with her parents in upstate New York when she began to make regular sorties into New York City to hang out at Max's, where she had previously worked as a waitress, and Mercers. In the late sixties Harry had been in, by her own admission, 'a pretty awful baroque folk-rock band' called Wind in the Willows, who had got as far as recording an album for Capitol in 1969, but she had not been involved in the music scene for some time. Hanging out at Max's, she learned of a girlfriend who was part of an all-girl band.

Debbie Harry: I heard that Elda Stiletto and Holly Woodlawn and Diane had a girl trio called Pure Garbage . . . I saw Elda one night at Max's and I said, 'Oh, I heard you have a trio. I'd love to come down and hear it.' And she said, 'Well, it broke up.' And I said, 'Well, if you ever want another singer, call me.'

The call never came, so Harry eventually took the initiative and in-vited Elda over to her New York apartment, also enticing Roseanne Ross, another girlfriend interested in singing, in the hope that some chemistry might occur. These original Stillettoes decided to become a dance combo, utilizing a musical director to choreograph their stage act.

Debbie Harry: Elda, me and Rosie Ross were the original Stillettoes. Tony Ingrassia was our director. He worked on the songs with us, projecting a mood through a song, stage tricks to give us a cohesive look. He and Elda used to fight about the image. She wanted 'True Confessions' trash, tacky.

Chris Stein, who was studying at the School of Visual Arts, had become a firm friend of Eric Emerson, leader of the Magic Tramps and perhaps the most talented Mercers musician not to be in the New York Dolls. Stein came along to the Stillettoes' second gig, at the Boburn Tavern on West 28th Street in the fall of 1973, at Elda's invitation. Elda knew Stein to be a competent guitarist – even though he was not a regular member of the Magic Tramps, he sometimes sat in with the band. Elda asked Stein if he would like to join the Stillettoes and he accepted, largely because of his interest in one of the other Stillettoes – Debbie Harry. As Stein would later admit, he had no real direction at the time he joined them:

Chris Stein: I was never very career-motivated until I met Debbie. I was just fooling around. There was always this gulf between you and the next generation [of bands].

The original Stillettoes wore out pretty quickly. In the winter of 1973–4 they lost their musical director, Tony Ingrassia, and shortly afterward a frustrated Roseanne Ross quit. At the same time the symbolic centre of New York's underground music scene, Mercers, crumbled to the ground, leaving Gotham's aspiring bands bereft of the one place they could play.

Just as later with Blondie, the Stillettoes proved resilient enough to reconstitute themselves early in the spring of 1974. With Ingrassia out of the picture, Elda Gentile could start to emphasize her own ideas for the band: '"True Confessions" trash, tacky', as Harry later put it. Elda found a black girl called Amanda to replace Roseanne and a new rhythm section: bassist Fred Smith – via a local ad – and drummer Billy O'Connor, whom the girls already knew. The Stillettoes Mk 2 now needed a place to play. Once again Elda Gentile's contacts proved propitious.

Chris Stein: Hell was going out with Elda, one of The Stillettoes, and she said [to us], 'Oh, I heard this bunch of guys and they dress like old men and they're very funny and they play in this weird bar downtown.' And we asked them where they were playing and they said CBGBs.

Elda Gentile soon talked the owner, Hilly Kristal, into letting the Stillettoes share Sunday bills with Television, who were hardly pulling in the crowds. The Stillettoes, who made their CBGBs debut on 5 May 1974 proved quite popular. Though they were considerably more derivative than Television, theirs was a more accessible appeal, or in Harry's words, 'the whole act became more gaudy and tacky.'

Harry and Stein had already started writing their own songs, initially reflecting the trash stance that the Stillettoes were peddling. 'Platinum Blonde', later recorded on Blondie's first demo, dates from this period and lasted the transition for self-evident reasons. The Stillettoes Mk 2 were soon branching out, playing the Club 82, and the Performance Studio, a small rehearsal studio which was the home of the Ramones.

Fred Smith: It was all glitter bands. That's what was happening. It was a lot of fun. It was exciting. There were all these groups forming on the Lower East Side. There was CBGBs and Club 82 opening. There was something happening. It was more fun than music. The Stillettoes, like most of the other groups, were probably more into presentation than music, but the girls wrote a few good songs.

By the summer of 1974, Harry and Stein had become unhappy with their roles in the Stillettoes. The band had become very much Elda Gentile's vehicle, was crafted in her image and represented her aesthetic approach. Harry and Stein had their own ideas, more in the pop vein.

Jimmy Wyndbrandt: Chris and Debbie were already thinking about what they wanted to do musically, and Elda's very into theatrics.

Debbie Harry: We had a lot of fun, but we weren't too musical. Three girls trying to get along together is pretty hard . . . I wanted to do my own thing again.

In fact, the difference in personnel between Blondie Mk 1 and the Stillettoes Mk 2 was only slight. It was more a bloodless coup that resulted in Harry and Stein assuming leadership of the band. The actual musicians – Stein, Smith and O'Connor – remained the same, while Elda and Amanda were replaced by the mysterious Jackie and

Julie. In the new ensemble Debbie Harry was lead singer and Jackie and Julie were restricted to backing vocals. Not surprisingly, given the Stillettoes' association with CBGBs, they debuted there in August, billed for the first two shows not as Blondie, but as Angel and the Snakes.

Anya Phillips: [When] I first met Chris and Debbie in 1974 ... Debbie was inviting me to CBGBs to see her band. At that time there would be maybe five people in the place. I don't think they even had a cover or admission at the door yet. It was really, really empty. The Ramones opened for Angel and the Snakes ... they knew they were changing the name to Blondie and adding two girl backup singers ... This was August, September 1974, still pretty much the heavy tail end of glitter. Debbie wore turquoise blue stretch leotard tops and red stockings.

The name-change to Blondie did little to change their luck. The day of their first gig as Blondie, Jackie dyed her hair dark brown. Julie and Jackie were soon replaced by the more empathic Tish and Snooky, two wacky sisters who were old friends of Harry. With Tish and Snooky, christened the Banzai Babies by Stein, Blondie began to alternate regularly between CBGBs and the Performance Studio, sharing bills with the Ramones and an embryonic Tuff Darts.

Blondie also recruited a second guitarist, the exuberant Ivan Kral. Kral had played in a mainstream New York rock band throughout the Mercer period. He had only recently returned from the West Coast when asked to help bolster Blondie's sound. With Tish and Snooky providing a link between Blondie and the Stillettoes in image, and with a more beefed-up guitar sound, the period between September and December 1974 saw Blondie begin to assert their identity on the budding scene. Though Blondie were never a hard rock & roll band, and remained more pastiche than pop, there was a lightness and humour to their performances which the small CBGBs audiences enjoyed.

Debbie Harry: When I split from the Stillettoes and decided that I wanted to do less schtick and more music, I dropped a lot of the more obvious theatrical things, but at this point we tried to think up as many tricks as we could.

Tish & Snooky: We opened for Television. We opened for the Ramones . . . We used to love wearing wigs and just wacky things . . . We were doing some originals, some covers, like Sixties Shangri-Las type stuff. Then towards the end of the time we were in the band they decided to do some disco covers like 'Lady Marmalade'. We were doing such a mixture of songs. There was 'Platinum Blonde', 'Giant Bats' [later 'Giant Ants'], 'In the Flesh'. At that time they had a completely different sound. There wasn't really anything wild but it was raw. It wasn't fast and loud like the Ramones . . . We fit in but didn't fit in at the same time. It was more poppy than the other bands.

Part of the difference between Blondie and their contemporaries was the fact that Television and Patti Smith played predominantly original material and the Ramones were entirely original – partly because they liked the conceptual integrity, but mainly because they couldn't figure out how to play other people's songs. Blondie were still largely reliant on covers. Though this made them popular with audiences, it meant that critics largely dismissed them.

Chris Stein: We did a hodge-podge of stuff: original stuff, things left over from the Stillettoes, cover songs, different things . . . We did a lot more covers. It took us a lot longer to find our own identity than the other bands. Like the Ramones would come out and not do anybody else's songs . . . We'd always do Stones songs, Shangri-Las stuff, 'I'll Be a Big Man in Town', the Frankie Valli song.

The early Blondie was neither tight nor professional. Despite the germination period in the Stillettoes, they had no real satisfactory direction. Their major problem lay with the musical makeup of the band.

Fred Smith: It was rougher. We worked a lot and just hoped that something would develop . . . We were a little erratic, you know. We had this drummer who kept passing out, he'd just collapse.

Debbie Harry would later suggest that there was some kind of 'art' approach to Blondie all along: that, though they were raw and required honing, the comic-book lyrics and the elements of 'True Confessions' trash carried over from the Stillettoes were absolutely deliberate.

Debbie Harry: Blondie always thought pop – i.e. dance music, movie themes, and the strict attitudes of modernistic Fifties design. We were definitely combining these ideas in rock & roll.

Contemporaries were less convinced. Even Blondie's 'musical director' admits that the band appearing at CBGBs and the Performance Studio through the winter of 1974–5 bore little resemblance to the Blondie that would record their breakthrough album, *Plastic Letters*, three years later.

Chris Stein: The way we played then was very funky and raw, sort of psychedelic punk, [with] feedback. We'd do [the theme to] 'Goldfinger' really psychedelic.

Between December 1974 and April 1975 Blondie began the transformation. The changes they went through in this period came very close to tearing them apart, and there was a considerable hiatus before a reconstructed Blondie could be unveiled.

In December 1974 Blondie were reduced to single-guitar status when Ivan Kral was 'purloined' by Patti Smith, whose prospects were considerably greater than Blondie's. It would be the start of what Harry and Stein came to feel was a concerted attempt to undermine Blondie's position on the scene.

Debbie Harry: Ivan just got bored. That was the non-period of rock. Television, the Ramones and us were just playing around, but there was no publicity, no attention focused on anyone.

Shortly afterward, Billy O'Connor left the band to go to law school. Fred Smith had been canvassing for O'Connor's removal for some time and Clement Burke's recruitment gave Harry and Stein their first figure in an equation for success. His first gig was at CBGBs in March 1975. Debbie, Tish and Snooky had dressed in jungle furs, which seemed to go down well with the largely male audience. But after the first set, Fred Smith informed them that Richard Hell was leaving Television and he was taking Hell's place.

Roberta Bayley: Fred Smith made the big error of his life when he quit Blondie to join Television. But at that point Television was the one tipped for big, big success. Blondie was the worst band in the city – they were just a joke. Everybody liked them personally but they didn't really have it together on a musical level. There were no set members. It was when they got Clem that he really had that Mr Anglophile idea and I think he had a lot to do with coalescing the idea, the energy and everything.

Harry was devastated at Smith's departure. He was the best musician in the band and, with a new drummer, they desperately needed Smith's solid bottom range to prop up the sound. At the end of the night she muttered to Tish and Snooky, 'Well, I guess there's no band.' Not surprisingly, Harry was extremely resentful of the forces she considered to have stolen Smith away.

Debbie Harry: We were struck dumb by the whole thing, by the whole movement against us. I may be paranoid but I think that whole clique wanted to destroy us.

The 'whole clique' was the art-rock clique forming around Television and Patti Smith, both of whom had now benefited from Blondie's line-up changes in recent months. The spring of 1975 represents the point when tell-tale cracks appeared in the small CBGBs scene. With the possibility of success, as the media began to take note of events on the Bowery, came the usual crop of jealousies and vanities. The main division was between the art-rockers and those who liked their rock & roll neat, without pretensions. A period of at least implicit cooperation was over.

Chris Stein: Patti helped coerce [Fred] away from us, helped take Fred over to the other side. Everything on the CBGBs scene was [cooperative] until the tension started being brought upon us and then it got very competitive immediately. For the first two years it was really very communal. I remember playing with all [Television's] equipment – using their guitars and amps. For some reason we had to do a show and we didn't bring any equipment. [It was] early on. First two years the audience was made up of fifty or a hundred followers and the other band members. That was it. A very intimate little scene. It was just something to do. We probably played [CBGBs] every week for seven months in a row. That was when we were living across the street.

The falling-out between Hell and Verlaine had ramifications which affected the entire scene. One was that Television moved away from the common ground they had previously held: art-rock for the straight rock crowd. When attempting to re-establish that ground through an alliance with ex-Dolls Johnny Thunders and Jerry Nolan, Richard Hell was searching for another guitarist to recreate the twin-guitar sound and – with Blondie temporarily in limbo – Chris Stein auditioned for the second-guitar slot in the newly formed Heartbreakers, though even Stein admits 'it was a half-hearted effort.'

The bewildering series of changes that Stein and Harry's ensemble underwent meant that Blondie was still largely perceived as merely a shifting vehicle for its photogenic lead singer. One of the earliest major features on the burgeoning CBGBs scene, written by Lisa Robinson for *Hit Parader* that spring, described Blondie in these terms:

There's Blondie, who used to be with the Stillettoes (real name Debbie) and she's pretty good. Backed by various musicians, she performs some of her own songs ('I Want to Be a Platinum Blond', 'Love at the Docks'), Chuck Berry's 'Come On', Nico's 'Sunday Morning' – with great deadpan delivery – Tom Verlaine's 'Venus De Milo' and the Shangri-Las' 'Out in the Streets'. Many feel she was the best of the original Stillettoes, projecting an appealing trashiness. She has been fairly successful with CBGBs audiences.

But resilience Harry had in abundance, and Blondie re-emerged after several months of splendid isolation. Tish and Snooky's roles in the band were deemed superfluous as the remaining flotsam from the Stillettoes' 'True Confessions' aesthetic was finally jettisoned.

Tish: Debbie was always calling me because she was very insecure about the group and stuff. So I suggested we have a group meeting. Two weeks went by without hearing from them, so I called I her and said, 'What's going on with the group?' and she said 'Oh . . . I guess there is no group.' I said, 'Oh . . . okay.' And then I ran into Chris at Max's, and he said, 'We're playing at such and such a place on such and such a night, are you gonna be there?' And I said, 'I thought there was no group.'

Tish and Snooky soon found their own niche, co-founding the outrageous schtick-rock outfit, the Sick Fucks.

Throughout this limbo Clem Burke, Blondie's newest recruit, stayed at home, patiently awaiting the band's reformation. Blondie resumed gigging just in time to appear at CBGBs' July festival of unsigned bands, at which they formally introduced their new bassist. Gary Valentine was an old school friend of Burke's and not only played bass, but also wrote fine pop songs. After jamming on the Stones' 'Live With Me' for an hour, Valentine was invited to join the band. The new Blondie proved to be one of the more popular acts at the festival, which attracted considerable media coverage.

But as they resumed gigging, Blondie were playing CBGBs less and less, partially due to a new booking policy. Terry Ork was now deciding which slots bands could take at the club, and as Television's biggest fan he was bound to favour them over more lightweight competition. But there were now several alternatives for so-called CBGBs bands. Mothers, Club 82 and the reopened Max's were all now prepared to book unsigned acts. Yet Blondie's relatively poor reputation as a live act was holding them back. Alan Betrock, a *SoHo News* journalist who had become excited enough by the new New York bands to want a more active role in the scene's development, recorded some demos with Blondie that summer.

Alan Betrock: Blondie were a real good recording band. I brought a couple of people to see 'em and I was really hurt and upset because they just couldn't play live, they'd stop in the middle of a song and start over again, the amps would go out, the guitar would go out, strings would break and they wouldn't have extra ones. I decided that the thing to do for them was just to make a tape and not to bring people down to see them.

The five songs Blondie cut included a cover of the Shangri-Las 'Out in the Streets', three of their best original songs – 'Platinum Blonde', 'Puerto Rico' and 'Thin Line' – and their parody of disco, 'The Disco Song', later reworked as 'Heart of Glass'. But the demos only confirmed that Harry's voice lacked depth and that Blondie were in need of its own garage to work in. Only 'Platinum Blonde', with its rinky-tink sound and Harry's fey voice working well in unison, had the potential to be vamped up into a releasable artefact. When Blondie asked Betrock to manage them he shied away, concerned about their ability to cut it up onstage.

Alan Betrock: They just weren't that experienced, they weren't that together, they didn't have any money and their equipment was always breaking down . . . [Debbie] was not all that comfortable. And I called her once and said, 'Well, look. I'm working with you and the Marbles and the Marbles can play live and I can't do both of you guys so I'm gonna work with them.'

Though Blondie would be recorded at the summer 1976 CBGBs festival, for the *Live at CBGBs* album, Kristal insists it was the inferior quality of the results that led to their omission from the album, not contractual reasons.

Hilly Kristal: Blondie didn't define the scene then. They were not known; they were more popular as the Stillettoes. They recorded and it came out badly. We went over it, and we wanted it to happen. They may have recorded for two days; we had them do it again, and it just didn't work. We couldn't even overdub. We couldn't do anything. And it was not fair to the band to do something that wasn't good.

Harry and Stein both insist that this was not the case, that Blondie had by this point already signed to Marty Thau's production company, Instant Records, and were not available for a CBGBs album. Whatever the case, Kristal's recollection that Blondie 'didn't define the scene then' clearly accords with the views of many contemporaries, who felt that Blondie were not going to 'make it' based on musical ability alone.

Yet by the time they joined Marty Thau's minuscule roster early in the summer of 1976, Blondie had figured out their own solution. In November 1975 they added keyboardist James Destri, making Blondie once again a five-piece band. His Farfisa organ added an extra dimension to their sound, providing the sort of instantly distinctive tone that harped back to the best of Brit-Beat and glam-rock.

Even as they were recruiting their third new member in a year, they were temporarily losing drummer Clem Burke, who high-tailed it to England for six weeks at the end of 1975. Blondie spent the time rehearsing with Destri. When Burke returned he brought with him some examples of what was happening in England. Blondie were particularly impressed by Dr Feelgood, who were leading England's short-lived pub-rock boom.

Clem Burke: If there's one group that must take the credit for giving direction to the New York scene, it must be the Feelgoods. I'd originally seen them in London and brought their album back with me and the fact that a band like the Feelgoods could pack Hammersmith Odeon, make it on to record and then into the charts gave many New York bands faith in what they were doing.

On 14 February 1976 the five-piece Blondie played their debut gig. Just as Patti Smith had managed to gradually piece together a band until she achieved the sound she wanted, so Stein and Harry had kept adding and subtracting – admittedly often unwillingly – until they had found a formula that worked.

Debbie Harry: We performed our first really recognizable gig as Blondie on Valentine's Day of 1976 at CBGBs, where else . . . We had worked really, really hard from the beginning of December all the way through to Valentine's Day. [We] went underground from that time until our gig. We had organized ourselves. We had also taken a turn . . . we were probably more punk before we got . . . Jimmy, and then we decided that we'd be straight pop.

From February 1976 onward, Blondie developed at a pace that took contemporaries by surprise. By the end of 1976 they were not only one of the more accessible but also one of the more distinctive bands on the scene. They had also secured the record contract that gave them the means to prove they could cut it on black plastic, where it really counted.

Joey Ramone: [Rock & roll] was a hodge podge of Pink Floyd and ELP and all this crap, so basically what we did was we stripped it right down to the bone and we disassembled it and reassembled it and put all the excitement and fun and spirit, raw energy and raw emotion and guts and attitude back into it.

The Ramones' unique sound, established at their very outset, was maintained throughout four years of regular gigging and studio outings with a uniform line-up. The 1974 model would serve them well.

If Blondie's progress was achieved by toning down the rough edges and asserting a keen pop sensibility, the Ramones were always determined to emphasize a red-raw edge to their music, submerging their equally rooted melodic sense beneath a primitive buzzsaw sound that made them largely inaccessible to American radio. Yet the Ramones would be the first CBGBs band to secure a record contract after the initial success of Patti Smith, whose reputation was established primarily away from the Bowery.

Tommy Ramone: The music was so different. Right from the start there were no solos and it had a unique sound, basically because the roots of it wasn't from the current music scene. Since John was playing the guitar, this was the music he used to play all the time. Then he gave up playing for a couple of years and [when] he picked up the guitar again all that was embedded in his nervous system. So when he started playing again, this time very loud, he'd get that kinda sustained, roary sound. It goes back to Love except they didn't have the roar, they had this nice, clean sound . . . It was absurd. It was [also] original. Especially in those days. It was so raw. There was Television who were also breaking away from the rock & roll look. So image-wise I [thought] what they were doing was good. But musically they were totally different. It was like, 'Television's real good but they're not rock & roll.' In a way it seemed like there hadn't been rock & roll for a long time. At that point the blues-rock had come in with Cream and everything revolved around the boogie-riff and blues-riff ... There was no pure energy type of thing. And we were doing that. We were as raw as awopbopaloobop must have been when it first came out. It wasn't planned or anything

In insisting that 'it wasn't planned or anything,' Tommy Ramone confronts a central conundrum in attempting to ascertain The Ramones' 'significance' – how (self-)conscious their original concept was. The notion of stripping rock music to its most basic components sounds both obvious and ingenious, but there still remains a nagging suspicion that it was a convenience brought on by technical ineptitude, only later solidifying into a *modus operandi.*

In fact the Ramones – even the original trio (Johnny, Joey and Dee Dee) – was not founded by non-musicians, even if none of its members could have successfully auditioned for Emerson, Lake and Palmer. Johnny, Joey and Tommy had all been in previous bands. In fact, the roots of the Ramones reside in Forest Hills high school, and a band named after a Donovan song – the Tangerine Puppets. The Ramones' first press bio, composed by Tommy, observed that 'kids who grew up [in Forest Hills] became either musicians, degenerates or dentists. The Ramones are a little of each. Their sound is not unlike a fast drill on a rear molar.' The same might be said of the Tangerine Puppets.

Tommy Ramone: John and I had ... a rather notorious band. We were quite frantic, especially John, who played bass at the time. I was the lead guitar player. He would just go crazy. The school would have yearly talent shows and we played one of them and John went so crazy the neck of his guitar went into this girl who was in the wrong place. So we were banned from the school after that ... We [played] the type of stuff that's now on the *Nuggets* album. At that point everybody was getting involved with all kinds of new things they were hearing ... All these bands had hit singles then disappeared.

Though Joey (né Jeffrey Hyman), Johnny (né John Cummings), Dee

Dee (né Douglas Colvin) and Tommy (né Thomas Erdelyi) all attended Forest Hills high school in the late Sixties, only the elder Ramones, Johnny and Tommy, shared years, graduating in the summer of 1967 (Joey graduated in 1968, Dee Dee in 1969). And it was Johnny and Dee Dee who came up with the original notion for the Ramones, though it was their mutual drug habits, rather than shared musical experience, that first brought them together in the early Seventies.

Dee Dee Ramone: I first met Johnny on the sidewalk by my house. We were checking each other out, and then we just started talking about the Stooges or something . . . Johnny had stopped doing hard drugs by then, but he really was a pot smoker. He was the first person to introduce me to really good pot. No one even knew about good pot, but John said 'Dee Dee I promise you three tokes of this and you'll be out of it!'– and I would be.

After graduating from Forest Hills, Johnny might have spent much of his time ruminating on whether to acquire a drug habit, but Tommy was determined to pursue his love of rock & roll. In these interim years his drive and sense of vocation were channelled into being a recording engineer.

Tommy Ramone: I was always enchanted by what you could do in the studio. The sounds of the records always fascinated me – how they got those dimensions in those records and stuff like that. I was watching some late-night talk show when I was a kid and Phil Spector was one of the guests . . . That was the first time I ever got the concept that there was such a thing as a record producer and as soon as I found that out it was like, 'Wow, I'd sure like to do that.' It was always at the back of my mind. And then an acquaintance of mine from high school, I met him on the subway and he told me that he was engineer at this recording studio . . . I kept pestering him and pestering him and finally he let me work for him. It was a famous studio [the Dick Charles studio]. Some of the people who started the Record Plant came from that studio. So eventually I went from there to the Record Plant. I worked there '68, '69. I left the beginning of '70.

Like many of his contemporaries Tommy turned away from rock & roll at the beginning of the Seventies. As he became disenchanted with the contemporary rock scene, he began moving into celluloid, where he felt he could further formulate his conceptual ideas.

Tommy Ramone: I was getting really disgusted with the music scene. Things get recycled and recycled. At that point it was starting to be the fifth generation Led Zeppelin bands. So I was saying: What about something new? ... And what made it really strong was that nobody seemed to really care that music had seemed to stop dead in 1969. That's when radio was changing. The programme directors started doing their strict adherence to the playlist and that's when things were tightening up. Frankly I was bored ... I was [getting] into film-making. I guess I was jumping around. I went to work for this film company. I was hanging around the Museum of Modern Art 'cause the company was right next to the Museum. I would take three-hour lunch-breaks and watch all the movies there and I got into avant-garde films. I started making some stuff like that. Which is interesting 'cause I was getting all these influences – from the recording world and the movie world. It changed me. It developed my aesthetics.

After working for the film company, two events served to remind Tommy of the latent power that rock & roll could still hold. The first was a visit to England, home of the Beatles and the Stones, which was once again moving to the beat of its own drum.

Tommy Ramone: I went to England on a vacation and something about the nightlife there got me excited about music again. This was '71. I wanted to get involved with music again but I wanted something different

Having witnessed the emerging glam-rock scene at a time when its most successful exponents – T. Rex, Slade and Sweet – were dominating the UK charts, Tommy made his way back to New York where he was invited to go see a new band performing at the Mercer Arts Centre.

Tommy Ramone: I knew the people who were in the Dolls. Their original drummer Billy, Sylvain and John used to hang out at Nobody's and Max's and we'd see them occasionally. We knew they were musicians ... [Mercers] was like a whole scene. It was an interesting aesthetic. Here was this band who really couldn't play that well but that was beside the point. That whole thing came right after the Eric Clapton/Cream thing, at which point musicianship was everything. All of a sudden from out of that comes this band who obviously are barely in tune and yet they have something about them that's good and everybody's having a great time. It was like attending a party. So I found that fascinating, especially because I was coming out of that film thing and I saw the co-relationship – 'cause those films were [also] made very haphazardly.

Instantly attracted to the Dolls' trash/glam aesthetic, Tommy soon put together his own Mercers band. Butch were strictly in the Dolls/Kiss mould. Like the other new New York bands, Tommy's outfit was restricted to the two New York venues where original, unsigned acts were welcome.

Tommy Ramone: I had a band called Butch, with Jeff Salen, [who was later] in Tuff Darts. It was sort of glam, that studded macho look. We played Mercers, then it fell down. We played [the] Coventry. There was absolutely no place. Max's had a small stage for recording artists. Long Island was just all Top 40 bands. That's what kinda killed that band. We were just rehearsing . . . [and] I was saturated with the glam look.

Making occasional appearances at the Coventry at the same time as Butch was an outfit by the name of Sniper, featuring one 'Joey' Hyman on drums (Hyman's brother had played in a band with Cummings). Like Butch, Sniper adopted a hard-glam image and sound and were consigned to a similar fate when Mercers collapsed.

Joey Ramone: [Sniper] was in the glitter vein, but more with an attitude. The music I had been into in that period were the Stooges, Alice Cooper, T. Rex, Gary Glitter, Slade, but . . . [Sniper were] harder, more Iggy and Alice Coopery.

Sniper's final gig was an ill-publicized affair at a small loft-cum-studio, sharing the bill with Suicide, who could make even Sniper sound harmonic.

Alan Vega: Sniper was coming across as a glitter band and there was Joey in these silver gloves and make-up and everything, and so they do a set and then Suicide does a set and we had a great night. But apparently, that night they had a fire and the place partially burnt down, so [the owner] blames Suicide for the fire, 'cos I was singing anti-Jesus songs that night, according to Tony Benelli . . . I was talking to Tony and there was this sign, Joey was looking for a new band, Sniper had fired him.

Cummings maintained only a marginal involvement with rock music throughout the Mercers period, despite being perhaps the most naturally gifted musician in this would-be quartet. On the occasions when he ran into his fellow ex-Tangerine Puppet, Johnny was generally reminded of the lost opportunities.

Tommy Ramone: I started a studio with a friend of mine, Monty Melleck, who's now tour manager with the Ramones ... I would bump into John every now and then and I'd say, 'Whadya doing?' And I always told him, 'Are you playing? You have something. You should be in a band. Why don't you get a band together?' And he would go, 'Oh well.'

Yet it was not so much any pressure Tommy may have brought to bear that finally persuaded Johnny to purchase a new guitar but rather the influence of his fellow drug-user, Dee Dee. Dee Dee wanted to learn how to really play, having auditioned – unimpressively – for the Neon Boys.

Dee Dee Ramone: John was a construction worker at 1633 Broadway. I got transferred there, and we'd meet every day for lunch. Usually we'd go over to a go-go place and have a few beers. And after we got a little tipsy we'd go over to 48th Street to Manny's Guitar Store and look at the guitars. Then one pay day, we both went over, bought guitars and decided to start a band. He bought a Moswright, and I bought a DanElectro.

Joey, who was sharing some 'accommodation' with Dee Dee at a paint store on Queens Boulevard, was an obvious candidate for Johnny and Dee Dee's new band.

Joey Ramone: I met Dee Dee first, 'cause [when] I was in Sniper he would come check me out and he liked what I was doing. We used to go see the Dolls, like at the Mercer Arts Centre or Kenny's Castaways, and Dee Dee would always be there. Then I met John. John was actually in a band with my brother, his name is Mickey Lee, and John would be hanging around the house ... John and Dee Dee were in the talking stages [when] John called me. He asked me if I wanted to play with them. I just thought it would be great working with them 'cause they were very unique individuals.

By January 1974, Johnny could finally call Tommy and inform him that he had a new band.

Tommy Ramone: He goes, 'Oh listen. I got a guitar and me and Dee Dee have been jamming together.' Dee Dee I knew through John, just from the streets. I didn't know him at school but I knew him. It was the same with Joey. Actually I knew his brother more than him . . . I knew Dee Dee was a colourful character and they needed a drummer [and] Joey was a drummer. So I said, 'Come down to the rehearsal studio.' They came down and they played and they were terrible. It was the worst thing I've ever heard. But I thought it was great. They had something. They would plug in and Dee Dee was half-drunk. Joey was a marvel on drums, really weird style. I said, 'Well it needs a little work but you got something there.'

The three 'original' Ramones shared the Hell–Kaye–Smith notion of rock & roll, built around a utopian ideal of Sixties music rooted in Brit-Beat and the US punk underground. They also considered the Stooges, the Dolls and a handful of English glam bands to be providing the only exciting rock music of the Seventies. It is thus not too surprising that they adopted a 'back to basics' approach, reflecting the sound of these bands though not their image. But copyists they were not destined to be!

Johnny Ramone: We decided we had to do other people's songs. And we sat down, and, well – we couldn't figure out how to play anybody else's songs.

From the beginning they were forced to perform nothing but their own songs, which were invariably built around chunging bar-chord rhythm guitars, with no lead breaks, and all clocking in around the ninety-second mark. Glam-rock it was not!

The duties in the prototype Ramones devolved thus: Dee Dee – bass and main vocals, Johnny – guitar, Joey – drums and an occasional lead vocal. Tommy's early role was managerial, while the enigmatic 'fifth' Ramone, bassist Ritchie, lasted only a couple of rehearsals before quitting, resulting in Dee Dee's demotion from second guitar.

Owning a part share in a rehearsal studio (which could double as a place to gig) enabled Tommy to organize a debut gig for the three-piece Ramones, just four weeks after Television's Townhouse Theater show and barely three months into their existence, at the Performance Studio, 30 March 1974.

Johnny Ramone: About thirty people or so showed up. We were terrible.

Dee Dee was so nervous he stepped on his bass guitar and broke its neck.

Just like Television, the Ramones realized that some further rehearsing was in order. Their main requirement was a drummer. Not that Joey was a poor beatmaster. Rather it had become self-evident that Joey was a more effective lead singer than Dee Dee. After six months of rehearsing and just one gig, the trio organized their first auditions, but every aspiring drummer proved incapable of fitting in with the Ramones' aesthetic. Their non-playing member was required to show them what they had in mind.

Joey Ramone: We auditioned these drummers and at the time we wanted to keep it simple, and everybody was very flash, so Tommy was trying to get on the drums to show everybody how to do it, more a beatkeeper than anything else. More of a Charlie Watts kind of a thing, [but] unconsciously he had his own style.

Tommy Ramone: All these drummers were coming from the Carmen Appice school of drumming 'cause that was the style then. It was just terrible. It just didn't mesh. Y'know – 'Give me a 4/4.' 'A what?'

After six weeks of rehearsing with Tommy, the Ramones made their CBGBs debut on the weekend of 16–17 August. Once again it had been word of mouth that had brought the small club on the Bowery to their attention. Chris Stein knew Tommy Ramone and was in the process of co-founding Blondie.

Chris Stein: I got the Ramones into CBGBs 'cause I had known Tommy from this band called Butch at Mercer Arts Centre . . . Tommy approached me and said, 'I hear you're playing at this weird bar. What's that?' And I said CBGBs . . . I remember thinking they were a Latin band because of the name.

After their first weekend at CBGBs the owner came up to the Ramones to give his own impressions about their performance. Surprisingly, Kristal liked them and agreed to retain them, despite informing them that 'nobody's [ever] going to like you guys'. They began playing double-bills with Blondie, whose performance art was at the same rudimentary stage. The bands were also sharing an occasional gig at the

Performance Studio, which despite its size could easily accommodate the Ramones' and Blondie's fans. Both of them.

The Ramones' early gigs at CBGBs were hardly well-ordered affairs. They rarely managed to complete their brief sets without some unplanned hiatus. Contemporaries recall that they often stopped playing in the middle of songs (several times a night) in order to start remonstrating with each other. It occasionally got as far as one or more band members leaving the stage or threatening to rearrange another's features. In these early days technical ineptitude was not merely an image.

Alan Vega: The Ramones were hilarious! I heard the name Ramones, so I went to see this gig and they go 'One, two, three, four!' and then someone breaks a string and off they walk, and they all come back in unison and 'One, two, three, four!' and someone else breaks a string and off they go again!

Craig Leon: The Ramones would get into fights [on stage] because they honestly didn't know how to end the songs ... they had these little ugly amplifiers – Mike Matthews amps – and they'd bust and they'd stop. [The set] would be like one long blur because they wouldn't end a song and start another one, it'd just be one long song and then it was over.

The notion of a band who played a dozen or more ninety-seconds-and-counting, seemingly neanderthal chants, every song stripped of embellishment beyond drilling guitars and repetitively abrupt lyrics, quickly endeared them not only to the rock & rollers but also to the art crowd, proof that the absurdity of it all had not been lost on everyone. With their stark, minimalist approach – and unaffected by mutterings as to a certain lack of proficiency – the Ramones were not long awaiting critical praise. Within six months of debuting at CBGBs, Alan Betrock was writing about them in *SoHo Weekly News* while Danny Fields, an enthusiastic convert, soon brought critic Lisa Robinson down to the rock & roll club.

Joey Ramone: Danny had told Lisa Robinson about us and Lisa came down to see us, she was blown away by us. She said that we changed her life. She started writing about us in *Rock Scene*, and then Lenny Kaye would write about us and we started getting more press like the *Village Voice*, word was getting out, and people started coming down.

Lisa Robinson of *Hit Parader* was a most important advocate, and she encouraged all her many contacts in New York to check the Ramones out.

Leee Black Childers: Lisa had *Hit Parader*, she had *Rock Scene*, she had a lot of things going internationally and she called me one night and said, 'Can you go to Madison Square Garden tonight? Sorry about the short notice, I need for you to photograph and I need for you to report, because I'm very ill.' And I said, 'Lisa, you know I'd do it, but I've got the 'flu, I can't move more than 12 feet from the bathroom, call Bob Gruen.' So she calls back and says, 'Bob can't do it, he's got the 'flu too, can you think of anybody who can photograph and report?' And I couldn't think of anyone else, so she said, 'I'll find someone,' and hung up. An hour and a half later, Bob Gruen, Lisa Robinson and myself ran into each other at the Ramones gig at CBGBs ... The Ramones were on stage and there we were, and no one was angry with anyone. Lisa just said, 'I guess rock & roll's changing, isn't it?'

The buzzsaw brevity of the Ramones' early songs was only one element of their incongruous appeal. The lyrics were as sparse as the sound – concise reflections on street-life, rarely more than eight lines long and with titles as memorably awry of traditional rock songs as the melodies. If legend is to be believed, the first Ramones set consisted of 'I Don't Wanna Walk Around with You', 'I Don't Wanna be Learned, I Don't Wanna be Tamed' and 'I Don't Wanna Go Down to the Basement'. As Dee Dee observed, 'We didn't write a positive song until "Now I Wanna Sniff Some Glue".' In fact several ·of their early songs were written by Joey and Dee Dee before the Ramones even formed. Joey had certainly written 'I Don't Care' and 'Here Today, Gone Tomorrow' between Sniper and the Ramones.

Nobody outside the band – and not even everyone in it – seemed entirely sure how self-conscious such early efforts were:

Joey Ramone: The earliest songs were 'I Don't Care', 'Judy is a Punk', 'Today Your Love (Tomorrow the World)', 'Loudmouth', 'Basement' ... There was 'I Don't Wanna Walk Around with You' but before that there was a song called 'I Don't Wanna Get Involved with You' ... then there was 'I Can't Be' and 'I Don't Wanna be Learned, I Don't Wanna be Tamed'

... We all had a dark sense of humour, we all shared that quality, that dark, warped sense ... When we started out to write, the songs were about our frustrations and feelings of alienation [and] isolation.

Tommy Ramone: The first songs were written somewhat seriously. Later on, maybe [not] ... I still don't know sometimes. They must have known that some of these lyrics sounded a little absurd. I just thought the lyrics were so strange.

Those that missed the humour in their material might have conceived of a deep nihilistic unrest in this set of I Don't Wanna songs. The Ramones, though, were no teenage delinquents, and if they were consciously replicating the essentially juvenile nature of the rock & roll lyric, they were trusting that, in a post-Nik Cohn world, such simplistic angst could not be interpreted as anything but ironic.

If the Ramones' unique sound soon slotted into place, their enduring image of four leather-clad punks was slower in coming. In the early days they lacked the consistent image of their CBGBs peers, Television. Their soon-to-evolve uniform look was not to the liking of all the band members.

Dee Dee Ramone: We were glamorous when we started, almost like a glitter group. A lot of times, Joey would wear rubber clothes and John would wear vinyl clothes or silver pants. We used to look great, but then we fell into the leather-jacket-and-ripped-up-jeans thing. I felt like a slob.

Late in 1974 the Ramones recorded their first set of demos. Unlike their contemporaries Television and Blondie, who were working on demos in the spring and early summer of 1975, the Ramones chose to represent a typical live set, recording fourteen songs, all of which clocked in at under two minutes.* Though recorded in a couple of days in an eight-track basement studio, the Ramones' demos give a surprisingly 'together' representation of their early sound. They naturally

---

* The demos were: 'I Don't Wanna Go Down in the Basement', '53rd and 3rd', 'I Wanna be Your Boyfriend', 'Judy is a Punk', 'Loudmouth', 'I Wanna Sniff Some Glue', 'I Can't Be', 'I'm a Nazi Baby', 'I Don't Wanna be Tamed', 'I Don't Wanna Walk Around with You', 'You're Gonna Kill That Girl', 'I Know Your Name', 'Sitting Here with Nothing to Do', 'You Should Never Have Opened That Door'.

benefited from having an experienced studio engineer producing the demos, Tommy successfully recreating the Ramones-esque 'wall of sound'.

Tommy Ramone: We used block chording as a melodic device, and the harmonics resulting from the distortion of the amplifiers created counter-melodies. We used the wall of sound as a melodic rather than a riff form.

The surprising thing, hearing these demos in a post-thrash world, is just how unmanic the early Ramones sound. Though much has been written about how fast the Ramones played, their songs were not intended to be a mere fuzzy haze, simply to the point. It was in relation to the blues-based grunge-rock passing for commercial rock in 1975 that the blur of the Ramones seemed as fast and furious as the industry perceived them to be. The response to their demo tape was predictable. There was, after all, no precedent for a band like the Ramones.

Joey Ramone: [The] fifteen-song (*sic*) demo, which we recorded for $2,000, we sent around to the record companies. [When] we got it back, you could see that they'd played the first 30 seconds of it.

If the industry was slow to respond to the band, the media was not, and the Ramones were one of the first bands to benefit from their association with CBGBs. In July 1975 the club generated international press coverage with the first of its summer festivals of unsigned bands. The Ramones received more than their share of this attention. With journalists from the *New York Times*, the *Village Voice*, *Rolling Stone*, the *Aquarian*, the *SoHo Weekly News* – and the *NME* and *Melody Maker* from England – all attending the festival, this amounted to considerable exposure for a young, unknown band.

Shortly after the festival's conclusion, Craig Leon from Sire Records expressed an interest in signing the Ramones, seemingly unaware of the degree of apathy that had greeted their carefully crafted demo tape.

Tommy Ramone: At one of the shows I'm on the way out and I'm stopped by Craig Leon – I was familiar with the name 'cause when I was with Butch, Sire was one of the companies we were interested in – and he seemed very excited. To me, it looked like he thought all these record companies were about to sign us.

With a set of demos, a rigorously defined image and a press bio (including notable reviews from *SoHo Weekly* and *Hit Parader*), it was perhaps logical for Leon to assume that the Ramones were the subject of record-label interest. But despite Patti Smith's success and Island's interest in Television – and even though the Ramones were the only other CBGBs band to be in a recordable state – they had met nothing but resistance from the Biz.

Tommy Ramone: At the time I thought [A&R people] would realize how great we were. I understand now. They'd listen to it and go, 'This is interesting but who's gonna buy this stuff?' I remember this guy at Warners – I accused him of not listening to the tape. [He said] 'I listened, believe me I listened to it. You guys are like Television. We can't sign a band like that 'cause they're not gonna sell any records' . . . We didn't sound like all the groups out there. Also we couldn't play – quote, unquote – It was that New York Dolls thing again. They didn't understand that aesthetic and most people still don't. 'Cause I guess that's a pretty strange aesthetic to ask people to understand: that there's something more than musicianship involved here. Blue Sky was considering signing us but somebody who worked there said, 'the MC5 didn't sell, the New York Dolls didn't sell and we shouldn't sign you.' And I said, 'We're gonna sell!'

The Ramones were the first of the CBGBs bands to discover that the process of signing a record deal was largely unaffected by enthusiastic local (or even international) media. It was not going to be cut and dried, despite Craig Leon's undoubted enthusiasm. After all, Leon was a junior employee at a small-time record label. Nor would it be any less problematic for their contemporaries down at the rock & roll club.

The Second Wave

Andy Shernoff: The original bands that were playing [New York] were formed before there was actually a place to play, and it was like there had to be a place to come out of all these bands that wanted to play.

Without the emergence of clubs where unsigned bands could play, there could hardly have been a new wave of bands in New York in the central years of the Seventies. The five boroughs had no club tradition – save for the folkdom of the Village – before the emergence of Mercers in 1972. The two central clubs in the scene replacing Mercers were CBGBs – with which the entire scene became associated in name as well as locale – and Max's, which changed its booking policy after the success of CBGBs, soon becoming its main rival.

Max's had been a rock & roll venue considerably longer than CBGBs. The Dolls had been regular favourites there from 1973 on, but they were a signed act and Max's booking policy was almost exclusively confined to record-label bands. The other bands on the Mercers scene were less successful in graduating from the arts centre, and when it collapsed in August 1973, New York's unsigned rock & roll bands were deprived of the one place they knew they could play.

In such a climate it was perhaps inevitable that, with a swell of underground bands in New York City – most from the fag-end of the glitter era – an alternative would be provided. There was, however, a period when very few options existed. As Lisa Robinson observed, in her June 1975 article on the New York scene in *Hit Parader*, the established clubs were slow to respond to this wave of original bands:

When the Mercer burned down (*sic*) in 1973 the scene shifted to the Coventry in Queens and the Club 82 on Wednesday nights [but] last summer, for some unknown reason, the 82 stopped booking bands and with Max's on the skids (only performers backed by record companies and using the upstairs stage for a showcase played there) there was no place [in Manhattan] for unsigned groups to play or hang out.

If the Coventry booked unsigned bands, it tended to favour techno- or glam-rock bands (for example, the Dictators, Kiss and Blue Oyster Cult) rather than the art-rock of Television and Patti Smith. As Robinson indicates, the Club 82 went through a period of not booking bands in the summer and fall of 1974, while Max's was experiencing serious financial difficulties. Though Max's policy regarding unsigned bands eased considerably throughout 1974, owner Mickey Ruskin was forced to cut the power on 20 December 1974. New York's premier underground hang-out was temporarily out of commission.

Inevitably CBGBs benefited from its virtual monopoly. It was in this vacuum that the club really established itself, first with Television and Patti Smith's joint eight-week residency in spring 1975 and then with its July festival of unsigned bands. A major difference between CBGBs and Max's was that nobody went to CBGBs to 'hang out' – seeing bands was the only real reason to be at CBGBs.

This had a lot to do with CBGBs' unique ambience. The club reflected its locale perfectly, though most genuine Bowery bums probably had better places to go. If New York had piles, it was a fair bet that this was their postal address. As the contemporary joke went:

Q: What's the difference between the toilets at CBGBs and a Puerto Rican whore?
A: In an emergency you can shit on a Puerto Rican whore.

However the club also had considerable virtues, particularly in the early days when it was largely unknown outside a small East Village circle. CBGBs did not enforce the rule of most other New York clubs to this day: once you pay, you stay. At CBGBs anyone could avoid some particularly bad band by going out on the sidewalk or even to a nearby bar, returning for a second set by their preferred outfit. The sound was also generally good, benefiting greatly from the shape and size of the club.

Jerry Harrison: It's a long narrow room, so even if there's only twenty people there, they'll be at the front so it at least feels like there's an audience. And if you didn't like a band, you could just go to the bar at the back . . . Hilly Kristal made it feel like our club, and thus allowed the scene to happen.

David Byrne: CBGBs was the kind of place where you'd sit at the bar and when your time came you'd just casually walk over and get onstage. When you were done you'd walk off and maybe wipe the sweat off your head, then walk back to the bar and have a beer.

It was inevitable that CBGBs would not maintain its monopoly for long. In the spring of 1975 Mother's, a gay bar on 23rd Street, began competing for the best new bands, while Club 82 also resumed booking rock & roll acts. The re-emergence of Max's in the fall of 1975, now also booking unsigned acts, meant that a fierce rivalry was inevitable between the clubs. Bands were soon perceived as Max's bands or CBGBs bands.

It would be unfair to give the impression that only when critical awareness of the New York scene began did Max's start to book these local, unsigned acts. In fact Max's change in attitude, though gradual, largely dated from 1974, after the collapse of Mercers. In response to the lack of alternatives available to popular Mercers acts like Wayne County and the Harlots of 42nd Street, Mickey Ruskin donated Tuesday nights to these bands, with the promise of a weekend residency if the audience response was positive. The first exponent of New York's punk scene to play Max's was Patti Smith, who performed there as early as December 1973, though the Smith/Kaye duo was just the support act (Phil Ochs was headliner). When Smith shared five days at Max's with Television at the end of August 1974, Television became the first regular CBGBs band to play the more esteemed establishment.

Nevertheless, when Max's closed in December 1974, its reputation was still for signed acts and the famous people who inhabited it in the small hours. The cross-section of habitués included everyone from Candy Darling to Zsa Zsa Gabor, via the perennial rock-stars-passing-thru-town. It had also played host to some of the most important rock & roll gigs in recent years: the Velvet Underground's final shows in the summer of 1970; Alice Cooper getting arrested one night for saying the word 'tits' repeatedly during his band's first major New York residency;

Iggy and the Stooges' 1973 shows, during which Iggy gouged his own chest with a broken bottle.

With such a heritage it was a considerable relief to New York's homegrown rock & rollers when Max's reopened under the new management of Tommy Dean in the summer of 1975. Yet Dean's initial intention was to retain Max's as a place for 'hanging out' and dispense with the live bands. For a few weeks he even tried to run it as a disco with flashing lights, but that decision proved short-lived.

What probably convinced Tommy Dean to compete with CBGBs was the considerable success of CBGBs' summer festival of unsigned bands. What is perhaps surprising is how many bands – around forty – CBGBs managed to muster for the festival, which was booked to run from 16–27 July (but was later extended to 1 August). According to Kristal, the most popular bands during the two week festival were the Ramones, Television, the Heartbreakers, the Shirts, the recently formed Talking Heads and, from Philadelphia, Johnny's Dance Band.

Tommy Dean decided to bring in Peter Crowley from Mother's to organize bands for Max's. This inevitably provoked mutterings from disaffected bands since Crowley was already managing Wayne County, though it opened the door for at least one important outfit unable to break into Kristal's kingdom – Suicide.

Alan Vega: Peter Crowley started us in that little club on 23rd Street [Mother's]. And when he got his foot in the door at Max's, he started bringing in Wayne and then Wayne started drawing . . . And then ironically we drew. [Tommy Dean] couldn't believe it and he kept having us back.

Though an early accord was struck between CBGBs and the reopened Max's, the peace was short-lived.

Leee Black Childers: When Max's decided to go rock & roll, they had a meeting with Hilly Kristal and decided to cooperate by not booking conflicting bands on the same night, but Max's were only offering one night's work compared to CBGBs three. As soon as Max's booked a band for Friday night, CBGBs would turn around and offer the band three nights. Obviously they'd prefer three nights' work, so Max's suffered. At one time there was an unwritten rule that if a band played CBGBs, they couldn't play Max's, but that's cooling down a bit now. Most bands can

play both clubs. Except of course the Dictators, who will never play Max's
. . . At the end of a three-day run, [the Heartbreakers] always make about
$2,500 at CBGBs. It's not bad money really . . . we're not starving at all.

The incident that resulted in the Dictators being banned from Max's
actually occurred at CBGBs, when Wayne County responded to some
– allegedly homophobic – heckling from 'Handsome Dick' Manitoba by
hitting him with the heavy end of his mike stand, breaking his collar-
bone and hospitalizing him for two weeks. Inevitably Crowley's association with County coloured his point of view and suddenly he was
attempting not only to place an embargo at Max's against Manitoba's
band, the very popular Dictators, but also anybody that played with the
Dictators.

According to Willy DeVille, Crowley even told at least one band
(Blondie) that they had to be either a CBGBs band or a Max's band.
Eventually a compromise was reached which restricted bands from
alternating between the venues until a reasonable timespan had elapsed.

Chris Stein: They had this rule where you couldn't play at one if you had
to play at the other one within two weeks or something like that. It was an
unwritten rule.

The rivalry did not end there. After the success of their 1975 summer
festival, CBGBs followed up with a Christmas festival. Max's responded
with an Easter 1976 festival and a reggae festival in the summer. The
Easter festival ran from 11–22 April and was as notable for its omissions
– Television, Talking Heads and the Miamis – as its inclusions: Wayne
County, Pere Ubu, the Marbles, the Heartbreakers, Suicide, Blondie
and the Ramones. Talking Heads pulled out at the last minute, having
been due to share the 13 April bill with Pere Ubu, who were making
their New York debut and who, according to *New York Rocker*, had 'the
most advance word-of-mouth publicity of any band involved in the
festival.' Presumably the Miamis saw themselves more as a CBGBs
band and refrained from appearing, though Television would continue
to play Max's on a regular basis.

The surprise hit of the Easter festival was the newly reconstituted
Blondie, now augmented by keyboardist Jimmy Destri. They caught
out many who previously thought they knew all about them. As Lisa
Persky wrote in *New York Rocker*:

Easter Sunday, another band's incubation period has ended and the award for the loveliest Easter Egg goes to Blondie who has finally hatched and presented us with five of the best pieces of chicken the fest has seen or heard. Having eliminated the between-song dreck we have never gotten used to, all of Blondie did much to convince us that they are now deserving of more concrete recognition than they have so far received.

If there were Max's bands and there were CBGBs bands, there was also a Max's audience and a CBGBs audience. Surprisingly, given Max's previous associations and CBGBs' rather aromatic ambience, it was CBGBs that appealed more to the art-rock crowd – despite attracting its fair share of the 'let's rock' brigade. The out-for-a-good-time regulars at Max's were less rigidly divided – just as long as they could groove to it. Suicide, who were very much a Max's band, had a marked preference for the Max's audiences.

Alan Vega: Everybody [came] from Brooklyn, Queen's punks, Bronx punks, New Jersey punks, there were a lot of New Jersey punks . . . That's who that [Max's] crowd was when they were teens. We were also getting the art crowd, who hated us more than anybody. Ironically, they were the ones we got the most trouble from, . . . CB's drew more of the art crowd, the intellectual crowd, without a doubt. Max's drew more of the Brooklyn kids . . . It was beer-drinking, carousing, they'd smash the glasses in front of me. They'd smash it in unison with me. They were rowdy [but] they weren't hurting me. If anybody'd talk to me, these kids'd kill 'em . . . The art crowd didn't go to Max's.

Max's also followed CBGBs' lead in releasing an album of the unsigned bands who habitually played the club, part of a gradually increasing awareness of the importance of the new New York scene. The CBGBs album was recorded at the club's second summer festival – a year too late to represent the 'real' scene that the club had helped to burgeon. By the summer of 1976 the first-rung bands had either signed to a record label, like Patti Smith or the Ramones, or were on the verge of signing, like Television, Blondie and Talking Heads. So the outfits that were happy to be represented on Kristal's album were the second-rung bands – and destined to remain that way.

Hilly Kristal: People have said to me that it doesn't represent the underground rock in New York because it didn't have Television or the Talking Heads, but I just took what was available.

The release of *Live at CBGBs* probably did more harm than good – and not only to the commercial chances of bands like the Miamis, the Shirts and Mink DeVille, all of whom were highly respected in New York but failed to impress on the CBGBs album. The entire scene was tainted in critics' eyes. Certainly the album's release in the fall of 1976, preceding all but *Horses* and the Ramones' debut, caused many reviewers to wonder what all the fuss surrounding the CBGBs scene had been about.

Max's 1976 album was an equally deliberate attempt to assert the club's claim to pre-eminence in the New York music scene. It was certainly better received than the CBGBs album, partially because it was entirely derived from studio recordings, and therefore not prone to the 'good night, not so good night' malaise that affected the CBGBs album. It was also a single album, and therefore less of an earful, and featured a few truly outstanding cuts, even if only Suicide (with 'Rocket USA') could really be considered representative of New York alternative bands. The other notable cuts were both reissues of existing singles.

Wayne County's 'Down at Max's' was an obvious choice, though County was really a throwback to the Mercers scene and destined to remain a figure of strictly local notoriety. Aside from 'Rocket USA', Pere Ubu's searing 'Final Solution' was the only cut on either album to suggest that the new American bands could match the intensity of the Pistols or the Clash, though the band who had recorded this stunning performance were no more by the time the Max's album reached the shops. The new Ubu had moved away from such unabashed rock & roll and, when commissioned to provide a track for a second Max's volume, Ubu came up with an early version of 'The Modern Dance', which was rejected as totally unintelligible.

Though a second Max's volume was released, Kristal abandoned any notion of a second CBGBs album after losing something in the region of $20,000 on his first effort. The second Max's album only confirmed the surprising haste with which the New York scene atrophied after the signing up of its first wave. It remains both the poorest and poorest-selling of the New York compilations.

The other New York venues that contributed to the city's mid-Seventies musical renaissance had fewer pretensions. Perhaps most notable were the Performance Studio and Club 82, both responsible for providing early hunting grounds for the first wave of CBGBs bands. The Performance Studio in particular, though no more than a loft on East 23rd Street, was a regular venue for Blondie and the Ramones.

Chris Stein: [The Performance Studio] was a place that Blondie and Tommy worked out of. It was a rehearsal/recording studio where they had an eight-track set-up. The Ramones did a lot of their early demos there. We played shows there. There would be fifty or a hundred people [who] would go up there and they would charge at the door. There was a small loft. We played there without Debbie and we played without the band one night, Debbie singing and me playing guitar, opening for the Ramones.

Like Max's, Club 82 had spent most of its long history in the guise of a late-night 'hang-out', not as a rock & roll venue – its transvestite reputation relating more to its employees than its customers – but it was one of the first places that the Stillettoes and Television were able to play. Though superseded in 1975 by Mother's as the main alternative to the CBGBs/Max's duopoly, it continued to be a popular meeting place for the CBGBs/Max's crowd.

Bob Gruen: Since the Club 82 had had this outcast image for so long, the punks and the early glitter kids were treated very openly by the management. They didn't think they were weird and didn't try and cash in on 'em – they'd been dealing with weirdos for forty years! So when bands started going there they brought the young rock & roll crowd.

By the time the bands that emerged in 1974–5 had either secured a record contract or been consigned to the eternal club circuit, there was a new wave of clubs to cater for the newer bands, including the Mudd Club and the various Village clubs that were now welcoming the new rock & roll crowd, notably the Bottom Line, where Patti Smith and Television played important gigs in 1975 and 1976, and the Bitter End, venue of the first Patti Smith Group gig.

From the end of 1975 New York's club scene had developed such a reputation that, for the first time in a decade, it was operating as a magnet for aspiring musicians in nearby cities – and some not-so-nearby metropolises. Though this second wave was a profound disappointment in terms of originality and inspiration, there were a few bands who represented new directions. The most notable would be Cleveland's leading art-rockers, Pere Ubu, and three students from the Rhode Island School of Design – David Byrne, Tina Weymouth and Chris Frantz – a trio of Talking Heads.

Lenny Kaye: In a sense every time we took another step towards the more traditional rock band we did limit ourselves in some ways, but it's a give and take and we also felt that we didn't want to have to play small art clubs the rest of our lives. To me that's not real integrity.

At the end of their spring 1975 CBGBs residency, Patti Smith and her band required just one addition to complete their assimilation into the rock & roll format – a drummer. At CBGBs the piano and bass had provided the essential rhythmic counterpoints to the lead guitar/vocals. But they knew they needed the steady 4/4 backdrop of a drummer if they were to pass beyond the art-rock coterie they had already converted and achieve mass acceptance. Tom Verlaine, who had been regularly guesting on a couple of songs during Smith's CBGBs sets – often the co-written 'Break it Up' or 'Space Monkey' – suggested a suitable candidate.

Tom Verlaine: She was thinking of getting a drummer and I told her this drummer in this band the Mumps was really good and I said that if I wasn't using Billy that I would go for that guy right away. He'd got a great attitude and he really played musically. So she had her manager go talk to him and he quit the Mumps.

Jay Dee Daugherty completed the Patti Smith Group barely in time to contribute to Smith's debut album. It was over four years since Smith had first played with Kaye. The album would need to reflect all stages of their development, to represent the Smith–Kaye–Sohl and Smith–Kaye–Sohl–Kral periods as fully as recent five-piece concoctions.

Having signed to Arista, Clive Davis snatching her from under the snouts of RCA, Smith was eager to fulfil her rock & roll ambitions. She was also the first member of the nascent New York scene to be recording an album. By the time *Horses* was completed, the major New York-based acts in this punk revival – Television, Talking Heads, Blondie, the Ramones and the Dolls/Television hybrid, the Heartbreakers – were all making regular appearances at CBGBs, the new centre of American rock & roll. The commercial success of Patti Smith's debut album, *Horses*, in the fall of 1975, would in all likelihood dictate the attitude of American labels to these contenders fighting it out on the Bowery.

Patti Smith: *Horses* for me was ... the culmination of four years of thought, processes of study ... of performance, of failure, building and rebuilding ... It was a document of years of work ... I listen to *Horses* and I think of it as the culmination of all my most heartfelt adolescent desires.

But Smith's debut album was never going to be simply an in-house version of her current live act. There would be a sixth factor in the process, one that Smith had not really considered – the producer John Cale.

Patti Smith: All I was looking for was a technical person. Instead, I got a real maniac artist. I went to pick out an expensive watercolour painting, and instead I got a mirror. It was really like *A Season in Hell* for both of us. But inspiration doesn't always have to be someone sending me half a dozen American beauty roses. There's a lot of inspiration going on between the murderer and the victim.

Horses, recorded over August and September 1975, is the product of Cale and Smith's battle for Electric Lady studio. If Smith had believed that, after the CBGBs residency, her songs were in recordable form, Cale was not convinced. Through his lack of conviction, he forced Smith to re-evaluate all that she had produced.

Patti Smith: I had to solidify everything I believed in ... We came into the studio really half-assed and glib, then I had to pound my fists into his skull day and night.

Lenny Kaye: The songs were already worked out. John came in and he didn't even look at the board, he went right to the songs, which resulted in numerous days of machine-gun fire throughout the studio. Everything wound up . . . the way it started . . . but we all understood it a bit more. His major contribution was setting up a psychological aura in the studio.

Despite Kaye's assertion that 'everything wound up . . . the way it started', this clearly was not the case. The more abstract songs became more rigorously defined. 'Birdland' grew from a four-minute rap-poem into a nine-minute *tour de force*. 'Land' was also transformed in the studio.

Patti Smith: We went through all kinds of voyages – usually there's Mexican boys and space guys, weird Burroughs stuff like Arab guys and Christian angels fucking in the sand, pulling out each other's entrails – or like there's Johnny in a blue T-bird going off the cliff while 'Thousand Dances' is playing on the radio. People used to come to CBGBs night after night to find out what was gonna happen to Johnny next – and I was curious to find out what was gonna happen to him on the record . . . On the second take something weird happened. The Mexican boys and spaceships were gone – instead there was a black horse, and all those electrical wires and a sea – a 'sea of possibilities' – I didn't know what direction the song was taking, there was all this strange imagery I didn't understand . . . On the last take it was obvious that I was being told what I wanted to know about Hendrix's death. The song is like eight or nine minutes long, so it's obvious I'm gonna lose control sometime – but I felt like it was *The Exorcist*, or somebody else talking thru my voice. I said 'How did I die . . . I, I tried to walk thru light' . . . and it ended up with 'in the sheets, there was a man' – it really frightened me. After I was done I felt like all three tracks had the total information of his last seconds, so I decided to mix them all together.

Horses was the summation of a decade of dreams for Smith. It is the album not of a sandblasted adolescent, but of an assured woman on the precipice of thirtydom. She inextricably links the history of rock & roll to personal experience. Using Rimbaud, Morrison and Hendrix as central figures in her explorations, the album relates a series of cathartic moments in her life. The voyage of discovery starts with Smith's rejection of the religion of her forefathers and a simple assertion of her own sense of responsibility – 'Jesus died for somebody's sins but not mine.' On 'Kimberly' Smith decides that, having rejected the living God, she will turn to man-made beauty.

Patti Smith: When I was thirteen ... my little sister Kimberly was born. I was outside and there was this huge storm brewing ... I was standing outside and I was sick ... sick of being a Jehovah's Witness, because ... they said there was no place for art in Jesus' world ... I said well, what's going to happen with the museums, the Modiglianis, the Blue Period, and they said it would fall into the molten sea of hell ... I certainly didn't want to go to heaven if there was no art in heaven.

In 'Break it Up' she recalled the moment in the summer of 1972 when she rejected her transferred idolatry for Arthur Rimbaud and Jim Morrison, and decided to seek her own voice.

Patti Smith: I went to Jim Morrison's grave in Paris, and I didn't feel anything. I couldn't even cry. I just stood there, completely hollow. I went to Rimbaud's grave afterwards, and stood there and felt totally cold. And then I just said, 'Fuck it. I'm going home and doing my own work. I'm not standing over the graves of these people.'

'Kimberly' and 'Break it Up' represent boundaries of previous existence pushed asunder. On the final song of the album, Smith finally learns to draw upon her heroes for inspiration rather than vicarious adulation.

Patti Smith: We had written this elegy for Jimi Hendrix and we recorded it 18 September, and that was the day Hendrix died ... You can really feel Jimi Hendrix in that studio ... Anytime I get in trouble, I shut my eyes and he's right there.

Horses surely signalled the beginning of the assimilation of America's underground rock bands into its mainstream. Without a hit single, but with considerable pre-release hype, *Horses* cracked the *Billboard* Top 50, something not achieved by any of Smith's precursors – the Velvets, the MC5, the Stooges or the New York Dolls. It still stands as one of the great debut albums of rock & roll.

If *Horses* could only ever be a partial representation of Smith's five years as a performer, her own pursuit of some reconciliation between her love of all forms of art and a deep-rooted sense of devotion was bound to drive her away from further recycling her past. When *Horses* was recorded, the five-piece Patti Smith Group was barely a working entity. Only with the year of touring that followed did the Patti Smith Group fully bloom.

After a two-month respite while *Horses* took its place in the market, the Patti Smith Group began a gruelling three-month tour of the States. These shows, which generated several high-quality bootlegs, went one step beyond *Horses*, combining Smith's own songs with her vision of a rock & roll heritage. The welding of the Velvets' 'We're Gonna Have a Real Good Time Together' and 'Pale Blue Eyes', the Kingsmen's 'Louie Louie', the Stones' 'Time is on My Side', Them's 'Gloria' and the Who's 'My Generation' on to her own rap-poetry and songs, both old and new, cemented her relationship with her past and the audience's future. The shows also allowed those fans only conversant with *Horses* to experience 'Space Monkey', 'Set Me Free' and 'Ask the Angels', songs which were in a more orthodox rock vein than 'Birdland' or 'Land'.

Patti Smith: When I perform, I just sort of mingle everything that I'm into at the moment. About a year ago it was the legend of Scheherazade and Patty Hearst. But it keeps changing all the time. I'm always on a tightrope, trying to keep all the stuff together. I got Rimbaud in my blood as strong as James Brown.

The abandon Smith brought to her onstage antics was certainly revolutionary, slowly chipping away at the barriers on which was painted 'Good girls don't let it all hang out!' Smith relished the opportunity to unleash on her audiences all the neuroses resulting from a strict religious upbringing, happy to shock the 'judges who dare to push fake morals'. Her participation in several forthright interviews in the months following the release of *Horses* betrayed her startling penchant for frankness:

Patti Smith: I don't consider writing a quiet, closet act. I consider it a real physical act. When I'm home writing on the typewriter, I go crazy. I move like a monkey. I've wet myself, I've come in my pants writing . . . Instead of shooting smack, I masturbate – fourteen times in a row . . . I start seeing all these strange spaceships landing in the Aztec mountains . . . I see weird things. I see temples, underground temples, with the doors opening, sliding door after sliding door, Pharaoh revealed – this bound-up Pharaoh with ropes of gold. That's how I write a lot of my poetry.

By the time she finished her first US tour in the early months of 1976,

Smith was already looking to her next album. *Horses* had been an album of old songs, even in August 1975. By May 1976, when the Patti Smith Group played a brief but influential European tour, she was more interested in playing new songs like 'Pumping (My Heart)', 'Ain't it Strange' and 'Pissing in the River' than attempting to replicate the studio recordings of 'Land' and 'Birdland'. The second album was going to be a Patti Smith Group album, a celebration of their uniquely primitive sound.

Patti Smith: If you're really relentlessly into something and you're into sound, it gets to the point where it doesn't matter whether you're good or evil or dream or whatever, you get into this rhythm of sound and you just have to be great no matter who you are.

Yet it was questionable whether Smith's new 'rhythm of sound' would be convincing enough to satiate the critics who wondered how she could surpass a first album composed over four years of relative isolation during a year inside the cauldron of fame. When she made *Horses*, Smith was not swimming in the rock & roll mainstream. With her second album she could continue to assert her independence from the conventions of rock music. Or not.

Despite their technical limitations, the Patti Smith Group had become an extremely flexible tool, and each song now contained more possibilities than at any point in their development. New songs like 'Pissing in the River' and 'Pumping (My Heart)', though considerably less free-form than 'Land', locked in a new intensity. In July 1976, at a concert in Central Park, Smith introduced the appointed heir of 'Land'. 'Radio Ethiopia' trod new terrain. It was the Patti Smith Group's most extreme statement, suggesting in Smith a renewed willingness to play explorer. On the second album, which would take its name from this, its most extreme, statement, 'Radio Ethiopia' would be bound to Smith's recitation of 'Abysinnia', for here lay the key to 'Radio Ethiopia':

everybody holds the Key of E that opens all vaults that lead to all roads to abyssinia. the kingdom of sheba . . . the true earth of rimbaud. abyssinia and all deeds belong to the people. there is no land but the land. there is no sea but the sea. and there are no boundaries no restrictions on the waves of radio ethiopia.

The official cut of 'Radio Ethiopia', recorded on 9 August 1976, was recording during a three-week stint that resulted in Smith's second album in less than a year. Though the song was attempted several times, the album take had a feel that none of the others had.

Lenny Kaye: 'Radio Ethiopia' was recorded totally live in the studio. There were no overdubs on it . . . nothing was done to it. It was very special the way it came about. It was really dark and there was a hurricane coming in around us, and we were in this studio in the middle of the night. We just did 'Radio Ethiopia' and it had this weird magic which we never recaptured, although we recorded it a few more times after that. We were gonna put other things over it, like radios, but we decided to just leave it how it came out. That track is what we've been working up to for a year.

'Radio Ethiopia' was the Patti Smith Group's 'Black to Comm', its 'Sister Ray', its 'Little Johnny Jewel'. It was what Kaye said it was, the track 'we've been working up to for a year'. And it reflected the same sense of unyielding expression as Television and the MC5 had sought from the free-jazz masters.

Patti Smith: There's rarely been a rock group into improvisation on the level of free jazz . . . The secret of improvisation is the movement within a song – like the way 'Radio Ethiopia' moves through its changes in a totally organic way – none of which is pre-planned.

But 'Radio Ethiopia' on the album was the bare bones of what the song became in the three months of touring that followed its release. Radio Ethiopia in the fall of 1976 was the Patti Smith Group's ultimate 'field' of sound, from night to night displaying its chameleon quality in a bewildering retinue of shades. Only the basic outline remained constant.

Lenny Kaye: Onstage 'Radio Ethiopia' . . . has less inbuilt barriers. 'Land' . . . was actually a song onstage, whereas 'Radio Ethiopia' is nothing but a field . . . a place where you can just run into it and have total freedom . . . an infinite field of exploration.

'Radio Ethiopia' became a suite built from a series of disparate elements. 'Abysinnia' had been jettisoned. The song now began with a rap-cum-poem, which could take any form, before the descent into

'Radio Ethiopia (version)'. An improvised instrumental section would then feed into 'Rock & Roll Nigger' and finally into 'Gloria'.*

Rock & Roll Nigger was now the working title for Smith's third album. For some time Smith had been fascinated by the concept of the artist as 'nigger', a minor variation on Rimbaud's idea of the artist as thief ('The poet, therefore, is truly the thief of fire.'). At one of her December 1975 Bottom Line shows Smith prefaced her rock & roll set with a poem called 'Nigger Book', later included on the rear cover of *The Night* (a pamphlet co-written with Tom Verlaine and published in July 1976):

the word (art) must be redefined – all mutants and the new babes born sans eyebrow and tonsil – outside logic – beyond mathematics poli-tricks baptism and motion sickness – any man who extends beyond the classic form is a nigger – one sans fear and despair – one who rises like rimbaud beating hard gold rhythm outta soft solid shit-tongue light.

A backlash, though, was also brewing. *Radio Ethiopia* had been poorly received by press and fans alike, seen as proof of Smith's deep-rooted aptitude for self-indulgence. Smith's 'holier than thou' pronouncements were also beginning to wear on her early advocates. Just as they were predicting a fall, the metaphorical became the literal. On 26 January 1977 Patti Smith plummeted from a twelve foot stage at a concert in Tampa, Florida.

'Radio Ethiopia' had not been the only song from Smith's second album to be subject to a little in-concert embellishment during the winter of 1976–7. Just a fortnight before her fall, Smith had talked to England's *Melody Maker* about the extended middle section to 'Ain't it Strange'.

Patti Smith: One night I became Alexander the Great's daughter! I was avenging (sic) the people who poisoned my father. Or I can go spinning off and get further and further into the Queen of Sheba's consciousness . . . It's just different things every night. But the ultimate person, of course, is always me. And when I dip totally into me and it's empty, I either get very

---

* A sixteen-minute 'Radio Ethiopia' from Smith's June 1977 CBGBs shows was issued in France as the B-side to a 12" single of 'Hey Joe'. It remains the definitive representation of the Patti Smith Group live.

angry or very afraid. Then I call out to God. Like I challenge Him . . . I shout 'Turn around God, make a move!'

Evidently God had decided to make His move. It was during 'Ain't it Strange' that Smith fell into grace.

Patti Smith: I was doing my most intense number, 'Ain't it Strange', a song where I directly challenge God to talk to me in some way. It's after a part where I spin like a dervish and I say 'Hand of God I feel the finger, Hand of God I start to whirl, Hand of God I don't get dizzy, Hand of God I do not fall now.' But I fell . . .

Smith would later begin to interpret her fall in a way that implied she had been offered a choice by God. In fact, though she needed a neck brace for a couple of months and twenty-two stitches in her head, the fall was not a life-threatening affair. But as far as Smith's own psyche was concerned, it represented a mystical point where she had nearly died for her sins.

Patti Smith: I did feel the finger [of God] push me right over . . . I feel it was His way of saying, 'You keep battering against my door and I'm gonna open that door and you'll fall in.' And that's how I think Hendrix died, that's what I was saying in 'Land' . . . I've had a moment where I had to make a choice, just as I was losing consciousness and I really felt like I was gonna die . . . Did I want a communication with God so intimate that I'd be dead, off the earth?

The resurrected Patti Lee would be a very different lady.

The originators of the CBGBs scene, the Hell–Verlaine incarnation of Television, never made a single vinyl representation. The most genuinely exciting band to play CBGBs during its 1975–6 heyday also failed to make any permanent record before losing their bass-playing wordsmith, a re-enactment of Television's great divide. Once again, the individual in question was Richard Hell. This time around, the band was the Heartbreakers, subsequently associated solely with Johnny Thunders of Dolls fame. However, the circumstances surrounding Hell's departure from the Heartbreakers were markedly different from those that caused the rift in Television.

The Heartbreakers' formation in April 1975 seemed like an inspired union of two leading lights on the Mercers and CBGBs scenes. Johnny Thunders' work with the Dolls had already established him in the pantheon of great American rock & roll guitarists. Richard Hell was exactly what Thunders needed, a songwriter of note and a frontman prepared to share the limelight.

Hell had expressed dissatisfaction with Television's set-up to Thunders when Television were playing support to the Dolls at the Little Hippodrome at the beginning of March. He was nevertheless surprised when Thunders approached him about forming a new band with Jerry Nolan, who had also quit the Dolls at the end of the month. After all, his reputation as bassist suggested only a bare competence.

Richard Hell: Johnny's always had really selective antennae for what's happening. I had run into some of them around town but I didn't know them. They weren't like friends and I was kinda surprised [when] something like two days after I'd left Television and the word had gotten out I got a

call from Johnny saying, 'Me and Jerry have split from the Dolls. You
wanna make a band together?'

The question of Hell's abilities as a bassist never became an issue,
partially because by this stage his poor reputation was largely unjustified
– his bass-playing had a rib-thudding resonance that dispensed with
niceties but was highly effective – and partially because the Heartbreakers were not interested in the ten-minute excursions that benefited
from Fred Smith's more jazz-oriented approach.

Richard Hell: To me, new wave is short, hard, compelling and driving
music. That's the first qualification, and people like Patti and Talking
Heads don't have it. Even Television doesn't now – when I was in the
group it was a rock & roll band.

Hell and Verlaine had always been divided as to the virtues of hard
rock & roll. Though Verlaine shared Hell's love of the Stooges and
early Stones, he was less enamoured of the bands that had followed in
their footsteps. His seeming distaste for the hard-rock sensibility had a
direct bearing on Television's move towards a more pronounced jazz/
rock fusion, reflecting his love of Ayler and Coltrane. This sat badly
with Hell, who much preferred to place the band's art-rock aesthetic
against a granite bedrock of sound. He saw a new opportunity to
explore his 'intelligent rock & roll' concerns with the Heartbreakers.

Richard Hell: I really liked the Ramones. They were around at the same
time and I felt a lot of affinities with the Ramones . . . [Tom] thought they
were beneath contempt. That was part of our whole difference. He basically
was a folk musician . . . Before I talked him into making a band the only
thing he'd ever done in music was to go to a hootenanny at a West Village
folkie bar on open mike night. But I thought we should make a real band
that was really going to turn things around.

While Thunders and his old Dolls sidekick Jerry Nolan provided the
necessary musical muscle, Hell's sardonic lyrics retained that sense of
many personal sleights committed against him by nature, man and God.
The songs Hell brought to the Heartbreakers were a remarkably
diverse series of expositions on the curse of life, including the likes of
'Blank Generation', 'New Pleasure', 'Hurt Me', and a rewrite of the

Neon Boys' 'High-Heeled Wheels', titled 'You Gotta Lose'. This last song included a verse pointedly directed at Verlaine:

> Not too long ago I knew a guy who thought he can't be beat
> But he got rabies on his rubies, now he can't unlace his feet.

Also introduced early into the Heartbreakers' live set was a rewritten 'Love Comes in Spurts', with a tightened-up riff and a new set of words. This soon replaced the original version in local affection. At the same time Hell gave the Heartbreakers their most famous song, the anthemic '(I'm Living on) Chinese Rocks', which he had co-written with Dee Dee Ramone.

Richard Hell: Dee Dee told me that he had an idea for a song that he didn't think the Ramones would wanna do, and he thought it would be good for us to do it, and he wanted to collaborate with me on it so he came over and we sat around, fooling around with it.

After Hell's departure, the song was retained by Nolan and Thunders, who subsequently appear alongside Dee Dee and Hell in the writing credits, a source of understandable acrimony for both Dee Dee Ramone and Hell (the Ramones eventually issued their own version in 1980). Sadly, the composition of 'Chinese Rocks' came at a time in both Dee Dee and Hell's lives when it was all-too-biographical in its depiction of living for that next fix of China White:

> I'm livin' on a Chinese rock
> All my best things are in hock
> I shoulda been rich
> But I'm just lyin' in a Chinese ditch.

Verlaine has suggested that part of his unhappiness with Hell at the end of his tenure in Television was due to Hell's steadily increasing drug use. But it was really during a year in the Heartbreakers that Hell's habit got seriously out of hand.

Richard Hell: None of us had habits at that time. It didn't take long, though. During the course of that year. We were all definitely inclined that way anyway. I think it was probably pretty inevitable.

Hell is being generous in suggesting that his fellow Heartbreakers

Nolan and Thunders did not have habits when he joined the band. All evidence contradicts his assessment. Thunders' and Nolan's habits had had a lot to do with the Dolls' fragmentation. As such, they were not the best of company for someone like Hell who was 'inclined that way anyway'.

Jerry Nolan: To begin with, it just seemed like part of the fun, part of the good times – and it was always around ... practically for free. After a while, you inevitably begin to try it. Then, after you'd tried it once, you always had this memory of how great it was to be stoned, and how easy it would be to recapture that feeling ... so really it's too cool for your own good. It has a habit of making it a habit.

Hell hints of early problems with his fellow Heartbreakers in his diary of the time, writing about their first headline gig at CBGBs, '[It] hasn't gone too badly though Johnny's got to be watched like a baby.' His account of their second CBGBs weekend continues, 'Using a lot of junk but not as much as Jerry.' As it happens, Bad Company had already been taken as a possible band name.

The Heartbreakers' live debut, which occurred two months after their formation, had not been auspicious. Both Hell and Thunders were used to playing in a two-guitar band, and the burden of responsibility proved to be too much. After this three-piece show at the Coventry, they set about searching for a second guitarist. As Hell would later describe it, 'finally on a dead night at CBGB, [we] heard the tall dark thin chords of a player named Walter in a local band called the Demons.' Walter Lure was a guitarist from Brooklyn 'who had always wanted to be in the Dolls'. The first pukka Heartbreakers gigs were on 25–27 July when they played three of the final shows in CBGBs' summer festival of unsigned bands. Not surprisingly they were among the most popular bands at the festival.

Their next shows as headliners came three weeks later – on 15 and 16 August, again at CBGBs. As agreed at the outset, the vocal duties each night were divided up, though the onus was mainly on Hell, who sang lead on 'Can't Keep My Eyes on You', 'Hurt Me', 'Chinese Rocks', 'You Gotta Lose', 'New Pleasure' and 'Blank Generation'. 'Going Steady', 'Pirate Love' and 'I Wanna be Loved' were sung by Thunders, while Lure got to sing a solitary song, 'Flight'.

Clearly Thunders had not been exactly prolific in the five months since the Heartbreakers' formation – despite Nolan's claim that 'we wrote songs every single day, for months'. 'Pirate Love' dated from the Dolls' final shows, and though Lure's one vocal did not survive the three weeks before their next CBGBs shows, it was not replaced by a Thunders original but by a cover of the Monkees' '(I'm Not Your) Steppin' Stone'.

The wired tension that would eventually stretch the Hell–Thunders alliance to breaking point was already in evidence. Hell was by far the more prolific songwriter. If Thunders had contributed a dozen co-written songs to the Dolls' repertoire, only 'Pirate Love' and 'I Wanna be Loved' matched Hell's contributions to the Heartbreakers live set. Though the Heartbreakers had been formed by two musicians who were tired of what they saw as the ego-mania of their former bands' frontmen and were craving a more democratic band, the truth is that Hell was the Heartbreakers' main asset, Thunders' flashy, cut-and-thrust guitar-playing notwithstanding.

This became most apparent in January 1976 when the Heartbreakers recorded their first set of demos, over a period of three days, at SBS Studios in Yonkers. Seven songs were recorded, only two of which were Thunders originals, 'I Wanna be Loved' and 'Pirate Love'. The others were all sung by Hell – 'Love Comes in Spurts', 'Blank Generation', 'Chinese Rocks', 'Hurt Me' and 'Can't Keep My Eyes on You'. The demos confirmed that Hell was dominating the band, and it was no surprise when Thunders expressed unhappiness with the situation.

Johnny Thunders: It was great when it first started, but when Richard was in Television, Tom Verlaine wanted to sing every song . . . and that's what Richard did to us; I could sing one song out of ten, and Walter could sing one song a night.

All the evidence contradicts Thunders. The Heartbreakers' final show of 1975, at Mother's (now issued by New Rose as *Live at Mother's*), featured the usual six–four split in favour of Hell. Thunders had recently introduced a gut-wrenching original into the live set, though 'So Alone' was based on an old Actress song from 1971.

Whatever Thunders' feelings, it was actually Hell who was most unhappy with the set-up. After just six months of regular gigging it had become apparent to him that he did not share the same aesthetic concerns as Thunders and Nolan. Sure, he wanted a hard-rock sound and the Heartbreakers had that in surfeit. But for Thunders and Nolan, 'short, hard, compelling and driving music' was the be-all and end-all of their ambitions. A year after his acrimonious departure from Television, Hell had reached the same point of disaffection with the Heartbreakers. His co-founders' aims and his own did not have a great deal in common, and he felt in danger of being left behind. American A&R men were already sniffing around the scene; the Ramones had become the first CBGBs band to secure a record deal – Patti Smith excepted – when they signed to Sire that January. In April 1976, after headlining one night at Max's Easter festival, Hell informed the Heartbreakers that he was leaving the band.

Richard Hell: We [had] agreed to take the same tack as I hoped to do in Television, where Johnny and I would sing the songs that we wrote and it would be about equal . . . [but] it was just that the music was too brutish for me. It was clear that it wasn't gonna have any kinda musical ambition except to stomp out rock & roll, which I like, but I wanted to be able to extend it more. The way I felt was that it was a perfectly amicable parting, but only recently I've seen all these places the guys say they kicked me out because I was too pretentious or something like that . . . I [just] realized I wanted a band that I led upfront.

The Heartbreakers had only just acquired their first manager, photographer Leee Black Childers, in an attempt to break out of the straitjacket of New York 'punk' clubs.

Leee Black Childers: It was Johnny Thunders who came to me and said that he needed a manager, he couldn't keep playing forever at Max's and CBGB, he needed to grow into more, would I manage them? So I said yes and that was right when the shake-up occured and Richard Hell left. Not because of me, he was already going.

Childers at least was aware that without Hell – who, to quote Childers, 'had more of an idea what a song was than Johnny' – the Heartbreakers had serious problems, and did his best to talk him into staying.

Leee Black Childers: Richard Hell . . . decided he [wanted to] quit. So I talked to him, and I tried to reason with him and get him to stay . . . and he couldn't. I think basically it was just a big ego conflict. Because it always was half the audience watching Richard Hell and half the audience watching Johnny Thunders and who did how many songs of their own and all that kind of thing, constant arguments . . . it couldn't have lasted.

Hell's grand experiment to align the two forms of New York rock & roll had failed. He would have to unlace his own feet. The time had come to create from within his own personal void.

Tom Verlaine: There's certain chronologies involved with CBGBs that nobody has gotten right ... There's two periods – there's like Television/ Blondie/Ramones. Then two years later (sic) there was the Talking Heads and umpteen other groups. In other words there were bands that were in New York that played there, then there were bands that came to New York, decided to live there and played there. Actually Ubu was before Talking Heads.

The difference between 'second wave' bands like Talking Heads and the Shirts and the first wave that Verlaine refers to is defined not simply in chronological terms, but also in terms of influence and artistic conceit. Though Talking Heads did not reflect the regressive poppiness or punk/metal of other bands in CBGBs' second wave, they always seemed at odds with the ongoing underground scene and its tradition, as defined by the Velvets and the Stooges. If the Heads' minimalism harkened back to the Velvets, head Head David Byrne gave no indication that he felt he was drawing on the Velvets' strand of American rock & roll.

Nor did his personal history suggest any link to the Velvets. There had been a brief pre-college flirtation with what one critic described as 'some sort of conceptual lounge act', a folk duo by the name of Bazadi, playing ukelele and violin, with a repertoire composed primarily of crooners' tunes, before Byrne made his first stab at rock & roll. The Artistics were composed from fellow students at the Rhode Island School of Art and Design, where Byrne had enrolled as a student in the fall of 1972. Formed in October 1973, the Artistics did not share the Heads' later minimalist pretensions.

Chris Frantz: The Artistics sounded like Television, only crazier and not as Messianic. We used to play to big crowds, but people would stand fifty feet away to hear us, since we had all the amplifiers we could get turned up as loud as they would go ... Our biggest gig was playing at the St Valentine's Day Masquerade Ball for the rest of the students. I think we were paid $200. That was where we first performed 'Psycho Killer'.

Co-founded by Byrne and drummer Chris Frantz – whom Byrne knew shared similar tastes in music – the Artistics were a two-guitar, one-sax band. Inevitably, as a collegiate band, they were largely restricted to playing covers. Byrne's choice of material betrayed an early interest in soul music but only a marginal connection with American underground rock.

David Byrne: The kind of community we were playing for, the people were more interested in your choice of material than in your execution ... We didn't look that much different than we do now. Maybe more concerned with a visual thing but nothing really striking. We didn't wear platform boots or make-up ... There were some Smokey Robinson songs we did. Things like 'Tears of a Clown' and 'My Baby Must be a Magician'. I think we did '(The Love I Saw in You was) Just a Mirage' as well, now I recall. Then there were '1–2–3 Red Light', and this old 1910 Fruitgum Company song which we carried through to playing at early Talking Heads dates.

Were it not for the fact that Byrne was already turning his hand to song composition, the Artistics would barely merit attention. In fact the Artistics worked up at least three Byrne originals that survived the transition to Talking Heads: 'Warning Sign', 'I'm Not in Love' and, most notably, 'Psycho Killer', a song that allegedly resulted from Byrne's attempt to write an Alice Cooper song. The Artistics' versions of these originals, though, were rather different from later incarnations, Byrne describing them as 'real frantic and cacophonous'.

The Artistics disbanded in the spring of 1974 as final exams approached. Byrne had decided to abandon RISAD and head for New York. Frantz and his girlfriend, Tina Weymouth, wanted to make the same journey, but chose to sit their exams. There remains considerable doubt as to Byrne's exact intentions in first coming to New York. If he had some particular artistic notion in mind, he may not have yet decided it should be rock-oriented.

David Byrne: We had an art orientation so that focuses towards New York. That's the place you're going to end up no matter what – at least at some point . . . We didn't know if there was any kind of scene.

Certainly Byrne's early months in New York were not spent making music or putting a band together. Perhaps he was waiting for his musical cohort Frantz to arrive from RISAD. Meanwhile he and Jamie Daglish, a conceptual artist, were jointly renovating a loft on Bond Street, just off New York's Bowery, barely a couple of blocks from CBGBs. It was inevitable that Byrne would soon investigate the seedy venue across the road, with its good jukebox and cheap bar. Byrne spent much of the summer hanging out at the club, assessing the small scene centering upon it.

Arriving in Manhattan in September, Frantz and Weymouth soon arranged to share a loft with Byrne while they attempted to secure gainful employment. With Frantz and Byrne's prior musical association and Weymouth's own musical background – mainly folk-oriented with a smattering of Brit-Rock – logic might suggest that they intended to form a three-piece rock band all along.

In fact Byrne seems to have been uncertain of a direction, and it was the CBGBs bands and Frantz's arrival in New York that revived previous convictions. Having resolved to make rock music the medium he would utilize, at least for now, Byrne needed to conceive of a sound considerably less orthodox than the Artistics.

Why Frantz and his girlfriend should want to become involved with Byrne's scheme-dreams remains a mystery. Yet it seems Frantz intended to join up with Byrne all along. According to Mary Clarke of Boston combo the Motels, Frantz told her that summer that he was going to New York to join a band with Byrne. Within weeks of Frantz and Weymouth arriving in New York, Byrne had moved permanently into their Christie Street loft, using Daglish's loft for his bathing requirements.

But Weymouth's position in the new set-up was considerably less assured than her boyfriend's, particularly when Byrne and Frantz began their search for the third component in their trio – a bassist. Evidently they already conceived of a far more stripped-down affair than the Artistics.

David Byrne: Every time I'd seen bands, I'd always thought there was too much noise. There always seemed to be too many instruments and they got mumbled so you didn't get a clear or clean-type sound. One way I thought of to get around this was to have only three instruments.

Byrne and Frantz realized that, like the early Television, finding a musician who shared their aesthetics was more important than an exponent of supreme technical proficiency, and Weymouth was finally allowed to become the Heads' female Hell. As they got down to serious rehearsals in the winter of 1974–5, the trio was duly christened by their friend Wayne Zieve, author of the lyrics to 'For Artists Only'. Talking Heads worked long and hard to ensure that they would have their own unique niche on the New York scene.

Chris Frantz: We figured we'd better have a pretty good angle, because there were so many people out there already who were a lot better at it than we were.

David Byrne: When we began, we felt there was this big hole. Very little that we were hearing appealed directly to us. We felt 'Nobody's doing anything for our crowd – we'll have to do it ourselves.'

If Television, Patti Smith and Blondie developed their sound by performing regularly over a period of many months, the sound of Talking Heads, like the Ramones, was largely in place by the time they debuted at CBGBs, in May 1975. Byrne had not squandered his time spent observing the other Bowery bands. Talking Heads were like no other CBGBs band.

Chris Frantz: A lot of people either laughed at us or shook their heads and said, 'What is this – a political band? an ecology band?' We had a song called 'The Girls Want to be With the Girls', so people thought maybe we were into sexual politics, or something. In fact, we were just trying to be . . . interesting.

Talking Heads' debut at CBGBs was astutely timed. The club's media profile had been steadily increasing since the Smith/Television residency that spring. The sense of a new scene was slowly permeating outward. Within two months of their CBGBs debut, Talking Heads were sharing the opening night bill at CBGBs' summer festival of unsigned bands, with the Ramones, Blondie and Tuff Darts. They were so well received that Kristal also booked them to play the final night of the festival, 1 August 1975, again with Blondie and the Ramones.

Talking Heads soon became the Ramones' regular co-headliners at CBGBs. If this pairing seemed incongruous – the Ramones' black-leather buzzsaw brevity the very antithesis of Talking Heads' ascetic appearance and funky quirkiness – they believed that they were mining similar veins.

Tommy Ramone: Hilly brought them in to open for us. Right away we saw that it worked. After that, whenever we had to find someone to play with us, we'd use the Talking Heads. Even though the Ramones played hard and raunchy, conceptually there were a lot of similarities: the minimalism. Even though their music was totally different, the concept was similar. We were so unique at the time that they were the first ones who played with us who actually fit.

The Ramones/Talking Heads bills inspired New York critics to write of a new minimalism in the city, though they were the only two CBGBs bands who can be said to have advocated such an approach. If there were conceptual similarities, this was also reflected in Byrne's terse lyrics, which were as pared down as the tunes. Talking Heads offered a marked contrast to Television and Patti Smith – the other side of the art-rock coin – both of whom were moving away from the three-minute over-and-out approach.

While Byrne may have chosen to adopt a Ramones-esque minimalism, slowed-down and funked-up, the Heads' image was more closely modelled on the 1975 Television. After Hell's departure, Television had quickly abandoned the personally monographed ripped-shirts but maintained a deliberately anti-glam 'we dress as we are' look. This appealed to Talking Heads, also looking beyond the remnants of the glam scene still inhabiting the backroom at Max's.

Chris Frantz: For a long time, CBGBs was the only place in the nation where we could play – when we started, we were a very way-out band. The New York Dolls had had their day, but kids in New York – or at least the hip kids – seemed to think that you had to wear platform shoes and tight leather pants and wild clothes and you had to lead a decadent lifestyle. We came on to the stage looking like a bunch of Jesuits . . . and we didn't do those rock & roll moves, we just played songs. It was deliberate.

In common with the Ramones, Talking Heads' minimalist approach was largely determined by circumstance – there were only three of them, they lacked a strong lead instrument and they were unlikely to find someone else prepared to fully embrace their aesthetic. Byrne was only a fair-to-middling rhythm guitar player, and as a lead guitarist he was a non-starter. His lack of ability in this area had resulted in his failure to be recruited into a New England band after the Artistics' disbandment (before he left Rhode Island for New York he had auditioned unsuccessfully for a glam-rock outfit that ex-members of local favourites the Motels were putting together). The heads-down/ foot-to-the-floor approach had already been taken by the Ramones, and Byrne was unlikely to be convincing as a manic rock & roller. Though he would later accept that there had been an air of deliberation in devising their sound, Byrne certainly took into account the very stringent parameters the Heads had to work within.

If Byrne was using the Heads as a vehicle for his own conceptual ideas, it would be foolish to underestimate the importance of Frantz and Weymouth. While critics expended much adjective-laden prose upon the 'radical' notion of a woman bass player, the actual quality of the Weymouth/Frantz rhythm section passed largely unobserved.

Lenny Kaye: Chris and Tina, the rhythm section, were really central. Talking Heads were a dance band. When I first used to go visit them at their loft they used to talk about Bohannon all the time. It was a great reference, especially since 'dance music' had a totally different connotation for avant-garde rockers in those days. That element of blackness shouldn't be underestimated. And it stemmed from the rhythm section.

So did the Heads ever consider themselves to be 'only rock & roll', or did they always conceive of themselves as a dance band working within a rock & roll framework? The bond between the other major CBGBs bands and the rock & roll form is self-evident – even for early Blondie. But this is not the case with Talking Heads. Here was a band who, from its earliest days, seemed to be drawing largely on black rhythms for the bedrock of their sound, while Byrne's notions of pop, rock and soul seemed mutually inclusive.

There remains the nagging suspicion that the Heads' association with a rock & roll club (indeed with rock & roll itself) was a convenience that, with the commercial success of their first vinyl flirtation with soul music, Byrne could discard. This would not make him greatly different in conceit from Richard Hell, Patti Smith or Malcolm McLaren, who all believed in rock & roll as a means to an end, even if each of these figures maintained an underlying belief in the power of the genre itself.

David Byrne: I don't think rock & roll is as direct as more specific kinds of protest. I don't think of it as being able to confront things issue by issue. On the other hand, it can imply that there is another frame of mind than the one that is generally accepted – that you don't have to think of things in the way people have told you to think of them.

To give Byrne the benefit of the doubt, the freedom that rock & roll offered the aspiring artist had an instant appeal to all the CBGBs art-rockers, even if it generally brought its own iconography with it. And the very austerity of the Heads' look and sound was, in one sense, an attempt to subvert the obvious divide between audience and artist that had been widening since the Beatles first hit American tarmac.

David Byrne: In most rock & roll there's the emphasis on the front person, or group of front people, on the stage living out this mythical archetype. They are given this role that they become possessed by and they live out that role in front of the audience . . . The basic consciousness [of our music] is quite different . . . We decided we wouldn't do guitar solos or drum solos, and we wouldn't make any grand gestures. We'd try and be very to the point. We were throwing out what we didn't want to be. It wasn't until we'd been performing for quite a while that we started to realize what we were.

Though a Heads song might develop in performance, Byrne was not looking to extend their length. As with the Ramones, there was an inevitable rigidity to a Talking Heads set. The amount of consideration that Talking Heads brought to their performance art, aligned to their limited musicianship, meant that the songs were never going to be a means of extemporization. The air of deliberation exuded by the Heads certainly seemed out of accord with CBGBs contemporaries' performance art.

Alan Vega: I never liked Talking Heads, I saw them one night, I mean they were the talk of the town, playing CBs. I went in to check 'em out and I went, 'I don't believe this! ... It was all studied, the songs were all there, all his moves were all plotted, he wasn't performing up there he was just going through the motions ... He didn't make any twitchy gestures without something in his head saying, 'Make a twitchy gesture now,' it wasn't for real. That always turned me off.

All the factors which ensured that the Ramones developed into a recordable state more rapidly than their fellow first wavers also served to benefit the Heads: the simplicity of arranging just rhythm guitar, bass and drums; the constant band line-up; the brevity of the songs; the rigid sets; and the opportunity to ride on the back of CBGBs' already established media profile. The *Village Voice* headline accompanying James Wolcott's review of the July 1975 festival of unsigned bands referred to a 'Conservative Impulse of the New Rock Underground'. The bulk of the review was taken up with praising Television and Talking Heads:

Repeated viewings (precise word) reveal Talking Heads to be one of the most intriguingly off-the-wall bands in New York ... They present a clean, flat image, devoid of fine shading and colour. They are consciously antimythic in stance.

The Heads had been up and gigging less than two months.

David Byrne: Writers seemed to like us very quickly – other important people liked us the first time, too. But the one problem we ran into since then was that we were dubbed as being intellectual ... We don't think we're smarties, we just don't particularly enjoy being stupid either. We don't get into ball scratching.

Inevitably, the For Artists Only label had a downside. The Heads were automatically assigned to the art-rock camp in the division that had begun to form between the 'fuck art, let's rock!' fans and the art-rock devotees. In fact the Heads had little in common with either camp. According to Craig Leon, the reason that Talking Heads are absent from the *Live at CBGBs* album was nothing to do with impending contracts – they simply 'didn't want to be part of the scene. They didn't want to be lumped in with all these other bands like Blondie.'

David Byrne: The term art-rock annoys me when it implies that this is a game for us, that we don't have sincere feelings about our music or we're just flirting with rock & roll.

Despite such protestations, the early labels attached to Talking Heads were largely warranted. There was a self-consciousness about everything that the Heads did which made them hard to stomach in such an unconscious medium as rock & roll, not just for those who preferred the more orthodox rock & roll bands that frequented CBGBs, but even more audacious art-rockers.

If the other members of the art-rock stable were known to 'rock out' – Television still reserved 'Friction', 'Psychotic Reaction' and 'I Don't Care' for non-believers, and Patti Smith's 'My Generation' finale could be as cardiac-arresting an experience as any Ramones set – Talking Heads seemed quite unable to 'let rip'. Inevitably the rock & roll crowd's disdain was suffused with a smattering of envy at the way the Heads had endeared themselves to the critics so rapidly. The Heads/ Ramones bills seemed a direct violation of a rock & roll aesthetic many CBGBs regulars held dear.

Tina Weymouth: In a way we were always outside the CBGBs scene. They were very snotty to us there because we didn't dress like the New York Dolls. The first time we played there was the second time we'd ever performed and we started getting publicity very quickly. The other bands didn't like it and they were very unfriendly . . . Our crowd was very different to the Ramones' and Television's. Very different to the girls who wear stilettoes.

Hilly Kristal loved them from the start, so their position at the club was always secure. Yet, with the early Heads, there operated a law of diminishing returns. At the 1975 summer festival, bands tended to be restricted to 20-minute sets. A standard five-song Heads set – which generally included the best of their early material: 'Psycho Killer', 'The Girls Want to be With the Girls' and 'For Artists Only' – could be a startling experience. The powerful rhythmic undercurrent and Byrne's disconcerting mannerisms were disarming in the extreme. Yet the very sameness of the Heads' early sound and the sheer austerity of their look were bound to wear on those who sat through them repeatedly, waiting for the amphetamine rush of the Ramones.

The Heads, like Blondie at this stage, were not a band best appreciated live. They were always likely to be an intriguing recording outfit, if their sound could be simultaneously harnessed and embellished. Yet a first attempt at appropriate embellishment, their recording of 'Love Goes to Building on Fire' as a single in the fall of 1976, was done against the better judgement of David Byrne. Though Byrne went along with producer Tony Bongiovi – adding strings and birds twittering – he knew what extra element of sound he wanted all along, and birds 'n' strings wasn't it.

Of all the bands to emerge from CBGBs, Talking Heads' 'rise' was the most considered, the most deliberated upon, the most self-conscious. Perhaps they were indeed the logical culmination of this most self-conscious of revolutions in rock & roll.

David Byrne: [We], along with a lot of other new groups, are very self-aware: about where they perform, what they look like, how they appear to the press . . . very aware of every move they make and what the supposed ramifications will be. It could seem very contrived but I think that's the way people are now. The days of naive, primitive rock bands are gone . . . The punk thing was a very self-aware reaction and in that sense it's very historically oriented. Part of its meaning and importance comes out of that historical perspective. Without that I don't think it would have seemed that important at all.

As the one figure willing to embrace both a Velvets version of rock and an Iggy-inspired form of rock performance, Peter Laughner was the one most caught up in the conflicts resulting from Rocket from the Tombs' demise. Attempting to preserve his friendship with all parties, he recorded a series of four-track demos with Craig Bell.* Shortly afterward Bell moved to Connecticut. Laughner also encouraged Gene O'Connor to form the Detroit/Dolls band he had long wanted. O'Connor quickly joined Stiv Bators and Johnny Madansky to form Frankenstein.

Stiv Bators: The Pere Ubu crowd hated us because we were just fuck art, let's rock and roll! And that's what really split us. But Laughner, he understood us, he liked us, and he understood the art crowd 'cause he was a writer. He was right in between. He tried bringing New York to Cleveland so bad, but Cleveland couldn't understand it . . . I really believed in Peter. Of all the people in Cleveland, Peter was the most hip. Peter made me believe in myself. I thought what I was doing was too far-fetched, and Peter said, 'No – you're right, do it, that's what it's all about'. . . He's what formed Dead Boys and he's what got me and Cheetah together, and his spirit was there, but he was too arty. That was his problem, he was caught right in between.

It wasn't just the Ubu enclave who felt that Frankenstein were a charlatan outfit. They were subjected to even more disdain from the

---

* These included Bell's own 'Muckraker', the co-written 'Rejection', Laughner's 'Life Stinks', which he prefaces with a hilarious Beefheart-esque monologue, and 'Amphetamine'.

Eels and Mirrors, for whom audacity was an essential ingredient in any rock & roll construct.

John Morton: We thought [Frankenstein] were pretty stupid and wrong . . . they pretty much ripped us off and they ripped off Rocket from the Tombs, we saw them and couldn't believe what they were doing, giving themselves names and everything . . . Rocket from the Tombs we respected [even if] we didn't like their music.

Frankenstein were evidence of O'Connor and Bators' willingness to ride a trend's tailgate. Forming a glam-rock band was an entirely regressive step. After all, this was the fall of 1975. Frankenstein still proved quite popular during their brief time in Cleveland, playing covers of Kiss, Mott the Hoople and Alice Cooper songs and a smattering of O'Connor's songs from the Rockets. Their first gig, just three months after the Rockets' collapse, was a Halloween show at the Piccadilly Penthouse. Their next performance, on New Year's Eve, was the one and only occasion that they played the Viking or shared a bill with the Rockets' other splinter group, Pere Ubu. Shortly afterward the Viking burnt down in mysterious circumstances and, deprived of their primary performance arena, Frankenstein decided to concentrate on creating a new image, before heading for New York, once again the magnet for all aspiring rock & roll bands, in the summer of 1976.

If Frankenstein were hardly stretching back the boundaries of rock & roll sound, Pere Ubu were an entirely different matter. Originally conceived as a one-off studio conglomeration, Ubu persevere as a productive outfit to this day. Pere Ubu's name, which may have been suggested by Thomas' teacher-father, was a reference to the grotesque central figure in Alfred Jarry's play *Ubu Roi*. The name had an obvious appeal to David Thomas.

Charlotte Pressler: Thomas was intensely into Jarry and the character of Pa Ubu, that's all the deepest, most unacceptable, most bestial and most banal impulses in the human being rolled into one, and it was that character that he wanted to impersonate.

Thomas's choice of name and his insistence on fronting the band made it clear that Ubu was no Rocket from the Tombs Mk 2. Thomas was more interested in drawing upon original musicians like those who had made up 'art projects' like Hy Maya. But he required the input of Laughner to bring the necessary strands together.

David Thomas: I was fed up and I just had this vague notion that I'd just do studio work and just record things and not try to do a band any more 'cause bands were too hideously painful ... I remember telling Peter that I was going to do this project and he said, 'Oh I'd like to do it,' and I said OK and I remember saying that I'd like to get Tim involved in some way, he'd been the sound man [for the Rockets], he didn't know how to play anything. I figured that he'd be an interesting musician 'cause he had interesting ideas ... At that point it was me, Peter and Tim. Scott lived at the Plaza and Peter had played with him; and Tom Herman was sort of a renegade there and it was known he played guitar and was an interesting person. Everybody knew Allen [Ravenstine] who owned the place and knew that he had a bunch of boxes.

Co-founder of Ubu Tim Wright remembers the band's formation slightly differently, implying that his participation was required to act as a mediator between Thomas and Laughner.

Tim Wright: An artist and myself had a loft in downtown Cleveland. It was gigantic and really cheap. So we had the Electric Eels and Rocket from the Tombs rehearsing there. When that band broke up everybody hated everybody. Since I was being a really nice guy and giving people a place to rehearse, David Thomas came to my house and said, 'What am I going to do. I have to have a band. Nobody will play with me.' [I said,] 'Peter's my best friend, you're a good friend of mine. Maybe we can do something. I know these other musicians. I know Tom Herman, who I've been trying to help get some of his tapes produced' ... Peter said, 'I'm not gonna work with David Thomas unless you're gonna be with me.'

Laughner remained the central link in the chain. He had already played with Krauss and Herman and it was he who first suggested asking the Plaza's landlord, Allen Ravenstine.

Allen Ravenstine: One of these guys in the Art Department was working as a janitor in this building called the Plaza, and he was hot that I should invest some money and buy this thing and it would serve as an occupation and we would have this 'Art Community' ... About the same time I started working on a symphonic piece that was called 'Terminal Drive' and it was about twenty minutes long and I did it on this four-track TEAC. I finished this 'Terminal Drive' piece and somehow Peter heard it, and he really liked it. He came over one night just to talk about it. Right around then Krauss was telling me about this band that was going to happen and the idea behind the band was that if you took a group of people of similar philosophy ... that even if they didn't know how to make music, they'd make something interesting. Then one day ... this big guy comes walking through the corridors, David Thomas. I said something to him and he had heard 'Terminal Drive', and I was in if I wanted to be.

The original intention was to record the Rockets' two most powerful songs – 'Thirty Seconds Over Tokyo' and 'Final Solution'. But Tim Wright arrived at Ubu's first rehearsal in September 1975, on West 6th Street, with the riff for what would become 'Heart of Darkness'. Rehearsal-time was largely spent working on 'Thirty Seconds Over Tokyo' and an as yet instrumental 'Heart of Darkness' (a recording of this first Pere Ubu rehearsal exists, and serves to confirm that Laughner was the dominant musical force in the early band, giving the bulk of audible instructions at the session).

Tim Wright: I had taught myself guitar in this interim period. But I couldn't decide whether I should play guitar or bass guitar so I bought myself a Dan-Electro six-string bass. I wrote one song [on it] which was the bass riff for 'Heart of Darkness'. We [also] had this seminal version of 'Thirty Seconds Over Tokyo' but it needed to be jazzed up a bit.

Though 'Final Solution' and 'Life Stinks' were also rehearsed by Ubu – a version of 'Life Stinks' was apparently attempted during Ubu's first studio session at the end of September – it was 'Heart of Darkness' and 'Thirty Seconds Over Tokyo' that were released as Pere Ubu's first single. Taken together they may well be the most astonishing debut single of the Seventies. Released on Thomas's own Hearthan label in December 1975, with sleeve-notes by Laughner – 'I was wired, all of a sudden, on some organic frequency that seemed to take hold of my motor responses and transmit ... use your muscles, your brain, your tissues NOW! MAKE A MOVE' – Ubu had made a quantum leap beyond the Tombs. The combination of the twin-guitar attack of

Laughner and Wright/Herman (who alternated on bass) and the aural soundtracks coming from Ravenstine's synthesizer created something totally original, while Thomas's delivery in the studio retained his in-concert growl but was now a wholly congruous part of this ominous miasma of sound.

Ubu had begun their 'dark period'. Though Thomas would later refute the notion that they were ever overly concerned with document-ing the darker side of life, a band whose central figures were Laughner and Thomas's *alter ego* 'Crocus Behemoth' could not fail to be bleak. As one Clevelander put it to me, 'Thomas is always influenced by some other personality. When he stops being influenced by the personality who has the dark period, he stops ever having had one.' According to Wright, it was the very darkness of the music that convinced Allen Ravenstine, synthesizer player and landlord at the Ubu's homestead, that he did not wish to continue his membership of the ensemble.

In fact, Ravenstine simply could not conceive of how he might do what he desired soundwise in a live environment.

Allen Ravenstine: I remember everyone being very excited and wanting to continue. All I could think was I had no idea how I was gonna take what I was doing and turn it into something that could be done live. I had never had any intention of being involved in it, I was interested in something that was more arty, I was thinking more in terms of symphonic stuff . . . Multi-layered stuff, and much more abstract stuff . . . If you heard 'Terminal Drive' you would know that it's much more dark than anything the band ever did, it's extremely dark . . . The only thing I remember, the first thing is: I am a primitive and I only know how to do what I did.

Thomas seemed perfectly willing to discuss Ubu's bleak aesthetic when interviewed for Cleveland's local paper the *Plain Dealer*, in December 1975, timed to coincide with the release of Ubu's first Hearthan single. He responded to a specific query about whether Ubu's music could be considered negative in these terms:

David Thomas: Negative? We see things as they really are. We're into reality music. People want to live in fantasy worlds. They think they're stars. They take dancing lessons Monday, foreign language on Tuesday and macramé on Wednesday and think they're artists. Reality is a scary thing ... What matters is that the listener in some way experiences what was in our minds. The emotion in 'Heart of Darkness' is desperation. We want to make the listener feel as if he is the narrator.

Yet Ubu, without even playing a single show, were undergoing a change. The original idea of Ubu – as a one-off 'art project' – had been abandoned, and Ubu was now seen as a vehicle for unspecified projects by Laughner, Thomas and Wright. Other members were considered ancillary to main operations. Ravenstine was uninterested in joining a full-time band, while Tom Herman, probably unhappy with his subordinate role, temporarily allowed himself to be replaced by John Horowitz.

Tim Wright: 'Thirty Seconds Over Tokyo' ... was fun, so Peter and Crocus and I wanted to continue doing it. We began trying people out, and we got some jobs because of the record.

Already it was apparent that Ubu corporate policy was only ever finalized after a tortuous process of debate. The central figures in Ubu were all highly literate, if clearly disenfranchised from their own class. These were very much third-generation rockers – entirely self-conscious in their quest for new directions.

Charlotte Pressler: We would sit around and elaborate the aesthetic. We'd just sit there and go, 'What's cool? How do you figure out how to live in the world?' This endless discussion about how can you possibly take an attitude to things that will let you live. We would go on for hours. It did have something to do with the Dexamyl.

The first Ubu gig, at the Viking Saloon on New Year's Eve 1975–6, was shared with black-sheep sister-group Frankenstein. Ubu were then offered a gig at the Agora, just thirteen days later, to help promote the Hearthan single. A friend of Wright's, Viet Vet David Taylor, was on synthesizer, while Herman had wisely returned to the fold. By this stage Ubu had augmented their repertoire with the lurching syncopation of 'Cloud 149' and the ironically titled 'Sentimental Journey', a song as intense and overwhelming as the two sides of their single – and as long! Combined with the two single cuts – plus 'Final Solution', 'Life Stinks' and a version of the Seeds' 'Pushin' Too Hard' – Ubu's early set still only stretched beyond the half-hour mark thanks to an extended, swirling synthesizer introduction to 'Heart of Darkness'. The Agora show convinced Ubu-ites that they were heading in the right direction.

On 26 February 1976 they recorded their second single, this time committing 'Final Solution' to vinyl. 'Life Stinks' was again passed over, this time in favour of the quirky 'Cloud 149'. 'Final Solution', thanks to its inclusion on the first Max's compilation album, remains the best-known of Ubu's early singles. The rumbling duosonics from Laughner and Wright aligned to the 'whirring chopper' of Taylor's synth made it a firm favourite in New York and Cleveland.

It seemed only a matter of time before Ubu would come to the notice of a larger audience, particularly when they were invited, on the strength of their second single, to play at Max's Easter festival of unsigned bands. The gig in New York, though, proved somewhat traumatic. For Laughner it had a real importance because of his brief tenure with Television, his habitual visits to New York and more than nodding acquaintance with many of the people on the New York scene. Now they could see and hear what his bravado about this Cleveland band was all about. Unfortunately an excited Laughner was usually an out-of-control Laughner.

Tony Maimone: He and David were butting heads and I remember when Pere Ubu went out to New York the first time Peter was so excited and out of his mind about everything, he was cutting coke up on the bar and just being outrageous and I think it was that incident that was used against him.

Save for Laughner and Wright, the residue Ubu-ites were not unduly impressed with the idea of taking their grotesque visions to the heart of America's underground scene.

Tim Wright: The rest of Ubu hated [playing New York]. They never wanted to play New York. They just wanted to be a Cleveland band. It was enough of an insult to do this weird music and then to have to give days off our jobs to travel to New York to play . . . Peter and I wanted to, but no one else did. Peter and I decided, 'Fuck these jerks, let's break up the band.'

Though Laughner and Wright did not disassemble Ubu, they were close to breaking point. Ubu's internal contradictions, unlike those of the Rockets, were not about musical direction but about personalities. New songs like 'Street Waves', 'Over My Head' and 'Can't Believe It' were all a continuation of the direction evident on the first two Hearthan singles, and Thomas, talking to *New York Rocker* during that first New York visit, continued to paint Ubu in black:

David Thomas: The whole way we do things is that we try to lay textures together. The essential breakdown of the band musically is we have a strong emphasis on rhythm, just a beat, and we use that beat to drive the psychedelic overtones. Hopefully, there's going to be a second psychedelic era ... People misunderstand what it's all about, because psychedelic music wasn't drug music ... It makes you experience different things and that's essentially where we're at. I wanted the name Pere Ubu 'cause ... it would be an added texture of absolute grotesqueness – a shadow behind everything that's going on, a darkness over everything.

Though the response to Ubu in New York was so favourable that Max's invited them back to headline their own show, they were heading in the same direction as the Rockets. Oblivion. Four weeks after their Max's debut, Ubu Mk 2 played their final gig at the Mistake, located in the basement of the Agora. Though they did not know it was their final gig, the 70-minute Ubu set that night showed how far they had come. The opener, as always, was Ubu's first composition, 'Heart of Darkness', while the inclusion of 'Pushin' Too Hard' and 'I Wanna be Your Dog' tipped a hat to their roots, and the final song, 'Heroin', sung by Laughner, cannot but take on a certain poignancy in the light of his subsequent stark decline.

If, as Wright asserts, a major problem in the band was a lack of commitment from certain quarters, Thomas attributes the disintegration of Ubu Mk 2 largely to Laughner's increasing drug habit. From an early age, Laughner had displayed a proclivity for excess that was legendary in Cleveland (while in high school he had written songs like 'I'm So Fucked Up' and 'The Alcohol of Fame'). His drinking habits were even more notorious than his pill-popping and it was starting to affect his playing. Laughner himself would write, at the very end of his association with Ubu, his infamous review of Lou Reed's *Coney Island Baby* album for *Creem* magazine:

This album made me so morose and depressed ... that I got drunk for three days ... I had a horrible physical fight with my wife over a stupid bottle of 10mg Valiums ... I called up the editor of this magazine (on my bill) and did virtually nothing but cough up phlegm in an alcoholic stupor for three hours ... I came on to my sister-in-law ... I cadged drinks off anyone who would come near me or let me into their apartments. I ended up the whole debacle passing out stone cold after puking and pissing myself at a band rehearsal, [and] had to be kicked awake by my lead singer.

Certainly Thomas and − Thomas insists − the entire band, including Tim Wright, were at the end of their tethers with regard to their friend.

David Thomas: There was a certain amount of unhappiness at that time with Peter. Everybody recognized it was impossible to play with him. Certainly of the decision-making people in the band there wasn't any question ... I broke the band up because Peter was doing too many drugs and I didn't want to play with Peter any more because it was becoming not worth it. That set the pattern in Pere Ubu which is whenever we want to change, the band breaks up. The plan at the time was that we were gonna break up and reform. I remember Tim and I planning this. Also ... part of the [situation] was that Allen was ready to play, and he made it known that he wanted to play, so the break-up of the band was also clearing the way for Allen to join up. This is the one thing that I feel bad about to this day − having to let Dave Taylor go − 'cause Dave Taylor was doing great stuff, was a great player, but Allen had 'dibs' − first call on it. So the band broke up.

Certainly Thomas had an ally in Tom Herman, who was resentful of what he saw as Laughner's domination of the band, was tired of his craziness, and wanted the lead-guitar slot in Ubu.

Allen Ravenstine: Tom had his own personality that he wanted to cut loose and Peter was extremely imposing and Tom was under his heel, and he hated it.

But it would be naive to think that it was only Herman who resented Laughner's domination of Ubu's musical direction. Laughner was the one figure in the band that even Thomas could not simply override.

Allen Ravenstine: For the length of time that Peter was involved, David was on his toes, because Peter was a force to be reckoned with.

The original Heartbreakers re-create the St Valentine's Day Massacre.
Iggy Pop and Richard Hell at CBGBs, circa 1976.

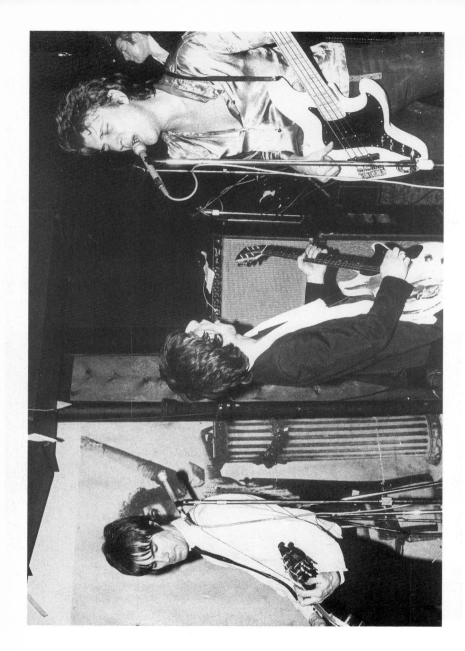

Hell leads the
Heartbreakers through
another rip-roaring
CBGBs set, 17 March
1976.

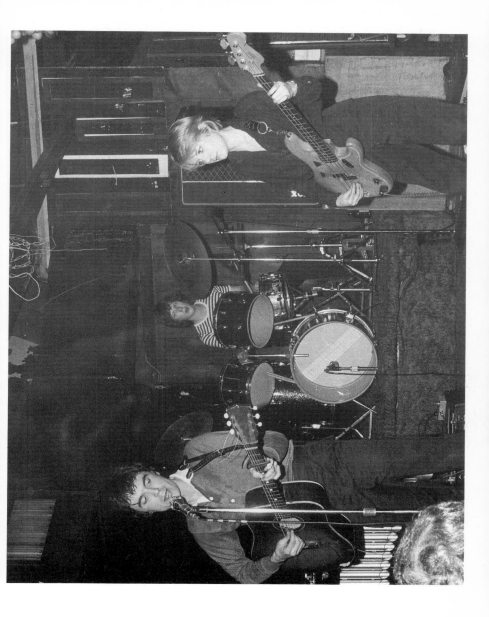

A three-piece Talking
Heads at CBGBs, circa
1976.

Pere Ubu Mk 2 (*left to right*): Crocus Behemoth, Peter Laughner (*top*), Tim Wright (*bottom*), Dave Taylor, Tom Herman, Scott Krauss.

The Dead Boys, complete with Nazi insignia, long hair and flairs, make their CBGBs debut, 26 July 1976.

The Dead Boys, cropped hair and straight jeans, minus iron crosses, at CBGBs, circa 1977.

The Dictators resume
gigging at Zeppz,
14 April 1976.

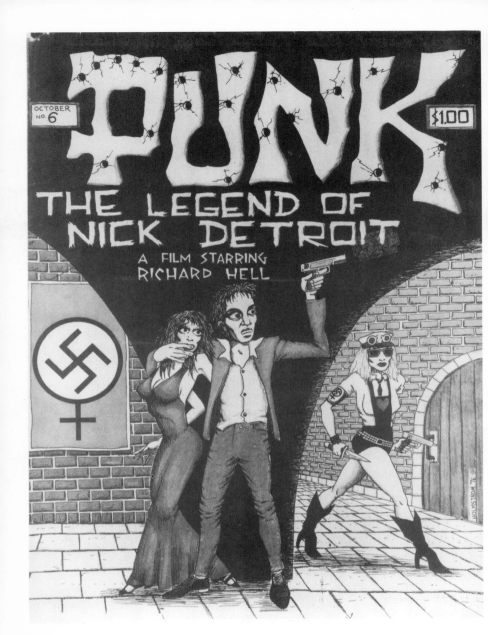

Front cover to *Punk* magazine's first comic-strip special.

Laughner's position in the band was based on his musical abilities – he was not an obvious exponent of powerplay politics – but his ability to push things to the limit made him a difficult combatant when it came to the lengthy Ubu decision-making process.

Allen Ravenstine: In any given situation the guy that's known to be the biggest asshole will win. Because everyone else will just go so far and no further. David was always willing to go to the end, but Peter would go further and David was still trying to figure out how far further was.

Laughner's departure was not the end of Ubu's reformulation. Tim Wright cannot have been happy with the idea of restoring Ravenstine to the band. As Thomas admits, Taylor was playing superbly in the band, and he had been recruited at Wright's behest. Also, it was evident that Wright and Ravenstine did not see eye to eye about Ubu's future direction.

Allen Ravenstine: I had prejudices against certain sounds. I didn't like anything that went 'Wheep!' or 'Whoo!' or any of that goofy stuff, and Dave did a lot of that, and I didn't like it . . . I wasn't being open minded about the sounds that a synthesizer could make, but I had my preferences and I liked big, heavy, dark things out of it.

This should have sat well with Wright, whose own bass-playing could be described as 'big, heavy, dark', but quite possibly Wright did not see such dissonance as the synthesizer-player's function.

Max's had provided the finance for Ubu to record a song for a second Max's compilation album.* Wright's suggested replacement for Laughner was guitarist Alan Greenblatt, who had been playing in a local r&b band for some time. The song Ubu recorded in June was a primitive version of what would become the title track of their remarkable debut album, *The Modern Dance.*

Tim Wright: I tried to do one more recording after [Peter left]. The library across the street from me was closed down and made into a modern dance studio. At the same time Peter was starting to lose his mind. So I

---

* Interestingly, the contract states that Tim Wright and David Thomas were the legal entity Pere Ubu.

was worried about the library. I was worried about Peter. That's how the lyrics came about. It was about him but it was also about the library. Musically [I wrote it with] Tom Herman. Al Greenblatt and I were involved in a big drug bust once so we spent time in jail together but I knew he was a slick guitar player. It was like my last attempt to save the situation.

Greenblatt was unwilling to join Ubu permanently, and when it became apparent to Wright that Thomas had no intention of finding another substitute for Laughner, he decided that the band he had co-founded with Laughner and Thomas now existed only in name.

David Thomas: There was this vague period during which we were to do the next single for the Max's album and we tried to get this hot-shot blues guitarist Alan Greenblatt to play with us which he did and was wonderful but he didn't want to join the band. The falling out with Tim was pretty simple. I didn't want there to be two guitars which meant that he was going to be the bass player. He didn't want to be the bass player. There was this big discussion about whether we should have two guitarists and . . . once it had been determined that we were going to have one guitar and the bass was going to be more of a traditional bass – quote, unquote – at this point Tim became alienated.

Though Ubu would resurrect itself in a new guise, Tony Maimone replacing Wright on bass, recording as the A-side to their third single one of the highlights of the early Ubu live set, 'Street Waves' (credited rather impertinently to the Mk 3 line-up), it would be a very different outfit from the one which had gigged so impressively between 31 December 1975 and 5 May 1976.

Aside from the loss of Taylor, Laughner and Wright, providers of principal tenets of Ubu's early sound, and the loss of two thirds of those responsible for Ubu's ideological impetus, they also gave up their two-guitar sound. From now on Ubu's main drive would come from Ravenstine and Thomas.

Tony Maimone: I think for a very long time Allen and David felt that they were the artists in the band and we were the Rockers. Once David said, this side of the stage is the artist's side of the stage and this side of the stage is the Panzer tank side of the stage.

As Thomas was to observe in the notes to *Terminal Tower*, by the time Ubu came to record *The Modern Dance* at the end of 1977 'Pere Ubu's so-called dark period was on the wane.' Tim Wright, on his return to the States from a lengthy sojourn in South America, would attempt to continue the fractured music he had envisioned with Ubu, but not in Cleveland. DNA would be one of the bands at the forefront of New York's late-Seventies 'no wave' movement. Wright had told *Plain Dealer* in December 1975: 'We're going beyond commercialism. We're going beyond music.' He remained committed to that ideal.

It is important to recall that a substantial number of bands played at CBGBs and Max's in the central years of the Seventies and that the vast majority catered to rock orthodoxy. Even among those bands saddled with the punk tag were outfits who just played a speeded-up hard-rock mutation of early heavy metal (Blue Oyster Cult/Black Sabbath, etc.), as if inbreeding had occurred between the Stones and the Ramones. Nor had the Mercers sound entirely faded away after the collapse of their Alma Mater. Both Wayne County and the Miamis remained among the most popular of the club bands throughout this entire period.

Leee Black Childers: There was a good deal of a backlash against glam, which the Dolls were. They were very much in the tradition of glam-rock, platform boots and a lot of make-up ... [but] if you look at the bands playing when Max's had its Easter festival, there was a glam-rock band every night mixed with the punk ones ... these are the bands that presaged the way Heavy Metal looks now, a lot of spandex ... so both those movements were coming out of Max's and CBGB at that time.

The two most notable New York bands to begin playing CBGBs or Max's in 1976 – the year that separates the original CBGBs bands from the later proto-punk bands who sought to emulate an essentially British aesthetic, derived from the Pistols and the Clash – actually predated all the 'first wave' CBGBs bands. Suicide had been gigging, albeit sporadically, since 1970, and the Dictators had been gigging since 1973, issuing an album on a 'major', Columbia's Epic subsidiary, before Patti Smith had even begun *Horses*. As Ira Robbins observes in the *New Music Guide*, 'scads of credit is due these pre-punk New Yorkers for being there first.'

While Suicide were certainly unique, the Dictators slotted easily into the 'fuck art, let's rock!' niche being carved out by the likes of the Dead Boys and the Hell-less Heartbreakers in the months after the summer 1976 CBGBs festival. Along with *The Ramones*, the Dictators' debut album was already having a direct influence on the wave of 'let's rock' bands – some still flirting with a glam look – that began to infiltrate the New York clubs.

The Dictators had been formed in upstate New York, quickly adopting a stance which can be seen to combine elements of the Dolls and the Ramones. They represent the bridge between these two bands, both in sound and image, predating the Ramones by a good year.

Andy Shernoff: The Dictators were formed in 1973. I was going to college and Ross [Funichello] was playing in a local band called Total Crud and he comes to me and says he's gonna quit Total Crud and wanted to form a new band. So we knew this guy Scott Kempner who had similar tastes. I knew of Scott 'cause we used to go record-shopping together. At that time to find somebody who had tastes like Stooges, MC5 wasn't that common so when you found the kindred spirits you became friends with them. We had a bunch of drummers coming in and out.

Despite their upstate location, the Dictators were fully aware of the Mercers scene. Like many of their Manhattan contemporaries, the Dictators drew direct inspiration from the New York Dolls, whom they realized were reclaiming rock & roll from the technocrats.

Andy Shernoff: I went to elementary school with Johnny Thunders. I used to go see [the Dolls]. It was completely sloppy, completely out of time, completely out of tune but it was exciting. It was actually inspirational. The connection that hit me was, 'You don't have to be a great musician.' We literally picked up our instruments and started playing. The only guy who really knew how to play was Ross, who'd been playing guitar since he was a kid. I bought my bass and then a year later I was making a record.

Though they shared with the Dolls a love for English glam bands, the Dictators were not interested in adopting a similar image, preferring one that was considerably more toned down and 'street-wise'. Their 'young punks' look may not have been entirely uniform but it was the antithesis of the glam look.

Andy Shernoff: We were like punk, we were leather jackets, wise guy know-it-alls. We were [certainly] anti-glitter.

Their fuzztoned guitars also predated the Ramones. This schizo Dolls–Ramones stance was reflected in the Dictators' choice of 'covers'. If their version of 'I Got You Babe' could have been a Dolls arrangement, their take on 'California Sun' was, if anything, even more frenetic than the Ramones'. As anti-glam exponents, the Dictators were largely restricted to one club in New York, the Coventry, where they managed to establish a small following.

Andy Shernoff: Coventry was in Queens. Mostly it was a glitter club. It was the only club you could play original music in New York City. There was no other place to play ... Joey Ramone used to play drums in a band called Sniper. He used to come see the Dictators. The interesting thing is that what the Ramones did and what the Dictators were doing was pretty much the same thing. They were more focused. The Dictators were trying to cover too many things ... It was really the same thing: fast, tight, funny, aggressive, similar influences, [same] ideas of what's good music and bad music. [We] also liked British [glam:] Sweet, Roxy Music, Slade, T. Rex. I didn't find American music interesting at the time. It was pompous, overblown and obnoxious. Scott Muny had a radio show – Hits from England – on Fridays in the afternoon and he'd play like the Top 10 hits. To me that was rock & roll. It was short, succinct, great hooks.

Unlike the CBGBs bands, though, the Dictators were allowed little gestation period in which to develop a coherent sound. While the Ramones were still auditioning drummers in the summer of 1974, the Dictators were signing to a major label.

Andy Shernoff: I'd been writing for a few music papers and magazines and had my own little fanzine, *Teenage Wasteland Gazette*. It was sort of a satirical take-off of a real rock magazine. So I knew a few people in the business and we got this guy Sandy Pearlman, who at the time was managing and producing Blue Oyster Cult, to come down. He saw the band, he liked the band. Got us to do a demo. Epic Records signed the band. We recorded the [first] record in 1974. It was released in 1975. This is all pre-CBGBs.

That first Dictators album – *The Dictators Go Girl Crazy!* – would become a firm favourite with New York's aspiring rock & rollers, who appreciated the tongue-in-cheek humour of cuts like 'The Next Big Thing', 'Teengenerate' and '(I Live for) Cars and Girls'. The Dictators' fascination with America's junk culture struck as much of a chord with their few aficionados as their frantic form of rock & roll. But in the climate that existed in the spring of 1975 – the Dolls in dissolution and po-faced arena-rock dominating the radio waves – the Dictators were never going to be the next big thing; and with a major label they were unlikely to be allowed a second chance. In the summer of 1975 the Dictators found themselves residing back at Square One.

Andy Shernoff: They couldn't get airplay on [*Go Girl Crazy!*]. They couldn't do anything with it. It was completely unmarketable, image-wise and sound-wise, so they dropped it – pretty quickly. The band never really played out that much. We didn't know what was going on. Then a few months after the record came out there is a place to play and there was a market for it, literally months: CBGBs, Max's, Washington had a club. There was a whole circuit you could play. If that record came out six months later it might have been a different story.

Go Girl Crazy! had not passed unnoticed in New York. After a period of reassessment, they decided to resume gigging in the winter of 1975–6 and found they had an unexpected base of new fans. With 'Handsome Dick' Manitoba promoted from 'secret weapon' to fully fledged front-man, the Dictators had no trouble re-establishing a reputation on the New York rock scene.

Andy Shernoff: We first played CBGBs in 1976 and there was this giant crowd, line around the block, packed full of people. We [started] playing around New York [again]. There weren't that many bands. Very often in those days bands would play Thursday, Friday, Saturday night and [on] Thursday night bands would come by and just check out the other bands. The East Village was like a little neighbourhood and most everybody knew each other. The Dictators were [only] semi-connected. Maybe we weren't as obviously artistic. We were more suburban in our approach.

Being 'more suburban', they had something in common with other CBGBs favourites that existed largely outside the scene. The Shirts, like those other local faves the Tuff Darts, were more interested in securing a record deal than in reviving rock & roll.

Annie Golden: We were like hicks from Brooklyn, never aspiring to go across the bridge, but we had read about the Mercer Arts Centre, which had just crumbled, and the back room at Max's, and we went down to see Patti Smith at CBGBs ... We were holed up in Brooklyn, we all had day jobs, we were rehearsing eight to ten hours into the morning, saving money for equipment. Bands in Manhattan were doing it another way. They were like artists; they were doing minimalist rock and they were starving. But we had this big light show and a big PA.

The Dictators managed to get netted by Asylum in one of the American record industry's trawl-fishing exercises, and in 1977 delivered *Manifest Destiny*, confirmation of a gradual movement towards orthodoxy on their part. The removal from Epic had obviously left the Dictators determined to avoid such traumas in the future. Their final album, 1978's *Blood-brothers*, made further concessions in a resolute attempt to be accessible. The gesture was futile. They still failed to ignite the mass market, and Asylum decided that they had given the band enough rolls of the dice. Rather than face another period of uncertainty, the Dictators decided that they had made their statement.

The other two bands who – following the Dictators' and the Ramones' lead – sought to appeal to CBGBs newly acquired 'fuck art, let's rock!' brigade were no more successful in their attempts to extend beyond this parochial club audience.

The Heartbreakers had willingly stripped themselves of any connection to the art-rockers with Richard Hell's departure. Their dilemma was no longer how to sound, but how to succeed, particularly with a certain sparsity of original material.

Jerry Nolan: We had [had] to cater to [Hell] a lot. The longer he was in the band the more he wanted. We got tired of it because it stopped us from our own creating.

In fairness to Thunders and Nolan, it may be true that Hell's contributions stopped the other Heartbreakers from writing songs. Certainly in the three months that elapsed between Hell's departure and the new Heartbreakers' debut gig (at CBGBs on 23 July) – with Billy Rath on bass – they worked up a radically revised set that included three new Thunders originals: 'I Love You', 'It's Not Enough' and 'Get Off the Phone'. 'Chinese Rocks' was the one survivor to carry Hell's name.

Without Hell, though, the sheer uniformity of Thunders' own songs and the regressive orthodoxy of the Heartbreakers' sound, allied to a 'more trouble than they're worth' reputation hanging over from the days of the Dolls, meant that they were not buried under an avalanche of recording opportunities.

Leee Black Childers: I was just stonewalled [by] everyone, even companies like Sire – even Terry Ork who had this little independent label . . . Johnny had the real bad-boy reputation.

Yet within two months of leaving the Heartbreakers, Hell had signed to Richard Gottehrer and Marty Thau's Instant Records production company, perhaps suggesting that the Heartbreakers had been holding Hell back, not vice versa. Thau had actually approached Hell while he was still in the Heartbreakers.

Marty Thau: My intent was to meet Richard Hell and see what the Heartbreakers were about. I certainly felt that he was the most alert person in that band. I have fond memories of Johnny Thurnders but I don't know that I would've ever wanted to work with him again.

By the end of 1976, the Heartbreakers had seen all the other major bands on the CBGBs scene signed up. So, when Malcolm McLaren approached them to play on a punk-rock tour of the UK with the Sex Pistols and the Clash, they decided that they had little to lose, despite Thunders' innate distrust of McLaren, dating back to the Dolls.

Leee Black Childers: Malcolm McLaren called me, and asked if we would like to come to London and do the Anarchy tour. To tell the absolute truth I had never heard of the Sex Pistols, much less the Clash, or the Damned, so I called Johnny, I said, 'There's this guy who wants us to go to London, and I would love you to go, he's called Malcolm McLaren,' and Johnny goes, 'Oh, yeah, you remember the guy who had us dress in red, managed the Dolls for a while, he's OK. Let's go' . . . And we arrived on the night of the Grundy show . . . the next morning Jerry Nolan, who never slept, had bought all the papers and they were full of it. So Jerry, who's very negative, comes into my room, throws all the papers on the bed and says, 'What have you gotten us into now?'

Though the legendary Anarchy tour was farcical in terms of actual opportunities to perform – thanks to the Pistols cursing their way to national notoriety – Leee Childers' instincts proved correct in bringing the Heartbreakers to London. The US record companies had already made their sweep of New York and any band left behind was likely to remain on the street, but London's A&R men were only just awakening to the commercial potential of punk.

With ill-considered haste the Heartbreakers signed to Track Records – of Who and Hendrix fame – and convened in a South London studio to record a debut studio album, the infamous *LAMF* ('Like a Mother Fucker', an old New York gang abbreviation). A Heartbreakers album was eagerly awaited by the English music press, impressed by the abrasive thrust that they brought to their live shows during a busy winter on the London club circuit. Unfortunately *LAMF* was a catastrophe. It finished the band, helped further Track's descent into receivership, and meant that any Heartbreakers' legacy went ignored for some time.

Leee Black Childers: We ended up in this studio across the river that was the Who's studio. And it did cost a fortune; and the engineers, although undoubtedly very good, were used to all this older type rock & roll stuff: So the mixing sessions began, and if you just keep mixing and adding on, and mixing and adding on and getting stoneder and mixing some more, you end up with mud. So we had mud. Jerry Nolan threatened to quit the band unless he alone was allowed to remix.

The released *LAMF* buried the Heartbreakers under a mountain of sludge. Amid the inevitable recriminations, Nolan's voice was heard the loudest. When it was made clear that he would not have the opportunity to remix the album, Nolan returned to the States. Though the Nolan-less Heartbreakers completed a UK tour, hoping to promote *LAMF* and a second single, 'It's Not Enough', the 45 had barely made it to the shops before Track were declared bankrupt. A radically remixed version of *LAMF*, which finally restored it to most of its ragged glory, was released in 1984 as *LAMF Revisited*, a belated reminder of how the Heartbreakers' story might have been different. If only . . .

After the Heartbreakers went the same way as the Dolls, Johnny

Thunders stayed in London to record his first solo album, *So Alone* – the record he had been working toward since he had left the Dolls three years earlier. The lack of many Thunders originals on this solo album, and the inclusion of two re-recorded Dolls songs and three covers, all suggested an intractable problem for one of America's finest guitarists – one that the Heartbreakers Mk 1 had never had: coming up with enough strong original material.

The Dead Boys were the last of CBGBs' hard-rock quartet to endear themselves to the 'let's rock' section of the CBGB fraternity, making their first New York appearance at the same CBGBs summer festival as the new Heartbreakers.

Frankenstein, the Bators/O'Connor combo formed from the debris of Rocket from the Tombs, had only recently become the Dead Boys. Their prospects had become extremely limited in Cleveland, playing largely covers to an audience unaware of the demise of glitterdom. Without the Viking Saloon, and with the undisguised animosity of the Ubu crowd, their options were limited, even if Bators' ambition was not. When they attended a Ramones show in Youngstown, Bators convinced the Ramones to secure them a gig at CBGBs.

Joey Ramone: We had played Youngstown, Ohio, and that is where I met Stiv Bators for the first time. We didn't know how to get back to Cleveland, so he said, 'Follow us.' They were driving ninety miles per hour and we were following them. Then all of a sudden Bators climbed out the driver's side window and he's still driving at ninety miles per hour. Then he mooned us, and I thought that was very impressive.

At this point Frankenstein needed a complete overhaul to even attain zombie status. Though their transformation into the Dead Boys involved no change in line-up, it was nevertheless a dramatic about-face. Abandoning their flirtation with the glitter/Brit-Rock aspects of Frankenstein, the Dead Boys self-consciously became a hard-rock version of Rocket from the Tombs – minus the pretensions. They took their name and the bulk of their best songs from the Rockets' songbook – 'Down in Flames' (with its line 'Dead boy, running scared'), 'What Love Is', 'Sonic Reducer', 'Caught With the Meat in My Mouth' (previously 'Never Gonna Kill Myself Again') and 'Ain't it Fun' were all seen as legitimate pickings from the carrion of the Tombs.

Retaining a smattering of Frankenstein's more raucous covers – Iggy's 'Search and Destroy', Mott the Hoople's 'Death May Be Your Santa Claus' and the Syndicate of Sound's 'Hey Little Girl' – the Dead Boys made their debut at CBGBs on 25 July, as part of a generally uninspiring 1976 summer festival of unsigned bands.

Joey Ramone: I said to Hilly, 'This band are amazing' and I hadn't seen them yet. But I had a feeling that they'd be good. I invited all the press and the hipper people to come down and see them. And they were amazing . . . So it'd be the Dead Boys, and the Dictators too, the Heartbreakers, it was that kind of a thing.

After witnessing the surprisingly enthusiastic response to their hard-driven rock & roll and Bators' copy-cat Iggy antics, and bolstered by a positive write-up in *Punk* magazine, the Dead Boys decided a relocation to New York was in order, even if they clearly disturbed some of the more erudite CBGBs regulars.

Craig Leon: [When] the Dead Boys drove up to the [1976] festival, [they were] a little bit out of the look of the scene, wearing Nazi uniforms and stuff. They came looking very right-wing. I was not that impressed. They did not have that pop sensibility.

The Dead Boys did have some things going for them – a slick rock & roll guitarist, a solid rhythm section and an energetic lead vocalist. What they could not achieve by original, inspired music could perhaps be compensated for by Bators' outrageous antics on stage.

If evidence were needed as to Hilly Kristal's misunderstanding of what had been happening at his club in 1974–5, his decision to manage two of the most regressive bands to play CBGBs – the Shirts and the Dead Boys – provides it. Kristal immediately loved the Dead Boys and decided that they should be the first band to sign to his very own record label, CBGB Records. Forced to abandon this idea after the economic setbacks that surrounded the *Live at CBGBs* set, he managed to sell them to Sire on the basis of a nine-song demo tape. Needless to say, the standout demos were a trio of Rockets songs.

Evidence of how reactionary the Dead Boys were came quickly enough. In April 1977, with the ink not yet dry on their Sire contract, the Dead Boys supported the Damned at CBGBs. As the first English punk band to play CBGBs, the Damned had a lot to live up to. They did not disappoint.

Roberta Bayley: The Damned came over and did a weekend with the Dead Boys – sort of a Battle of the Bands. The Dead Boys were doing like 'Anarchy in the UK'. They were goofing on the English bands and stuff. The Dead Boys were just rock, they weren't really punk rock when they came out of Cleveland. They quickly adapted to what the scene needed – which was their own punk-rock band doing Iggy stuff on stage and throw[ing] themselves around and be[ing] outrageous and bleed[ing]. But to me the Damned were really original. They were just so weird. They were also very fast and very manic and they had really good songs.

Though the Dead Boys were loath to admit it, everything changed with the Damned's US debut. The Damned wrote better songs, played faster and were a lot funnier than their Cleveland cousins. The Dead Boys' response seemed to be to turn up the excessometer.

Bill Shumaker: They had heard and read about what rock stars were supposed to do, and whether it was true or not, they tried to do it.

The inclusion on Sire's *New Wave* sampler that summer of their version of David Thomas and Cheetah Chrome's 'Sonic Reducer' perhaps suggested that the Dead Boy's reputation for hard-hittin' raw rock & roll was warranted. But their debut album, issued in October 1977, was only sporadically impressive. Yet, whatever their shortcomings, by 1977 the Dead Boys and their kind now represented the CBGBs scene and it was their crowd that filled the club.

Maureen Nelly: When the Dead Boys happened, the club changed, it became punk. Pre-Dead Boys it was Television, Talking Heads, Mink DeVille, Shirts, all those type of people, which had a more underground-poet-beat sort of feeling to it. Allen Ginsberg would hang out there. People like that. And then when the Dead Boys happened it was the whole punk English scene with the Sex Pistols, and it became a different crowd. When the Dead Boys came in a new generation came in. That's when the first wave of younger kids started coming around. Previous to that it was all people in their late twenties, people who lived in the city.

After the small buzz the first Dead Boys album created, they were quick to record a second album, the close-to-the-knuckle *We Have Come for Your Children*. Released in June 1978, the album confirmed that the Dead Boys had little original material of worth. Without the benefit of foot-to-the-floor 'covers' and remnants from the Tombs, they were a band without songs. The one impressive track was Laughner and O'Connor's 'Ain't it Fun', and even here Bators failed to deliver such a painfully sad epitaph to his friend with any real sense of the wastefulness at the heart of the song.

Though the Dead Boys stumbled into 1979 – hampered by a brief hiatus while Johnny Madansky was temporarily out of commission, after being knifed in a stupid fight with some Spanish hoods – their removal from the Sire roster in the summer of 1978 indicated that the Dead Boys' fifteen minutes of fame was up. Ironically their flaying-to-death mode of live performance and Bators' mock dementia on stage would assure them of a hallowed place in the annals of the nascent thrash scene, perhaps the logical consequence of the more brutal aspects of the punk sound.

Though it was 1976 before the bands at CBGBs and Max's began to attract the interest of recalcitrant record labels, media awareness of a new musical movement came earlier. This was down to a handful of periodicals that sought to spread the news. From the summer of 1975 the New York daily and weekly press, and to a large extent the English music weeklies, began to write about an exciting new scene centered on the Bowery. But the primary commentators remained the new periodicals inspired by the sounds emanating from the Lower East Side, in particular *Rock Scene*, *Punk* and *New York Rocker*.

Rock Scene was a spin-off from the long-established *Hit Parader*, and its content was pretty minimal. Essentially a photo-magazine, it relied on a form of pictorial gossip. It chose to devote considerable space to all the new New York bands; one of its earliest issues included Patti Smith's two-page feature on Television, their first major press exposure.

Hit Parader, which had considerably more content and a substantial national circulation, included among its roster of occasional writers Patti Smith and Richard Hell. Its main contributors were Lenny Kaye and editors Richard and Lisa Robinson. The Robinsons, enthusiastic fans of the new bands, allocated column inches to the New York bands in what was very much a mainstream magazine. Lisa Robinson's June 1975 article on 'The New York Bands' must be considered the first major feature on the nascent scene. Its four pages were devoted to Wayne County, Patti Smith, Television, the Heartbreakers, Blondie, the Miamis, the Ramones, Cherry Vanilla and the Mumps.

If the repeated coverage by *Hit Parader* of Patti Smith was a major factor in her assimilation into the consciousness of the record-buying public in the crucial years of 1975–6, the Robinsons also ran features on unsigned artists like the Ramones – commissioning the part-time pen of Richard Hell to provide this particular item. Like Smith and Kaye, Hell used his journalistic features to espouse the New York creed:

The Ramones were among the original five or six groups drawn to CBGB in New York by Television's 'success' there in late 1974 ... The scene is frantic and the most exciting thing happening in rock music today and probably for the next few years. The ambition level is staggering, but what distinguishes the scene as exemplified in the five or six best groups is that they really mean what they're doing. Without being pretentious, they're not killing time. They use their stagelights like blowtorches to burn away whatever garbage lies can't take the heat, and light up what's left.

Hell adopted no less of a polemical slant when writing for the Robinsons about David Johansen:

The Dolls were the real thing – on stage and off they were real life rock & roll stars because they wanted to feel that way, the way they imagined it would be like, and so they did it ... Rock & roll has continued on this track of self-consciousness, as witness Bowie, Ferry, Smith and Springsteen. Like Johansen's, their works are filled with allusions to other rock & roll, their stage acts are studied, they have carefully designed the image of themselves that they mean to project. In fact you could make a good case that, with the possible exception of Springsteen, they all probably perceived themselves as stars before musician or vocalist or writer and that their greatest talent is for attracting media attention. I think this is great. The art-form of the future is celebrityhood ... the occupation of rock & roll is so appealing to inspired people now – it's an outlet for passions and ideas too radical for any other form.

Inevitably a scene populated by writers like Lenny Kaye, Patti Smith and Richard Hell was going to use all its media opportunities for self-promotion.

Lenny Kaye: We were certainly pushing a position. [But] the whole *Rock Scene* philosophy was [not] us and them. We didn't draw the line as the English punk rock bands did. I'm gonna draw the line against Jeff Beck? You must be kiddin' me. I love him. But one of the reasons we felt a need for our band to go out there ... [was] because the music we loved was in danger of stratifying and solidifying and certain of the impulses – the almost naive lust for the music and its raw self-expression – were definitely being sucked up ... New York had a scene that was not only very accessible to the media but was a lot broader 'cause each of the bands was like a little idea of its own ... The rock scene was drawing a lot from the different arts ... then you had a really aggressive press trumpeting a certain aesthetic about rock, Lester Bangs writing about the Count Five [in] *Creem*. *Rock Scene* was a complete promotional organ for the entire New York scene.

If *Hit Parader* and *Rock Scene* were important in disseminating knowledge of the New York bands nationwide, in local terms they were of less importance than two magazines which first hit the news-stands in the winter of 1975–6. The first was *Punk*, a *Mad*-style magazine that took as its principal theme the new rock & roll. Its first issue was published at the turn of the year. The original idea had been to make the new rock & roll just one aspect of the magazine, not its *raison d'être*, but the immediate response to issue 1 changed all that.

John Holmstrom: I went to the School of Visual Arts on East 23rd Street from '72 to '74, and a lot of people from the CBGBs scene were there. Chris Stein was there at the time. Eric Emerson and the Magic Tramps played our Christmas party. Upon leaving school I kicked around for a few months and then we started the magazine. I went back to Connecticut to visit and I ran into Eddie McNeil, known as Legs. September '75 we put our money together, rented a storefront [and devised] the idea for the magazine. I wanted it to be more of a regular rock or general magazine. The fact we did New York groups was that we were in New York and they were accessible ... [and] we were getting a good reaction. People were buying the magazine to read about these New York groups.

If the idea of calling the magazine *Punk* was partially a reflection of the sort of music Holmstrom and McNeil intended to feature, it was also an act of confrontation. Punk was not an acceptable name for a magazine at the time, and when posters were plastered up around New York announcing 'Punk is coming' everybody at CBGBs thought it was some cheesy out-of-town band trying to instigate a little hype.

John Holmstrom: We thought of the name *Punk*, we talked to the Ramones, and Lou Reed was there and we had the whole magazine together in one night. Punk rock was rock & roll, like the Stooges and garage-rock. Basically any hard rock & roll was punk and that's the kind of music we wanted to write about, to differentiate it from Paul Simon or the soft-rock that was dominating. But then the term got very narrowly defined. We thought it was a general term for anything that was hard rock & roll. Then it became the Sex Pistols and everybody who sounded like the Sex Pistols . . . Punk was a dirty word at the time. Us putting Punk on the cover was like putting the word fuck on the cover. People were very upset. It was a very controversial thing. We were in a mode of being hippy-conservative so if you put a swastika on the cover that was the worst thing you could do. We were being refused news-stand space.

Punk quickly established a unique niche on the scene. It ran anything, from a pastiche of 'the rock star reveals all' interview in which Legs McNeil and Richard Hell would drink themselves unconscious and record the results, to a spoof piece like 'How to write your own porno novel' or an interview with Jonathan, the CBGBs dog, complaining about all the dog shit in the place. *Punk* was never intended as a critical periodical, yet it was too professional and art-oriented to be a fanzine. Refreshingly irreverent, it allowed members of the New York scene the opportunity to participate in its comic-art activities, best exemplified by its two comic-strip specials – 'The Legend of Nick Detroit', starring Richard Hell and Debbie Harry, and 'Mutant Monster Beach Party', with Joey Ramone and Debbie Harry.

Debbie Harry: *Punk* became an organic part of the whole scene, as it was the most interesting magazine in the world when it came out. It was very cool to be in it, too. Chris contributed photographs frequently after the first issue . . . *Punk* was a lot sharper than the other fanzines before it eventually collapsed under financial and personal strains.

Though the other magazine founded during the winter of 1975–6, *New York Rocker*, may have been a considerably more conventional rock & roll magazine, it still had its own specific rationale. *New York Rocker* was created by Alan Betrock, a respected rock journalist who was already writing regularly about the CBGBs bands for *SoHo Weekly News*, which at this time was attempting to subvert the *Village Voice* monopoly of the New York 'cultural weeklies' market. *NYR*'s first issue was dated February 1976.

Alan Betrock: I [had] had a magazine called *The Rock Marketplace* ... it was [like] an early version of *Goldmine* ... I enjoyed doing it and it was doing well but I was getting excited about the New York scene and all the bands and no one was covering them and I thought it'd be important for them to get coverage ... I went down to see Television and they were great. It was rudimentary but it was energetic. There was the Club 82 and [the bands] would rent a loft and they would play. CBGBs became the focal point but in the beginning they didn't play there every week, so on the weeks they weren't there or at Max's they'd find some other small club or bar.

On the front cover of its first issue, the new magazine offered features on the Ramones, Wayne County, Talking Heads, Marbles, Milk'n' Cookies, Miamis, Blondie, Patti Smith and the Heartbreakers. A close examination of the contents reveals that the feature on the Miamis was written by Blondie, aka Debbie Harry. The feature on Blondie was written by T. & J. Wyndbrandt, better known as co-founders of the Miamis (and Harry's ex-backing musicians in the early Stillettoes). A feature on the Heartbreakers appeared in a section marked 'Opinion':

The Heartbreakers exist in the images they create out of desperation. For love and money. A couple of them want to die as well. In other words the Heartbreakers are imaginary, the desperation is real ... Hell is a master rock conceptualist ... On stage he generally appears completely blank, very tired, extremely angry or profoundly agonized. That's because he feels that way ... Rock & roll has become more than its own history. The best rock & rollers ... are human beings of rock & roll. Like mutations. Having been born roughly simultaneously with the sound, they've absorbed it, it's modified them and they have an unprecedented and mysterious ability to turn a teardrop into a driving question mark. Time after time.

This would have been a surprisingly intense overview of the Heartbreakers were it not from the pen of Theresa Stern, 'authoress of a book of poetry', available from R. Meyers of East 12th Street. Its inclusion showed that *New York Rocker* was at this stage more about propaganda than perspective.

Betrock's tenure at *New York Rocker* only lasted eleven issues. His final issue as editor came out just over a year after the first issue, in which time the magazine unflaggingly promoted the most vibrant local scene in rock & roll. The switch to Andy Schwartz's editorship – with the April/May 1977 edition – marked a change, not only for the magazine, but in the axis of rock & roll. The front cover was graced by the Clash, the first non-New York band to make the cover of *New York Rocker*. Though *NYR* would continue to cover the New York bands, it no longer operated largely as a vehicle for them.

Alan Betrock: [*New York Rocker*] was the first coverage of a lot of these people and I think it fostered a lot of the sense of a scene and got more people from the outside who would read about these bands. Initially it was just a lot of people who were all friends and who knew each other ... When I did *New York Rocker* ... I thought the important thing was to get these New York bands known and publicized and signed and on the way ... After a couple of years of that the scene had really expanded and everybody had picked up on it and a lot of the bands had gotten signed. [It was time to quit] – partly because I was exhausted and partly because my goal had been fulfilled ... People were kinda surprised when [Andy] put the Clash on the cover.

The existence of these magazines was partially a result of the lack of press about this new rock & roll in the mainstream music press. *Rolling Stone* and *Crawdaddy* virtually ignored the New York scene in its three years of growth, while *Creem* gave disappointingly little coverage to the CBGBs bands, despite general in-house enthusiasm for Patti Smith and Peter Laughner's very personal enthusiasm for Television.

Such taciturnity was not displayed by New York-based journalists writing for the English music press, who were among the first to give the scene extensive coverage. The need to fill weekly music papers and the traditional English interest in New York's music scene had a direct bearing on early English press coverage of the New York Dolls, Patti Smith, Television and even Blondie.

The summer 1975 CBGBs festival began an eighteen-month period when the three main English music weeklies – *New Musical Express*, *Melody Maker* and *Sounds* – regularly devoted space to the New York scene, sometimes to the detriment of its own punk explosion. Among the first features was Steve Lake's somewhat jaundiced report of the summer festival in the 16 August 1975 issue of *Melody Maker*, which reflected Lake's perverse idea of who was at the forefront of the CBGBs scene:

Time was when the best band in New York was the one that wore the highest platform heels. But times change, and the outrage scene, which spawned groups like the Harlots of 42nd Street, Teenage Lust, and Queen Elizabeth, featuring Wayne County, is in decline. But there are plenty of new bands around ... The *MM* visits the oddly named CBGB & OMFUG bar, in the heart of the Big Apple's wino and junkie area, to see the Heartbreakers, the Shirts, Stagger Lee, Second Wind and other pioneers from New York's answer to London's pub-rock scene.

A year later *Melody Maker* was attempting to contrast and compare the English punk scene with its New York equivalent. Again *MM* got it dramatically wrong by placing the lamentable Slaughter & the Dogs and Eddie & the Hot Rods at the forefront of English punk, but at least Caroline Coon was perceptive enough to recognize one of the essential differences between the two scenes:

While New York cultivates avant-garde and intellectual punks like Patti Smith and Television, the British teenager, needing and being that much more alienated from rock than America ever was, has little time for such aesthetic requirements. British punk rock is emerging as a fierce, aggressive, self-destructive onslaught. There's an age difference too. New York punks are mostly in their mid-20s. The members of the new British punk bands squirm if they have to tell you they are over 18.

By the end of 1976 the difference between the English and American punk scenes was becoming a major issue in the music press, as the direction of the New Wave was dictated by its strongest propellent force. The sheer uniformity of the post-Pistols first wave of English bands ensured that theirs would be punk's dominant sound.

No Wave – Goodbye!

The main figures to establish the CBGBs scene – the Ramones, Blondie, Talking Heads, Richard Hell, Television – all secured recording deals between January 1976 and the winter of 1976–7, as did several of the bands who existed on the scene's outer edges, but whose reputations were also made at CBGBs and Max's – notably the Dictators, Suicide, Tuff Darts and Mink DeVille. After a year and a half of regular gigging, the leading bands had all refined their material and sound to the point where they were ready to take their music to the American consumer, and the commercial success of *Horses* set an example that they could all draw inspiration from.

1976 might seem like the year when the American record industry woke up to its own new music. In fact it was only because of three industry figures with their fingers on New York's pulse that these acts were finally able to get their sounds down and out. The trio in question were Marty Thau, Seymour Stein and Craig Leon, none of whom would qualify as major music-biz moguls.

All three played their part in the first post-Patti New York combo to sign a record deal. The Ramones had been gigging with an unchanged line-up since July 1974. Craig Leon, working for Sire, first witnessed the Ramones early in the summer of 1975. Though impressed, he had an uphill battle convincing Sire proprietor Seymour Stein that they were 'recordable'.

Craig Leon: Nobody thought that the Ramones could make it to tape in those days ... There was quite a long time between when they were first seen and when they actually got the deal together. I saw them and Talking Heads in the same gig. I was like Seymour's junior guy. I was actually down at CBGBs looking for Patti Smith. I'd heard some of her stuff and [thought], 'This is hot. This is brilliant' . . . [Seymour] was looking for new bands so we went around New York looking for bands. He came down after I told him to go and see Talking Heads . . . Marty knew I was going for this band the Ramones . . . and he took them into 914 Studio, an ex-bowling alley on Long Island [and] cut some tracks with them.

As a result of Sire's prevarications, which stretched through the fall of 1975, the Ramones ended up recording a single with Marty Thau. They had originally asked Thau to be their manager, something they badly needed, but after his experience with the Dolls, Thau was uninterested in taking on management duties again. He suggested that they do a record together, which he would sell as a one-shot deal. They cut 'I Wanna Be Your Boyfriend' and 'Judy is a Punk' (now both issued on *Groups of Wrath*), two authentic slugs of Ramone-rock, but the deal that Thau offered in order to sell the single was not one that the Ramones could be happy with.

Tommy Ramone: Sire [had] got interested in us but I guess there was some hesitancy. Then we were dealing with Marty Thau and as we were involved with Marty Thau, Craig Leon calls up and says, 'We're interested in signing you.' We had already done the [single] with Marty Thau. He wanted one of those 50–50 deals. I said to myself, 'What is this? Colonel Parker?'

In fact, unbeknown to the Ramones, the recordings with Thau - which Stein had been allowed to hear – played their part in convincing him that the Ramones' unique sound could be transferred to vinyl. The other significant factor was Leon's assurances that they could record an album, with him as producer, for little more than a pittance. The Ramones finally joined the Sire roster in January 1976.

Craig Leon: They signed for basically a PA system and a very small amount of money. I promised Seymour that we could make the album incredibly cheaply – beyond cheap – and if I was producing the record that I would do it after work and not charge them for it. I'd work A&R during the day and then go down to Plaza Sound at night to make the record. I think he gave us a week to make the record.

The Ramones had waited a long time to make a vinyl statement. Upon signing they began preparatory rehearsals and within a month they were in Plaza Sound recording their first album, finishing it on schedule in just seven days. The lack of time meant that the sound of the album largely duplicated their existing demos.

Tommy Ramone: The [first] record was cut very fast and it's got a unique sound, but it would have been nice to have had a slightly more leisurely time of doing it and maybe work on the sounds. The band, meaning Johnny, wanted to get it over with. It wasn't budgeted high ... [and] Craig Leon wanted to prove that he could bring it in under a certain amount of money. And it was done. On the demo we experimented with certain sounds – in other words we were doing a left/right ping-pong stereo – to make it sound different. Also we were listening to old Beatles records which were done on 4-track and 2-track and they were doing that and I produced the demo. So then when we did the real record it was just transferred to that. That's also done like that, ping-pong, guitar left, bass right, voice in the middle.

Craig Leon: [There were] problems with the demos. There just wasn't sonically enough to translate to vinyl [and] get it on the radio.

Achieving the same 'ping-pong stereo' in a modern studio without reducing the sound to Roaring Guitars required a little ingenuity. The likelihood of producing an album of guitar noise was greatly increased by the Ramones lack of certitude about how to get the best sound out of the new Marshall amps they had inveigled out of Sire. As Dee Dee later commented, 'we just turned everything up all the way.' The results do not sound like *White Light/White Heat*! Despite being an experienced recording engineer in his own right, Tommy had only a subsidiary role in the album's production (he would be credited as 'associate producer'), and as he observed, 'The studio engineers didn't know what the hell was going on.'

Craig Leon: The only reason I engineered on those records was because none of the stupid engineers would do anything [adventurous] ... 'What do you mean you're using a distorted guitar, let's turn it down.' That stuff still existed then. [I was] wanting to go to Radio City Music Hall and set up three amplifiers in three different rooms and have them blasting and have total separation and still the loudest sound ever at the same time ... Plaza

Sound had a lot to do with why that record and *Blondie* sounded like they sounded – why they were so cavernous . . . The concept of the [Ramones] album was to be very, very separated, based upon like a mid-Sixties Beatles album, which was done simply because they didn't have enough tracks. But what the hell did we know? This massive amplifier [was] leaking into everything. If you recorded by conventional Seventies techniques, you would have had this tremendous amplifier, and no clean drums and no bass. You would have just had this big, big noise. So the idea was basically to isolate the sound without baffling. I was always wanting to make a record at least as loud as Phil Spector ever did . . . but a clean, individual wall of sound, very much with sonic impact but with no echo. There's walls of guitars 'n' stuff mashed down to one on certain things [on that album]. It was done on sixteen-track, wide head – technologically average for the time – but it had these massive rooms and so you could put the drums in one room; there was a rehearsal hall off to the side so you put the guitar amps in there, and then down in the other hallway was the bass amp . . . They'd watch this little metronome that was constantly set to like 208 bpm and it would flash on and off and everything was totally isolated within the three separate parts of the studio.

If Leon had succeeded in transferring the Ramones' sound to record – and cheaply – it was not an album that brought their harmonic hooks high enough in the mix to attract any serious radioplay, and in that sense at least *The Ramones* was destined to be a failure.

Craig Leon: Hell, I thought they were going to be massive off their first record and so did they. They were thinking they were in like Beatles, Herman's Hermits territory, not any kind of underground Stooges/ performance-art damage. The Ramones were thinking they were going to revitalize pop music.

Though the album has passed into rocklore as something of a classic – due primarily to the seismic effect on a generation of first hearing the Ramones's take on rock & roll – the buried melodies and the unrelenting nature of its sound were probably responsible for the relative commercial failure of the album (though its highest chart position – 111 – equalled the Dolls' considerably more hyped debut). The impact of that first Ramones album may have been considerable, but it certainly does

not equal the patently ludicrous claims made on its behalf in the notes
to the CD version of the album:

With the Ramones, Punk Rock was born. Certainly there were the forebears,
like the Stooges, MC5 and Patti Smith, but the Ramones hoisted the banner,
declaring themselves punks and their followers punk rockers. All subsequent
punk bands, from the Sex Pistols down, owed allegiance to the Ramones.

By this point, the Sex Pistols had been gigging for over six months and
were already performing the bulk of their recorded material. Indeed the
Ramones were already aware of the buzz that the Pistols were creating
on the other side of the pond.

Tommy Ramone: All of a sudden I pick up a magazine and there's a
picture of a band called the Sex Pistols and I look at it and I read about it
and about their type of music and these guys seem to be doing the same
thing we're doing. And it mystified me ... Pretty soon after that we played
the Roundhouse and when we played Dingwalls, the day before [the
Roundhouse], they came there.

The Ramones come at the end of America's first wave of underground
rock & roll – after the Velvets, the Stooges, the Dolls and the original
Television – not at the forefront.

   Though the reviews of *The Ramones* were generally favourable, Alan
Betrock's in the scene's own magazine, *New York Rocker*, was less than
gushing. Betrock concluded by reflecting – unfavourably – on the speed
with which the album had been recorded:

For people who have experienced the Ramones in person, this record should do
just fine, but for the 99% of the record-buying public who haven't, it may
present some problems. For starters, the production is erratic and often nonde-
script. I would've preferred the guitar more upfront and powerful; searing,
rather than the somewhat muffled effect it now sports. I would have liked to
hear the drum sound vary from track to track, with a crisper, punchier effect ...
The band's flaws become obvious here ... the lack of proficient dexterity and
musical depth leaves some songs sounding unfinished, and occasionally the LP
sounds just too rushed, more like a good demo than the real thing.

Despite the initial failure of the Ramones to break into the mass
market, Sire still endeavoured to mop up the remainder of New York's

best bands. In particular, Seymour Stein was anxious to gain the signature of Talking Heads. Talking Heads would soon provide the sort of commercial success that even the majors considered acceptable – particularly when attached to critical kudos – while Stein's sweep of the New York bands gave Sire something it previously lacked – a moniker to attach to the label.

Marty Thau: Seymour is a great historian. Seymour knows the stories of the Chess Records and the Motowns and he understood that, for an independent, newly developing label, it was important to have an identity to hang your hat on. To be known as something, 'the house of . . .' At some point he realized that this [scene] was valid and went for it. He coined the phrase New Wave because punk was too tough to digest as a word for the record industry in conservative America, because of the connotation of punk. It was a Thirties, Forties prison term. If you were a punk in prison you were the girlfriend of someone in Cell Block Five.

However, Sire was still very much a small independent label, Stein's financial resources were extremely limited, and he was forced to restrict his interest to four or five bands.

Craig Leon: I don't think Seymour had the resources to sign like eight or nine bands and become the CBGBs label, which is one of the reasons Instant Records started later. He went for the Ramones and Talking Heads. He pared it down to those. Talking Heads had offers from other labels. Talking Heads were unsigned at the time of the *Live at CBGBs* [album] because we actually recorded them for that . . . There was competition involved. I guess there had to be a lot of hustling done by Seymour . . . He was finally swayed on the Ramones when they got a cool manager, Danny Fields . . . and they were very inexpensive records by industry standards, so why not? And they had an art connotation.

Stein was also interested in signing Television, but Verlaine remained confident that his band warranted, and could command, the sort of signing-on fee a major might offer, even though it seemed at times that Television were being left behind.

Craig Leon: He started some negotiations with Terry Ork and Television. Tom Verlaine came up a few times but they never got it together. They were looking for massive money which Sire didn't have.

Talking Heads were almost as hard to land, though Stein had been one of the first industry figures to realize the Heads' potential. Talking Heads had been spotted by Leon back in the summer of 1975 and, when Stein came to CBGBs to see them for himself, he was soon convinced that here was a truly original band. Though the Heads initially refrained from signing to Sire, they also refused all other offers. In April 1976 Talking Heads recorded their first demo tape, just three songs – 'Psycho Killer', 'Care Free' and 'For Artists Only' – but despite interest from RCA (at Lou Reed's behest), CBS and Capitol, the Heads finally did sign with Sire – after checking with Danny Fields how the label had treated the Ramones.

Danny Fields: I told them there wasn't going to be much cash. There wouldn't be suitcases full of dollar bills on the doorstep. But they would see the royalties and have artistic control of everything, from packaging to product.

It was a full year after Stein had first seen them. To record their debut single, Stein put them in the studio with Tony Bongiovi, co-producer of the Ramones' second album. Bongiovi decided that the sound of the trio was too sparse, and embellished the A-side with strings – and birds twittering! Though Byrne described the results as a 'sort of experiment', he was later very critical of Bongiovi's approach. Yet 'Love Goes to Building on Fire' remains one of the Heads' most arresting works and, despite his distaste for Bongiovi's 'additions', the single served to confirm something Byrne had suspected for a while; that the sparsity of the trio's sound required some immediate and permanent bolstering.

David Byrne: It seemed to be very difficult to capture all the nuances of what we do live, and make it sound exciting on tape. Somehow with just bass, guitar and drums, the way we had it in all the [early] recordings, it sounded real pathetic. It didn't have the richness it could onstage.

Unlike the Ramones, Byrne chose to reflect on the Heads' first Sire session before hurtling into recording a debut album. Not until spring 1977, and then as a four-piece, would the Heads commence '77.

Stein, because of his direct control of even Sire's threadbare purse-strings and the apathy of rival companies, was able to take his pick of the New York bands. The other central figure in the process of transferring the CBGBs bands to vinyl was required to sift through Stein's scraps. But if Marty Thau was required to hustle a little more, he had a keener awareness of who might best make the transition to record. After all, it had been Thau who had recorded the Ramones when Sire were still prevaricating, and who, in the spring of 1976, came up with the idea of a live compilation album of CBGBs bands.

Even before recording his aborted single with the Ramones, Thau had been interested in producing some of the CBGBs bands and had begun to bring Richard Gottehrer, Seymour Stein's ex-partner and co-founder of Sire, down to the rock & roll club, hoping to inspire him too.

Marty Thau: Jerry Nolan [had] called me, he said, 'You should be the guy that comes down and checks out what's going down in this CBGBs scene. You would understand what to do with the talent here.' I went down to CBGBs one night and felt the vibration of this ongoing movement. I was recording a single with a group called the Dirty Angels and I thought it would be good for Sire Records. I was trying to reach Seymour Stein who never returned my phone calls and then realized that I knew his partner Richard Gottehrer, not knowing that they had broken up their partnership. When I finally got Richard on the phone to sell him on the idea of listening to this single he told me that he had split and I said, 'What are you doing?' He said, 'I'm working with this Scottish bagpipe player.' I thought he was a little off the beaten track. I said, 'Richard, why don't we go down and take a look at what's going on at CBGBs.' He said OK. We went and we looked ... I was able to convince Richard that there were a number of interesting groups that were emerging. I had to sell him through the fact that these groups are not on the level of groups that [he was] accustomed to working with: 'This is not focused. These are not finished, polished rock & roll things. These are things we have to read between the lines, interpret and go for certain values within them that are different than values that were used before.'

Thau's original concept was to produce a live album of the best CBGBs acts, hoping to represent the entire ongoing scene in a favourable light. It was exactly what these bands needed to reinforce the sense of a new movement in public perception (much like the *Live at the Roxy* album in Britain in the summer of 1977). Thau also had credibility in the eyes of the important bands because of his association with the Dolls, his business know-how and his enthusiasm for the scene. What Thau did not have was access.

Marty Thau: It was my idea to do what became the CBGBs compilation, which was not the compilation that I envisioned. Hilly took it upon himself to conclude, 'Well, look. I own the club, I own the name, so I own the project.' I didn't own the club, the name or the project. But I had the idea. I knew what it should be: the Ramones, the Heartbreakers, Blondie, Television, Patti Smith. All the most high-profile, interesting acts connected to the punk/New Wave movement. We had meetings . . . Hilly lifted the project for himself and really didn't have the wherewithal to bring in the best acts for it. Didn't know how to approach these acts. Maybe didn't even know who was who. He knew who the best attractions were but I don't think that he connected any of that to a worldwide change in music. The Shirts were totally meaningless. Tuff Darts had a good guitar player but they were not of the same persuasion at all to what was going on with Patti Smith or Television . . . I think that Hilly missed the point and that was a very critical factor in the whole thing, because he controlled the ability to make the record.

Despite Kristal's naivety when it came to securing permissions, and his misunderstanding as to the import of the scene, all the bands who played the 1976 summer festival at CBGBs were recorded for the project, even if what Atlantic received for release were bands who signified nothing.

Craig Leon: Mink deVille were [already] signed by Atlantic Records and that was one of the main reasons for doing the *Live at CBGBs* album. The original concept of *Live at CBGBs* was on Hilly's label, OMFUG Records, but the bands that were originally [going to be] on that record and were recorded were everyone that was part of that scene. Needless to say at that point a lot of them couldn't be used. But I do believe Atlantic thought they were getting Television, Talking Heads, Blondie. The actual rough mixes of the *Live at CBGBs* album that we were unable to issue were brilliant . . . All the bands that ended up on *Live at CBGBs* were all these other bands that Hilly kinda liked that had virtually nothing to do with the scene.

While Kristal was busy putting together his double album of second-rate CBGBs acts, Thau and Gottehrer decided to set up their own production company, Instant Records. Craig Leon also joined the organization, primarily as a producer, but also as one of the few industry figures to understand what was going on here. For their initial roster they wanted Blondie and Richard Hell, neither of whom appeared on Kristal's *Live at CBGBs* set, though Blondie performed at the festival where the recordings were made.

Thau had already convinced Blondie to sign with Instant Records before the '76 summer festival, committing them to two singles under Instant's auspices, the first of which was recorded early that summer, with Richard Gottehrer and Craig Leon co-producing: X Offender/In the Sun. Though Leon spent some time with Blondie in pre-rehearsals and admits, 'they weren't that together,' the actual results surprised everyone. Recorded at Plaza Sound, the single gave early notice that Blondie were capable of evolving into supreme pop exponents, measuring a discreet flirtation with a Sixties girl-group sound against a more abrasive garageband beat.

Clem Burke: 'X Offender' totally amazed everybody, 'cause they didn't know what to expect from us and it was a total production, not just the live sound at CBGBs ... I think what [everyone thought] Blondie was all about at that point was going totally crazy onstage, making as much noise and racket as possible.

Rather than putting the single out as an independent release, Thau sold it to the Top 40 label Private Stock, who had all-important national distribution. They were pleasantly surprised by the response to the single's release.

Marty Thau: Howard Rosen was the director of promotion for Private Stock. We grew up together and I called him when we'd finished the [Blondie single] and said, 'I wanna play you something. I think this act should be on Private Stock.' I went up to his house. I must have played 'X Offender' thirty-five times in the course of the night. I wouldn't let up and he said, 'Well, it has the hook like Bruce Springsteen's "Born to Run". I guess if that could be a hit for Springsteen, this'll be a hit for Blondie.' I knew that if Blondie put out a single there would be more attention to this from the punk circles of the country than Private Stock would ever realize.

I made sure that it was written into the contract that they would have an option to pick up within thirty or sixty days to do an album, at $20,000, if they chose. And I knew that it would happen. I made the deal so attractive, 'You wanna buy this single it'll cost you $2,500,' which was so minor. They're always buying something at $2,500 or $1,500 or $3,000 and they say, 'What the hell! We'll throw it up against the wall. If it sticks, great, we'll work it. If not, what did we lose?' So once that was accomplished Blondie, who 'would never get a record deal', had a record deal. I had a view of the independent small-label game. I worked in the Sixties at Buddah Records and I thought you could, like a baseball player, go through the minor leagues up to the Yankees, which is the way it worked for Blondie.

By August 1976 Blondie were back at Plaza Sound, recording their first album, Richard Gottehrer acting as sole producer. The sound Gottehrer conjured up was richer than that achieved by Leon with the Ramones, though retaining the same sense of space. Gottehrer also managed to toughen Harry's voice up in the recording process.

In May, Harry had told *New York Rocker*, 'every time we go onstage, I try to do something different. It's like a process of elimination; something works and we keep it, it doesn't work and we throw it out.' The debut album was a closet-clearing exercise. Using material from all periods, including favourite oldies like 'In the Flesh' and 'Return of the Giant Ants', the album laid out the gradual development in Blondie's sound. The next album would prove that they had gone beyond early 'prime-time' preoccupations.

Debbie Harry: The concept of that first album was based on the personality Blondie brought to the subject matter. When you listen to the whole thing you notice a predominant theme of violence and gunfire. I don't think there's a song without a reference to someone getting shot, stabbed, degraded, or insulted. It's prime-time television on record.

The other Instant Records act signed by Thau in the weeks leading up to CBGBs' second summer festival represented even more of a gamble than the underrated Blondie. Thau had always been impressed by Richard Hell and knew that he had (co-)written several of the scene's finest anthems, including 'Chinese Rocks', 'Love Comes in Spurts', 'You Gotta Lose' and, most important of all, '(I Belong to the) Blank

Generation'. Yet in May 1976 Hell was still in the embryonic stages of forming his own band. Thau and Gottehrer had offered Hell a production deal before he'd even quit the Heartbreakers, but Hell considered their lack of financial backing problematic.

Instant's offer stayed on the negotiating table while Hell set about forming his own band. The first part of his quest was for a guitarist. Having already played with two of New York's finest in his brief career, finding a player of comparable flair, particularly with all the fierce competition now surrounding the CBGBs scene, seemed an impossible task. Yet the key link in Hell's new band was not a member of any CBGBs outfit, but a friend he had known for years, Robert Quine.

Richard Hell: We [had] worked together in the packing department of this bookstore called Cinemabilia, it was a bookstore about movies. I used to go over to his house after work – this was all the time I was in Television and the Heartbreakers – where he had this fantastic record collection, and listen to records.

Quine had had a semi-audition for the Heartbreakers, just like Chris Stein, and he was already a highly accomplished guitar player, having been playing his axe for nearly a decade, though since his arrival in New York in the early Seventies he had not played in any bands, concentrating on a legal career. Because of Quine's unorthodox tastes, Hell was not sure whether he could combine the dexterity of Verlaine with the gutsiness of Thunders.

Bob Quine: One night [Hell] was over at my house with Ork right 'bout when he was leaving the Heartbreakers. I had this cassette of some band I was with in 1969 playing outside somewhere and I was doing 'Johnny B Goode', bunch of solos on that, 'Eight Miles High' . . . Before then I think he just thought I played strange, outside stuff. Then he heard I could do a Chuck Berry thing or 'Louie Louie' and that was it.

Hell was equally prompt in securing a second recruit. Drummer Marc Bell had been playing with Wayne County for some time.

Richard Hell: Marc [Bell] was a guy who was known to everybody in New York . . . he'd just left Wayne County and he came up to me at Max's one night and said he'd heard I'd split with the Heartbreakers and asked if we should get together and immediately I said yeah.

For several weeks the unnamed combo was rehearsing as a trio. However, after the disaster that passed for the three-piece Heartbreakers, there was never any question in Hell's mind that this would be a two-guitar band.

Richard Hell: I always pictured the sound of rock & roll as two guitars . . . it's like, syncopated rhythms among the guitars during the entire song. There's a guitar part that follows the melody, and there's one that hits everything the other player doesn't hit . . . It's essentially the idea of getting every nuance of beat on the guitar during the entire length of the song and you really need two guitars to do that.

Having spent most of May looking for a suitable player, a local ad caught Quine's attention.

Bob Quine: We were all set to put an ad in the *Village Voice* [when] I just happened to see this ad in this little free giveaway paper called *Musicians Classified* . . . [Ivan Julian] said . . . something about being into the Stones . . . All I said was, 'We don't play no Eagles.' He loved the Stones, the way me and Richard did – the same stuff for the same reason.

Richard Hell now had his four-piece band, but very little time to get them in shape. His diary entry for 25 June 1976 reads:

I've signed contract with Instant Records to produce and sell my tapes in exchange for 50% of record royalties. I have right of approval of any contract we obtain with a label, and if they haven't gotten me a decent contract within four months of completion of my ten-minute demo I may cancel the contract . . . I will find out next week (we begin recording on Wednesday) how well we'll work with Gottehrer and Co. in the studio.

The 'ten-minute demo' that Hell and Co. recorded in the last week of June would be released in its own right in November of 1976, as an independent release on Ork Records, though the primary function of the *Blank Generation* EP was to help secure the band a record deal.

Among the three songs that constitute the EP – 'Blank Generation', 'You Gotta Lose' and a new six-minute opus entitled '(I Could Live

With You) (In) Another World' – the release of 'Blank Generation' was bound to generate the most attention, though 'Another World' suggested that punk music did not need to be 'short and hard' to be 'compelling and driving'. It also proved that Hell was as capable as Verlaine of producing songs with constantly shifting moods, painted within a two-guitar framework. Julian and Quine, though, were considerably more angular and staccato in their approach than the Television duo. The recording of the EP was the beginning of a highly fertile period for Hell and his band.

Bob Quine: When the group was formed we had two weeks to play together and that was our project – three songs for this EP and that's all we did. We did some [more] demos in December. I would guess those demos had more effect [on Sire] than the EP. We had a lot more confidence. The most creative period was after the Ork single, the five months before we played live and we were in a very small rehearsal studio, our amps in each other's faces.

If the EP provided much-needed evidence that Hell's new outfit could finally confirm his importance to American punk, it was only part of a strategy for whipping the band into a recordable state. Spending July to October in intense rehearsals, working on at least half a dozen new songs, Hell was reluctant to gig until the new combo was in shape.

Having christened his band after an unfinished novel he had written in 1973 – though only after dispensing with alternatives like the Savage Statues, the Junkyard, the Morons, the Dogbites and the Beauticians – Richard Hell & the Voidoids made their debut at CBGBs on 18 November 1976. The songs carried over from the Heartbreakers – 'Love Comes in Spurts', 'New Pleasure', 'Blank Generation' and 'You Gotta Lose' – were supplemented by new songs like 'Time Stands Still', 'Betrayal Takes Two', 'Look Out Liars' (released as 'Liars Beware'), 'I'm Your Man', 'Another World' and 'The Plan'.

The most instantly accessible of these new songs, 'Betrayal Takes Two' and 'I'm Your Man', were recorded in December as a further demo, this time under the auspices of Richard Gottehrer (Craig Leon had co-produced the EP with Hell himself). Hell was clearly happier with the sound on these demos, and Gottehrer would get to produce the Voidoids' debut album. By this time, though, Thau and Gottehrer were in the process of disbanding their short-lived partnership. Inevitably the question of money had reared its greenbacked head.

Marty Thau: In the course of my period with Richard Gottehrer all of a sudden the deal changed . . . Initially it was to be that Richard would have 50% of the company and I would have 50% of the company. Richard, being the slick baron that he is and the person that was financing it, but very begrudgingly and on a very limited level, all of a sudden changed the terms of the deal. He was saying, 'Well, instead of you being a 50% partner maybe you'll be a 25% partner.' I didn't like that because I felt that most of the acts that were coming to us were [doing so] because they were attracted to me. I introduced him to what the scene was about and had to explain it him, so if he put up a couple of thousand dollars – Big deal!

But it was not just about money. Gottehrer had never really been 100 per cent convinced as to the importance of these bands and at each turn his conservative impulses and concern about funds – his funds – acted as a brake on Instant's potential. The final proof of Gottehrer's lack of ambition came in the fall. Leon and Thau had high hopes of striking a deal with Stiff Records in London – who were releasing the *Blank Generation* EP in the UK – that would result in an Instant–Stiff alliance, Instant securing for America the best of Stiff's small London roster and Instant responding in kind.

Craig Leon: What was gonna happen was a partnership between Stiff and Instant, based upon the bands Marty and I wanted to do, like Suicide, Television, at that point even Talking Heads were a consideration. Basically Richard [Gottehrer] was very, very conservative and didn't think that Marty's and my stuff was worthwhile. Marty and I were a little more radical and we got very pissed [off].

Gottehrer decided to concentrate on trying to get his old label to sign the Voidoids. Given that they were now a working unit, it was surely only a matter of time before a major label took them up. Stein was greatly impressed by the new demos, and in January 1977 Hell finally secured his own record contract. On 14 March, two years on from Television's aborted Island album, Richard Hell began recording a pukka debut album.

While Hell's trials and tribulations had certainly played their part in delaying his vinyl debut, his old band Television, once considered 'The

Band Most Likely . . .', had only just completed their own debut album. Having generated label interest as early as the fall of 1974, it had been expected that they would be among the first CBGBs acts to secure a contract. They had gone through relatively few pangs of rebirth after the loss of Hell and had quickly emerged the stronger. Their August 1975 single proved that Television could be as impressive on vinyl as on stage, unorthodox a choice as 'Little Johnny Jewel' had been.

But after the problems resulting from the Eno/Island approach, Verlaine had clearly decided to take his time before signing any contract, confident that Television had no serious competition waiting in the wings. For some time it seemed as if they would sign to the same label as Patti Smith, Arista. Smith had recommended them to president Clive Davis, who had seen Television during their famous residency with Smith in the spring of 1975. His hesitancy led to a suggestion from Smith's boyfriend, Allen Lanier, keyboardist for Blue Oyster Cult.

Tom Verlaine: Clive Davis had made us an offer . . . there were various companies making bids . . . but I think Allen [Lanier] went up to him and said, 'You haven't really heard this band, you should hear what they sound like when they're produced' . . . He persuaded him to let us do the demo. We did about five songs in two nights, working fourteen hours a night . . . it was a much warmer sound than Eno got.

The demos – which included 'Torn Curtain', 'I Don't Care', 'Guiding Light' and 'Oh Mi Amore' – finally convinced Davis to make a serious bid for Television, but he was competing with at least one other major label. In August 1976 Television finalized a record deal with Elektra, a label with a pedigree that included the Doors, MC5 and the Stooges. An important factor in Elektra's favour was their agreement to let Verlaine produce Television's debut album.

Verlaine had had enough of others attempting to capture Television's sound and decided that he could do the job best himself, despite his inexperience in the studio. Elektra, though, did stipulate that he had to work in conjunction with a respected recording engineer. Andy Johns, Verlaine's eventual choice, may have engineered three of the first four Led Zeppelin albums but it was apparently his work on the Rolling Stones' *Goat's Head Soup* which had impressed Verlaine. Johns would receive co-production credits on *Marquee Moon*.

After nearly three years of stockpiling material, a whole series of songs were rejected during preparatory rehearsals – the ever-popular 'Double Exposure' ('too old'), 'Kingdom Come' ('too long') and 'Oh Mi Amore' among them. According to Verlaine, very little material, save for the album's eight cuts, was actually attempted at the *Marquee Moon* sessions. He knew how he wanted the album to be structured, even before recording began. Virtually all the songs were recorded live, a couple – including the transcendent 'Marquee Moon' – in just one take. Released in February 1977, two years after the bulk of the album was written, *Marquee Moon* closed the book on the peak years of the New York scene.

If all the significant CBGBs bands were having to make shifts in their methodology in order to translate to vinyl, for many it was inconceivable that Suicide could be among the New York bands able to make that necessary adjustment. Yet, by the beginning of 1977, a year after they had resumed gigging at Max's, they were in the studio with Thau and Leon, recording 'Frankie Teardrop' and other atonal howls from the abyss. After the collapse of Mercers, Suicide had spent most of 1974 and 1975 detached from the scene.

Alan Vega: We would go out to town occasionally, or we would play some lofts or an art gallery or something ... We couldn't get into CBs, right away Hilly goes 'No way,' now he's successful he doesn't want us ... It was Marty Thau who finally convinced him.

Though Vega was a regular at CBGBs and Max's during these years, it was in the guise of observer and philanderer.

Alan Vega: I was picking up girls and hanging out at Max's, CBs, other little clubs. I'd be hanging out with Johnny Thunders or Richard Hell. It was a closely knit scene. And we'd all hang out every night. We'd go to Max's at two in the morning and everybody'd be there, seven nights a week, drinking. And [Dean would] keep it open till five in the morning ... By being around, by [Marty] befriending the Dolls and my befriending other people and talking to club owners and hanging out with them and drinking they'd go, 'Hey, Al's a great guy, he's a regular guy, he likes things like we do, he goes to the racetrack.' They all thought – God knows – I was from Mars or something!

In a post-Mercers world, Vega realized that for Suicide to be anything more than an experimental art project, an evolution that linked them to the art-rock aspect of this new scene was required. Vega and Rev spent these two years working on developing their highly original sound, rehearsing and recording demos but making few performances.*

Marty Thau: Alan realized that they'd have to make shifts. They can't play non-music, they have to play music-music – within their style. And that's what he worked on for those years between '72 and '76, when it started clicking. They were trying to reinterpret rock, forseeing the electronic world that was coming and to make some point that was a little bit more real lyrically, [though] most of the bands in New York thought Suicide were the doormats of New York.

If their shift was intended to tone down the element of confrontation in a Suicide performance, one of their first post-Mercers gigs, at Boston's Rat Club at the end of 1975, was not auspicious.

Alan Vega: The first time we did a gig in Boston it was like, 'Wow, they're letting us out of prison' . . . It was at the Rat, which was kinda the Max's or CBs of [Boston]. We almost got killed. I love that reaction. The place was packed because we had the reputation and the reaction was mixed. I'd say one half wanted to kill us and one half loved us.

Some things never changed. An air of confrontation was an essential environment for Suicide, something that Vega thrived on, and sought to compound if he sensed even a whisper of incomprehension. Whatever shifts were required to transform Suicide from Art Project to art-rockers, the element of confrontation needed to remain firmly implanted. The actual change in Suicide was more like the one required by the early Stooges when they passed from a band who played at happenings to one who recorded an album. For Suicide the process of recording demos probably convinced them that something less abstract was needed on tape than what worked in performance.

Alan Vega: In our stupid, naive way we always tried to get a record deal happening so we did try to get more commercial. Of course, we kept

---

* Four demos from this period can be found on a ROIR cassette, *Half-Alive.*

rehearsing all the time. We did play at least three or four times a week . . .
we started getting into songs – not arrangements. We were never into
verse–chorus types of [songs but] we started getting into my vocal thing,
and I started writing a lot more. I started [out] going 'Rocket Rocket USA',
y'know, and that was a lyric . . . Slowly but surely I was getting words . . .
Musically it happened too in a way. Marty always had a good dance thing.
'Cheree' and 'Dream Baby Dream', [which] started out as chaotic plays,
suddenly started to form [into] songs with a dance beat.

Even when they resumed regular gigging at Max's at the beginning of
1976, thanks to the continued support of Peter Crowley, they found
entry into CBGBs barred by an obstinate owner. They did not play a
return gig at Hilly's on the Bowery until the beginning of 1977, Vega
having extended his confrontational approach to a certain club
manager.

Marty Thau: They were not playing CBGBs . . . because Hilly didn't like
them. I think it had something to do with Alan going down one day and
asking for a show and Hilly saying, 'I don't think so.' Alan confronted him,
'Whaddya mean you don't wanna play us? Who the fuck do you think you
are? You don't own this. This is beyond you. You have to play us. You
have no choice. Or is this some game that has to do with how much
money you're gonna make?' And Hilly heard it. I remember going down
after that and confronting him [also], 'You do have to play them. You
have no choice. You must play them.' [I was] yelling at him outside of the
club in the street. It was really funny. And he said, 'Okay, okay, give me a
break. We'll play them.' This was early '77.

By this point Gottehrer and Thau had disbanded their partnership and
Thau was attempting to set up his own record label, with funds again
provided on an extremely limited basis, from a couple of small-time
entrepreneurs in search of a tax dodge. Thau wanted the first release on
his new label, Red Star, to be Suicide's debut album. Thau convinced
Leon, who was residing upstate after the dissolution of Instant Records,
to return to New York to help him attempt to put Suicide across in an
entirely aural medium. A little lo-tech hocus pocus was required, but
the results were certainly innovative.

Craig Leon: [The *Suicide* album was done] at Ultimate Sound [which] wasn't the most high-budget studio . . . over a weekend. There was an engineer so to speak, called Larry, who had made some horrible synthesizer records of the 1812 Overture and things like that. But this guy was getting such a weak sound [I said], 'I'm gonna go in there and overmodulate everything,' . . . That place had a system where you could actually distort the echo and then you could run a delay off of it and that would get the repeat effect that's on [Vega's] voice . . . They played everything at once through an amp and a radio [but the album] is absolutely stereo 'cause it was done even to the point where I would have them double-track things so I could put different EQs on them and split it.

The characters that populate the album – Johnny, the ghost rider, Cheree and Frankie Teardrop – are adrift in a world of existential terror intercut with moments of symphonic beauty. *Suicide* was a genuinely avant-garde album. It was also an unmitigated commercial flop. Yet it has become an immensely influential artefact. In an obvious sense all electropop and synth outfits from the original two-piece Human League (modelled very deliberately on Suicide) to Depeche Mode (who to this day play Suicide over the speakers before their concerts) have based their sound on the one Vega and Rev originally formulated.

However, their real progeny would be the 'no wave' bands that were forming around the time that the Red Star album rolled off the presses. It was these bands who would develop the aesthetic of noise, atonality and repetition in a direction that had been directly anticipated by Suicide. If Suicide had stripped rock bare, the no wavers wanted to exercise a little flagellation with its emaciated frame – and record the results! Sucide was the signpost on the route from art-rock to 'no wave', as the New York scene began to mutate into diverse forms and the first wave passed beyond the confines of the clubs.

Sometimes it takes but one record – one cocksure magical statement, to cold cock all the crapola and all purpose wheatchaff mix'n'match, to set the whole schmear straight and get the current state of play down, down, down, to stand or fall in one dignified granite-hard focus.

Such statements are precious indeed. *Marquee Moon,* the first album from Tom Verlaine's Television is one: a 24-carat inspired work of pure genius, a record finely in tune and sublimely arranged with a whole new slant on dynamics, centred around a totally invigorating passionate application to the vision of mastermind Tom Verlaine – Nick Kent, *NME,* 5 February 1977.

Recorded in November 1976 at A&R Studios in New York, *Marquee Moon* remains probably the most dramatic debut of any American rock band. It was a perfect match of early frenetic Television ('Friction', 'Venus De Milo' and 'Prove It'), their live *tour de force* 'Marquee Moon' and complex new works – the serene 'Guiding Light' and the psychodrama of 'Torn Curtain' – indicating that Verlaine was still thirsting for new vistas. It also gave the lie to those who thought New York's punk bands couldn't play.

Tom Verlaine was holidaying in London when the debut album became an unexpected British success, an ecstatic two-page review from Nick Kent in *New Musical Express* helping to turn anticipation into units.

Tom Verlaine: Nick Kent wrote the first great review of the record. When we finished the record I wanted a week off and I'd never been to London so I flew to London just to hang around. And the day before I was to leave I went to a little Notting Hill Gate magazine store and the band was on the cover [of NME]. So I thought maybe I should call Elektra and I called and spoke to this girl in press and she said, 'Are you in London?' And I said yeah. She said, 'What are you doing here? Why didn't you call a week ago. Everybody wants to talk to you and all this stuff.' And I said, 'Yeah? What's going on?' She said, 'Well this record's a huge hit. Everybody wants to talk about it. Everybody's playing it. You have to come and tour right away, etc.' I thought [the review] was accurate in terms of nailing certain things. I remember he talked about the Byrds' *5D* record. He nailed it in terms of the record had a lot of contrast which is a thing I still like.

Yet eighteen months after the release of *Marquee Moon*, Television would disband, dispirited by a lack of concommitant success in their homeland, the first CBGBs casualty of unrealistic commercial expectations.

Before Television could even play a much-awaited English tour and reinforce their new-found commercial success (a 12″ single of 'Marquee Moon' even made the UK Top 30), Elektra had organized a support slot on ex-Genesis frontman Peter Gabriel's first US tour. Playing small theatres and some larger clubs, the tour may have brought Television a degree of exposure, but the Gabriel/TV line-up was a mismatch. Television were not readily accepted by Gabriel's prog-rock aficionados.

As Television's first real experience of mid-American audiences, the Gabriel tour proved a little unnerving. Despite a positive critical response to the album, *Marquee Moon* failed to make the Top 200 in the US, selling less than 80,000 copies.

The other side of the coin was on display in May, when Television played a highly successful theatre tour of the UK, with the ill-suited Blondie as support act.

Tom Verlaine: It was the first time we'd played big theatres and they were packed and people were extremely enthusiastic, which was really a great thing after playing clubs for four years.

The experience was less rewarding for Blondie. First off, Television were not so happy with the idea of a TV/Blondie bill as they may have been in yesteryear. Both bands had developed along mutually exclusive lines and Verlaine found himself saddled with a support act he did not want.

Chris Stein: We had done that tour with Bowie and Iggy and they were totally helpful and Bowie was completely into making the show like a totality, and then when we toured with Television they were so competitive. The first show we showed up and all our equipment was shoved up at the [Glasgow] Apollo and we had like three feet of room so that Tom could stand still in this vast space.

But Television were now experiencing the problems resulting from an association with an established label like Elektra rather than an 'independent' like Sire. Though Elektra never queried Television studio budgets and provided a highly efficient means of distribution, they never really knew how to promote a band that, though technically profound, had been tarnished by their association with 'punk'.

Returning to the States, Television found that Elektra had largely written off *Marquee Moon* as a commercial non-starter. Rather than launching an assault on American hinterlands, they were consigned back to New York. The period between Television's two spring tours of England was punctuated by just three live gigs. Television seemed reluctant to go out on the road themselves and promote *Marquee Moon*, Verlaine preferring to start work on a second album.

The recording of *Adventure* would be considerably more tortuous than *Marquee Moon*. The first problem was ordinary enough – years working up material for album number 1, just months writing songs for album number 2.

Tom Verlaine: The first Television record was stuff we'd been playing live for three years, so we just went in and played them live. Most of the solos I did were live. Second album was stuff we developed in the studio, taking a break for a week to work up and then recorded.

Verlaine was reluctant to draw upon the archive of Television songs passed over for their debut, even though extensive workouts like 'Kingdom Come', 'Breakin' in My Heart' and 'Poor Circulation' still constituted part of Television's live repertoire. Of the songs on *Adventure*, only 'Foxhole' and 'I Don't Care' (renamed 'Careful' because of the Ramones' song) could be considered 'old' songs.

Verlaine had always been interested in exploring the possibilities offered by studios. New technology offered a previously unavailable opportunity to experiment, particularly on songs he felt the need to kick life into after years of performance.

Tom Verlaine: That whole album was like a series of moods. I remember trying to weird up ['I Don't Care'] in the studio. I told the engineer that I wanted to sing it from across the room – I wanted the mike fifteen feet away and he got really annoyed. I said, 'Well, let's just try it' and we did it and then I wouldn't sing it again.

Though Verlaine later insisted that *Adventure* was completed in just six weeks, it was a far more arduous undertaking than that, using up most of September and October, and half of November and December 1977. Final mixing ran into the first week of February 1978. Part of the problem was a lengthy false start. The first series of sessions yielded just 'Days' and 'Glory', before Verlaine decided to draft in John Jansen to fulfil Andy Johns' engineer role.

The Lloyd/Verlaine guitar-interplays on this album were also less overt, largely because Lloyd was out of action in hospital for much of the time, though Verlaine's increasing determination to decide Television's direction cannot be discounted as a factor. Verlaine worked long trying to capture the elusive sound he was searching for.

Tom Verlaine: I remember Lloyd being very crazed . . . He also wasn't around that much. He was in the hospital for two or three weeks. We started that record with some guy who had worked on a demo . . . Then we decided to get this guy John Jansen. We did the rest of the cuts with him. There was a cut called 'Adventure' which didn't make it to the album . . . We took three weeks off in the middle of this period . . . After doing the first record there was a lot of disenchantment about the way it sounded. Me and Fred would play records and think, 'Why can't we sound this way?'

Many critics consider *Adventure* a failed experiment, but with hindsight it convinces as a logical continuation of certain facets first revealed on *Marquee Moon.* 'Carried Away', 'The Fire' and 'The Dream's Dream' all developed the sensibility first introduced on 'Guiding Light'. 'Glory', 'Foxhole', 'Careful' and 'Ain't that Nothin'', though retaining the abrasive quality of 'Prove It' and 'Friction', were more musically ambitious. But the lack of any obvious anthems, save perhaps for 'Careful', or a major opus around which the album could revolve – plus the nagging suspicion, commented on in several reviews, that Television might just be in the process of becoming the Tom Verlaine band – ensured that *Adventure* was not well received.

If an album as acclaimed as *Marquee Moon* had suffered the ignominy of chart-failure Stateside, *Adventure* was not likely to be the album to establish Television in their homeland. In England some typically malevolent British reviewers rejoiced in dubbing last year's model 'the Ice Kings of rock & roll'. With the storms of imminent backlash a-risin', Elektra organized a UK tour in April 1978, then failed to get the new album out until after the tour. Though *Adventure* still became Top 10 album, Verlaine was increasingly disenchanted with Elektra, sensing an unwillingness to put the full weight of the company behind Television, despite their proven commerciality in the country with the most exciting contemporary pop scene.

Tom Verlaine: I was disappointed in the record company. They gave us tour support, but there was nothing in terms of letting people know about the record. Next to no advertising . . . I think they had the attitude, 'Well, this is an interesting new band that we don't really know what to do about, so, rather than do something they'll hate, we won't do anything.'

Early in the summer of 1978, Television made a final attempt to break down American consumer resistance to their new brand of rock & roll, embarking on a brief coast-to-coast tour. They had never played better. Bootlegs of West Coast shows in Portland and San Francisco illustrate the sheer inventive dynamism of the four-piece. Verlaine and Lloyd's scintillating, almost telepathic interplay had never been stronger, their quicklime leads sliding easily around Smith's granite bedrock. Songs like 'Marquee Moon' and 'Little Johnny Jewel' were reaching new heights of extemporization, rarely clocking in at under fifteen minutes.

But the will to keep banging their heads against the brick wall of *Hotel California* was no longer there. Lloyd had begun to tire of Verlaine's total domination of Television's repertoire and direction. His previously suppressed songwriting instincts were now asserting themselves. He had composed and co-produced a new single by Chris Stamey and the dBs, and the prospect of a longer-term association hung in the air.

Tom Verlaine: I know Richard always wanted to write songs and have his own group. He was writing songs he knew weren't quite right for Television in terms of the sound they put out. I don't know how badly he wanted to do them because he never tried to force them on the rest of us.

Television gave their final shows at the Bottom Line in July 1978. It is tempting, in the light of Verlaine's reputation for imposing his ideas on his co-workers, to see their demise as inevitable. In fact it seems to have been largely unplanned and unexpected.

Tom Verlaine: Me and Lloyd and Fred were walking somewhere one day and I just said, 'God, I really just want to do something else.' And Lloyd said something that really surprised me, 'Yeah, maybe we should have a change.' And that was sort of it. Fred was scratching his head and I think he told Billy.

Just as the Dolls, the originators of the Mercers scene, had never transcended their initial New York appeal, so the originators of the CBGBs scene also disbanded after just two albums, without making serious inroads into the mainstream – except in the one country where the New Wave was not merely a cult phenomenon but a genuine commercial movement.

The break-up of Tom Verlaine's Television confirmed that the buoyancy had gone out of New York's fledgling scene. A band's association with New York was no longer a useful endorsement in the eyes of America's A&R representatives. Within a year the bands formed by the other leading lights of New York's mini-renaissance – Patti Smith and Richard Hell – would go the same way as Television.

When low hit i was in a period of disgrace. of total immobility. low. the fall and potential rising of thomas jerome newton. the sound track of Bowies escape into film. a backdrop for months of head-motion, low provided a state of connective id-mutual non-action. of dream and beyond into creation. a stiff neck person can indeed inter/enter the wrath of the creator. and so i was remembering. i was sliding into the dark backward. revisiting all the carnal landscapes of the bruised interior.

For someone as hyperactive as Patti Smith, the three months of 'total immobility' that followed her Miami fall was bound to prove irksome. But, much like Dylan's fabled motorcycle accident, it allowed an opportunity to take stock of the situation, unchained from touring schedules and recording sessions. Listening to records again, it was Bowie's *Low* that provided Smith with a surprising solace. Her thoughts again turned to writing poetry.

This initially took the form of a book of joint poetry, to be written with Richard Hell. Only a few Hell/Smith poems were completed before Hell realized that the dual commitment of recording his debut album and reviving his poetic career was too demanding. Smith began working alone on a series of new poems. Collected with the best of her earlier efforts, they would be published in 1978 as *Babel*, intended to be a definitive representation of her poetic work to date.

Patti Smith: I was able to clean up a lot of loose ends and best of all, I wrote a book – which I'm really proud of . . . I was able to do a lot of work I hadn't been able to do for a long time . . . the other books were like very spontaneous efforts . . . I haven't published anything since early '73, because I was so intensely involved in performing and verbal expression that I lost contact with the word on paper ... [*Babel*] is entirely different. Firstly, it's mostly prose pieces, they're longer and there's much more voyage ... I wrote a lot of [*Babel*] in a very unusual state of mind, because I had special prescriptions from doctors, so I think that it deals with a very subliminal landscape.

Anxious to confirm that the flame still burned, Smith arranged a couple of shows at CBGBs – where else? – to celebrate Easter, and her own resurrection. Given that she played the shows in a neck brace, it is not too surprising that they were somewhat stilted performances, though fans were happy to queue around the block just to see her alive 'n' kickin'.

Further shows at CBGBs in June and the Elgin Theatre and Village Gate in July confirmed her gradual physical and mental recovery, but there was an audible contraction of the Patti Smith Group's chosen parameters. Though Smith was 'out of traction, back in action', the 1977 shows were very different from previous efforts. No mistaking, this was a rock & roll band!

Lenny Kaye: When she fell off the stage that was the realest of moments. We were so good that night. We were so locked as a band. We were so into that particular moment in 'Ain't it Strange' where she challenges God. 'Come on God, make a move.' And at that point we would always, when we were really locked, wobble the music, make it dizzy. And she whirled off the stage. That was the turning point. After that our music definitely changed. To me it was the apex ... After moving outwards to see how far we could push [it], the envelope [was] coming back.

If 'Radio Ethiopia' was still an integral part of the Patti Smith Group live set, it was devolving into a more accessible form. As Smith said, 'It's shorter and faster. It's still improvisational, but it's shorter, stronger and it's not so much groping around.'

The remainder of the show was composed of short, sharp shocks; songs like 'Free Money', 'Redondo Beach', 'Ask the Angels', 'Time is on My Side' and – restored to the set – 'Space Monkey'. The shows did not resolve what direction the Patti Smith Group intended to pursue on their third vinyl expedition. Smith, talking about her next album before her fall, had said it was going to be called *Rock & Roll Nigger*, which suggested an even more rock-oriented effort than *Radio Ethiopia*. Within a week of her fall she was talking about the album in terms of a celebration.

Patti Smith: It's [gonna be] more of a resurrection . . . it's more creatively sparking, more celebratory, we're bouncing right back! It's gonna be a celebration of the whole new scene, the whole new wave.

The producer for this 'resurrection' album was not a propitious choice. Jimmy Iovine was Main (as in Mammon) Stream. Their early discussions suggested that he was looking to temper the band's more radical explorations.

Patti Smith: [Jimmy] calls the kind of music that I like 'building-burning music'. He says, like, 'Your next record can't be a bunch of building-burning music.' That's what he calls *Radio Ethiopia*.

After the commercial and critical lambasting the second album had received, the third album needed to affirm Smith's desire to reinvent the form. As it is, *Easter* may well be the Patti Smith Group's definitive rock & roll expression. A relentless catalogue of anthems, it confirmed their place in the rock & roll pantheon. But *Easter* also proved that Smith was never going to extend herself beyond the boundaries previously set by *Horses* and *Radio Ethiopia*. *Easter* may have been a beautifully crafted album but it was built largely around old songs. The album's most powerful expressions were the song Iovine obtained from Bruce Springsteen, 'Because the Night'; a trilogy of pre-*Horses* live favourites, 'Space Monkey', 'Privilege (Set Me Free)' and 'We Three'; and the pre-fall showstopper, 'Rock & Roll Nigger'.

The unexpected success of the 'Because the Night' 45 gave Smith a renewed commercial standing, without recovering her previous favour with the critics. An extensive tour to promote *Easter*, lasting most of the spring and summer of 1978, may have showed her determination to re-establish herself, but she was still going adrift as far as most critics were concerned and her public statements failed to assuage their sense of disillusionment. The critical backlash to *Radio Ethiopia* was nothing to the one that greeted Smith's passage into mass acceptance. She was not helping matters herself.

Patti Smith: I don't talk to most press people, 'cause they don't care any more. I wanna talk to somebody that cares, that isn't interested in writin' a bunch of gossip and bullshit and their own twisted ideas of what we're doin' . . . I think that a true hero can only be criticized by himself. A true hero is his own highest critic. What he needs is support, he needs confidence, he needs the energy and the strength of the people. He doesn't need criticism.

At a press conference in England in 1978 she harangued the English press simply for reporting that she had recently left her long-standing boyfriend Allen Lanier and moved in with ex-MC5 guitarist Fred 'Sonic' Smith, instructing them to 'put more integrity in[to] your writing, because there's people out there who believe.'

Patti's relationship with Fred Smith was only part of a radical change in her life. The first intimation of the psychological consequences of her fall was a quote from the New Testament in the sleeve-notes to *Easter* – 'I have fought a good fight, I have finished my course . . .' (2 Timothy 4:7) – implying that Smith had abandoned her apostasy and allocated a finite span of time to her pursuance of the rock & roll dream. All the evidence suggested that Smith was re-evaluating her beliefs, increasingly unsure that Jesus only died for 'somebody's sins!' In interviews she began to rationalize her previous oath of disobedience.

Patti Smith: I wasn't saying that I didn't like Christ or didn't believe in Him, just that I wanted to take the responsibility for the things I do – I didn't want some mythical or ethical symbol taking the credit for what I do . . . I'm a very Old Testament kind of person in that in the Old Testament man communicated with God directly; in the New Testament man has to communicate with God through Christ . . . I'm learning to accept a more New Testament kind of communication. So as part of that acceptance I have to re-evaluate exactly who Christ was.

The album she began work on in the winter of 1978–9 was her most overt testament to a new-found spirituality. Lenny Kaye sees the *Wave* album as the culmination of Smith's spiritual journey, from agnostic to advocate. It was to be the final wave.

Lenny Kaye: The whole band's movement is from 'Jesus died for somebody's sins' through that final little track on *Wave* which is a complete *rapprochement* with the spirit – not the actuality 'cause Patti didn't really believe in religious dogma – of Christianity ... She utilized rock & roll as an intense examination of her entire spiritual core – and to her the spiritual core is the creative ideal. That was our synonym for God. Basically she had certain questions when she began as an artist and through her art she was able to answer them and come to the end of the rainbow.

By the time that Smith was promoting *Wave* on the road in the spring of 1979, she was prefacing 'Gloria' with a brief rap. It is tempting to see the rap as some kind of apologia for the song's sentiments: 'For now this is my answer: I must accept the Truth. But then again, is this answer forever? Is it just one simple question in the quest from my youth?'

Wave was the first product of a relocated Patti Smith. In the fall of 1978 she had moved to Detroit to set up home with 'Sonic' Smith. It was the end of Patti's symbiotic relationship with New York. If Detroit was no Abyssinia, it suggested that her energies were no longer so intensely directed into her work.

Patti Smith: I love New York, but it's a matter of heart why I've been living in Detroit ... I just felt I did everything I could have done in my twelve years in New York. It's my spiritual home, where I flourished as an artist and gained confidence as a person. But I've never been afraid of change.

Though it produced another hit single with 'Dancing Barefoot', *Wave* was not well received. The inclusion of a lacklustre rendition of the Byrds' '(So You Wanna be) A Rock & Roll Star' came in for much ridicule. It seemed that the critical backlash, rather than waning, was reaching new heights. The entire Patti Smith Group was made aware of it. Even previous supporters like the staff of *New York Rocker*, and Jane Suck in London, expressed bitter disappointment at both the album and recent live performances.

Lenny Kaye: Our attempts at reaching beyond expectations of what we did and what people were listening to weren't meeting with very much success. We felt a lot of resistance on all levels.

Despite critics' hostile reception for *Wave*, Smith's summer tour of Europe was an itinerary of large arenas, culminating in a series of shows in Italy. 'Radio Ethiopia' had finally been excised from the set. The inclusion of rock standards like Dylan's 'Mr Tambourine Man', John Lennon's 'It's Hard', the Who's 'The Kids are Alright', Manfred Mann's '5–4–3–2–1', Presley's 'Jailhouse Rock' and Spector's 'Be My Baby' – but with lead-vocal duties taken by assorted members of the Patti Smith Group – helped to create an arena-style show. Smith was taking fewer and fewer gambles with her music. On *Wave*, she had mined her early efforts to provide 'Seven Ways of Going'. Considering the erratic quality of the new originals, perhaps the well had indeed run dry.

Lenny Kaye: She couldn't have gone out there and done a jukebox of her greatest hits and towards the end that's what people wanted. We'd be playing these places eight to twelve thousand. Size of that place you can hardly play 'Radio Ethiopia'. People wanted to have their cork popped at the right moment. In a sense I agree with her because we were done. We didn't have any songs in the pipeline.

The final Italian shows were dispiriting affairs. There were even reports of Smith being pelted with fruit by a certain member of the audience. When Smith suggested a respite after the August shows, her group was not to know that she was really calling time. Smith had tired of the industry, of critics, of false expectations.

The Patti Smith Group would make one final appearance before being consigned to the barbs of posterity. When Smith agreed to appear at a benefit for Detroit's symphonic orchestra at the Masonic Temple in June 1980, fans must have hoped it would signal the start of a third era. Though the benefit proved to be no more than a footnote to Patti Lee Smith's story, there were a couple of instances which suggested the PSG need not have ended this way.

Lenny Kaye: The first part was Patti reading poems from her book . . . her reading was as strong as I've seen it since the early days when that was primarily what she was, a poetry reader. Then she read a segment from the Bible – I'm not exactly sure what chapter and verse. Then Richard Sohl played 'Hymn', from the last album, on this big pipe organ, and Patti sang it . . . Fred 'Sonic' [Smith] and Patti came out and they lowered a screen, and on the screen they showed a film of Jackson Pollock painting. They turned a guitar on to feedback, leaned it against the amp, and they played

– Fred on saxophone and Patti on clarinet . . . It was real, actual improvisatory jamming, and as the soundtrack to this Jackson Pollock film very, very heavy. [Then on came the Patti Smith Group.] We opened with 'The Hunter Gets Captured By the Game', an old fave, and then we did an oldie we used to do, 'It's All in My Mind' by Maxine Brown. We did a Cole Porter standard, 'I Concentrate on You' – Patti's always been into that kind of Chris Connor/Julie London '50s school of heart-throbbing. Then we did two new songs which probably form a direction we'll be moving in. One is called 'Torches', which is a kind of Appalachian reel or English folk-dance tune. Then we closed the set with a song we've been working on, on and off for about the last year, called 'Afghanistan'. It's a very moody, chant-oriented song in a kind of Arabic mode – Patti played clarinet, Sohl on piano and synthesizer, and I played bass. It's very open ended in the sense of 'Seven Ways of Going'.

If there was some impatience in the audience at Smith's abstract approach to the performance, her fans were considerably more bemused by her decision to read Chapter 28 of the gospel according to Matthew (dealing with Christ's resurrection).

The new songs, though, suggested a new development. 'Afghanistan' in particular implied that Patti had been listening intently to her Albert Ayler records and that her clarinet lessons had not been entirely in vain. Though more instrumental than previous 'fields', it was very much a return to the direction at the time of 'Radio Ethiopia'. When Smith made her vinyl return, some eight years later, minus any of the group who had served her so well, it was clear that she had abandoned such intriguing avenues of exploration.

If the August 1979 shows mark the effective end of the Patti Smith Group, they had at least managed three vinyl statements which attempted to replicate the innovative flair of Smith's remarkable debut album. When Richard Hell & the Voidoids disbanded in the fall of the same year – three and a half years after their formation – Hell had just one long-player to his name. Yet *Blank Generation* remains as noteworthy, if not quite as renowned, a landmark in American rock & roll as *Horses*.

Though *Blank Generation* was the only significant result of forty months in the Void, Hell – by the time he completed the album – had recorded most of the songs for between two and four separate 'projects'. Several songs had already been recorded prior to any Sire sessions. The prototype 'Love Comes in Spurts' had been recorded with the Neon Boys, its finished form with the Heartbreakers. 'Blank Generation' had also been recorded with the Heartbreakers and as the title track for the Voidoids' first EP. 'You Gotta Lose', 'I'm Your Man', 'Another World' and 'Betrayal Takes Two' had all been demoed by the Voidoids in 1976. Of the songs intended for the album when sessions commenced in March 1977, only 'Down at the Rock & Roll Club' had not formed part of the Voidoids repertoire in the late fall of 1976.

Blank Generation was completed in just three weeks, at the same studio and in the same time span as *Horses*, and Hell seemed genuinely enthusiastic about it. However, this would not be the album that would belong to the blank generation. While it was being recorded, Sire had been negotiating a new distribution deal through Warner Brothers. The deal would ensure that Sire product could compete with the major labels, thus giving its roster of acts a fair crack at the American consumer. Sire convinced their new acts, including Hell, Talking

Heads and Tuff Darts, to await the completion of the distribution deal before releasing their debut albums. During the delay, Hell began to have serious doubts about the results secured at Electric Lady.

Richard Hell: It was frustrating ... when we finished the whole album and they couldn't release it because they were going from ABC to Warners. We'd recorded it and and it was due to come out right away and there was this delay of seven to eight months until all this business had been taken care of with Warners. And after a couple of months of this waiting I was thinking I'd like to do this and that song over again.

Richard Hell & the Voidoids began re-recording parts of their long-awaited debut at Plaza Sound Studios in June. They ended up re-recording almost the entire album. Among the songs discarded in the process were versions of 'I'm Your Man', 'You Gotta Lose' and Frank Sinatra's 'All the Way'. Only 'Another World', 'Liars Beware' and 'New Pleasure' survived the transition. Superior takes of 'Love Comes in Spurts' and 'Down at the Rock & Roll Club' were early casualties. After four years, three bands and a seemingly endless series of demos, Hell was beyond caring. As he dispassionately observed at the end of the second set of sessions:

My heart wasn't really in the record's re-recording and I didn't sing as well as at Electric Lady, but we're using most of it because the arrangements are so much better. I'm [just] so sick of hearing all the material and postponements and the attempt to concentrate while mixing, supervising the album's design, etc.

In the same diary entry, Hell betrayed his own doubts about following through on the promise of the album, despite the favourable hype that the prospect of its release seemed to be generating:

I have no idea what to expect when the album comes out (except I expect critics to like it). I don't know at all how much I will (like it). I do know that with Warners distributing and promoting, and with such attention as I've gotten in *Time, Newsweek* & the *NY Times* recently – even before a record appears – that I've finally got real shot at getting what I want and that what I make of things – my consciousness – will soon be out there having what impact it will [but] I don't know whether I have the stamina to take it all the way.

Though *Blank Generation* had undoubtedly been impaired by some of the changes, it still affirmed Hell's importance. Any album featuring the adrenalin rush of 'Love Comes in Spurts', the subterranean sensuality of 'Another World', the Voidoids' staccato rendition of Creedence's 'Walking on the Water', the anthemic title track and the psycho-waltz 'Betrayal Takes Two', would be deserving of serious attention. Unfortunately it also represented the culmination of Hell's rock & roll ambitions. The mundane aspects of promotion, in particular the prospect of incessant touring, held little appeal for him.

Richard Hell: I realized shortly after our first album came out that I wasn't ambitious to become a pop star more than I was determined to do what I wanted to do every day. Success is a record company's top priority. I just wanted to sleep late more often . . . As a matter of fact, when that record came out I felt like quitting rock & roll. I'd accomplished what I set out to do and I felt like I wanted to disappear, pack my handkerchief and catch a boat to Africa.

In an early entry in his diary, Hell had written of the French symbolists that he so admired: '[they] die young because they have the courage to lay the heart bare and write the book after which only death (or maybe conversion . . .) remains.' Hell considered that he had now written his book. Unlike his friend, Patti Smith, conversion was not an option. Death was certainly a possibility.

Hell's fear of the chimera of fame was partially a corollary to a spiralling drug habit. Since his days in the Heartbreakers the sentiments of 'Chinese Rocks' had become all too real in his life. His drug dependency contributed to a torturous first UK tour in the autumn of 1977. If Hell was unsure whether he wanted to follow through with the promotion of his debut album, i.e. going 'on the road', his first experience confirmed his worst fears.

Despite his standing as one of punk's true originals and stylistic innovators, plus the small-time success of the *Blank Generation* EP (which had apparently sold out of its original UK pressing of 5,000 in just four weeks), Hell had been consigned to support the Clash on a UK tour.

Richard Hell: We were all miserable. I realize that in retrospect we were kinda naive and very arrogant but we thought we were really being mistreated by the record company. We had to travel all around the country – the five of us in a minibus. But that's what every young band really has to go through starting off. It infuriated us with the label and the Clash would come on, opening up with 'I'm So Bored with the USA' ... they were encouraging the tendency to reject anything American that was a part of punk in England ... To me it was a little disappointing and humiliating to have to open for a British punk group – period. So it was kinda miserable and I was kinda strung out. As a matter of fact on that tour when we first got there I was hanging out with some girl in London who was flamboyantly self-destructive – just my type at the time – and we were doing a lot of drugs and one night she had some English drug that I didn't know what it was and she said it was great and it was shootable and I wanted to shoot it even though it was a pill and so we had to go through this elaborate mashing it up and cooking it and filtering out the mush and then we're in a nightclub and we have to go into the girls restroom to shoot up. We're already drunk. It's about four in the morning and I'm trying to shoot this awful gunk into my left arm. I miss the vein and inject the whole thing – turned out it was like a Mandrax – and when you miss your vein with one of these tranquilizers like that you get an incredible bruise like an abcess. My whole left arm was one big, mushy bruise for the entire tour and it hurt. So I was half-incapacitated.

Though the Clash would have been among the first to acknowledge Hell's importance, their fans were wont to show appreciation and/or disgust by gobbing at the band. Playing to a hardcore punk audience, who had no time for the sinuous melodrama of 'Another World', the Voidoids were given a very rough ride.

Bob Quine: [We were] getting hit in the head with unopened cans of beer ... I remember one night the drummer had blood in several places streaming down his forehead. The gobbing thing was at its full peak. I can't say I appreciated that ... That was the turning point for the end of the band ... [Hell] was totally fed up. He was totally disillusioned with Sire. It poisoned me permanently against tours. I couldn't have gone on another day [with] what we were subjected to.

Hell recorded his feelings of total alienation in a diary entry for 1 November 1977:

I'm in Sheffield, on tour with Clash and it's become completely clear that I've lost interest in rock & roll. It's the exact eternal feeling that I want to leave, which seems to be my most profound characteristic. I began to suspect it as soon as we'd finished the album and I actually knew it by the time we arrived in England.

The failure of Sire to release *Blank Generation* in the UK until the end of the tour totally soured Hell's relationship with his record label. Their final gig on the tour was a one-off show at the Music Machine in London, which they were actually headlining. The Voidoids sounded (as indeed they were) positively demented, playing at last to a packed Music Machine crowd, there to see Hell, not some English Stones-clones. At the end of the show, Johnny Rotten climbed on to the stage and demanded that the audience cajole the Voidoids into coming back one more time, to deliver the most intense 'I Wanna Be Your Dog' since the Stooges had been put to sleep.

Despite such moments, Hell's manic-depressive demeanour remained largely unchanged. Before his first album had even been released, Hell had developed a – partially justified – reputation for espousing a dangerously nihilistic aesthetic. The author of 'Love Comes in Spurts', 'Hurt Me', '(I Belong to the) Blank Generation' and 'You Gotta Lose' could hardly be considered to paint an assuredly positive view of the world. Though Hell insisted at the time that he was searching for 'a positive method for believing in the worth of life that doesn't exclude the horror – a way of perceiving it that ultimately means its inherent worth', his serious junk habit accentuated the natural lows and diluted the highs.

Richard Hell: It got worse and worse as my drug problem got worse and worse. Everything seemed futile or impossible . . . That was the way I saw things. I was pretty hopeless. The drug thing followed as much as it led from this state of mind . . . I did actually say all those things and I was thinking that way. It was partly being a Devil's Advocate. It was partly in response to the ludicrousness of the sentiments you hear in pop music.

The drugs also began to colour Hell's judgement. His first miscalculation on returning to the States was his decision to disentangle himself from Sire at all costs. Despite the difficulties back in 1976 in first securing a contract, it does not seem to have occurred to Hell that he might not find a more sympathetic outlet for his records than Sire – however he may have felt they had treated the band.

Richard Hell: After that tour we had a little loophole that allowed us to [quit Sire] . . . So we got off Sire. I thought it was gonna be a breeze. I thought as soon as we got off, somebody's gonna snap us up but NO! I was totally fucked up and strung out. I thought of myself as a prize item from a record [company] point of view. I realize now, why should we be? We were talking for a long time to Earl McGrath who was running Rolling Stones Records. He told us that Mick and Keith liked us and he was coming to our shows and we thought it was pretty well certain. But they backed out at the last minute and that was our last good prospect.

Given that he had decided to extricate himself from the Sire contract, Hell was unwilling to tour the US to promote the Sire album. What few shows the Voidoids did play in the winter and spring of 1978 featured a new bassist, Jerry Antonius. Hell had abandoned the bass to concentrate on his lead vocals, feeling that it 'interferes too much with my attempts to communicate with face, flesh, and voice'. At least one Voidoid felt it was a mistake.

Bob Quine: By early '78 [Hell] would not play bass. Between him giving the bass chores to somebody else and the drummer problem – we went through several drummers – it was never the same . . . There's no substitute for his bass-playing, the way he played 'You Gotta Lose' with his brutality . . . [The others] had no fuckin' balls to it!

The most serious interference to the Voidoids' plans for regeneration, though, resulted from Hell's new-found interest in acting. A long-standing fan of *film noir* and Orson Welles, Hell was offered the opportunity to 'star' in a new film which took its title from Hell's most famous song, 'Blank Generation'. Directed by Ulli 'Tenderness of the Wolves' Lommel, it was to feature the Voidoids in concert and Hell as the 'romantic' lead – playing a disillusioned rock star.

Bob Quine: At that point Hell seemed more interested in [the film]. This took several months to do and the band was extremely inactive. That's when Marc Bell got his offer from the Ramones . . . [We] got out of [our] contract with Sire. There was one point where we were ready to, and they wanted us to, do a second album – early '78 – and we would have except for the movie. And by the time we got around to it we decided we didn't want to be with Sire Records.

The film ended up mutating in mid-shoot, the results retaining little of the original concept. Hell would observe in February 1978, '[Lommel] wrote himself into it just cuz he couldn't stand ceding the attention of the beautiful women to me even when they're acting . . . Lommel was bringing in new scenes to shoot every day, none of which had any perceptible relationship to the original script and which he refused to explain.' By the time the Voidoids played their second UK tour, in January 1979, Hell was disowning the film for the cul-de-sac it had proved to be. However, it would not be the end of his movie ambitions.

When the Voidoids finally resumed activities, they not only featured a new bassist but a new drummer, Frank Mauro. Marc Bell had replaced Tommy Erdelyi in the Ramones, after a final show with Tommy at CBGBs on 4 May 1978. Throughout the summer and fall the Voidoids kept hoping that Rolling Stones Records would come through with their promised record deal. Hell even put off a firm offer from Private Stock in the interim. By the time it became evident that the Rolling Stones were just toying with the idea of a record label, the one remaining offer was from the newly established English label Radar Records.

Radar had been set up by Elvis Costello's manager, Jake Rivera. Costello, undoubtedly Radar's prime asset, was a fan of Hell's, joining him to perform 'You Gotta Lose' on a New York radio broadcast, and Costello's producer, Nick Lowe, was keen to produce Hell. At the end of October 1978 the Voidoids recorded a single with Lowe, the recently composed 'Kid with the Replaceable Head', paired with the old stalwart 'I'm Your Man'. It was intended as a taster for a second Voidoids album, to be recorded in England in the New Year.

Bob Quine: Nick Lowe came over to my house one day and sat around. He wanted to produce us . . . We were originally going to do an album with him but meanwhile we would do this single – we did it in like two days – and on the strength of that we'd tour with Elvis Costello [in the UK] . . . [Radar] were presented with a band that was fairly well demoralized despite what they were doing for us. They put us in a pretty nice houseboat

Patti Smith, 'out of traction, back in action', at a benefit for *Punk*, May 1977.

Johnny Thunders'
Heartbreakers in London,
circa 1977.

Richard Hell & the Voidoids Mk 1 (*left to right*): Bob Quine, Richard Hell, Ivan Julian, Marc Bell.

After Iggy & the Stooges, cometh Iggy & the Ramones, CBGBs, circa 1976.

Debbie Harry and Chris Stein enjoy the fruits of their labour, circa 1979.

'No, you first.' Crocus Behemoth and Peter Laughner go on the air, 13 April 1976.

Crocus Behemoth caught smiling, 13 April 1976.

Television, poised to pose, circa 1976.

but we were not getting along well enough to live in a houseboat together, in any kind of communal situation whatsoever. We were allegedly going to do an album when this tour ended. That's the only reason we did the tour. I think what probably happened [was] they didn't see a lot of new material. They saw a band who did not get on. Then after staying in London they said, 'Okay. Go back to the States. We're gonna postpone it a while.'

Though their January 1979 UK tour with Costello was less traumatic than the previous one with the Clash, it signalled the end of the Voidoids Mk 2. Another rhythm section had had enough of the lack of any obvious direction from Hell and the continual bickering between Hell and Quine. Hell seemed happy enough to see them gone.

Bob Quine: We got a new bass player and drummer after a lot of rehearsals. They were good [but] it was never like the first band. They walked into a fairly poisonous situation. We did a last set of demos in late '79. We could have gone on indefinitely. Certainly we were making good money. He had some booking agency sending us around.

When the Radar deal fell through, the Voidoids had no outlets for vinyl output. Reasons for persevering with the Voidoids were fast diminishing.

Yet Hell had more than enough original material to record a second album.* What Hell no longer had was the opportunity to release these songs. Further demos that summer failed to secure the recording deal that might have saved the Voidoids, and though 'Don't Die' and 'Time' became part of a *Richard Hell – Past and Present* EP released at the beginning of 1980 on Alan Betrock's Shake Records, the Voidoids Mk 3 had already folded. Hell had had enough of rock & roll, and Quine was heartily sick of Hell.

Robert Quine: [Richard] can't seem to make up his mind whether he wants to be a rock star like Elvis Costello or just go die.

Though Hell has indulged in occasional discreet flirtations with rock &

---

* Aside from the two sides of the Radar single, the Voidoids were performing songs like 'Funhunt', 'Lowest Common Dominator', 'Staring in Her Eyes', 'Don't Die', 'Time', 'Ignore That Door' and 'Crack of Dawn'.

roll throughout the succeeding decade, even managing a second Voidoids album of sorts, 1982's *Destiny Street* (only Quine remained from the
original band), the demise of the Quine/Julian Voidoids marked the
end of any serious ambitions he held in the pop arena.

If their experiences on their two UK tours had played a large part in
the Voidoid's disillusionment with rock & roll, it was not only Hell who
was being subjected to the intolerance of European punk audiences. In
the year between the Voidoids' support slots on Clash and Costello
tours, Suicide were the special guests of first Costello – on a summer
tour of the Continent – and then the Clash, on their fall '78 tour of the
UK. The treatment they received on the Clash tour was considerably
more severe than that meted out to Hell.

Alan Vega: I got beaten up a couple of times on that tour with the Clash.
The skins got me a bunch of times, the Nazis, the National Front, the
swastika armbands. I got my nose busted on stage in Crawley. The Sham
69 guy got a thousand skins with him to come to the gig . . . they didn't like
me. They jumped me from both sides [even though] they had these huge
barricades. They crawled over the barricades. They got me and busted me
up. I was bleeding like a pig . . . In Glasgow somebody threw an axe by my
head! . . . in Plymouth the Nazis . . . got me in the dressing room. Marty
was still on stage with his keyboard thing and I got into the dressing room
and there's all these guys with armbands [and] I don't know why . . . I used
to improvise a lot. Maybe I did start singing anti-Nazi songs. I would tend
to do things like that. Maybe someone screamed at us and I answered
back. That would happen all the time . . . The problem was all the kids that
hated us fought all the kids that loved us. They'd push them to the back if
they caught anybody applauding us and beat them up.

If Suicide's brand of music induced a particularly violent reaction at the
Clash shows, their support slot on Costello's tour caused something
between bedlam and full-scale riots at every turn. In Brussels on 16
June 1978, the crowd actually trashed the venue and Costello's set had
to be cancelled. This performance was immortalized on a flexi-disc
album, *23 Minutes in Brussels*, included with the 1980 reissue of Suicide's
debut album. As Lester Bangs observed, it was Suicide's *Metallic K.O.*,
and provides the best exposition on Suicide's performance art. Not

surprisingly it was 'Frankie Teardrop' that finally precipitated the violence.

Alan Vega: [It] didn't start with the Clash, it started with Elvis on the Continent ... There was a riot every night with Elvis. Some nights they wouldn't go on. They were crazed. When we [hooked up] it was the ninth, tenth month of their tour and I think they'd been doing a lot of speed ... one night we had this big thing in Belgium and it was a major riot – they never even got on! It was a police riot – they came in with tear gas. We played and started a whole riot – just doing Suicide ... There were times Marty would look at me and go, 'It's your performance thing!' and then there were times I'd go, 'It's your music that did it!' That sound, that grungy kinda thing. It wasn't like the Sex Pistols, it didn't have that guitar thing, it didn't have that drum thing they could immediately relate to ... 'Where's the guitar player – it's only two guys!' I think that had a lot to do with it. The two-man thing ... So after the gig in Belgium, Elvis catches me and he goes, 'Al, do you think you could do that for us tomorrow?'

As a further parallel to the experiences of the Voidoids, Suicide – after their support stint with the Clash – decided to play their own British mini-tour on the back of some extremely positive European press and the belated UK release of their debut album. This time the audience response was refreshingly positive. Indeed, it was enthusiastic enough to be of concern to Vega, who was not entirely at ease when an element of confrontation was removed.

Alan Vega: We went on an eight-day tour after the Clash, and Edinburgh was like the third night of the tour, of our own tour, and I remember the place – [Tiffany's], a great club – it was packed! Must've been a thousand people in there. And we're playing and suddenly I noticed people were moving all over the place and I go, 'Oh shit!' Like, they're getting ready to charge ... At Tiffany's they had these revolving lights. They came on and I noticed everyone was dancing and I walked back to Marty and I said, 'What am I going to do? It's over. I have no one to intimidate, no one's intimidated – they love this shit. No matter what we do tonight, how crazy we are – look at 'em, a thousand people are dancing – what are we gonna do?' I knew from that day, it's all over with. That's why I like that hostile reaction. It means you're still doing something.

Even Suicide, in a climate that tolerated the likes of Devo and Pere

Ubu, with Suicide-copyists like the original two-piece Human League also gaining kudos, and with the gold stamp of music-press approval plus an album which gently introduced the listener to the Suicide concepts, were being assimilated. Like Ubu, they found a degree of acceptance among the UK's considerable swell of New Wave fans, at least when removed from those Clash devotees who were one step down the evolutionary ladder from even New York's 'fuck art' fraternity.

Yet even in 1980, when their second and 'final' album was released, produced by Ric Ocasek of Cars fame, Suicide attracted minimal interest (or sales) in the US, however well the children of Suicide might have been selling.

Alan Vega: We got signed to Ze, and Ric did the record! . . . [but we] came back to America to nothing again. Punk was dying and what was happening was something that Suicide really created — the techno-pop thing, and again they weren't letting Suicide have it . . . it was still too crazed. We tried to be commercial but it was too much . . . Suicide is easy listening music to me . . . And you can never understand, when you put it out, people going, 'What the fuck is this?' . . . to you it's the most ordinary thing in the world.

New York's prophets of punk were destined to remain honoured save in their own house.

Peter Laughner's choice of name for his post-Ubu band, Friction, was intended not as a comment on his relationship with his ex-outfit, but a direct reference to his enduring love for Television. Which is not to say that Laughner did not have grounds for grievance. If being expelled from Ubu was not bad enough, purloining the bassist in his new band, Tony Maimone, as replacement for the disgruntled Tim Wright, was adding insult to injury. Maimone had been very much a Laughner protégé.

Tony Maimone: I [had] heard about this building downtown, called the Plaza. I was tending bar at this place called the Piccadilly Penthouse, where a lot of bands were starting to come through, mainly on Peter's recommendation . . . So I got a place in the Plaza, I got a couple of amps, and I just decided I was gonna learn how to play. I was basically playing to records, blues records mainly, and Peter just loved music and he loved playing and as soon as he found out that there was someone who was always sitting around there playing, he just started showing up. He'd always be coming home with his guitar, he'd have his sixpack, and he'd just start bringing records over, like *The Harder They Come*, the Springsteen album which had 'For You' on it? . . . [Peter], more than anybody else, really opened it up for me, he just showed me how easy it was.

After Ubu, Laughner was quick to recruit Maimone, and Anton Fier – then playing part-time in the Styrenes – for his new band. After rehearsals at Fier's house, they made their debut at a birthday party for the manager of a Shaker Square bookstore, at a club called Earth By April. Two familiar faces were in the audience.

Tony Maimone: I was looking out into the audience that night at Earth By April and seeing David in his black raincoat and seeing Tom [Herman]. I could see them checking me out as we played, and after [the set] they came up and asked me if I'd like to get together and jam one night, and back then, with Ubu, if you were being invited to jam with the band, you were being invited to join the band. It was an easy decision for me to make, 'cause Peter was going up to New York a lot. Even though he said he wanted to be in a band he was coming and going, and these guys were rehearsing a couple of nights a week.

Maimone's change in loyalties benefited both Ubu and Friction. Friction in its original three-piece form was breaking little new ground with its standard rock-trio sound and a set primarily composed of covers, albeit perverse in both selection and execution – largely Stones, Velvets, Dylan and Television – interspersed with a couple of Laughner originals. As such Friction was really a continuation of Laughner's previous covers band, Peter and the Wolves, which had been composed of three Ubu-ites (Laughner, Herman and Krauss) and had played regularly at the Bottleworks in the winter of 1975–6, a part-time alternative to Ubu.

The second version of Friction, which debuted alongside the reconstituted, five-piece Ubu at the Pirate's Cove on 2 November 1976, was a four-piece recreation of Laughner's Cinderella's Revenge outfit, with Fier substituting for Eric Ritz on drums. Deborah Smith, who was contributing bass and violin, had played regularly with Laughner as a bass/electric guitar duo in the years between Cinderella's Revenge and Friction.

The new Friction managed to achieve a far more satisfactory balance between covers and Laughner originals, and a more original sound. Aside from the aching 'Don't Take Your Love Away', graced with Smith's sawing violin and a soulful counter-vocal by Sue Schmidt, there was the jazz-tinged 'Hideaway', an explosive 'Dear Richard' – 'an answer to an unwritten suicide note' – and a song to suggest Richard Thompson's profound influence, 'Old Song Resung' (actually a W. B. Yeats poem Laughner had set to his own folk-rock tune). Of Friction's many covers, the highlights were a reggaefied medley of Dylan's 'Knockin' on Heaven's Door' and 'Billy', and a ten-minute virtuoso guitar and violin arrangement of Richard Thompson's

'Calvary Cross', which Laughner insisted on playing in the original open key rather than transposing to an easier key.

The 2 November Pirate's Cove gig was also the live initiation of Pere Ubu Mk 3. The new five-piece Ubu's first activity had been to record a third single, 'Street Waves', before searching for a regular place to gig. Since the Viking had burnt down, there had been no real local alternatives. Ubu used a tactic similar to the one used by Television to convince Hilly Kristal to book them at CBGBs. They had located a club called Pirate's Cove in the Flats. Business tended to verge on the deathly mid-week.

Tony Maimone: [The owner of Pirate's Cove] just didn't have anything going on on Thursday nights and I can't remember who actually asked him, we just said, 'Let us come in and we'll play for the door, there's no risk to you.' We brought in the PA system.

If the fall 1976 Friction/Ubu gigs marked the rebirth of Ubu, they provided only a final, exasperating hint of Laughner's fading brilliance. Less than eight months after the first Friction Pirate's Cove gig, Laughner was dead – from acute pancreatitis – and he wasn't even 25. Friction itself barely lasted out the fall, metamorphosing into a new version of Peter and the Wolves in which Laughner's new girlfriend, Adele Bertei (Pressler was in the process of divorcing Laughner), contributed guitar/vocals.

Tony Maimone: Peter had different guitar players, sometimes it was Doug's brother Pat [Morgan], sometimes it was Rick Kallister. And Anton was the drummer, then they had two drummers . . . In the beginning Adele was definitely Peter's protégé, he brought her all the way out. He gave her, very graciously, a chunk of his stage.

This new Peter and the Wolves – in which Laughner shared both vocal and composition duties with Bertei – was equally short-lived. If Bertei's vocals were as unimpressive as some of her early songs, she still felt she could expel the erstwhile leader of the Wolves from his own band – for much the same reasons as his earlier expulsion from Ubu. By now Laughner was dangerously out of control. In his famous obituary of his friend, Lester Bangs would recall:

Around the time I moved to New York from Detroit (last fall), he called me up and told me that the doctors had informed him that he was going to die if he didn't stop all drinking and the use of drugs. 'It's gonna hafta be Valium and grass from here on out,' he said. 'Shit, you gotta have somethin'.' It was around this time that his midnight phone calls began to take on a creepy tinge.

Laughner had always perceived some dubious correlation between inspiration and artificial stimuli. His penchant for excess, and the comfortable income his parents provided, ensured that he was always able to concoct unhealthy mixtures of drugs and drink. Though it was largely drink that caused his early demise, as one New Yorker observed 'the guy would shoot up cough drops.' If weed was strictly *verboten*, pills and cocaine regularly chased the booze home.

Charlotte Pressler: The worst thing, the most totally uncool thing you could do in the early punk scene was smoke marijuana. But pills were pretty easy to get. You could get a bottle of a hundred Dexamyl and it didn't cost that much.

The notion that somehow a life of blowtorching the candle was an integral part of rock & roll repeatedly crept into Laughner's writings. Writing about the Modern Lovers in *Creem*, Laughner remarked:

[*She Cracked*] reminds me of a conversation I had with a 15-year-old on a bus in 1968. She had just gotten out of the psycho ward after kicking a meth habit . . . She later picked up a mild junk habit, and once when presented with the opportunity to ball her my own meth use negated my abilities. I digress.

'Never Gonna Kill Myself Again', 'Dear Richard', 'Life Stinks' and 'Ain't it Fun' all affected a world-weariness that drew upon an aesthetic of excess considered *de rigueur* in certain rock & roll circles. It was perhaps inevitable that Laughner's life would be reduced to this one component by the Dead Boys, with their 'tribute' recording of 'Ain't it Fun' on the *We've Come for Your Children* album. 'Ain't it Fun' represents Laughner's most self-conscious exposition on the aesthetic:

> Ain't it fun, when your friends despise what you've become,
> Ain't it fun, when you break up every band you ever begun,
> Ain't it fun, when you know you're gonna die young.

That Laughner could write this when he was just 21, and be prepared to die for it when only 24, suggests just how beguiling this aesthetic had become for him.

Charlotte Pressler: Peter did have a real death-wish . . . It was a form of suicide. I hate that stuff – that early-death romanticism. I can't tell you how much I hate it.

That he was a consummately accomplished guitarist and an adept poet and lyricist makes his death a tragic waste. The night before his exit, 22 June 1977, Laughner made one final recording – Adele Bertei would later describe it as 'a little biography' – at his parents' home.

The sixty-minute acoustic tape contained some new Laughner originals and some personal favourites. The favourites were drawn from such diverse writers as Tom Verlaine, Richard Thompson, Van Morrison, Richard Hell, Jagger and Richards, Jesse Winchester, Lou Reed, Eddie Cochran and, most pertinent of all, Robert Johnson, the blues singer who died in his late twenties, poisoned by a jealous husband. Laughner chose for his nocturnal digression the voodoo of 'Me and the Devil Blues':

> Early this mornin'/ when you knocked upon my door,
> Early this mornin'/ when you knocked upon my door,
> I said, 'Hello, Satan/ I believe it's time to go.'

If Friction's tenure at the Pirate's Cove was brief, the fall 1976 shows began a year-long lease for Ubu. Though all but two of the songs that appear on Ubu's 1978 debut album, *The Modern Dance*, were performed at the outset of their Pirate's Cove residency, the songs were undergoing radical changes over the ensuing months, particularly those retained from Ubu's original conception. 'Heart of Darkness', 'Sentimental Journey' and 'Thirty Seconds Over Tokyo' all allowed Ravenstine full scope for his unique sonic soundtracks. Ubu frontman David Thomas still recalls this period with great fondness.

David Thomas: The conceptual, spiritual heyday was some point between May and September '77 . . . [it was a] particularly formative and most intensely influential period . . . We were playing in the Flats and we had built up an audience enough that the shows were very well attended. We were getting interest from all over the world. We knew that we were special and everybody knew that it was a very special time. It has to do with [being] down in the Flats. It was a period where we really felt we owned them. It's very deserted down there and we sort of claimed it as our own and there was a very tight-knit, intense community at that point, [it] was a very inspiring period – lot of ideas, lot of enthusiasm, lot of naivety.

Playing every Thursday at Pirate's Cove, Ubu shared the bill with some of the old regulars of the Cleveland scene, Robert Kidney's 15–60–75 (generally referred to as the Numbers band) and Akron's Tin Huey, as well as a second wave of local bands from Cleveland and its sister city Akron: Sue Schmidt and Deborah Smith's post-Friction combo, Chi-Pig; the Styrene Money Band and X-Blank-X, both composed of ex-members of the Electric Eels and Mirrors; and an outfit called Devo, an abbreviation of Devolution, the pseudo-concept around which their live performances were based. Devo and Tin Huey were providing an essential link between the twin cities. Tin Huey had been around for some time, sharing bills at the Viking with Mirrors.

Michael Weldon: People from Tin Huey and the Bizarros would come to Cleveland and see bands and check out the bands, and after a while we went to Akron to see Devo and Tin Huey play and realized there were things going on that were maybe even more happening than Cleveland.

Formed in 1973 from the embers of an acoustic group devoted to 'early Marc Bolan and smoking hash', Tin Huey drew upon Soft Machine/Robert Wyatt notions of jazz-rock, playing highly precise, formal and intricate original material. Despite such handicaps they were able to establish a healthy local following in the years preceding their regular shows at the Pirate's Cove and Akron's the Bank. It was Devo who located the Bank, an Akron equivalent to Pirate's Cove, doubling the potential gig opportunities for all these bands.

Allen Ravenstine: Devo had managed to chip out a club to play in Akron, the Bank, we'd go down to their club and play and they'd come up here and play at our club. That was the root of the Cleveland/Akron connection, because the group of people doing this was so small and the group of people who wanted to see this stuff was so small, that had everybody not united on some level or other, it probably would've died right out.

Devo also became regular favourites at the Eagle Street Saloon, opened by Clockwork Eddie after Clockwork Orange had been forcibly shut down. There also remained the occasional gig at the Agora's basement club, the Mistake. Tin Huey had shared a once-a-week residency there in spring 1976 with the original Ubu.

Devo had been in existence almost as long as Tin Huey, playing their first gig at Kent State University at the rear end of 1973 and recording their first home demos at the beginning of 1974. Composed of Mark Mothersbaugh, 'the only mellotron player listed in the Akron Musician's Union book for 1974', brother Bob, Jerry Casale – 'chief theoretician', brother Bob II, and drummer Alan Myers, they spent two years working up a sound with home demos, playing just two gigs. The demos Devo recorded in these first two years* show the development of a basic concept. On one of the earliest of their demos, 'Mechanical Man', recorded in April 1974, Devo established a notion that the common man was becoming an underling in this increasingly mechanistic world. The strict, metronomic precision of Devo's sound was presumably intended to illustrate that they were no less devolved than their audience. And then there were the lyrics:

Devo's songs lyrically are almost exclusively concerned with the pursuits of apemen, pinheads, rubber workers, mongoloids, and similar specimens of de-evolved humanity – Charlotte Pressler, *CLE*, No. 1.

Devo only fully emerged from their home-studio chrysalis in October 1975, when they were part of Cleveland radio station WMMS's Halloween Concert at the WHK Auditorium. The response was not encouraging. To quote Pressler again:

If they had been beer-can collectors, it would have been a good gig. Probably there were some rare varieties among the ones the audience threw at them.

Undeterred by the reaction, Devo played their first Akron gig on New Year's Day 1976, sharing a rather incongruous bill with Frankenstein. Throughout 1976 and into 1977 they established a local reputation by gigging regularly at the Bank, Pirate's Cove and the Eagle Street Saloon, but their Akron homestead and aloof image meant that they were kept at arm's length by the Ubu partisans, who were never

---

* Found on Rykodisc's *Hardcore Devo Vols. 1 & 2* and the *Devonia* bootleg album.

entirely sure that Devolution wasn't all an elaborate put-on. One incident at the Pirate's Cove certainly was a put-on:

Allen Ravenstine: I remember the imitation of [David] because it was Jerry dressed in a dark coverall stuffed with newspaper and he came on and stripped this thing off and started throwing the newspaper and David went ballistic . . . and we almost didn't play that night 'cause he wouldn't go out! . . . They were doing it in good fun, it's just that David didn't have a particularly good sense of humour about himself.

If Devo were as much art-rockers as the early Ubu, their influences were more mainstream, and they retained the two-guitar/synth set-up that Ubu had abandoned in May 1976. The coherence of their concept enabled them to be singled out very early on, particularly by ex-art students like David Bowie and Brian Eno, constantly on the prowl for new ideas to appropriate, and new artists to endorse and maybe even produce.

Shows at Max's Kansas City in the summer and fall of 1977 showed that Devo had achieved a highly persuasive fusion of Roxy Music, Sparks and Kraftwerk and something akin to Suicide and Ubu in their more accessible moments. Their first single (on their own Booji Boy label), released to coincide with these shows, paired the cunningly simplistic 'Mongoloid' with the anthemic 'Jocko Homo', with its call-and-answer hook, 'Are we not men? We are Devo', the eventual title of their debut album.

The success of the single on import got them an English record deal with Stiff Records. Their second single, released early in 1978, was a mechanical jerk-off, set to the Rolling Stones' 'Satisfaction', and convinced Warners to sign them in the US, though only after Marty Thau had failed to persuade them to join the same label as Suicide, Red Star. As with Talking Heads, Devo's out-of-kilter rhythm, uniform image and dance sensibilities were unorthodox enough to intrigue, but not so avant-garde as to disconcert conservatively inclined A&R people.

The rapid-fire ascent of Devo proved that Ohio origins and originality were not anathema to success. However, parochialism was. Ubu's attitude to New York had always been at best ambivalent, even if Ubu's previous reluctance to extend their frontiers beyond Cleveland had slightly dissipated by 1977. They did make occasional sorties to New

York, playing at both Max's and CBGBs, notably a set of shows at Max's in February 1977, and they continued to develop their reputation without becoming the 'overnight sensation' that Devo seemed to become. Of course Ubu's music was considerably more demanding than Devo's, whose sound was made subservient to an overall concept. Ubu were never likely to cross over to the mainstream, as Devo were able to do. However, Ubu also failed to make a concerted effort to take their music to America at a time when they were in their 'conceptual, spiritual heyday'. The attitude largely stemmed from the Art side of Ubu's neatly divided stage.

Tony Maimone: We were going to this rehearsal place and rehearsing twice a week and then we would play a gig at the Pirate's Cove, that made up a big chunk of Ubu activity and I know that Ubu at that time could have done anything it wanted to do ... David never seemed to like being on the road ... and it wasn't what Allen wanted to do because he had a responsibility to this building [the Plaza]. It was because of that situation that the band didn't tour much ... [but] David had a problem with New York, he never liked it. There was a certain provincial attitude that the band was attached to Cleveland and there was this anti-New York feeling that I perceived.

In fairness to Ubu, the period 1976–7 was a time of immense interest – both locally and internationally – in the very active Cleveland–Akron scene. With the single releases on Thomas's Hearthan record label, which had now been extended to include the likes of Mirrors archive material, and Paul Marotta's Mustard label, the *CLE* magazine and Ubu's debut album, there was a lot of local excitement, largely centered around Pirate's Cove and the Drome record store.

Michael Weldon: The Drome record store was just mutating from an eccentric hippie store into the punk store for the region. Peter Laughner was working there [shortly before] he died ... One of the other employees there was David Thomas. Pere Ubu was practising in the basement and everything was happening at once. That's when the Pagans came along and Hearthan Records was [being] run by David Thomas out of the basement at Drome. He was interested in putting out a few records that weren't Pere Ubu, and of course he knew about Mirrors and he ... ended up putting out this single which sold decently considering the band had broken up some years earlier ... and not long after that the Electric Eels single happened on Rough Trade [in England] and all these people at the Drome store were putting out *CLE* magazine, which was very interesting. For a short while there the Drome was a focal point for what was happening. They had Devo and the Pagans playing in the store ... John put on these Extermination Night-like shows at the old WHK Radio Hall which was in disastrous shape. He put on these two big shows with all these bands: Pere Ubu, the Styrene Money Band, Destroy All Monsters, Devo, Chi-Pig, the Suicide Commandos ... [but] in '79 the Drome moved to the westside.

Like Devo, Ubu managed to secure a record deal – with a 'major' – as a result of their independent singles. A Phonogram A&R man had heard one of their Hearthan releases, at a Chicago record store, and decided to investigate. Ubu released two Hearthan singles during their year-long residency at Pirate's Cove, now assured of adequate sales in Cleveland, New York and London, where Rough Trade were advocating the Ubu creed.

A&R man Cliff Burnstein's first exposure was to Ubu's 'comeback' single, Street Waves/My Dark Ages, issued in the fall of 1976. 'Street Waves' was a nod to Ubu's still discernible rock & roll roots, spiced up by Ravenstine's sonic reductions, while 'My Dark Ages (I Don't Get Around)' was as disorienting an experience as either side of Ubu's debut single.

Ubu would issue one more single – The Modern Dance/Heaven in August 1977 – before signing with Phonogram and beginning work on their long-awaited debut album. While the single version of 'The Modern Dance' was largely transformed from its June 1976 prototype, 'Heaven' was a discreet flirtation with reggae rhythms, and may well be Ubu's most seductive studio recording. Meantime, Burnstein was busy creating Ubu's very own label under the Phonogram umbrella.

David Thomas: [Cliff Burnstein] was our first manager from about '77 to about '81 or '82 ... He's a real music fan and managed to find our records in some store ... He found my number somehow and called me up and said, 'I really like what you do but I don't want to sign you to Mercury/Phonogram because this is just a disaster' ... So he put Blank together on

Mercury, to sign us to, so he could control our release[s] more than if he had signed us [direct] to Phonogram.

The fall of 1977 saw Ubu not only begin work on *The Modern Dance*, but audibly move away from the dark aesthetic with which they were associated, willingly or not. Thomas would observe, in his *Terminal Tower* sleeve-notes, that the change was signified by two new Ubu compositions, 'Chinese Radiation' and 'Humour Me':

The two new songs written for the *Modern Dance* sessions reflect this change. 'Chinese Radiation' insisted on a disciplined, pragmatic optimism while the frustrated anger of 'Humour Me', in response to the death of Peter Laughner several months earlier, was directed against the destructive illusions essential to certain popular rock & art aesthetics.

'Humour Me' had been transformed during album rehearsals from what Thomas describes as 'one more in a series of "mystic" love songs'* into the expression of 'frustrated anger' that its released form took.

Tony Maimone: With 'Humour Me', we had the music and David had a whole different lyric to it, we were already out at Suma making the recording and David came in, he had been sitting in the car, and he had rewritten the lyrics intact to what they are now. I remember David saying it was about Peter.

'Humour Me' was the essential counterpoint to 'Life Stinks', the one song to survive from the Rockets. It concluded an album that seemed haunted by the spirit of Laughner. Ravenstine certainly considers *The Modern Dance* to be Peter's album. 'Humour Me' was not the only song about Laughner's demise. There can be little doubt that it is Laughner who is the poor boy on the title track who, because he 'believes in chance/will never get The Modern Dance.'

Recorded in November 1977, *The Modern Dance* is one of the most important signposts on the frontier of modern music. It would be voted number 32 in NME's 1986 poll of the All-Time Top Hundred Albums, and though it may have remained largely unknown in Ubu's home country, it had considerable influence in England, where bands like Joy

---

* This version is included on *390 Degrees of Simulated Stereo.*

Division learnt its fractured sensibility well. Perhaps the response at the American pressing plant whence *The Modern Dance* had been despatched gave Ubu an early intimation as to the likely response to their work.

David Thomas: We weren't trying to be different. This was the way we heard music. When we got the first test pressing [of *The Modern Dance*] back the record plant said, 'There's something wrong with this thing. There's noise all over it. You'd better check your masters.' We said, 'No, that's the way it's supposed to be.'

By the time *The Modern Dance* was released early in 1978, Ubu were already looking beyond Dance and into Dub. Save for 'Chinese Radiation' and 'Humour Me', the songs on *The Modern Dance* were old hat when they were recorded ('Over My Head', 'Life Stinks', 'Street Waves' and 'Sentimental Journey' all dated from the Laughner incarnation). Thomas in particular was determined to disavow this image of Ubu as a band from the industrial wastelands of Ohio reflecting the angst of a mechanized, modern world. Devo were welcome to that tag!

David Thomas: People kept on saying this is all really dark and we kept on saying no it isn't and so we had discussions and we'd say what we're doing here isn't very dark really and there's quite a bit of humour in this but people aren't perceiving it so we need to push it. Need to adjust the mix of things. It all had to do with the fact that we'd kept getting these stupid reviews that were going on about industrial wastelands. Well, it had nothing to do with industrial wastelands ... We figured this can't be allowed to happen so we tried to adjust it. This was all conscious stuff. And a matter of discussion. Most of these discussions [were] between me and Allen ... The irony level of things is intensified [on *Dub Housing*] because it was something we had decided to consciously do because the humour of 'Sentimental Journey' and some of those other things seemed to us to have been totally mistaken or ignored or missed. Y'know, the breaking glass was such a pivotal point [on that song] because the last thing you hear is all the glass being swept up. It seemed to us to be the finest, subtlest touch. It seemed so apt after this extravagant thrashing around and chest-beating and adolescent sort of psychodrama [that] in the end, after all this thrashing around, you gotta sweep it up.

If none of their American contemporaries were entirely successful in their attempts to advance beyond the sound they developed for their debut albums, Ubu were the exception. *Dub Housing* was released just nine months after their ground-breaking debut, and may well be the greater work.

Tony Maimone: The band went to Europe, and when we came back we started to make *Dub Housing* and I think Europe had a profound effect on Pere Ubu. I think *Dub Housing* is a reflection of that.

Dub Housing once and for all advanced Ubu's sound beyond its Laughner/Wright/Thomas origins, suggesting that Ubu now preferred to inherit the mantle of Beefheart and Zappa, rather than that of the Stooges and Velvets. Its creepy soundtrack sensibility and its offbeat sense of rhythms proved so innovative that it would take Ubu themselves some ten years to come to terms fully with their achievement. Its tragi-comic face was a subtler version of the monochrome *Modern Dance*.

Allen Ravenstine: I think *Dub Housing* was one of those kind of spurt things, we had a lot of pent up stuff and it just kinda blurted out . . . *Dub Housing* is probably Tom's record and he got away with it. *Modern Dance* was Peter's, *Dub Housing* was Tom's, after that they were all David's.

Ubu's music was never going to be accessible enough to reach an American mass market that had scorned the pop sensibilities of the Ramones and Television. *Dub Housing* and *The Modern Dance* passed largely without comment, outside the established havens of Cleveland and New York. Ubu's primary market was England, where Rough Trade had provided the groundwork by distributing the Hearthan singles, and where Ubu managed two tours in April and November of 1978, both critically acclaimed and well attended. Ironically, despite directly benefiting from the climate established by the English New Wave, Thomas has nothing but contempt for England's punk exponents.

David Thomas: Punk to us was an alien thing. It wasn't what we were doing. We weren't doing loud, thrashing, anti-social, adolescent music. We saw ourselves as being more mature than that, more serious than that. We were embarrassed to be associated with the punk movement. We had done that three years earlier, four years earlier. We were doing the same thing in Rocket from the Tombs, but we had passed that stage and I hate to see things regress 'cause we were very serious about pushing music forward. You hate to see things cycle back which is what they always do.

The November 1978 UK tour was the culmination of two and a half years spent trying to recapture the intensity of the original Ubu shows. Before Joy Division, Wire and Magazine, Ubu were venturing into uncharted territories of sound and returning to place them in a rock context. Shows in London were taped for a possible live album, but Ubu preferred to go to work on a follow-up to the audacious *Dub Housing*.

Unfortunately, internal tensions had returned to gnaw away at the roots of the band. The primary source of tension this time was Thomas's reversion to the God-fearing ways of his Jehovah's Witness parents. In an almost exact parallel with Patti Smith, Thomas had spent most of the Seventies confronting moral certitude before collapsing into the bedstead of a comforting Christianity. Tom Herman was particularly disconcerted by the change.

Allen Ravenstine: I remember specifically being in a van somewhere out west and somebody saying 'Goddammit' and David just pulled the plug and said, 'Look . . .' and spilling this whole thing about how he had gotten religion and that he would not stand for hearing the Name of God taken in vain any more, and so that was it, Tom Herman said 'Goddammit' over and over again for six weeks after that, just to twist that blade. There were numerous stops at roadside areas while various members called up Cliff Burnstein and said 'I can't bear this' . . . In the studio somewhere in there Tom said 'This is going the wrong way, this is just getting weirder and weirder and weirder and we're never gonna get it anywhere' . . . The weirder it got, the better I liked it. Every time we finished a record I'd call Burnstein and say 'Cliff, this is great. This is the most commercial record we've done, wait till you hear it!'

Perhaps inevitably, Ubu ventured too far with their third album. Like Wire and PiL, Ubu's third album did not advance on a remarkable second vinyl excursion. Instead, when they returned again to Britain in August 1979 to present their new visions, the results were entirely unintelligible to the natives.

David Thomas: The first time around the record companies would just let us do anything we wanted, which was really a mistake for us because it just encouraged us to try and go further and further. Every time we'd get away with something, we'd think, 'Wow, I wonder what else we can do.'

New Picnic Time – whose working title was *Goodbye* – was the last album from Ubu's most stable and enduring line-up. At the end of the summer, Tom Herman quit the band and Ubu 'lay dormant 2–3 months'. The sheer unlistenability of *New Picnic Time* also cost them their contract with Chrysalis, who had stolen them away from Mercury after *The Modern Dance*, only to discover that they had signed up a band who did not feel inclined to tour to promote their highly unorthodox sounds.

Tony Maimone: I think one of the things that really soured the grapes for Chrysalis [was] that they signed this band that wouldn't go out with the Buzzcocks. I think that demonstrated to a lot of people on a lot of levels that the band was operating on a different frequency from what everybody else was.

Though Ubu stumbled on through 1980–81, only marginally bolstered by a contract with the independent Rough Trade label, *New Picnic Time* marked the end of Ubu as an innovative force in modern music. The introduction of Mayo Thompson and Anton Fier, who replaced the disaffected Scott Krauss after 1980's *Art of Walking*, only confirmed that Ubu had stepped beyond the bounds of their brief – to reformulate the modern dance.

Tony Maimone: Mayo and I never could write the way Tom and I could. I remember writing the music for 'Heaven' and 'Humour Me' in one week. Tom would stop over at my house and we'd have coffee and beer and a couple of amplifiers and we were writing that stuff right there.

Dub Housing had not sacrificed melodic sensibility, nor deflated Ubu's desire for exploration. Subsequent efforts became intrepid for intrepid's sake – and the bailing men were a limited audience at best.

For the three CBGBs bands that endured into the Eighties – Blondie, the Ramones and Talking Heads – 1977 was an equally frustrating year. Their debut efforts struggled to gain a place in America's commercial sweepstakes, and only Talking Heads fared discernibly better in 1978. Though Blondie and the Ramones both secured albums in Britain's Top 40, they were making little headway in the home market.

Blondie in particular, while achieving unparalleled commercial success outside the US, failed even to scratch the surface of American public perception. It would be January 1979 before 'Heart of Glass' finally dented the *Billboard* charts, by which time Blondie's two previous albums, *Plastic Letters* and *Parallel Lines*, had both topped the English album charts.

When Blondie followed up their support slot on the 1977 Television UK tour, headlining a tour in the autumn in their own right, they had already recorded *Plastic Letters*, which contained the two singles that broke the band in Britain and Europe: a cover of Randy & the Rainbows' 'Denis' and Gary Valentine's 'Always Touched by Your Presence, Dear'. Yet America remained obdurate and once again events conspired to deny Blondie the momentum they desperately sought. By the time 'Presence, Dear' reached the UK Top 10, its composer had left the band.

Gary Valentine: I started to not like it . . . after we did the first album, and especially when we went on tour . . . Everybody took it too seriously . . . The music of the band was changing . . . I told my manager, 'I don't feel I can get along with these people artistically any more.'

The recording of *Plastic Letters* was a somewhat disjointed affair. Though Blondie retained Richard Gottehrer as producer, Gottehrer was not convinced that they knew what direction they wanted to head in. It is surprising that the album packed such a commercial punch, in Europe at least. The actual results were very erratic.

Richard Gottehrer: On that second record it was hard for me to grasp the point that they were trying to make. There were conflicts in general about just which songs to do, almost like 'We gotta do a few of Jimmy's songs, a few of our songs.'

The Blondie that toured the UK that fall had reverted − for the first time in three years − to its two-guitar status, switching Frank Infante, temporary bassist on *Plastic Letters*, to guitar and recruiting English bassist Nigel Harrison. The new Blondie quickly became an increasingly commercial tool for Stein and Harry's mass-audience aspirations, even if they were uncertain how much of their rock roots to jettison. They had to play the game of accepting their New Wave status in England and resisting it in the US where, throughout the late Seventies, punk was treated as some kind of malignancy in modern music.

Chris Stein: The stigma of the word 'punk' is something that could not be absorbed into today's American culture as representing anything remotely positive. And that's one of the things that held Blondie back for so long.

In June 1978 Blondie began recording the album that would finally bury their so-called 'punk' origins and tide their passage over to true mass acceptance. *Parallel Lines* remains Blondie's ultimate populist statement. They had replaced Gottehrer with the much-scorned but nauseatingly successful Mike Chapman, the very man who had told *Rolling Stone*, 'If you can't make hit singles you should fuck off and go chop meat somewhere.'

Mike Chapman: [*Parallel Lines*] is good light listening − that's what Blondie's all about . . . I didn't make a punk album or a New Wave album with Blondie. I made a pop album. If the radio stations would only forget this evil word 'punk rock'. It's modern rock & roll.

Stein insists that he was not conversant with Chapman's earlier work and that Blondie made their choice more on reputation, apparently unaware that a band's internal chemistry was not a factor in the Chapman recording process. All sound and fury had to be subservient to his Spectoresque sense of 'perfection' – minus the benefit of Spector's unerring vision. Chapman had a justifiable reputation for fastidiousness. His approach required multiple takes and mind-numbing track-building, something that was the complete antithesis of the spontaneity that Gottehrer had largely adhered to.

Chris Stein: Mike's theory is that if you can do something once, you can do it again better. He would make us do things over and over again until we got up to his standard. And nobody was prepared for that.

Stein and Harry would later become very defensive about accusations of 'switching camps' following the mega-success of 'Heart of Glass'. In an article in *Circus*, entitled 'Why are Rockers Going Disco?', Stein suggested that too much was being read into the choice of 'Heart of Glass' as a single.

Chris Stein: We did it as a novelty item to put more diversity into the album. We thought 'Picture This' and 'Pretty Baby' would be [the] big hits in the States . . . it's only one song.

Yet it was clear that 'Heart of Glass' was no mere 'novelty item'. The song had been recorded on Blondie's first demo, with Alan Betrock, back in the summer of 1975, under the title 'The Disco Song', at which time Blondie tended to include the occasional disco hit like 'Lady Marmalade' in their live sets. Destri suggests that Stein in particular always had an enduring interest in the genre.

Jimmy Destri: Chris always wanted to do disco songs. He's a dadaist. We're running through this new wave-'I hate disco'-punk rock scene, and Chris wants to do 'Disco Inferno' and 'Love to Love You Baby'. We used to do 'Heart of Glass' to upset people. It was his idea to bring it back, but as a funky song.

In fact recording 'Heart of Glass' was more indicative of a discreet flirtation with electronic music than disco-rock, and it was this direction that Blondie chose to pursue on vinyl, after they got over their 'we're a rock band and don't you forget it' reaction to the 'Heart of Glass' controversy, with the underrated *Eat to the Beat*.

Latter-day Blondie rarely deviated from Stein and Harry's dance-floor notions of electro-pop. 'The Tide is High' and 'Rapture' confirmed the commercial success of their approach, Chapman continuing to produce their new sounds right up to their penultimate album, *Auto-american*. The final Blondie album, 1982's *The Hunter*, failed to maintain their commercial ascendancy, and suggested that their sassy synthesis of black and white dance forms had been assimilated and surpassed by more authentic exponents of this form of disco pop.

Blondie were not the only ones who, by disavowing prior association with the CBGBs scene, aligned to a discreet flirtation with black dance rhythms, unlocked the door to commercial success. While the 1978 Blondie had been clocking up mega-units outside America – if failing to impress their mother country – Talking Heads had been nudging the US Top 20 with their dreary cover of Al Green's 'Take Me to the River'.

The trio that had played CBGBs never got to record an album before their sparse sound was augmented by a fourth element, ex-Modern Lover Jerry Harrison. Byrne had been looking to embellish the Heads' sound for some time when Harrison was invited to New York to sit in on a set at the Ocean Club in September 1976.

David Byrne: After a while I started to feel it was limiting. If one of us stopped playing for an instant then the whole song would sound really spare. You couldn't change the dynamics of the song because you had to be playing all the time.

Talking Heads were already conversant with Jerry Harrison's work in the Modern Lovers. They often included a version of 'Pablo Picasso' in their early live sets and had been holed up in Rhode Island during the years of the Lovers' brief ascendancy in New England. As such they would have found it hard to be unaware of Boston's premier rock & roll outfit.

Harrison had been attempting to revive his academic career after the 'wasted' years with the Modern Lovers, enlisting in architecture school. Nevertheless, he welcomed the opportunity of some New England shows in January 1977 to play with the Heads again. Talking Heads were on a brief tour of the north-east when he joined them for shows in Boston and Providence. Though he did not join the Heads officially until April 1977, the January shows proved decisive.

Jerry Harrison: I thought [after the Ocean Club], 'I can't quit school once again. I gotta think about this.' I knew it sounded really good, but I just didn't know enough at that point to forget about school again. That kept me away until the band came up to Boston and I took a week and we played. That was when I really knew it was going to work.

The addition of Harrison came just in time for sessions for the Heads' debut album, to be followed immediately by their first European tour. It was soon apparent that Harrison was fulfilling an important role. The British leg of the European tour, at the end of April, restored a familiar CBGBs bill, Talking Heads/Ramones. With the equally resonant Television/Blondie bill crossing Albion at the same time, CBGBs' brand of rock & roll was avenging the British Invasion in style! The Heads/Ramones tour was a marathon effort, six weeks across Europe, finally ending on 7 June. It allowed crucial practice on the killing floor, testing Harrison's mettle in front of the 'fuck art, let's rock!' brigade.

The sessions for the Heads' debut album were a less happy experience. For a band who had been so careful about most career decisions, it is surprising that they left the decision about which songs to record to Tony Bongiovi, who was producing the album.

Tina Weymouth: We did this rough rehearsal demo for Tony Bongiovi when we were doing the first record. He selected the songs that he thought were the best because his job was to make us sound like a real BAND. Maybe they were the most conventional songs – maybe not – but they were his favourites.

'77 was not concluded until July, so did not suffer the fate of Hell's first stab at *Blank Generation*, being released untouched in September. '77 sidled into the nether regions of *Billboard*'s Hot Hundred, but it would be the beefier *More Songs* that would make Talking Heads the first post-Smith New York band to achieve mass acceptance.

What their second producer – the redoubtable ex-Roxy Music noisemaker Eno – did was turn up the funk quotient and turn down the quirkiness. The Heads on *More Songs* were no novelty combo. Recorded ten months on from '77, *More Songs about Buildings and Food* sought to deploy mostly stockpiled material. The first two Talking Heads albums were products of the same era, drawn from the same corpus of CBGBs songs. The distinguishing factors were the producer and the Heads' increasing confidence.

David Byrne: I think there was a certain amount of excitement about changing things structurally ... We were looking at the process and breaking it apart and saying here's a slow part and here's a fast part and what would happen if we slowed this one down and speeded this one up and played this one at half speed. Just things like that. It was a very structuralist approach.

It was this 'structuralist approach' that took over on subsequent Talking Heads artefacts. Their next album, *Fear of Music*, was 'composed' virtually from scratch – everything being built up from fragments and ideas in the studio. Eno, again playing at producer-cum-Devil's Advocate, encouraged Byrne's experimental bent.

David Byrne: There were lots of notes taken on the American tour, ideas for songs. I would just write instructions to myself to write a song about something ... I also had a lot of tapes of musical ideas that didn't immediately fall together and we worked together on doctoring them so they formed particular songs.

In fact, the tour to promote *Fear of Music* represented the end of Talking Heads as a full-time, four-piece rock outfit. Throughout the Eighties, Talking Heads would be a sporadic ensemble reconstructed to fund many solo ventures and commercialize Byrne's increasingly avant cul-de-sac ideas. Talking Heads' fourth studio album, *Remain in Light*, their last for three years, represented the culmination of Eno and Byrne's 'structuralist approach'.

If Blondie had been determined to assert their continuing relationship with their rock & roll roots throughout the disco-rock controversy, the Byrne who recorded *Remain in Light* felt no such need. Loyal fans may have convinced themselves that the Heads were still operating on some tangent to American rock & roll, but Byrne was unconcerned with maintaining the connection.

David Byrne: It's not Talking Heads with a new style. The whole concept has changed. There is a little bit of the old concept left in there but the main emphasis is totally different ... I'm cynical about rock music ... A lot of what remains to be done is squeezing the last drops of water out of something . . . The innovations in popular music seem to be more often in disco and funk in the last ten years.

The final Talking Heads tour, promoting their 1983 album *Speaking in Tongues*, allowed the gradual introduction of ancillary musicians from a starting point of the original trio, performing 'Psycho Killer'. Talking Heads were presenting their history, from minimalists to maximists – and the new maxim was world music. Their subsequent gatherings in the studio may have retained the name but not the sense of Talking Heads. They stopped making that when they moved into the light.

The two CBGBs bands to alter their sound dramatically in search of something palatable to the American consumer were also the ones that achieved commercial success in their homeland. Ironically, the one band that seemed bent on maintaining their original sound until they witnessed the Four Horsemen of the Apocalypse lost what little commercial ground they had secured when making a leap towards orthodox wisdom.

In October 1976, just eight months after recording their debut, the Ramones were back in the studio, recording a second selection of songs stockpiled over two years of gigging, before most of their contemporaries had even begun recording vinyl debuts. This time the album was co-produced by Tommy Ramone (under his real name Erdelyi) and Tony Bongiovi, Leon having left Sire for Instant. The results may have the edge on their debut. According to Tommy, there was a very real sense of working on something groundbreaking during these sessions.

Tommy Ramone: When we were making the second album, I was thinking that we were making *Sgt Pepper's*. That was the mentality. In other words, 'This is gonna be great.' I was having a great time. I was in my element. I was a producer. They were great songs. It was all very glamorous. It was that kinda feeling. I didn't think it was gonna sell millions of copies but I was making it like it could. At the same time [I thought], I really don't care whether this sells two records. I just want it to be good. I want it to be something that'll last . . . that's what I meant by *Sgt Pepper's*, I wanted it to be special.

The release of *Leave Home* in January 1977, coinciding with the English punk explosion, may have given them a Top 50 album and a Top 30 single ('Sheena is a Punk Rocker') in the UK, but it was not even as successful as their debut in the US, peaking at a disappointing 148 in the *Billboard* charts. The curiosity that had preceded the Ramones' vinyl debut seemed to be subsiding.

An eleven-month respite between *Leave Home* and *Rocket to Russia* might suggest that the Ramones were considering how to advance beyond their original sound. This was not the case. They had already decided to persist with their trademark sound, retaining Bongiovi and Tommy's co-production, even before they knew how *Leave Home* had fared commercially.

Tommy Ramone: That [third] record was conceived when we put out *Leave Home*. So we didn't know whether *Leave Home* was gonna be big. We knew we were good. Everybody was telling us we were good. Phil Spector was telling us we were good. We thought at that point that we were the next big thing. To us it seemed like we should be – if the aesthetic of you don't have to be a great musician works. So, yes it was a continuation: now here comes the pay-off. It was like a polishing. We were very pleased with [*Rocket to Russia*]. But then we weren't number one, we weren't even number one hundred.

Not quite true. *Rocket to Russia* was actually the Ramones' most successful vinyl venture to date. Coming after 'Sheena is a Punk Rocker', it did crack the Top 100 and included two minor hits in 'Rockaway Beach' and 'Do You Wanna Dance'. It seemed that the continual reinforcement of their original message, along with a smattering of suitably Ramones-ized pop classics, was beginning to pay dividends.

But they were still not a Top 40 band, and began to feel that only by deviating from their formula could they become one. Tommy Ramone had announced his intention to quit at the end of an arduous American tour in April 1978, hoping to concentrate on production. Ex-Voidoid Marc Bell was drafted in on drums, adding a new punch to their sound. With Tommy making his last contribution for six years as producer, they began recording album number 4, *Road to Ruin*, in May 1978, just two years on from the release of *The Ramones*.

Road to Ruin reflected not just the Ramones' enduring love for Sixties pop, but a nagging desire to expand beyond the confines of 120 seconds in search of a new vocabulary of harmonic hooks, albeit linked to the guitar-crunching sonics established on their first three albums. The riff-driven gabba-gabba fury was still in evidence on 'She's the One' and 'I Wanna be Sedated', but something was missing. *Road to Ruin* was a flop Stateside, even though it had been a very deliberate attempt to secure American radioplay.

Tommy Ramone: Now comes the next album. Now what do we do? What's wrong? Why can't we make it? This is what happens at this point in every band's career. What do we do next? We can't keep doing the same thing. Who's big? This is where the rot sets in. Now we start listening to other things. What's successful, what's not. See, that's bound to happen. You can't keep putting the same album out. On *Road to Ruin* we solidified a sound, 'Let's make the drums humungus, let's make the guitars roar like crazy' ... It was the first semblance of different structures that came in. The first song, 'I Just Wanna be with You', that has a different feel, a different beat. To me that's not really the Ramones, that beat, that structure. 'I Wanna be Sedated', [which] is an extension of 'Beat on the Brat', that's the Ramones!

If Talking Heads' movement away from rock & roll conventions – like Blondie's – sought mass acceptance, the Ramones' sideways shift was simply perceived as a dilution of their original form. Though the Ramones managed to make their very own trash version of *Blackboard Jungle*, with *Rock & Roll High School*, and even fulfil some kind of ambition by recording an album with Phil Spector in 1980, their Eighties' status has been largely the result of their influence on the speed-merchants. The Ramones' trademark buzzsaw sound has been pushed to previously unimagined limits of amphetamine-rock, blurring the boundaries between rock & roll and distorted noise so that they have become largely indistinguishable.

The central axis of a resuscitated rock & roll may have passed from New York to London in the winter of 1976–7, but New York remained a centre for new American music. This was largely down to its thriving club scene, rather than the continuing emergence of exciting New York bands. The new bands that were playing at Max's, CBGBs, the Mudd Club and in the Village were now largely composed not of New Yorkers, but of musicians who had been attracted to New York by its renewed reputation.

In particular, there was a small coterie of Cleveland musicians who treated the city as a second home. The Dead Boys had relocated in the fall of 1976, while Ubu and Devo made regular expeditions to the one city outside of Cleveland/Akron where they could be sure of an enthusiastic reception, though Ubu seemed to be recalcitrant rockers when even temporarily required to abandon their domain in the Flats. Several important musicians from Cleveland's mid-Seventies mini-renaissance also moved to the five boroughs.

With the solid grounding in eclecticism that they had enjoyed from Cleveland radio, its 'alternative' record stores and friends like Peter Laughner, three of his ex-musical cohorts – Tim Wright, Anton Fier and Adele Bertei – all made a contribution to the next generation of New York bands. Wright and Bertei were to be prime movers in the short-lived 'no wave' movement.

The main 'no wave' exponents were the Contortions, Teenage Jesus & the Jerks, DNA and Mars, all four appearing on the Eno-produced *No New York* compilation album, though not necessarily in their most innovative formations. *No New York*, designed to represent a buoyant new scene, was devised after a five-day festival of these bands at SoHo's Artist Space in May 1978.

The original Teenage Jesus & the Jerks had been formed in 1977, by a lady with the *nom de plume* Lydia Lunch and a squalling saxophonist who had been jumping onstage at gigs by r&b combo the Screws to wail along to 'long, crazy jams'. His name was James Chance. The early Teenage Jesus was an attempt to remind the new wave of its free-jazz roots. Their form of free jazz/punk combined the aggression of punk with the structural freedom of free jazz. But the Jerks were short-lived. Chance soon decided he would rather make his own statement and Teenage Jesus became a vehicle solely for Lydia Lunch.

The Contortions, James Chance's new combo, continued his experiments with a de-structured form of rock & roll, augmented by two ex-Screws, Jody Harris and Don Christensen, bassist George Scott and Adele Bertei, recently arrived in New York after the dissolution of (Peter and) the Wolves. Bertei had her own avant-garde approach to playing keyboards, hammering at the keys with her elbows and fists, all the while providing some of the best melodies that the Contortions could muster.

The Contortions, though, proved no more enduring than the original Teenage Jesus & the Jerks, as manager Anya Phillips pushed Chance in a direction more funk than free jazz; a halfway house being represented by the more lightweight of the two Contortions albums, *James White and the Blacks' Off White*.

It was not until after their embryonic recordings for the *No New York* album that the three-piece DNA welcomed ex-Ubu Tim Wright into their ranks, at the expense of keyboard/vocalist Robin Crutchfield, who departed to form his own band, Dark Day. On the *No New York* cuts, Arto Lindsay's vision of a new percussive sound, stripping the songs of the conventional verse-chorus-middle-eight form, was subsumed to Crutchfield's electro-synth pop.

Arto Lindsay: Robin wanted it more pop, more structured in the sense you know where every little thing is gonna be. I'm interested in ideas of structure that are just as obvious to the ear; but not so much like arithmetic.

For the notions Lindsay held so dear, Tim Wright was the perfect foil. Here was a man who as early as December 1975 had insisted that he wished to go beyond commercialism, beyond music. Lindsay, who also wrote lyrics for Mars, was equally determined to sail beyond traditional rock & roll structures in search of something less rigid, more spontaneously formed. Though only a single and an EP resulted from Wright and Lindsay's three-year association, DNA were a notable addition to the New York scene.

Arto Lindsay: Mars was the first band who dared to start out with a Roxy-ish or Velvets-influenced song and, by the end of it, be playing noise . . . I was jealous . . . [but] Tim and I both play very melodically. We're not anti-melody. There's just a lot more to music than rock & roll.

Yet no wave represented no more than a brief fluttering of art-rock's wings and, if many of the pre-no wave New York bands had been short-lived by chance, it seemed that the no wavers were determined to build in their own obsolescence.

Lydia Lunch: All the 'no wave' bands just self-destructed. They were all so concise in the music, the delivery, the point and they just ended. It wasn't a premature death, it was an immediate and accurate one, they didn't extend the boundaries of their short lives.

Also abandoning Cleveland for more enticing climes had been Anton Fier, ex-Styrenes, Friction and (briefly) Ubu drummer, who joined New York outfit the Feelies in the fall of 1978, as they worked up the material that would later appear on their ground-breaking debut album, 1980's *Crazy Rhythms*. Fier also shared a part-time band with DNA's Arto Lindsay, the Lounge Lizards, playing a cocktail-lounge version of free jazz.

Other Clevelanders who found New York's no wave/art-rock scene more intriguing than their insular hometown scene included Bradley Fields, drummer in Teenage Jesus & the Jerks, Cynthia Sley, who formed the Bush Tetras with Adele Bertei after the dissolution of the Contortions, and Paul Marotta and Jamie Klimek, who took the Styrenes to New York in 1980 after barely registering a blip of media interest from three years of gigging in Cleveland.

Though few of the bands that stayed on in Cleveland made it to New York to gig, there were other buoyant scenes closer to the East Coast mecca, notably in Boston, where the Rat Club was playing host to everyone from the Real Kids to Willie Alexander, both of whom made the transition to wider acceptance in New York.

Even the West Coast was waking from its decade-long torpor, beginning to create a scene whose exponents played a music so frantic that the Ramones and Sex Pistols seem somnambulent by comparison. Despite having their own fanzines from the earliest days of American punk (*Slash* and *Search and Destroy*), as late as 1977 the Los Angeles and San Francisco punk scenes seemed strangely backward.

Chris Stein: The first or second trip we made [to the West Coast] there was this band called the Hollywood Stars and they were the tail-end of the glitter scene and they had just signed a deal after being out there for years and years. Of course [they] didn't amount to anything [but] they butted heads with the New Wave. When we went out there everybody was still wearing flares. Blondie and the Ramones kicked off a lot of that [LA post-punk] stuff. The first time we went out there in '77 all the kids were all dressed in bell bottoms and stuff and we all wore our little suits and narrow lapels. Then next time we came back they were all dressed like that. It was the same phenomenon as all the Patti Smith audiences showing up dressed like the album cover – a sea of white shirts with black ties.

In the summer of 1977 Los Angeles became the centre of one of the most unexpected explosions of communal inspiration in the history of rock & roll. At the Masque, a dingy basement off Cherokee Avenue, new bands rehearsed and began to perform. When the Masque was shut down by the fire-marshals at the beginning of 1978, two 'Save the Masque' benefits were organized at the Elks Lodge. These benefits, on 24 and 25 February, were the real beginning of the LA thrash scene. The bills included the Zeros, the Dils, the Germs, the Weirdos, the Dickies, the Plugz, the Flesh-Eaters and, way down on the second night's bill, X.

But that, as they say, is another story.

The LA scene, like London's, was based on a series of bands adopting the same musical approach. Ironically the very uniqueness of each of the 'first wave' New York bands had probably proved their commercial undoing. The sheer diversity of their sounds meant that each band had to be sold separately to the record-buying public. No 'if you loved the Ramone's debut album, you'll just lap up the first vinyl excursion of Richard Hell & the Voidoids' ad campaign for these guys.

Lenny Kaye: [The New York bands] were all kinda weird takes on life, slightly intellectual and artistically conscious of the moves they were placing themselves along the rock spectrum. But then New York is a very artistic city, [and] especially at that time.

If the early English and LA punk bands shared a common sound, the New York bands just shared the same clubs. As such, while the English scene never became known as the '100 Club' sound, CBGBs was the solitary common component in the New York bands' development, transcended once they had outgrown the need to play the club. Even their supposed musical heritage was not exactly common – the Ramones preferring the Dolls/Stooges to Television's Velvets/Coltrane to Blondie's Stones/Brit-Rock. Though the scene had been built up as a single movement, when commercial implications began to sink in, the differences that separated the bands became far more important than the similarities which had previously bound them together.

Tom Verlaine: I didn't feel it was really a scene. Newspapers were making it into a scene but to me it was just a club we played for three years. It was nice that it was now packed every time we played instead of having eighteen people and a couple of Hell's Angels hanging out.

In the two years following the summer 1975 festival, CBGBs had become something of an ideological battleground, if not between the bands then between their critical proponents. The divisions between a dozen bands, all playing the same club, all suffering the same hardships, all sharing the same love of certain central bands in the history of rock & roll, should not have been that great. But the small scene very quickly partitioned into art-rockers and exponents of a pure let's-rock aesthetic.

Chris Stein: The critics never thought we were artsy enough. There was a real heavy artistic focus in the CBGBs scene with Television and Patti. We were always too poppy for that, so critically we were passed over in the early days.

Roberta Bayley: The more you continued to see [Patti Smith's] act the more it seemed like artifice to me. Wayne County did a big parody of her where he came on and he had a black wig and white shirt, a tie and he did this whole thing about following one of Jim Morrison's pubic hairs down the sewers of Paris. It was like 'Horseshit, horseshit, horseshit, etc.' There was something a bit pretentious about her. Then when Talking Heads came out it was like, 'Oh these people have really found their band.'

It was this division which became more acute as the first wave of bands passed beyond the club scene or dissolved. Though the centre of thrash lay 3,000 miles away, CBGBs soon provided an even more absurd version of mock dementia rock & roll than the Dead Boys, in the form of Wendy & the Plasmatics. Not as funny as Tish & Snooky's Sick Fucks combo, nor as confrontational as Suicide, nor as outrageous as the early Wayne County, Wendy O' Williams nevertheless generated considerable press for her orchestrated stunts on stage, most notably sawing a car in half during one particularly excruciating song. Unfortunately, whatever the form, the Plasmatics' music was totally devoid of substance.

If no wave had pushed art-rock entirely beyond the bounds of commercial considerations, the thrash bands soon stripped any pop sensibility from their 'pure rock' approach. While the English New Wave developed its own finely tuned commercial charm, the American bands began to allow their artistic conceits to get in the way of populist instincts.

The failure of the CBGBs bands marks a very significant divide in the history of 'pop' music. It was the last time that a new wave of American rockers – at least those refraining from using the most blatant knee-jerk ways of eliciting a response – set out to reform rock music, believing in an immutable alliance between pop and rock. Their failure suggested an irrevocable breach in this supposed compact.

26 June 1992. A balmy evening it is not, but Glastonbury's mystical qualities, previously transparent, are finally revealed by a raggedly familiar twin-guitar refrain. Television are into 'Glory', back on the boards after a fourteen-year hiccup. It has all come around again.

Fifteen years on from punk's heyday, Television's return, with their power seemingly undimmed, only affirms the sense of *déjà vu* that permeates Rock '92. As the hard-rock bands of Seattle and other satellites of London, LA and New York draw self-consciously on the lessons and sounds of punk's vanguard, so this renewed interest seems to have induced a spurt of activity from America's first wave.

New albums by Television, Richard Hell, the Ramones, Pere Ubu and Suicide, archive releases from Talking Heads and Devo, and Patti Smith's first book in fourteen years, all suggest that the third wave may yet be upon us. At a time when American consumers are feeling the weight of corporate clout like never before, voices like Vega's, Verlaine's Hell's and Thomas's are vital cries, from individuals determined to resist the undertow of conformity.

Their continued presence is a reminder that, however transitory the scene that spawns him may be, the artist (and his message) endures, seeking always to transcend that moment when it was all there for the taking. Tom Verlaine has not stopped making albums. Richard Hell has not abandoned writing prose and poetry. David Thomas has not rejected his sense of vocation as a performer.

Even Patti Smith, after twelve years in virtual silence (broken only by 1987's *Dreams of Life*, seeming to confirm an irreversible loss of vision), has produced a pocket-size collection of prose-poems that summon up all the phantoms of language she had at her command twenty years ago.

Woolgathering is Patti's 'When I Paint My Masterpiece'. It is a work that confronts inspiration and its wellspring – youthful aspirations:

I always imagined I would write a book, if only a small one, that would carry one away, into a realm that could not be measured nor even remembered.

I imagined a lot of things. That I would shine. That I'd be good. I'd dwell bareheaded on a summit turning a wheel that would turn the earth and undetected, amongst the clouds, I would have some influence; be of some avail.

Richard Hell's recent return to the rock & roll forum, after spending most of the Eighties working to establish himself as the serious writer he undoubtedly is, may have been more expected but was no less welcome. Though his relationship with rock since 1982's *Destiny Street* has been fitful, he has been unable to definitively turn his back on the medium – despite the parting shot in his 1985 sleeve-notes for *R.I.P.*, written as Lester Myers: 'He's tired of Hell and is moving on.'

Dim Stars, the album-length collaboration with Sonic Youth's Thurston Moore, is a typically infuriating mish-mash. If the Hell wordplay remains, sometimes dazzlingly, intact ('I want to leap upon her throat, and chew my way through every coat/of fear and pain, but she's so shy, she just says, "Yes," and wants to die'), his vocals lack the confidence that Hell the Performer normally exudes, while Moore's sonic waves often overwhelm the half-formed melodies. Hell certainly feels that the project was rushed. It lacks his usual attention to detail. However, it has inspired Hell to attempt a further resurrection of his rock & roll aspirations. He may yet prove it.

The other neon boys have also decided to prove it, if not all night. After eighteen months of speculation, and a brief European summer sortie, September 1992 saw the release of Television's eponymous third album. Fourteen years after their second, *Adventure*, *Television* has Verlaine reverting to the two-guitar context within which he has invariably produced his best work. If the drums sound a little too contemporized, the Lloyd/Verlaine interplays still ring clear, the rhythmic weight of Ficca's and Smith's playing remain intact, and 'Call Mr Lee', the album's first single, shows all would-be pretenders that the original remains the best. Above all, it sounds like Television.

However, ever-determined to negate their hard work, Television seem reluctant to embark on the kind of serious touring stint needed to remind today's concert-goers why these guys are a primary source behind all of rock's contemporary twin-guitar exponents. As such, it looks like *Television* will not tide their passage into mass acceptance. Whether they or Capitol will allow them(selves) another shot at the target remains to be seen.

The fact that Pere Ubu were able to spend the spring of 1992 recording a fourth album since their reformation in 1986 suggests a remarkable degree of faith on the part of their label, Phonogram. If their second 'comeback' release, 1989's *Cloudland*, did not achieve the requisite breakthrough – despite being their strongest since *Dub Housing*, containing the irresistible 'Waiting for Mary' single, and garnering their best reviews in years – a fourth album, recorded as Ubu begins to implode once again, is unlikely to do the job.

As it is, Thomas is unable to muster any cohorts among his fellow Ubu men to tour with the new material, and has taken to playing with minimal accompaniment, billed as Petit Ubu. After a brutal tour in the support slot for the Pixies, Thomas has seemingly alienated all potential allies in the Ubu corporate structure.

Ubu's concessions to popular tastes, evident on all three Phonogram albums to date (*Tenement Years, Cloudland* and *Worlds in Collision*), can never circumvent the band's (justifiably) avant-garde reputation, acquired in the Seventies. And though Thomas's vocals have come on in leaps, if not bounds, since the bellowing of Rocket from the Tombs, for as idiosyncratic a voice to be mass marketable the entire band would have to effuse a benevolent eccentricity belied by the 'shadow of grotesqueness' the name will always allude to.

The other band to share that historic 14 April 1976 Suicide/Ubu bill at Max's – surely the most avant garde double-bill in Seventies rock – have also spasmodically insisted on reminding the rock fraternity that they remain a long-term project. 1992 saw the release of the first Suicide album in five years (their 1987 opus, *Way of Life*, having been their first studio album since Ocasek's 1980 effort). As Rev insists, both he and Vega, whatever their solo projects, remain committed to pushing the Suicide aesthetic, and their rare live performances remain events to be treasured. If Suicide's new work, like Ubu's, recognizes the need to produce sounds for the marketplace, Vega and Rev remain unregenerate about preserving notions of atonality, dissonance and repetition in rock music.

And that is good news – that Television and Hell and Patti and Ubu and Suicide (and, indeed, the Dee Dee-less Ramones, who also have a new album imminent) can all be at work in 1992, within and without the system, hopefully continuing to influence the bastard children of the revolution instigated in New York and Cleveland in 1975, in Sydney, London and Manchester in 1976, and in Los Angeles and San Francisco in 1977.

Richard Hell: That is the ultimate message of the New Wave: if you just amass the courage that is necessary, you can completely invent yourself. You can be your own hero.

Patti Smith: Any man who extends beyond the classic form is a nigger.

3 August 1973 – The Mercer Arts Centre collapses.

November 1973 – Patti Smith and Lenny Kaye resume performing together, playing their first show in thirty-three months at Les Jardins on the roof of the Hotel Diplomat.

December 1973 – Patti Smith and Lenny Kaye play support at Max's Kansas City to Happy and Artie Traum.

2 March 1974 – Television make their debut at the Townhouse Theatre.

30 March 1974 – The three-piece Ramones make their debut at the Performance Studio.

31 March 1974 – Television make their CBGBs debut.

7 April 1974 – Television share a second CBGBs bill, with a band by the name of Leather Secrets.

14 April 1974 – Patti Smith and Lenny Kaye attend their first Television show at CBGBs.

5 May 1974 – The Stillettoes play their first show at CBGBs, supporting Television.

26 May 1974 – Television/the Stillettoes play CBGBs.

5 June 1974 – Television/the Stillettoes play CBGBs.

August 1974 – Angel & the Snakes make their debut at CBGBs. They change their name to Blondie before their second gig, also at CBGBs in the same month.

16 August 1974 – The Ramones, now a four-piece, make their CBGBs debut.

28 August to 2 September – Patti Smith and Television share the bill at Max's Kansas City.

20 December 1974 – Max's Kansas City closes down.

17–19 January 1975 – Television resume playing CBGBs, with Blondie as support.

14–15 February 1975 – Patti Smith Group make their debut at CBGBs as part of a Valentine's Day weekend of shows.

28 February to 2 March 1975 – The New York Dolls premiere their 'Red Patent Leather' show at the Little Hippodrome. The support act is Television. These are Richard Hell's final shows.

20 March to 20 April 1975 – Patti Smith Group and Television, with new bassist Fred Smith, play four days per week, Thursday to Sunday, in a five-week residency at CBGBs.

May 1975 – Talking Heads make their debut at CBGBs.

May 1975 – The three-piece Heartbreakers make their debut at Coventry's in Queen's.

27–29 June 1975 – Tuff Darts, billed as Tough Darts, make their CBGBs debut, sharing a weekend bill with the Demons, whose guitarist – Walter Lure – is subsequently purloined by the Heartbreakers.

16 July to 2 August 1975 – The CBGBs Festival of Unrecorded Rock Talent. 16–18 July: Ramones, Tuff Darts, Blondie, Talking Heads, White Lightning. 19–20 July: Jelly Roll, Pretty Poison, Mink DeVille, Sniper, Antenna. 21–22 July: Planets, Day Old Bread, Rainbow Daze, Mantis, Ice. 23–24 July: Patrick David Kelly & Toivo, Demons, John Collins, Johnny's Dance Band, Trilogy. 25–27 July: Heartbreakers, Shirts, Stagger Lee, Mad Brook, Second Wind. 30 July: Uncle Sun, Sting Rays, Johnny's Dance Band, Hambone Sweets. 31 July: Ramones, Blondie, Sting Rays, Johnny's Dance Band, Hambone Sweets, Silent Partners. 1 August: Ramones, Blondie, Talking Heads, Punch, Dancer. 2–3 August: Television, Marbles, Talking Heads, Ruby & the Rednecks, Mad Brook, Uneasy Sleeper, Stagger Lee.

15–17 August 1975 – The Heartbreakers headline a weekend at CBGBs. Support acts are Talking Heads and Blondie.

11–21 December 1975 – The CBGBs Christmas Rock Festival. 11–12 December: Heartbreakers, Keiran Liscoe, Best, Kid Blast, Zabnick. 13–14 December: Shirts, Tuff Darts, Poppees, Smoker Craft, Hambone Sweets. 16–17 December: Rice Miller Band, East Steel House, Wild Child-Cats. 18–19 December: Ramones, Tricks, Baby Moon, Mink DeVille. 20–21 December: Talking Heads, Joe & Blake, Bonjour Aviator, Buzzy Weiler.

26–28 December 1975 – The Heartbreakers and Mink DeVille play a weekend of shows at Mother's on West 23rd Street. The 1991 *Live At Mother's* Heartbreakers album dates from the final night.

14–15 February 1976 – The new five-piece Blondie, with keyboardist Jimmy Destri, make their debut at CBGBs. Support act is the Miamis.

11–22 April 1976 – Max's Easter Rock Festival. 11 April: Wayne County, Planets, Day Old Bread. 12 April: Honey Davis, Denise Marsa Band, Keiran Liscoe Band, Manster. 13 April: Pere Ubu, Suicide, Harry Toledo (Pere Ubu's New York debut). 14 April: Marbles, Just Water, Mumps, Dancer. 15 April: Heartbreakers, Tuff Darts, Mong (Richard Hell's final gig with the Heartbreakers). 18 April: Ramones, Blondie, Poppees. 19 April: August, Dicey-Ross Blues Band, Rice Miller Band, Rags. 20 April: Miamis, Shirts, Uncle Son, Tricks. 21 April: John Collins Band, Billy Falcon's Sunshine Thunder Band, Clear Cloud, Moonbeam. 22 April: Kid Blast, Best, Somebody Good, Startoon.

23 July 1976 – Johnny Thunders' Heartbreakers make their debut at CBGBs.

25 July 1976 – The Dead Boys play their first show at CBGBs as part of an audition night for CBGBs 2nd summer festival.

26 July 1976 – The Dictators make their CBGBs debut.

5 August to 6 September 1976 – CBGBs Underground Rock Festival.

18 November 1976 – Richard Hell & the Voidoids make their debut at CBGBs.

February 1977 – Pere Ubu and Devo play at Max's Kansas City.

5 April 1977 – Patti Smith plays her first show after breaking her neck in Florida at CBGBs.

31 May to 8 June 1977 – Patti Smith Group plays a nine-day residency at CBGBs.

27 December 1977 – The CBGB Theatre opens with a first night bill of Talking Heads, the Shirts and Tuff Darts.

28 December 1977 – The Dictators, the Dead Boys and the Luna Band play the CBGB Theatre.

29–31 December 1977 – The Patti Smith Group play the CBGB Theatre. On the second night the fire-marshals shut the theatre down because of excess capacity. After the third show, the theatre closes permanently.

Appendix 2   **Bibliography**

This is a selected bibliography citing those articles and books used as primary source material and/or quoted in the text. It does not aim to detail every source used to corroborate factual information or provide background material. However, it does aim to provide a cross-section of the most useful published sources on American punk.

Interviews

Ron Asheton by Toke – *Motorbooty* No. 5

Stiv Bators by Cindy Black – *New Wave* No. 3

Clem Burke by Jim Green – *Trouser Press* September 1982
by Roy Carr - *New Musical Express* 29 September 1979

David Byrne – *New York Rocker* No. 2
by Patrick Goldstein – *Creem* March 1979
by Mark Abel – *New Wave* No. 3
by Richard Grabel – *The Face* January 1981
by Ian Birch – *Melody Maker* 29 July 1978
by Nick Kent – *New Musical Express* 22 December 1979
by Greg McLean – *New York Rocker* No. 43

John Cale by Roy Trakin – *Creem* November 1987
by Mary Harron – *Punk* No. 11
by Mark Kemp – *Option* No. 33
by Peter Blauner – *New York* 27 November 1979
by Christian Fevret – *New Musical Express* 6/13 October 1990

Leee Black Childers by Chris Charlesworth – *Melody Maker* 27 November 1976

Jimmy Destri by Jim Green – *Trouser Press* September 1982

Billy Ficca by Allan Jones – *Melody Maker* 18 June 1977

Jerry Harrison by Mat Snow – *Q* No. 49
by Kris Needs & Sarah Lewis – *Zigzag* No. 97
by Caroline Coon – *Melody Maker* 21 May 1977
by Bill Flanagan – *Trouser Press* November 1979

Debbie Harry by Richard Robinson – *Hit Parader* 1982
by Craig Gholson – *New York Rocker* No. 3

Richard Hell by Moira McCormick – *Trouser Press* November 1982
by Andy Schwartz – *New York Rocker* No. 53
by Giovanni Dadomoni – *Sounds* 23 April 1977
by Richard Hell – *New York Rocker* No. 28
by Chris Brazier – *Melody Maker* 29 October 1977
by Paul Rambali – *New Musical Express* 6 January 1979
by John Tobler – *Zigzag* No. 81
by Kristine McKenna – *New Musical Express* 12 February 1983
by Craig Gholson – *New York Rocker* No. 5
by Lester Bangs – *Gig* January 1978

David Johansen by Stanley Mieses – *Melody Maker* 15 April 1978

Lenny Kaye by Kris Needs – *Zigzag* No. 72
by Karen Rose – *Trouser Press* No. 10
by Andy Schwartz – *New York Rocker* No. 32
by Mat Snow – *New Musical Express* 15 February 1986

Richard Lloyd by Roy Trakin – *New York Rocker* No. 15
by John Tobler – *Zigzag* No. 89
by Craig Gholson – *New York Rocker* No. 4
by Jon Young – *Trouser Press* February 1980

Lydia Lunch by Don Watson – *New Musical Express* 24 November 1982

Paul Marotta – *Ragnarok* No. 7

Sterling Morrison by Mary Harron – *New Musical Express* 25 April 1981
by Thomas Anderson – *Creem* November 1987
by Christian Fevret – *New Musical Express* 6/13 October 1990

Jerry Nolan by Colin Keinch – *Zigzag* No. 74
by Kris Needs – *Zigzag* No. 71
by Pamela Brown – *Punk* No. 2

Bob Quine by Lester Bangs – *New Musical Express* 2 June 1979

Joey Ramone by Caroline Coon – *Melody Maker* 30 April 1977
by Kris Needs – *Zigzag* No. 81
by Mat Snow – *Q* No. 49

Johnny Ramone – *Punk* No. 2

Tommy Ramone – *Punk* No. 2
by Clin Keinch – *Zigzag* No. 81

Lou Reed by Bill Holdship – *Creem* November 1987
by Bill Flanagan – *Musician* April 1989
by Peter Blauner – *New York* 27 November 1989
by Christian Fevret – *New Musical Express* 6/13 October 1990

Fred Smith by Allan Jones – *Melody Maker* 18 June 1977

Patti Smith by Caroline Coon – *Melody Maker* 15 January 1977
by Andy Schwartz – *New York Rocker* No. 19
by Roy Trakin – *New York Rocker* No. 11
by Lisa Robinson – *Hit Parader* April 1975
by Stephen Demorest – *Sounds* 21 January 1978
by Steve Weitzman – *Gig* June 1977
by Lisa Robinson – *Hit Parader* January 1976
by Michael Gross – *Blast* August 1976
New Musical Express 9 June 1979
by Tony Parsons – *New Musical Express* 5 February 1977
by Chris Brazier – *Melody Maker* 18 March 1978
by Chris Charlesworth – *Melody Maker* 29 November 1975
by Robb Baker – *Gallery* May 1976
by Lisa Robinson – *Hit Parader* June 1976

by Nick Tosches – *Penthouse* April 1976
by Susan Shapiro – *Crawdaddy* December 1975
by Tony Glover – *Creem* January 1976
by Jane Suck – *White Stuff* No. 8
by Lisa Robinson – *Hit Parader* 1978
by John Tobler – *Zigzag* Nos. 83–4
London press conference – *Zigzag* No. 88
by Lisa Robinson – *New Musical Express* 12 April 1975
by Penny Green – *Interview* October 1973

Chris Stein by Roy Carr – *New Musical Express* 29 September 1979

David Thomas by Rich Shupe – *Reflex* No. 8

Maureen Tucker by Thomas Anderson – *Creem* November 1987
by Byron Coley – *New York Rocker* No. 30
by Christian Fevret – *New Musical Express* 6/13 October 1990
What Goes On No. 4

Gary Valentine by Jeffrey Lee Pierce – *New York Rocker* No. 11

Tom Verlaine by George Elliot – *Crawdaddy* January 1977
by Hendrik Geller – 'Quote Unquote' (private pamphlet)
by Dave Schulps – *Trouser Press* May 1978
by Allan Jones – *Melody Maker* 18 June 1977
by Allan Jones – *Melody Maker* 15 April 1978
by Roy Trakin – *New York Rocker* No. 22
by Paul Kendall – *Zigzag* No. 73
by Richard Grabel – *New Musical Express* 13 October 1979
by Caroline Coon – *Melody Maker* 7 May 1977
New York Rocker No. 1

Tina Weymouth by Ian Birch – *Melody Maker* 29 July 1978

Tim Wright by Glenn O'Brien – *Interview* February 1981

Features

Anon. – Sleeve-notes for *Life Stinks* by Rocket from the Tombs

Lester Bangs – 'Roots of Punk Part III' in *New Wave* No. 3
   'Peter Laughner' in *New York Rocker* September/October 1977

Richard Hell – 'The Ramones Mean Business' in *Hit Parader* June 1976
   Sleeve-notes for CD reissue of *Destiny Street*
   'Punk and History' in *Discourses* (New York Museum of Contempory Art, 1990)
   'David Johansen: Secret Messages' in *Hit Parader*
   'How I Invented Punk Rock' in *New Musical Express* 5 April 1981

John Holmstrom & Mark Rosenthal – 'The Dictators Story' in *Punk* No. 11

Lenny Kaye – 'The Velvet Underground' in *Zigzag* No. 16

Matthew King Kaufman – Sleeve-notes for 1990 CD reissue of *The Modern Lovers*

Peter Laughner – 'The Modern Lovers' in *Creem* August 1976
   Cleveland Plain Dealer 11 October 1974

Alan Licht – 'A History of La Monte Young's Theatre of Eternal Music' in *Forced Exposure* No. 16

Jerry Nolan – 'My Life as a Doll' in *Village Voice* 16 July 1991

Charlotte Pressler – Rocket from the Tombs Mutual Admiration Society Newsletter No. 1
   'Rocket from the Tombs' in *PHFUDD* No. 6
   'Those Were Different Times' in *CLE* No. 3
   'The De-evolution Band' in *CLE* No. 1

Dee Dee Ramone – 'My Life as a Ramone' in *Spin* April 1990

Allen Ravenstine – 'Music Lessons' in *The Penguin Book of Rock & Roll Writing*

Lisa Robinson – 'The New York Bands' in *Hit Parader* June 1975

Deirdre Rockmaker – 'Too Much Too Soon?' in *Spiral Scratch* No. 1

John Sinclair – *Zigzag* Nos. 74–5
   MC5 concert programme May 1968

Patti Smith – 'Ou est Baudelaire' in *Creem* May 1977
   'Edgar Winter After Dark' in *Creem* March 1977
   'HERoes' in *If Not Now, When?* (bootleg)

'Flying Saucers Rock & Roll' in *If Not Now, When?* (bootleg)
Cowboy Mouth (with Sam Shepard) in *Fool for Love and Other Plays* (Bantam, 1984)
'Fantasy Gave Me Fire' in *Creem* September 1971
'Jukebox Cruci-Fix' in *Creem* July 1975
'Television' in *Rock Scene* October 1974
Chris Stigliano – 'Cinderella Backstreet' in *Black to Comm* No. 14
Deanne Stillman – 'Put on Your High Heel Sneakers' in *Crawdaddy* June 1973
David Thomas – Sleeve-notes for *Terminal Tower* by Pere Ubu
Richard Williams – *Melody Maker* 22 January 1977

Fanzines:

Black to Comm Nos. 1–17
New York Rocker Nos. 1–52
Punk Nos. 1–12
Search and Destroy Nos. 1–11

Books:

Anon. – *Patti Smith: High on Rebellion* (Babylon, 1979)
  Velvet Underground Scrapbook Vol. 1 (1991)
Antonia, Nina – *In Cold Blood* (Jungle Books, 1987)
Bangs, Lester – *Psychotic Reactions & Carburetor Dung* (Heinemann, 1988)
Bockris, Victor with Gerard Malanga – *Uptight: The Velvet Underground Story* (Omnibus, 1983)
Davis, Jerome – *Talking Heads: A Biography* (Omnibus, 1987)
Doggett, Peter – *Lou Reed: Growing Up in Public* (Omnibus, 1991)
Frame, Pete – *Rock Family Trees* (Omnibus, 1980)
Gans, David – *Talking Heads: The Band and their Music* (Avon, 1985)
Harry, Debbie with Chris Stein and Victor Bockris – *Making Tracks: The Rise of Blondie* (Dell, 1982)
Hell, Richard – *Artifact* (Hanuman, 1991)
  The Voidoid (1991)

Henry, Tricia – *Break All Rules!: Punk Rock and the Making of a Style* (UMI Research Press, 1989)

Julia, Ignacio – *Feedback: The Legend of the Velvet Underground* (VUAS, 1987)

Kozak, Roman – *This Ain't No Disco: The Story of CBGB* (Faber & Faber, 1988)

Miles – *The Ramones* (Omnibus, 1981)
  Talking Heads (Omnibus, 1981)

Nilsen, Per with Dorothy Sherman – *The Wild One: The True Story of Iggy Pop* (Omnibus, 1988)

Pop, Iggy with Anne Wehrer – *I Need More* (Karz-Cohl, 1982)

Roach, Dusty – *Patti Smith: Rock & Roll Madonna* (And Books, 1979)

Rolling Stone No. 507 ('The 100 Best Albums of the Last 20 Years')

Velvet Underground Appreciation Society – *What Goes On: A Critical Discography* (VUAS, 1986)

Woliver, Robbie – *Bringing it All Back Home* (Pantheon, 1986)

Ron Asheton – guitarist in the Stooges until 1972, he was demoted to bass guitar in the reformed Iggy & the Stooges.

Lester Bangs – considered by many to be the godfather of punk, Bangs was an abrasive critic whose work for *Creem* in the early and mid Seventies constantly championed America's rock underground. He died in 1982. A posthumous collection of some of his writings was published in 1988, *Psychotic Reactions and Carburetor Dung*.

Stiv Bators – Bator's first band was Mother Goose, after which he was briefly drafted into Rocket from the Tombs in July 1975. He then formed Frankenstein, who became the Dead Boys, and subsequently founded the Lords of the New Church. He died in 1989 in Paris.

Roberta Bayley – as Richard Hell's girlfriend, Bayley was a regular at CBGBs in 1974, before becoming doorperson at the club. From 1975 she also photographed all the most important bands at CBGBs and Max's, her work regularly appearing in *New York Rocker* and *Punk Rock*.

Alan Betrock – was reviewing the CBGBs bands for *SoHo Weekly News* when he decided to record some demos with Blondie in the summer of 1975. By the beginning of 1976 he had founded *New York Rocker*, which he edited until the summer of 1977.

Clem Burke – joined Blondie as their drummer in March 1975.

David Byrne – as guitarist, vocalist and main songwriter, Byrne provided the general direction for Talking Heads from inception in 1975 to their formal demise in 1991. However he has spent most of the last decade embroiled in various solo projects.

John Cale – co-founder of the Velvet Underground, he was ousted from the Velvets by Lou Reed in September 1968. His solo career has included notable production duties with the likes of Nico, the Stooges, the Modern Lovers and Patti Smith, as well as fine solo efforts like *Fear* and *Vintage Violence.* He reunited with Reed for the *Songs for Drella* project in 1990.

Mike Chapman – as part of the Chinn-Chapman team, was responsible for some of the more ephemeral hits of the early Seventies with labels like RAK and bands like the Sweet. His subsequent work with Blondie was even more successful, though he was subject to considerable criticism for 'sanitizing' the band.

Leee Black Childers – was a photographer for *Hit Parader* when he began regularly attending shows at CBGBs. In 1976 he began managing the Heartbreakers, taking them to London in December 1976.

Tony Conrad – as co-member of the Theatre of Eternal Music, shared an apartment with John Cale in 1964–5. Conrad briefly became part of the Primitives, though he declined to join the Velvet Underground.

Michael Davis – joined the MC5 in the summer of 1965 as bassist.

Jimmy Destri – joined Blondie in November 1975 as keyboardist.

Danny Fields – as A&R man at Elektra in 1968, signed both the MC5 and the Stooges to the label. Maintaining his interest in America's rock underground throughout the early Seventies, he was an active supporter of the New York Dolls. He began managing the Ramones in 1975.

Chris Frantz – played with David Byrne in a college band called the Artistics in the early Seventies before co-founding Talking Heads in the early months of 1975.

Annie Golden – lead singer in New York band the Shirts.

Richard Gottehrer – co-founder of Sire Records with Seymour Stein, Gottehrer then set up the Instant Records production company with Marty Thau, producing notable debut albums for Blondie and Richard Hell & the Voidoids.

Bob Gruen – was already a noted rock photographer when he discovered the New York Dolls. Throughout their brief career he photographed and filmed them extensively. He subsequently photographed all the major CBGBs bands, primarily for *Hit Parader* magazine.

Jerry Harrison – from 1971 to 1974 Harrison played keyboards in Jonathan Richman's Modern Lovers. After a brief spell with Elliott Murphy, Harrison resumed an undergraduate education before being enlisted into Talking Heads in January 1977.

Debbie Harry – her first band, Wind in the Willows, recorded an album for Capitol in 1968. She formed the Stillettoes in 1972, before taking Chris Stein with her to found Blondie in the summer of 1974.

Richard Hell – Hell's first collaboration with schoolfriend Tom Miller (aka Tom Verlaine) was a book of poetry entitled *Wanna Go Out?*, published under the pseudonym Theresa Stern. After forming and disbanding the three-piece Neon Boys, Hell and Verlaine finally formed Television at the end of 1973. Hell left Television in March 1975, co-founding the Heartbreakers with Johnny Thunders and Jerry Nolan. In April 1976 he quit them to form his own band, the Voidoids, with whom he recorded two albums. He recently released his first new album in ten years, a collaboration with Thurston Moore of Sonic Youth, *Dim Stars*.

David Johansen – joined New York quartet Actress as their vocalist in the winter of 1971–2, during the process of evolving into the New York Dolls.

Lenny Kaye – was a regular contributor to America's best-known rock magazines when he began performing as a guitarist with Patti Smith in February 1971. He remained an integral part of the Patti Smith Group until its dissolution in 1980. He has subsequently enjoyed a varied career as a record producer.

Hilly Kristal – owner of CBGBs.

Peter Laughner – Cleveland's leading advocate of the rock underground, Laughner moved from Cinderella Backstreet to Cinderella's Revenge to the Finns to Rocket from the Tombs to Pere Ubu to Friction to Peter & the Wolves without ever finding a satisfactory vehicle for his music. He also wrote regularly for *Creem* magazine, championing the New York scene, even spending three days in Television in 1975. He died in June 1977.

Craig Leon – as (co-)producer, Leon was responsible for some of the New York scene's most important artefacts: the *Blank Generation* EP, Blondie's first single, the Ramones' first album and Suicide's Red Star debut.

Arto Lindsay – leading light in New York no wavers, DNA.

Richard Lloyd – was, throughout Television's five-year history, the essential foil to Verlaine, providing a more abrasive approach to the guitar.

Lydia Lunch – co-founded Teenage Jesus & the Jerks with James Chance. After Chance left the Jerks late in 1977, they became solely a vehicle for Lunch. After disbanding the Jerks in 1979, Lunch has spent her time indulging in a series of short-lived collaborations.

Tony Maimone – was recruited into Pere Ubu from Peter Laughner's Friction in July 1976, after Tim Wright departed from the band, and has remained a permanent member of the Ubu set-up ever since, whilst managing to indulge in extra-curricular activities with the likes of Bob Mould, the Golden Palaminoes, the Pixies, the Mekons and They Might Be Giants.

Gerard Malanga – assistant to Andy Warhol, Malanga was an active participant in the Exploding Plastic Inevitable. He also documented the Velvet Underground both visually and aurally. He would later co-author, with Victor Bockris, *Uptight: The Velvet Underground Story*.

Paul Marotta – after providing guitar and 'electronics' for the Electric Eels in the early Seventies Marotta temporarily played the keyboards for fellow Cleveland outfit, Mirrors, in 1975 before co-founding the Styrenes with Mirrors frontman Jamie Klimek.

Sterling Morrison – guitarist in the Velvet Underground.

John Morton – Co-founder of the Electric Eels, for whom he contributed guitar, vocals and ideology.

Maureen Nelly – a bartender at CBGBs.

Jerry Nolan – After Billy Murcia's death, Nolan became drummer in the New York Dolls. He left the Dolls at the same time as Johnny Thunders, co-founding the Heartbreakers with Hell and Thunders. He died in January 1992.

Iggy Pop – Lead vocalist and performer extraordinaire in the Stooges, Pop has enjoyed a sporadically successful solo career since 1976.

Charlotte Pressler – As the wife of Peter Laughner, Pressler played an extremely active role in the Cleveland underground in its mid Seventies heyday. She contributed articles to *CLE* and *New York Rocker* throughout the New Wave years.

Bob Quine – Lead guitarist in Richard Hell & the Voidoids from 1976 right through to the recording sessions for 1982's *Destiny Street*, Quine then played a significant role in Lou Reed's return to form, *The Blue Mask* and its successor, *Legendary Hearts*. He has remained in demand as a versatile, innovative guitarist.

Dee Dee Ramone – bassist for the Ramones.

Joey Ramone – After being drummer in Sniper, Joey was promoted to lead singer in the four-piece Ramones.

Johnny Ramone – lead guitarist for the Ramones.

Tommy Ramone – After serving time as a recording engineer, Tommy became the Ramones' drummer and, from their second album, co-producer, until 1978's *Road to Ruin*. He continues to work as a producer to the present day.

Allen Ravenstine – synthesizer player in Cleveland's premier art-rockers Pere Ubu. 1989's *Cloudland* was his swansong. He has subsequently concentrated on developing a career as a commercial pilot and short-story writer.

Lou Reed – co-founder and leading light in the Velvet Underground, Lou Reed's subsequent solo career – which now spans two decades – has had more highs and lows than just about any other major rock artist, Dylan excepted. His 1989 album *New York* restored some critical kudos and gave him his most successful album in over a decade. *Songs for Drella* and *Magic and Loss* may not have consolidated *New York*'s commercial success, but have him reaffirmed as a darling of rock critics once more.

Bill Schumaker – worked for Hilly Kristal at CBGBs throughout the mid to late Seventies.

Andy Shernoff – co-founded the Dictators with Ross Funicello and Scott Kempner in 1973. Aside from his bass-guitar duties, Shernoff sang most of the vocals on the Dictators' first album prior to 'Handsome Dick' Manitoba assuming the main vocal duties.

Gene Simmons – bassist in American techno-rockers Kiss.

John Sinclair – was a jazz critic for *Downbeat* magazine when he first saw the MC5 in 1966 and convinced them to let him manage them. He provided the band with much-needed radical impetus until 1969, when they dispensed with his services and he was jailed for handing two joints to an undercover cop.

Patti Smith – had already published two volumes of poetry, *Seventh Heaven* and *Witt*, before recording her first independent single, 'Piss Factory', in 1974. Between 1974 and 1979, augmented by the Patti Smith Group, she concentrated on a rock & roll career, recording four albums and gigging extensively before her sudden retirement after a tour of Europe in the summer of 1979. Since 1980, and her relocation to Detroit, she has released just one album, 1987's *Dream of Life*. In September 1992, Hanuman Books published her first book in fourteen years, *Wool-gathering*.

Pete Stampfel – co-founded the Holy Modal Rounders in 1963 with Harry Weber. A permanent resident of the Village since the early Sixties, Stampfel has remained on the outer edges of New York's underground for three decades. He continues to issue stimulating, unorthodox records, destined to remain at a tangent to the mainstream.

Chris Stein – After joining the Stillettoes as a guitarist in 1973, Stein co-founded Blondie with Debbie Harry in the summer of 1974. Stein and Harry were the only constant members of Blondie throughout its eight-year existence.

Marty Thau – After working as an in-house producer at Buddah for most of the Sixties, Thau took up personal management in 1972 with the New York Dolls. After the Dolls' dissolution, Thau attempted to put together an album of CBGBs acts before forming the Instant Records production company with Richard Gottehrer. After their partnership disintegrated at the end of 1976, he formed Red Star Records, whose roster included Suicide and, later on. Richard Hell & the Voidoids.

David Thomas – began writing about rock music for Cleveland magazine *The Scene* in the early Seventies, under the pseudonym Crocus Behemoth. After forming the Great Bow Wah Death Band and then Rocket from the Tombs, Thomas co-founded Pere Ubu, with Peter Laughner and Tim Wright, in September 1975. After a brief solo career in the mid-Eighties, fronting the Pedestrians and then the Wooden Birds, Thomas joined the reformed Ubu in 1986.

Johnny Thunders – Lead guitarist in the New York Dolls and co-founder of the Heartbreakers, Thunders pursued a solo career from 1978 – interspersed with the occasional Heartbreakers reunion gig – until his death in 1990.

Tish and Snooky – two sisters who first sensed their true vocation when singing backing vocals in the early Blondie. During the CBGBs years they fronted the outrageous Sick Fucks.

Maureen Tucker – drummer in the Velvet Underground.

Gary Valentine – bassist in Blondie from the summer of 1975 to the summer of 1977.

Alan Vega – co-founder and vocalist in avant-garde synthesizer duo Suicide.

Tom Verlaine – After coming to New York to become a poet, Verlaine (né Miller) founded first the Neon Boys and then Television with Richard Hell. After Television's demise in 1978, Verlaine pursued a solo career with three different record labels until 1991, when Television finally decided to reform.

Michael Weldon – drummer in Cleveland's Mirrors in the mid-Seventies, Weldon is best known for his two volumes of *The Psychotronic Film Guide*.

Tina Weymouth – bassist in Talking Heads.

Richard Williams – worked for Island in A&R in 1974, when he first saw Television live. In March 1975 he took them into the studio to record some demos with a view to a possible record deal. He has subsequently worked as a journalist.

Tim Wright – was the soundman for Rocket from the Tombs before co-founding Pere Ubu. After departing from Ubu in the summer of 1976, Wright attempted to revive the Electric Eels before leaving Cleveland. In 1978 he became bassist in New York no wave trio DNA.

Jimmy Wyndbrandt – guitarist in the Miamis, a regular favourite at Mercers and CBGBs, Wyndbrandt was also a backing musician for the Stillettoes in 1972–3.

This discography relates primarily to CD releases, as this appears to be the medium in which these recordings will be most easily accessible to the reader. Only where a recording is not available on CD is reference made to a vinyl version. Singles are generally referred to only when they contain cuts unavailable on album or CD. The references to bootlegs are necessarily selective: this discography is by no means intended to be a definitive representation of all relevant bootleg titles.

Precursors

The Velvet Underground

There are four official studio albums by the Velvets: *The Velvet Underground and Nico* (1967), *White Light/White Heat* (1968), *The Velvet Underground* (1969) and *Loaded* (1970); plus two albums of studio out-takes, *VU* and *Another VU*. All are available on CD, though vinyl copies of the first and third albums include important variants. On the CD version of *The Velvet Underground and Nico*, a previously unknown alternate take of 'All Tomorrow's Parties' has replaced the original vinyl version.

The CD versions of the third album are rather confusing. There are two different versions of *The Velvet Underground*: the so-called 'closet' mix (the original US release) and the Valentin mix. Aside from a radically different mix, the 'closet' version features an alternate take of 'Some Kinda Love'. The standard CD release is the Valentin mix. However, due to a blunder at the mastering stage, the first German pressing of the CD (identifiable by a -1 at the end of the matrix on the

CD itself) features side 1 of the closet mix and side 2 of the Valentin mix. An original 'closet' mix vinyl version is preferable.

There are also two official Velvets live albums, *Live at Max's* and *1969* (now released as two separate volumes on CD), though both represent the latter-day incarnation with Doug Yule. Both are available on CD, in the case of *1969* with bonus cuts of 'Heroin' and 'I Can't Stand it'. However the *Live at Max's* CD fails to correct the speed fault on the original album and continues to omit the other four cuts recorded at this final show − 'Who Loves the Sun', 'Cool it Down', 'Candy Says', and 'Some Kinda Love'. Fans must seek out the three-album bootleg boxed set *Everything You've Ever Heard About . . .* to obtain these four songs.

The complete October 1969 Dallas show, from which Polygram culled four cuts for *1969*, is also available − in superior quality to the official release − as a double bootleg CD, *Live at the End of Cole Avenue.*

The only officially available recording of the Velvets with Cale − a three-minute version of 'Booker T' from an April 1967 show at the Gymnasium in New York − is on Cale's 1992 soundtrack album, *Paris S'Eveille.* Frustratingly, a promo-only French CD single for the above album includes an unedited version of the same cut, which clocks in at a full six minutes. Though Cale retains the full 58-minute tape of this show, only one other cut is available to collectors: 'Guess I'm Falling in Love', which Cale broadcast on New York radio, can be found on the aforementioned *Everything You've Ever Heard About . . .* set, or alternatively on the quasi-legit *And So On.*

For a cross-section of the few live recordings of the Velvets with Cale, readers are advised to seek out *Down for You is Up*, a mediocre but fascinating CD bootleg of the Velvets playing live in Ohio in November 1966; *A Symphony of Sound*, a double bootleg album which includes part of the EPI set from the above gig, a section from the instrumental soundtrack *A Symphony of Sound* and two cuts from Poor Richard's, Chicago July 1966 − 'Heroin' and 'Venus in Furs' − sung by Cale; and finally, and most importantly, *Sweet Sister Ray*, a double album which includes a complete 40-minute 'Sweet Sister Ray' from a show at La Cave in April 1968. A version of 'Heroin' from the previous night appears on the *Live '68* bootleg and is also worthy of investigation.

There are considerably more recordings of the post-Cale Velvets in concert, and, though none are exceptional quality, several are quite listenable, providing a better representation of the Velvets in full flow than the slightly stilted performances that make up the bulk of *1969* and *Live at Max's*. Unreservedly recommended is the CD bootleg *The Wild Side of the Street*, which includes the entire Hilltop Festival gig from August 1969, featuring definitive versions of 'Run Run Run' and 'What Goes On', plus a crunchy 'Sister Ray' from the so-called 'guitar amp' tape, a March 1969 show at the Boston Tea Party.

Though collectors enthuse about the various Tea Party shows from December 1968 to March 1969, the bootleg equivalents are all slightly disappointing, though *A Symphony of Sound* includes a clean copy of most of the 'guitar amp' tape. Better performances and comparable sound can be found on two bootleg albums compiled from shows at La Cave, Cleveland in October 1968 and January 1969, *Live '68* and *The Murder Mystery*.

The best representation of the *Loaded* period can be found on a fine bootleg compilation, *Praise Ye the Lord*, which includes a staggering seventeen-minute edit of 'Train Round the Bend' and 'Oh Sweet Nuthin'' from a May 1970 show at the Second Fret, as well as a fine 'Head Held High' from the same performance. Finally, a three-album bootleg boxed set spanning the entire Velvets career, entitled *Searchin' for My Mainline*, provides probably the best cross-section of those Velvets live performances preserved on tape, but copies remain extremely scarce.

The Stooges

Like the Velvets, the Stooges' recordings need to be divided into two basic incarnations: the Stooges (1969–71) and Iggy and the Stooges (1972–4). Their original incarnation recorded just two studio albums, *The Stooges* (1969) and *Fun House* (1970). Both are available as CDs in the US though only as imports in the UK. Sadly there are no complete, listenable live performances by the Stooges, either on bootleg or officially (a particularly excruciating 1971 tape has been released by Revenge but should be avoided at all costs).

The Iggy and the Stooges period, with James Williamson on lead guitar, is considerably better documented, though little of great significance has been released outside of this incarnation's one studio album, *Raw Power*, and the Skydog live 'artefact' *Metallic K.O.*, derived in part from Iggy and the Stooges' final show. A more complete version of *Metallic K.O.*, entitled *Metallic K.O.* × 2, has now been released as both a double album and single CD, and is an essential document.

Devotees are also advised to seek out the pre-Bowiefied mix of *Raw Power*, which circulates on tape, having been broadcast on an American radio station at the time of the album's release. Four of the cuts appear on a bootleg album, *Duet at the Mantra*. Of the seemingly endless flood of French quasi-legit Stooges product from the Fan Club and Revenge labels, only Fan Club's *Rubber Legs* – which collects together the best of the hours and hours of 1973 rehearsal tapes that exist – and Revenge's *Live at the Whisky A Go-Go* – from a September 1973 gig in LA, simply for its inclusion of a monstrous if muddy 'She-creatures of Hollywood Hills' – warrant serious investigation.

MC5

The most important MC5 recordings all predate their signing to Elektra. In the eighteen months before *Kick Out the Jams*, they released just two independent singles: I Can Only Give You Everything/One of the Guys and, perhaps their definitive vinyl release, Borderline/Looking at You. An alternate version of the first single, which substituted 'I Just Don't Know' for 'One of the Guys', was released, also on their own AMG label, shortly after signing with Elektra, and is equally recommended. Skydog pirated the 'Borderline' single in 1977 and copies of this version are relatively easy to locate. Though the MC5 compilation cassette/CD *Babes in Arms* collects all three cuts from the first single plus 'Looking at You', the searing single cut of 'Borderline' is sadly absent and the quality of the other cuts – poorly transferred from vinyl copies – makes *Babes in Arms* a slightly disappointing, if important, release. All four cuts also appear, in slightly better quality, on *Michigan Nuggets*, a late-Seventies various-artists compilation album on Belvedere Records.

Also important to an understanding of the MC5's early sound is at least one recording of their magnum opus, 'Black to Comm'. There is a bootleg single taken from a September 1968 performance, which also appears on Revenge's *Live 68–69* CD. An alternate version appears on the *Sonic Sounds from the Midwest* bootleg album. However, the most fascinating performance dates from the summer of 1967, a live version on a local TV show on Channel 57, which exists as a black and white video.

Kick Out the Jams in uncensored form has now been released on CD and remains a vital document. Of less significance, but with flashes of former glories, are the second and third albums, *Back in the USA* and *High Time*, which have now been released as a 'twofer' single CD.

Alice Cooper

In relation to this book, there is only one Alice Cooper album recorded when they were based in Detroit, the seminal *Love It to Death* (1970). However, for its influence on American punk and for its abiding commitment to that garageband sound, *Killer* (1971) remains an equally important artefact. Readers may also wish to check out the second of the Straight albums, *Easy Action* (1970), which anticipates aspects of the breakthrough on *Love It to Death*. A live recording from the *Love It to Death* era has been released on bootleg CD under the title *Alice in Rockland*, but poor packaging, mediocre sound and copying from a vinyl source all conspire to make this a largely redundant release, though the ten-minute 'Black Juju' warrants a listen.

The Modern Lovers

The Rhino reissue of *The Modern Lovers* remains the essential document from the Lovers' all-too-brief career. Originally issued as a nine-song album, Beserkley added 'I'm Straight' on reissuing the record in 1986. The Rhino version, released in 1989, adds a further two cuts, 'Dignified and Old' and 'Government Center', previously only available on the Warner Brothers sampler *Troublemakers*. The sleeve-notes which accompany the Rhino reissue also provide a lot of useful background (as well as featuring the only live shots of the Lovers I've ever seen).

A second collection of Lovers studio material, compiled from tapes made by Kim Fowley in 1972 and 1973, is also available on CD from the German label Line Records. *The Original Modern Lovers*, as issued on vinyl by Bomp Records, accidentally omitted the ubiquitous 'I'm Straight' but the CD rectifies this oversight. However, little of the best residual Lovers studio material is found on this album.

A bootleg EP, entitled simply *Modern Lovers*, largely duplicates the Fowley material on *The Original Modern Lovers*, but includes a fine alternate version of 'Modern World'. This version also appears on a Richman bootleg album, *For All the Modern Lovers*, along with two cuts from a 1974 Harvard University gig, 'Walk Up the Street' and 'She Cracked'. Four further cuts from the same gig – 'Cambridge Clown', 'Wake Up Sleepy Head', 'Dignified and Old' and 'Womanhood' – appear on a bootleg album called *Route 128 Revisited*, which also includes four Modern Lovers studio cuts – 'Such Loneliness' from the 1972 Cale demos and three songs from the abandoned 1973 album, 'Plea for Tenderness', 'Song of Remembrance' and 'Ride On Down the Highway'.

An even rarer Richman bootleg, which is untitled, collects together studio material from the 1973 Fowley sessions. Again the album duplicates parts of *The Original Modern Lovers* but versions of 'Fly into the Mystery', 'Hospital' and 'Winters Get Hard in New England' are unique to this volume.

The New York Dolls

Both of the Mercury studio albums by the Dolls are now available on CD: *The New York Dolls* (1973) and *Too Much Too Soon* (1974). A collection of nine demos recorded with Billy Murcia in New York in the summer of 1972 has also been released on CD by ROIR, under the title *Lipstick Killers*. Four further studio recordings, made in Kent, England, shortly before Murcia's death, have recently been released as a CD EP on the Classic Tracks label, after endless repackagings as 12″ singles, picture discs, etc.

Also recently released in CD form is the French Fan Club album *Red Patent Leather*, derived from the Dolls' final New York shows at the Little Hippodrome in March 1975. The CD version has added four tracks to the eleven-track album – 'Stranded in the Jungle' from the Little Hippodrome, plus three cuts from a show in Paris in December 1973: 'Trash', 'Chatterbox' and 'Puss 'n' Boots'. The Little Hippodrome material has been remixed, though not necessarily for the better, while the three Paris cuts are taken – complete with pops and crackles – from a French radio transcription disc. The complete broadcast, from a considerably cleaner transcription disc, has recently been bootlegged on CD as *Live in Paris* and provides the best example of the Dolls in performance currently available. A bootleg album from their 1974 US Tour, *Dallas '74*, is poor quality but features the demonic 'Lone Star Queen' which needs to be heard.

A double bootleg of the demos recorded for Mercury in March 1973, *Seven Day Weekend*, provides the broadest cross-section of the Dolls' repertoire, giving twenty-two tracks in superb quality. A single CD, *Endless Party*, is copied direct from the vinyl and deletes three tracks. The vinyl version is preferable. Talk of an official Dolls video release continues, without any definite result. However videos of their perform-ances on Don Kirschner's *Rock Concert* and *The Old Grey Whistle Test* freely circulate.

The First Wave

Television

The original three-piece incarnation of Television, the Neon Boys, can be heard on *Richard Hell – Past and Present*, a 1980 EP on Shake Records, which features the original 'Love Comes in Spurts' and 'That's All I Know (Right Now)'. The CD version of this EP, released by Overground in the UK in 1991, adds 'High-Heeled Wheels'.

Marquee Moon (1977) has been issued in both UK and US on CD, with the full, unfaded ending to 'Marquee Moon' restored. *Adventure* (1978), a Top 10 album in the UK, did not register a single blip in the Top 200 Stateside. It is available on CD only in the US. Tele-vision's first single, 'Little Johnny Jewel Parts 1 + 2' (1975), was reissued as a 12″ single in 1979, with both parts included on a single A-side. The B-side was a previously unreleased live version of the song.

In 1982, New York cassette-specialists ROIR issued a double-play cassette of Television derived from shows at My Father's Place in

March 1978. *The Blow Up* is now available as a double CD set. However the original bootleg from which the tapes were taken, entitled *Arrow*, is considerably superior quality to either the ROIR cassette or CD, and includes a live version of the unreleased 'Poor Circulation'.

The complete studio take of 'Little Johnny Jewel' appears on the *Double Exposure* bootleg CD, along with several demos from the same sessions, including 'Fire Engine' and 'Hard On Love', plus the five Island demos with Richard Hell, generally erroneously referred to as the Eno demos, and three live cuts with Hell, including '(I Belong to the) Blank Generation'. The quality of both material and recording are impressive and make this an essential item, at least until Television put together their own anthology of 'lost' studio recordings.

The best live representations of Television currently available – at least in terms of performance – can be found on two bootlegs from their last US tour. *Portland, Oregon 1978* is a double album from a show in Portland in July 1978, supplemented on side four with five cuts from a 1976 show at CBGBs, including versions of 'Oh Mi Amore' and 'Adventure'. A radio broadcast from a San Francisco show shortly before the Portland gig has also been bootlegged as a single CD, *Live Adventures*. Though 'Marquee Moon' does not scale the heights of the Portland version (which has to be heard to be believed), the overall performance has the edge.

Finally, there are two cuts on the first Tom Verlaine solo album which originated as Television songs, 'Grip of Love' and 'Breakin' in My Heart'. A live version of the latter, from July 1975, completes the *Double Exposure* bootleg CD.

Patti Smith

Though all four Patti Smith Group albums are available on CD – 1975's *Horses*, 1976's *Radio Ethiopia*, 1978's *Easter* and 1979's *Wave* – there is precious little else currently on catalogue. Talk of a live compilation set of the Patti Smith Group in 1980 rapidly subsided, while a consider-able amount of B-sides and various-artist-album appearances remain confined to vinyl.

Of major importance is the first Patti Smith single, when they were just three: Piss Factory/Hey Joe, released as early as August 1974.

Though a French 12″ single of 'Hey Joe' was released in 1977, 'Piss Factory' is best heard on ROIR's *The New York Years* CD compilation. The B-side of the French 12″ of 'Hey Joe', a sixteen-minute version of 'Radio Ethiopia', complete with part of 'Rock & Roll Nigger', is an essential Patti Smith recording. A further European 12″ single of 'Privilege (Set Me Free)' includes live versions of '25th Floor' and 'Babelogue', while the French 7″ of 'Ask the Angels' includes a rather untogether live version of 'Time is on My Side' on its B-side. Further live recordings hidden away on B-sides include a take of 'My Generation' on the reverse of 'Gloria', a live 'Frederick', B-side to its studio counterpart in the US, and a live '5–4–3–2–1' on the derriere of the 'Dancing Barefoot' 7″.

Patti Smith also contributed to several of the 'Dial-a-Poet' Giorno Poetry Systems Records, providing the seven-minute 'Histories of the Universe' on the *Big Ego* album, the six-minute 'Parade' on *Sugar, Alchohol and Meat*, and 'Poem for Jim Morrison' and 'Bumble Bee' on *Nova Convention*.

Studio recordings that remain unavailable on CD include the *Wave* out-take 'White Christmas', issued as a bootleg single along with a live recording of 'No Jestering'; 'Godspeed', issued as B-side to 'Because the Night'; and 'Fire of Unknown Origin', a long-standing live favourite, released in the UK as B-side to 'Frederick'.

There are a considerable number of Patti Smith bootlegs, the majority originating from her live shows in 1975–6. However, the earliest recording is an EP featuring three cuts – 'Stockinged Feet', 'Brian Jones' and 'Oath' – from a 1973 performance by Patti Smith and Lenny Kaye. A recent CD version of the famous *Free Music Store* bootleg at last releases the complete May 1975 WBAI radio broadcast of a four-piece Patti Smith Group, with such rare gems as 'The Hunter Gets Captured by the Game', 'Snowball', 'Scheherazade' and 'Aisle of Love' all included. Two songs from the 'War is Over' rally in Central Park in the summer of 1975 complete the CD.

Of the bootlegs from the *Horses* tour, the best are *Teenage Perversity and Ships in the Night*, from a January 1976 show at the Roxy in LA, *Live at the Bottom Line*, from a December 1975 New York radio broadcast, and *In Heat*, from another radio broadcast, this time from Washington. Single- and double-album bootlegs from Patti's two shows in London in

May 1976 manage a fair amount of duplication in both content and title, *Live in London* for each, but feature early versions of 'Pumping (My Heart)' and 'Pissing in the River'. However, the best of the *Radio Ethiopia* live bootlegs must be the October 1976 Stockholm album *I Never Talked to Bob Dylan*, taken from a TV broadcast, and featuring an early version of the 'Radio Ethiopia/Rock & Roll Nigger' medley. A CD version derives from the original vinyl.

Of her post-accident performances, the best is a radio station transcription disc, the syndicated 'Rock Around the World' show, which features a gig from Cleveland in the spring of 1978, though copies are hard to find. The bootleggers preferred to issue less exemplary shows from Paris – *Paris '78* (also on CD) – and Santa Monica – *You Light Up My Life*. A good-quality double album from a 1979 radio broadcast from Philadelphia – *To the Ones She Loves* – is the best of the latter-day bootlegs, though pressing faults and inexplicable omissions from the full broadcast mar an otherwise exemplary product.

Blondie

Blondie's six albums are all available on CD in the US: *Blondie* (1976), *Plastic Letters* (1977), *Parallel Lines* (1978), *Eat to the Beat* (1979), *Auto-american* (1980) and *The Hunter* (1982).

There are also a plethora of Blondie bootleg albums, though the vast majority date from the 'Chapman years' and are less than exciting. *Quarters to Dollars*, from a show at Max's Kansas City in July 1976, offers a good idea of the Blondie sound at a formative stage. Equally recommended is the *Demos* EP, which features four of the five demos recorded with Alan Betrock in the summer of 1975 (omitting 'The Disco Song').

The Ramones

The first four Ramones albums are now available on CD as two 'twofers', combining *The Ramones* and *Leave Home* on *All the Stuff (and More) Volume One*, with pre-Sire demos of 'I Don't Wanna be Learned, I Don't Wanna be Tamed' and 'I Can't Be' and B-sides 'Babysitter' and live versions of 'California Sun' and 'I Don't Wanna Walk Around with

You' added as bonus cuts. *Rocket to Russia* and *Road to Ruin* constitute *All the Stuff (and More) Volume Two*, which has demos of 'Slug', 'I Want You Around' and 'Yea, Yea', and the B-side 'I Don't Want You to Live this Life (Anymore)' in addition. However, *Leave Home* omits 'Carbona Not Glue', originally included on the album but soon replaced by 'Sheena is a Punk Rocker', presumably in an attempt to avoid controversy.

Also now on CD is Marty Thau's *Groups of Wrath* compilation, which includes the two songs he cut with the Ramones before they signed with Sire: 'I Wanna be Your Boyfriend' and 'Judy is a Punk'. 1980's *End of the Century* is available in Germany as a single CD, as is the live double set *It's Alive*, though the 1979 soundtrack album *Rock & Roll High School* is currently unavailable on CD.

Like Blondie, there are few bootleg albums of early Ramones shows, though *Live at the Roxy* is drawn from an August 1976 radio broadcast, and a double bootleg, *At Your Birthday Party*, collects together this broadcast and a March 1977 performance at the Rocker Tavern in Washington.

The Second Wave

Talking Heads

All Talking Heads studio albums remain in catalogue on CD, including '77 (1977), *More Songs about Buildings and Food* (1978), *Fear of Music* (1979), and *Remain in Light* (1980). However *The Name of this Band is Talking Heads* (1982), a composite live double album, derived from performances in 1977, 1979, 1980 and 1981, appears to be still available on vinyl.

A double-CD anthology, titled *Popular Favorites 1976–92*, was recently released and features two unreleased cuts from 1976, 'Sugar on My Tongue' and 'I Want to Live', as well as the Heads' first single, 'Love Goes to Building on Fire', and the B-side to 'Psycho Killer', 'I Wish You Wouldn't Say That'. However the set omits the alternate version of 'Psycho Killer' (credited inaccurately as an acoustic take) found on the B-side of the 12″ 'Psycho Killer' single.

Perhaps the best Talking Heads 'in concert' album remains *Talking*

Heads Live on Tour, a Warners promotional album drawn from a show at the Agora in Cleveland in March 1979, at the tail-end of the tour to promote *More Songs about Buildings and Food*. The set includes 'Electricity', the prototype for 'Drugs' on *Fear of Music*, and has been bootlegged extensively, as a single album, *Why Did the Artist Cross the Road?*, and as a double album, *Electricity*, which also includes a 1978 'Saturday Night Live' appearance and the three demos recorded as a three-piece in April 1976 – 'Psycho Killer', 'For Artists Only' and 'Care Free'. These are also available as *The Psycho Killers* EP.

As to bootlegs of early Heads performances, the double set *Workshop Image*, from an August 1977 CBGBs show, is a useful document. *Compassion is a Virtue, but . . .* and *Electrically* are from West Coast shows on the fall 1978 tour, while at least a couple of bootleg CDs have derived from an August 1979 radio broadcast from Berkeley on the *Fear of Music* tour, Great Dane's *Memories Can't Wait* being the best.

The Dead Boys

The Dead Boys were responsible for just two albums during their short existence, *Young, Loud And Snotty* (1977) and *We Have Come for Your Children* (1978), though a CD also exists of a 1979 Dead Boys reunion show, *Night of the Living Dead* (1981). Though the second album remains unissued on CD, there are now two versions of the first album in this medium. The first CD release is misleadingly called *Younger, Louder and Snottyer*, implying early demos and such. However this quasi-legit French CD is simply a first rough mix of the released album with one 'bonus' cut, a live version of 'Search and Destroy', a fairly desperate attempt at enticement. Despite the claims made in the notes to the CD, this is a patently inferior mix to the released Sire album, now available on CD under the correct title and with the pukka mix.

The Heartbreakers

Though the Heartbreakers with Richard Hell never released any product there have recently been a steady trickle of bootlegs and quasi-legit releases. An EP on Nowhere Records called simply *The Junkies Live NYC 1975* contains four tracks – 'Blank Generation', 'Flight', 'Pirate

Love' and 'Goin' Steady' – from their first weekend at CBGBs in August 1975. Then, in 1991, French label Fan Club issued their own bootleg-in-all-but-name, *Live at Mother's*, on both vinyl and CD. Though credited to 1976, the tape dates from a 28 December 1975 show at Mothers.' Though the quality is not at all bad, and as a document of the Heartbreakers with Hell it is fascinating, *Live at Mother's* clocks in at barely thirty minutes and represents poor value for money.

Following hard on Fan Club's heels, American label Bomp decided to issue their own unauthorized CD. Despite a gorgeous front cover shot of the original Heartbreakers in full flight, *What Goes Around* is considerably inferior to *Live at Mother's* in all aspects. The tape runs at the wrong speed, the quality is pretty grim and the credits for the tracks are all wrong. 'So Alone', credited to a show at Mother's on 16 November 1975, was not played that night, and the bulk of the set is credited to a show two weeks before they made their live debut. And to top it off, the sleeve-notes are plain embarrassing as both English and history. Avoid.

Hell himself had the decency to issue three of the seven demos he recorded with the Heartbreakers in January 1976 – 'Love Comes in Spurts', 'Can't Keep My Eyes on You', and 'Hurt Me' – on his own career retrospective *R.I.P.*, which is now available via ROIR on CD.

As to the post-Hell Heartbreakers, the bulk of the essential recordings have been conveniently collected on a single CD by Jungle Records. *D.T.K. – L.A.M.F.* combines a live recording of the Heartbreakers at the Speakeasy in the winter of 1977, previously released as *D.T.K. – Live At The Speakeasy*, with the 1984 revamped version of the Heartbreakers' one and only studio album, *L.A.M.F.* This 1984 version, christened *L.A.M.F. Revisited*, attempted to salvage the album tapes and remix them into something approaching an enjoyable listening *mélange* (even adding a welcome take of Nolan's 'Can't Keep My Eyes on You').

The other notable Heartbreakers recording was also released by Jungle, back in 1983: a 12" EP entitled *Vintage '77*, which features three demos recorded for Track – 'Let Go', 'Chinese Rocks' and 'Born to Lose'. A live album of the Heartbreakers minus Nolan, with a repertoire marginally changed from 1976, was recorded in 1978 and released in 1979, and has recently been released on CD in Germany. *Live at Max's Kansas City* was originally released on Max's Kansas

City's own label. Also recently released on CD, complete with the previously absent title-track, is Johnny Thunders' first solo album, *So Alone* (1978).

Richard Hell & the Voidoids

The vast majority of Hell's concise catalogue is now on CD. However one of the few omissions is his first recordings with the Voidoids, the *Blank Generation* EP. All three cuts – 'You Gotta Lose', 'Blank Generation' and '(I Could Live with You) (In) Another World' – are more brutal than the takes issued by Sire. This EP may well be Hell's finest fifteen minutes.

Despite Sire's release of an expanded version of the *Blank Generation* album on CD in 1990, there are at least three items from that project still only available on vinyl. Of the original version of the album, compiled from the March 1977 Electric Lady sessions, only three cuts actually made it to the released record – 'Liars Beware', 'New Pleasure' and 'Another World'. On the subsequent CD reissue, three further March cuts were added – 'I'm Your Man', 'All the Way' and 'Down at the Rock & Roll Club' – and the album version of 'Down at the Rock & Roll Club' was deleted. However, the March versions of 'You Gotta Lose', 'Love Comes in Spurts', 'The Plan' and 'Blank Generation' were not utilized on the CD. This version of 'Love Comes in Spurts' was included on the 1977 Sire sampler *New Wave*, while this take of 'You Gotta Lose' appeared on Sire's second New Wave sampler, *The Sire Machine Turns You On* (1978). Both are only available on these vinyl compilations.

Hell issued only one further album with the Voidoids, 1982's *Destiny Street*. This is also now available on CD, on Line Records in Europe and Red Star in the US, though the intrigued are advised to seek out the American release as it includes new sleeve-notes, written by Hell himself, as well as full lyrics to the songs.

There are also two ROIR compilations, originally only available on cassette but now on CD as well, which cover the Voidoids career on stage and in the studio. *R.I.P.* concentrates on studio material and, aside from the three Heartbreakers demos already mentioned, includes two Voidoids demos from December 1976 – 'Betrayal Takes Two' and 'I'm

Your Man' – plus four songs from 1979. The final Voidoids recording on *R.I.P.* is a live version of 'I Can Only Give You Everything' from 1983. The other ROIR compilation, *Funhunt*, concentrates on the Voidoids' late-Seventies heyday and is entirely derived, save for one cut from a non-Voidoids performance in 1985, from live recordings made in New York between June 1978 and June 1979. The fifteen cuts include several covers, notably the Stones' 'I'm Free' and 'Ventilator Blues', Hendrix's 'Crosstown Traffic' and the Stooges' 'I Wanna be Your Dog', though the recording quality is only fair-to-middling. The bootleg EP *Into the Void of Hell* contains a more manic version of 'I Wanna be Your Dog', along with 'You Gotta Lose' and Creedence's 'Walking on the Water'.

The other Voidoids recordings on CD come from the *Richard Hell – Past and Present* EP, originally released in 1980. 'Time' and 'Don't Die' come from what was intended to be the final Voidoids session at the end of 1979. Both appear on the five-track Overground CD reissue of this EP. The other single recorded by the Voidoids after their departure from Sire – Kid with the Replaceable Head/I'm Your Man – released by Radar in December 1978, is only available in this form. Both songs are alternatives to the album takes subsequently released on CD.

The Dictators

Of the Dictators' three studio albums, only the first and best, *The Dictators Go Girl Crazy* (1975), is currently available on CD and this only in the US. *Manifest Destiny* (1976) and *Bloodbrothers* (1978), both on Elektra/Asylum, remain deleted. However, ROIR's live cassette of a February 1981 reunion show, *Fuck 'em if They Can't Take a Joke*, has been issued on CD in Europe by Danceteria.

Suicide

The two Suicide studio albums, *Suicide* (1977) and *Alan Vega – Martin Rev* (1980), are available as a single CD on Restless in the US. The UK label Demon have released *Suicide* on CD but without the second album. This version represents extremely poor value and readers are advised to seek out the US release. In fact Demon's CD, had it been the 1980 UK re-release of *Suicide*, would have warranted release in its own right. The 1980 version of the first Suicide album is quite different from the original. Though 'Girl' is omitted, the album includes two live cuts, including a version of '96 Tears' from CBGBs, plus the single version of 'Cheree' and its B-side 'I Remember'. Both this version of 'Cheree', which features a radically different mix, and 'I Remember', have now been issued on CD on the *Groups of Wrath* compilation.

The 1980 reissue of *Suicide* also included a flexi-disc version of *23 Minutes in Brussels*, a live recording originally issued in a limited edition of a thousand copies by Bronze in 1978. If *23 Minutes in Brussels* remains the best available document of a typical Suicide live performance, live cuts on the 1981 ROIR compilation cassette *Half-Alive* only further the cause of disorientation, mostly notably a wild 'Sister Ray Says'. *Half-Alive* also features three demos from 1974, including a prototype version of their 1979 European 'hit' single, 'Dream, Baby, Dream' – the 12″ single of which is well worth seeking out – and provides a useful overview of Suicide's first career, temporarily suspended in 1981.

The Cleveland Bands

Cinderella Backstreet

See Peter Laughner.

Mirrors

Only one single, issued posthumously on David Thomas's Hearthan label, documents Mirrors' existence. She Smiled Wild/Shirley adequately conveys the nature of the Mirrors sound. It is rumoured that a CD retrospective along the lines of Homestead's Styrenes and Eels compilations will soon do the same for Mirrors.

The Electric Eels

For many years a 1978 Rough Trade single, Agitated/Cyclotron, was all that the outside world had heard of the Electric Eels. Finally, in

1989, a ten-track album of recordings from the Eels' final sessions in the summer of 1975 was released as *Having a Philosophical Investigation with the Electric Eels*. Then, in 1991, a CD version of that album, retitled *God Says Fuck You*, came out in the US on Homestead. This seventeen-track CD gives a fair idea of how the Eels thrived on noise, though sadly only three cuts – 'Natural Situation', 'Cards and Fleurs' and 'As if I Cared' – feature Paul Marotta, thus representing the two-guitar-no-drums approach that the Eels pursued for most of their fraught career. The addition of Nick Knox, later of Cramps fame, on the remainder of the tracks adds an unnecessary element of orthodoxy. It is to be hoped that some brave soul may yet release the Eels' set from the second Special Extermination Night at the Viking (preferably with Mirrors' set as well).

Rocket from the Tombs

Though a Rocket from the Tombs retrospective similar to the Eels' was issued in 1990, *Life Stinks* was only ever available on vinyl (with a free 7″ single included, featuring Ain't it Fun/Transfusion) in a limited edition of 600, and remains hard to find. Although the quality is a little disappointing considering the source tapes, the album as a whole is very listenable, the mixture of the WMMS demos and the May 1975 Agora broadcast working very well, not to mention providing an opportunity to hear original RFTT versions of 'What Love Is', 'Down in Flames', 'Life Stinks', 'Thirty Seconds Over Tokyo' and 'Final Solution'. The sleeve-notes, credited to 'Th' Cle-Man', are extremely informative and detailed.

The Styrenes

At the same time as their Eels CD retro, Homestead also gave the world a Styrenes compilation CD, *It's Artastic (Cleveland '75 to '79)*. The twenty-one-track anthology covers the period from June 1975 ('Circus Highlights', in truth the final Mirrors session) to December 1979 and a final studio session in Cleveland before relocating to New York. The first nine cuts, which go up to September 1977 and maintain the guitar-piano-bass-drums set-up, develop aspects of the Eels and Mirrors in a positive direction. The 1979 cuts – the remaining twelve – tend to be overwrought and unduly intricate.

Pere Ubu

Despite a concerted reissue of the bulk of Pere Ubu's back catalogue on CD by Rough Trade in 1989, the most renowned Ubu album remains virtually inaccessible on CD. *The Modern Dance* (1978) was released on CD by Fontana in the UK in 1988 in a limited edition of a thousand copies, intended to promote the recent reformation of the band and the release of *Tenement Years.* However, due to legal problems, the CD was never re-pressed in the UK or elsewhere and copies are now extremely hard to find. Suffice to say, *The Modern Dance* has lasted extremely well, and its transfer to CD has made it no less rewarding an aural experience.

The other CD to represent the early studio recordings of Ubu – i.e. the six non-album cuts released on the Hearthan singles between December 1975 and August 1977 – is *Terminal Tower,* a near-as-dammit-definitive collection of Ubu A-sides and B-sides. Aside from all four sides to HR101 and HR102 (Thirty Seconds Over Tokyo/Heart of Darkness and Final Solution/Cloud 149), *Terminal Tower* includes the original version of 'The Modern Dance', previously only available on the UK 12" *Datapanik in the Year Zero,* 'My Dark Ages' and 'Heaven' from HR103 and HR104 respectively, and a live B-side of 'Humour Me' from the 1978 Ubu Mystery Tour. Unfortunately *Terminal Tower* has steadfastly failed to appear in the UK on CD and must be sought out as a Twintone US import, minus the lyrics and discography that accompanied the original vinyl version.

The remainder of the Ubu *oeuvre* first time around was released in its entirety by Rough Trade in 1989. That is, the four remaining studio albums, *Dub Housing* (1978), *New Picnic Time* (1979), *The Art of Walking* (1980) and *Song of the Bailing Man* (1982), and two live compilations designed to cover the full gamut of Ubu incarnations.

390 Degrees of Simulated Stereo, subtitled 'Ubu Live Volume One', originally released on vinyl in 1981, features three songs from the final show of the Laughner–Wright–Taylor–Thomas–Herman incarnation – 'Can't Believe It', 'Over My Head' and 'Sentimental Journey'. A further cut from this 5 May 1976 show was included on a flexi-disc single given free with issue 3B – an Ubu special – of *CLE* magazine. Though the recordings on *390 Degrees* go as far as March 1979, all the actual material is derived from *The Modern Dance* or the Hearthan singles. Two cuts are drawn from a show at the WHK Auditorium in Cleveland in February 1978. The complete recording of this show had already been issued as a bootleg album called *The U-Men*.

A second volume of Ubu live, not released until 1989, *One Man Drives While the Other Man Screams*, sought to cover the band's career from *Dub Housing* through to *Song of the Bailing Man*, though the CD concentrates primarily on a show from London's Electric Ballroom on the November 1978 Ubu Mystery Tour as the *Dub Housing* material develops live. Both live albums are highly recommended.

Peter Laughner

Aside from the two singles and four live cuts from his time in Ubu now released officially, and the Rocket from the Tombs quasi-legit album *Life Stinks*, there is little officially available from Laughner's various projects. A 1982 album on the local Koolie label, long deleted, and simply called *Peter Laughner*, features two lengthy excursions with Friction from a November 1976 Pirate's Cove show – 'Dear Richard' and 'Hideaway' – plus several acoustic originals, including two of Laughner's most intense cuts, 'Sylvia Plath' and 'Baudelaire'. Despite clocking in at barely half an hour, this album is well worth tracking down.

The only other two vinyl releases are both singles. The first, released by *Forced Exposure* magazine, coupled a version of 'White Light/White Heat' from the final Cinderella Backstreet show with an acoustic version of 'Cinderella Backstreet' itself. And most recently SOL/Dutch East India have released two of the cuts from the summer 1974 Finns tape: a searing 'Baby's on Fire' and the ubiquitous Velvets cover, 'What Goes On'.

Finally, a double-album/single CD compilation of Laughner's work, entitled *Take the Guitar Player for a Ride*, is due to be released in 1993 by T. K. Records.

Devo

Thanks to a recent spate of CD releases on Rykodisc, the years before Devo's debut album have now been well represented in their official output. 1990's *Hardcore Volume One* released fifteen demos recorded between 1974 and 1977 on a 4-track recorder in their home studio, including demos of 'Mongoloid' and 'Jocko Homo' and two of the cuts previously available on the famous *Mechanical Man* bootleg EP, the title track and 'Auto Modown'. A further twenty-one demos from the same period made up the 1991 release *Hardcore Volume Two* and included demos of 'Be Stiff', 'Can U Take It' and 'Clockout'. However, these clearly are not all the demos that date from this fertile period, as the *Devonia* bootleg album includes demos of 'Sloppy (I Saw My Baby Gettin')', 'Secret Agent Man', 'Smart Patrol', 'Uncontrollable Urge', and 'Blockhead' – all of which are absent from the *Hardcore* CDs.

Also recently added to the Devo corpus was *Devo Live – The Mongoloid Years*, a seventeen-track CD spanning the same period as the demo collections. Beginning with five cuts from the Halloween 1975 radio broadcast at the WHK Auditorium, the bulk of the CD derives from a September 1977 show at Max's Kansas City, previously bootlegged as *He, She, or It's Devo*. A further 1977 show from the Mabuhay Gardens, San Francisco, has been extensively bootlegged, notably as *Workforce to the World*, and is equally impressive.

Of the three Devo singles recorded for Booji Boy in the US and Stiff in the UK prior to signing to Warners, neither side of the third single – Be Stiff/Social Fools – has been included on Devo albums and/or CDs (though 'Social Fools' reappeared as the B-side to the first Warners single 'Come Back Jonee'). The first album, *Q: Are We Not Men? A: We are Devo* (1978), which includes both sides of the first two Booji Boy singles (Mongoloid/Jocko Homo and Satisfaction/Sloppy (I Saw My Baby Gettin')), has been issued on CD in the US, as has the third album *Freedom of Choice* (1980). However, the second album, *Duty Now for the Future* (1979), is apparently only available on CD in Japan.

Index